T. F. H. ALLEN
BOTANY

ATLAS OF CAERNARVONSHIRE

ATLAS OF CAERNARVONSHIRE

Edited by

T. M. BASSETT & B. L. DAVIES

1977

GWYNEDD RURAL COUNCIL

ISBN 0 903935 05 8

Published by Gwynedd Rural Council, 2 Slate Quay, Caernarfon, Gwynedd,
and printed by Gwasg Gee, Denbigh.

Contents

CONTENTS (Cont'd)

Illustrations

EDITOR'S NOTE

We wish to thank the Arfon Rural Community Council for promoting this work and for the happy co-operation of their secretary, Mr. Albert Jones, D.M.A., as well as the valuable typing assistance provided by Mrs. E. H. Jones and Mrs. J. M. Jones in the office. We also wish to acknowledge the ready co-operation of all the contributors. Dr. Thomas Parry was always prepared to answer any queries, and Mr. H. Stanley Jones, B.A., B.Litt., read through the English text. We are particularly indebted to Emeritus Professor E. G. Bowen for his counsel and good advice in all matters. We also wish to express our thanks to Miss M. H. Bigwood of the Department of Botany, University College of Wales, Aberystwyth, for her exceptional work and patience in the preparation of the maps. The photographs were gathered from various sources and we acknowledge our indebtedness under each photograph, but we must mention in particular the Controller, H.M.S.O., for permission to use the photographs from the various volumes of the Royal Commission on Ancient and Historical Monuments in Wales, and the Snowdonia National Park Authority for permission to use photographs in their possession. Finally, Mr. Bryn R. Parry, M.A., D.A.A., Gwynedd Archivist, was especially helpful in making available the resources in the archives and lending a guiding hand in the selection.

T. M. BASSETT.
B. L. DAVIES.

FOREWORD BY THE ARCHBISHOP OF WALES

I cannot conceive that anyone, however well versed in the history of the old county of Caernarfon, will fail to find in this invaluable Atlas much that is new and exciting. All praise to the Rural Council for its conception and for assembling so rare a team of scholars to produce it for our pleasure and enlightenment. It deserves, and will surely receive, widespread acclaim and appreciation.

Llawenydd o'r mwyaf yw cyflwyno'r Atlas gwerthfawr hwn i sylw darllenwyr yn hen Sir Gaernarfon ac ymhell tu draw i'w chyffiniau. Mae enwogrwydd y cyfranwyr yn eu hamryfal feysydd yn gwarantu gwerth y gwaith. 'Rwy'n edrych ymlaen at bori'n broffidiol ar ei dudalennau. Llyfr yw hwn y byddaf yn ei dynnu'n aml oddi ar y silff a chael fy hun yn gallach a mwy difyr o'i astudio.

✠ GWILYM CAMBRENSIS

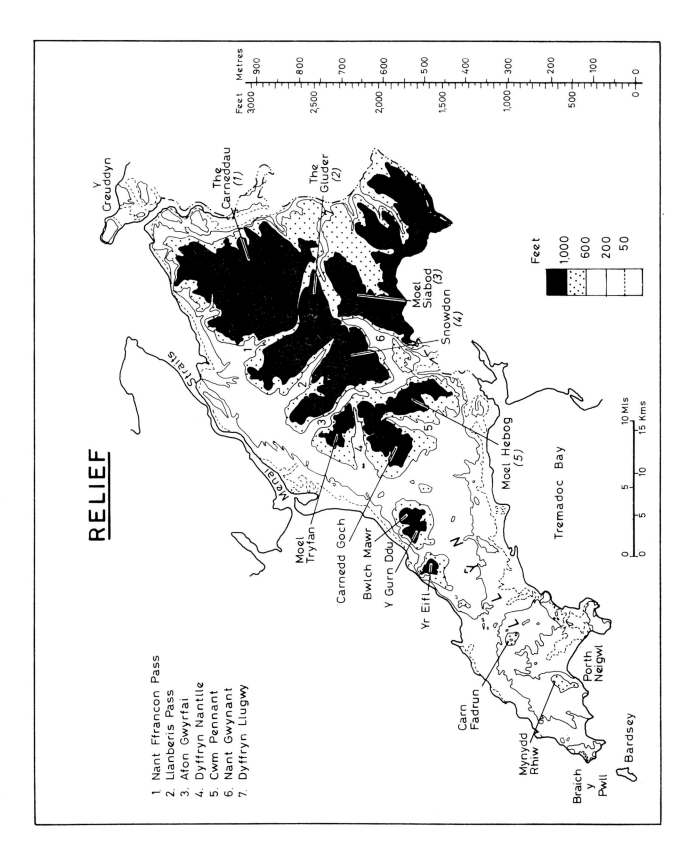

RELIEF

1. Nant Ffrancon Pass
2. Llanberis Pass
3. Afon Gwyrfai
4. Dyffryn Nantlle
5. Cwm Pennant
6. Nant Gwynant
7. Dyffryn Llugwy

The Carneddau (1)
The Gluder (2)
Moel Siabod (3)
Snowdon (4)
Moel Hebog (5)

Moel Tryfan
Carnedd Goch
Bwlch Mawr
Y Gurn Ddu
Yr Eifl
Carn Fadrun
Mynydd Rhiw
Braich y Pwll
Bardsey

Y Creuddyn

Menai Straits

Tremadoc Bay

Porth Neigwl

Feet
1,000
600
200
50

Feet Metres
3,000 — 900
— 800
2,500 — 700
— 600
2,000 — 500
— 400
1,500 — 300
— 200
1,000 — 100
500 —
0 — 0

10 Mls
15 Kms

0   5   10
0   5   10   15

Relief

Some of the most spectacular scenery in the whole of Wales lies within the county. Snowdonia, a great mountain mass of over 3,000 feet, forms the heart of the area, but equally beautiful and varied scenery is found along the narrow coastal plain to the north, in the deep Conwy valley to the east, and in the lowlands and hillocks of Llŷn to the west. The county has a more varied relief than any other in Wales. The present landscape reflects not only the nature of rock outcrops but also the impact of considerable volcanic activity, earth movements, glacial action and subaerial erosion over countless ages.

In Snowdonia, the peak of Snowdon — the highest in England and Wales — rises to 3,560 feet, whilst north-eastwards are other summits of similar heights in Gluder Fawr (3,279′), Carnedd Ddafydd (3,426′), Carnedd Llywelyn (3,484′) and Y Foel Fras (3,091′). In this central core, the land rises sharply on all sides, and it is only a matter of four miles from Beddgelert at approximately 100 feet above sea level to the summit of Snowdon. Deep valleys with swift-flowing streams open from this central core in every direction and leave no more than seventy square miles of the county above the 1,500 foot contour line — some twelve per cent of the total area of the county.

Valleys and passes have divided the mountain core into five fairly distinct blocks. The first division, the Carnedd Group to the north-east, between the rivers Ogwen (Nant Ffrancon) and the Conwy is an extensive upland of over 2,500 feet with at least four summits over 3,000 feet. From high tarns such as Dulyn, Melynllyn, Ffynnon Llugwy, and the long, narrow lakes of Eigiau, Cowlyd, Crafnant and Geirionnydd, swift-flowing streams drain east-wards and cascade over abrupt slopes to join the river Conwy. Below the bleak and barren upper slopes, rolling moorlands of rough pasture are extensively used for sheep grazing, and much afforestation has taken place along the steep valley slopes.

The second area, consisting of the Gluder group, lies between the Ogwen and the Pass of Llanberis. Though not as extensive as the previous upland, most of the land is above 2,000 feet, with five peaks rising to over 3,000 feet — Y Gluder Fawr reaching 3,279 feet. Y Gluder Fach (3,262′) and Tryfan (3,010′) tower above Llyn Idwal and Bochlwyd on the eastern slopes overlooking Llyn Ogwen. From Elidir Fawr (3,029′), the land slopes northwards towards the Menaian platform. The eastern and western slopes of this upland sector are greatly disfigured by the terraces of the Penrhyn and Dinorwig slate quarries.

In the third area, which extends westwards from the Llanberis Pass as far as the valley of the Gwyrfai with Llyn Cwellyn, rise the pyramidical peak of Snowdon and the associated ridges of Crib y Ddysgl (3,493′), Crib Goch (3,023′) and Lliwedd (2,947′). These rugged slopes are probably the most popular haunts of tourists, climbers and hikers in the whole of upland Wales. Cwms and hollows are deeply carved into these craggy slopes, and many a lake and tarn nestle beneath precipitous cliffs.

West of the river Gwyrfai, the fourth upland area includes Moel Ddu (1,811′), Moel Hebog (2,566′), Y Garn (1,190′) and Mynydd Mawr (2,290′). This is a more extensive even if less impressive upland than the previous sector. The beautiful valleys of Cwm Pennant and Cwm Ystradllyn open to the south-west.

South and east of these upland blocks, and south of the rivers Llugwy, Gwrhyd and Glaslyn, the land rises to Moel Siabod (2,860′), with the splendid Cnicht (2,268′) on the county boundary. Dotted throughout this upland, too, are remote but very attractive tarns and lakes and the three attractive valleys of the Lledr, Machno and Upper Conwy.

To the north of the upland core, a narrow belt of lowland extends along the south shore of the Menai Strait. Here there are remnants of more than one platform of marine erosion which have been cut across geological strata, irrespective of age, degree of hardness, or the extent of folding, faulting and metamorphism to which they may have been subjected. The best known of these erosion surfaces is the Menaian platform which is preserved on both sides of the Strait. The average elevation is about 270 feet, and although interrupted by the Strait, the uniformity of levels and the rolling nature of the land surface on either side are unmistakable. Further south, the terrain rises to a second shelf of gently rolling landscape known as the Llanrug-Llanllyfni platform. It has a general elevation of approximately 430 feet, and extends as far as the Snowdonian foothills where there is a sudden change of slope as the land rises abruptly to the interior uplands. Eastwards, the very narrow coastline extends from Llanfairfechan to Conwy. Throughout the ages this narrow lowland has provided man with more congenial conditions for settlement and a very convenient routeway.

The Conwy valley, to the east of the mountain core, extends from south to north for nearly twenty miles. The main valley has a flat alluvial floor of between half and three-quarters of a mile wide which reaches only 30 feet above sea-level even at Betws-y-coed, 14 miles inland. This largely explains the constant flooding suffered in the valley in wet weather. It is not primarily a glaciated U-shaped or an over-deepened valley, but a fault-shattered belt which pre-glacial rivers were able to excavate rapidly after changes in base-level. To the west of the valley, especially south of Tal-y-bont, the sides rise very abruptly from 30 feet to over 900 feet, but to the north of this village the valley sides become much gentler. Permanent diversion in the lower course of the Conwy occurred in glacial times. Instead of reaching the sea in Penrhyn Bay, Irish Sea ice forced the river to divert its course to the west of the Great Orme.

Westwards of Snowdonia for some 30 miles extends the peninsula of Llŷn, where lies the most extensive lowland within the county. The 270 foot platform of marine erosion is again the basic element in the relief, especially in the southern and south-western region. The lowlands, which seldom exceed 600 feet in height, are, however, sharply interrupted at intervals by bold peaks and dome-shaped hills of igneous rocks as in Garn Boduan (918'), Mynydd Nefyn (750') and Yr Eifl — a composite mass of three peaks at 1,458', 1,849' and 1,591' — and Garn Fadrun (1,217'). All these owe their prominence to the resistance of hard intrusive igneous rocks.

This highly varied relief within the county has had a significant influence upon the activities of man throughout the ages — in peace and war, in work and play, in patterns of settlement and in lines of movement.

BIBLIOGRAPHY

Bowen, E. G., *Wales: A Physical, Historical and Regional Geography,* Methuen, 1957.

North, F. J., Campbell, B., Scott R., *Snowdonia,* Collins, 1949.

Carr, H. R. C., and Lister, G. A., *The Mountains of Snowdonia,* Crosby Lockwood, 1948.

Howell, E. J., *Land Utilisation Survey of Britain, Parts 41-43, North Wales,* London, 1946.

Stamp, L. D., *Britain's Structure and Scenery,* London, 1946.

Dury, G. H., *The Face of the Earth,* London, 1959.

Snowdonia, National Forest Park Guide, H.M.S.O., 1954.

Snowdon from Crib Goch

LAKES AND RIVERS

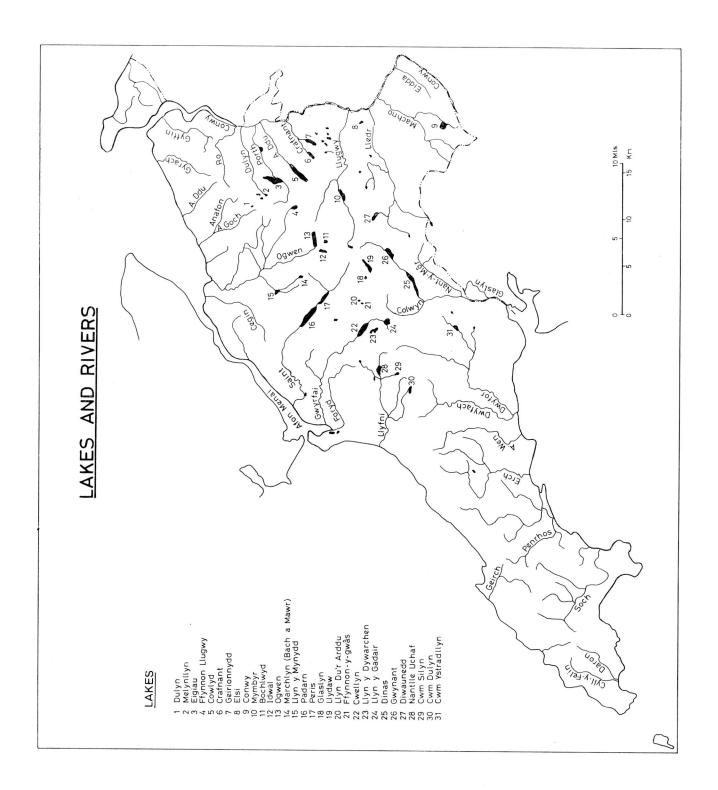

LAKES

1 Dulyn
2 Melynllyn
3 Eigiau
4 Ffynnon Llugwy
5 Cowlyd
6 Crafnant
7 Geirionnydd
8 Elsi
9 Conwy
10 Mymbyr
11 Bochlwyd
12 Idwal
13 Ogwen
14 Marchlyn (Bach a Mawr)
15 Llyn y Mynydd
16 Padarn
17 Peris
18 Glaslyn
19 Llydaw
20 Llyn Du'r Arddu
21 Ffynnon-y-gwâs
22 Cwellyn
23 Llyn y Dywarchen
24 Llyn y Gadair
25 Dinas
26 Gwynant
27 Diwaunedd
28 Nantlle Uchaf
29 Cwm Silyn
30 Cwm Dulyn
31 Cwm Ystradllyn

Lakes and Rivers

With such high altitudes, steep slopes, widespread distribution of impervious rocks and soil, very heavy rainfall and land which was so extensively glaciated, it is not surprising that the county abounds in lakes and rivers. It is claimed that there are more than sixty lakes in Snowdonia alone, ranging from small rounded tarns such as Llyn Glas, overlooking the Llanberis Pass, to Llyn Padarn, which is over two miles long. These lakes are likewise scattered at all levels from valley floors, as in Llyn Dinas, 176 feet above sea-level in Nant Gwynant, to Melynllyn, at 2,094 feet, nestling beneath Y Foel Grach. Of particular interest, too, is the highly varied depth of these lakes. Some, such as lakes Ogwen and Idwal, with maximum depths of only 10 and 36 feet respectively, are unexpectedly shallow, whilst the majority have maximum depths varying from 40 to 60 feet. Compared with their area, many of the valley lakes are shallow, with a depth of 122 feet in Cwellyn, 114 feet in Peris and 94 feet in Llyn Padarn. More impressive depths are found in lakes at higher levels, with Llydaw 190 feet, Dulyn 189 feet, and Glaslyn 127 feet deep. The variation in the depths of these lakes can be directly related to glacial erosion and deposition.

On the upper mountain slopes throughout Snowdonia there are several classic examples of cwm or cirque lakes, such as Glaslyn, Llydaw or Marchlyn. These cwms have characteristic steep headwalls — particularly in volcanic rock — with a general armchair shape and reversed floors impounding lakes, as in Cwm Idwal or Cwm Dulyn. These are clearly not features due to water erosion, and the majority face between north and east, in which positions there would be maximum shade and the best conditions for the collection of snow. The hollows in the floors of the cwms were excavated by the familiar processes of glacial action, and, later, as the ice melted, it deposited moraine across the lip of the rock basin. This deepened the cavity in which water could accumulate when the ice finally disappeared. Streams from these lakes are short and usually cascade to a main valley below, as in Cwm Bochlwyd, hanging 800 feet above Llyn Ogwen, or Cwm-llan, 600 feet above the floor of Nant Gwynant.

By contrast, in all the valleys radiating from the Snowdonian peaks are lakes such as Cowlyd, Eigiau, Padarn, Gwynant, which are long, narrow and even-sided, and in which the shape of the lakes follows the contours of their valleys. These lakes are in the hollows gouged by powerful glaciers as they moved along the valleys to sea-level. Morainic materials strewn at the lower ends of the hollows also contributed to the ponding back of these waters.

Most of the lakes were at one time very much larger and considerably deeper than they are today, for most lakes are gradually being silted up. Padarn and Peris, for instance, were originally one lake, and the alluvial flat separating them is really the delta of the river Hwch which cascades down into the valley from the western side. There is also an expanse of flat alluvial land above Llyn Peris, and a further marshy track below Llyn Padarn extends as far as Cwm-y-glo. This flat tract must at one time have been submerged under a very long lake of some 4 or 5 miles. Even today, Llyn Peris — the upper lake — has a depth of 114 feet as opposed to Padarn which is 94 feet deep, indicating that the valley was not gouged simply by normal river erosion.

In several valleys in the area, there are alluvial flats marking the sites of lakes that have been filled up or drained because the streams leaving them have cut through to the bottom of the dams or rock ridges that held back the water. The flat land around Beddgelert, for example, marks the site of a lake that has disappeared; so also does the much larger area which forms the floor of Nant Ffrancon.

Very many of these lakes and rivers are being used for leisure pursuits; several attract fishermen, others are used for boating or canoeing or swimming. The lakesides are also popular picnic sites and are visited by thousands every year. Many of the lakes are in clean, unpopulated areas, and have been used to generate hydro-electric power, as at Cwm Dyli and Dolgarrog. In the near future, the Llanberis lakes will also be used in connection with a Pump Storage Scheme, constructed by the General Electricity Board. In the past, some of these lakes were used to provide hydraulic power for the slate quarries; Marchlyn Mawr provided such power for the Penrhyn Quarry.

Generally, short swift-moving tributaries drain the central mountain core in every direction, and link up with the main streams at lower levels. The Conwy, Ogwen, Saint and Gwyrfai are the main rivers flowing to the northern coast, whilst the Glaslyn is the only river of note draining southwards. The straightening and deepening of the main valleys by glaciers can be appreciated from the map. Many examples of truncated spurs are seen, and the lower parts of the valleys subjected to the passage of large glaciers have become U-shaped, although the flat floors are often due to alluvial infilling, as in Nant Ffrancon. Breaks in the long profiles of the main valleys are equally common — as in the Ogwen Falls and the Aberglaslyn Pass. Many of the rivers are strongly discordant with structure, cutting across folds indiscriminately or flowing against the dip of the rocks, yet often possessing remarkably straight courses.

Much of Llŷn is covered with glacial drift which caused permanent diversion of the pre-glacial drainage by the obstruction of the original channels by glacial deposits. A classic case of complete glacial diversion is that of the Soch, which flows from the north and west to within half a mile of the sea at Hell's Mouth (Porth Neigwl) and then turns back on itself at Llanengan, before flowing north and east and then through a deep gorge to the sea at Abersoch.

The principal changes in the landscape of this area in post-glacial times have been due to slight subsidence in land levels. To this post-glacial subsidence may be attributed the separation of the island of Anglesey from the mainland, by the drowning of the low watershed between two short valleys to form the Menai Strait. Recent theories suggest that the Strait functioned as a spillway for the meltwaters of Irish Sea ice which stagnated in Conwy Bay and around Anglesey during deglaciation. The Menai Strait channel was then cut deeper as it drained a larger area of ice.

The rivers, lakes and coastal scenery enhance the beauty of this area very considerably, and this has been of great benefit to the tourist industry.

BIBLIOGRAPHY

Ward, Frank, *The Lakes of Wales,* London, 1931.

Howe, G. M. and Thomas, P., *Welsh Landforms and Scenery,* London, 1965.

Howe, G. M., *Wales from the Air,* Cardiff, 1957.

George, T. N., *The Welsh Landscape,* Science Progress, 1961.

Steers, J. A., *The Coastline of England and Wales,* London, 1946.

Embledon, C., *The Geomorphology of the Vale of Conway, North Wales, with particular reference to deglaciation.* Trans. Inst. Brit. Geog., 1961.

Snowdonia, National Park Guide, Number 2, National Parks Commission, H.M.S.O., 1960.

Llyn Idwal

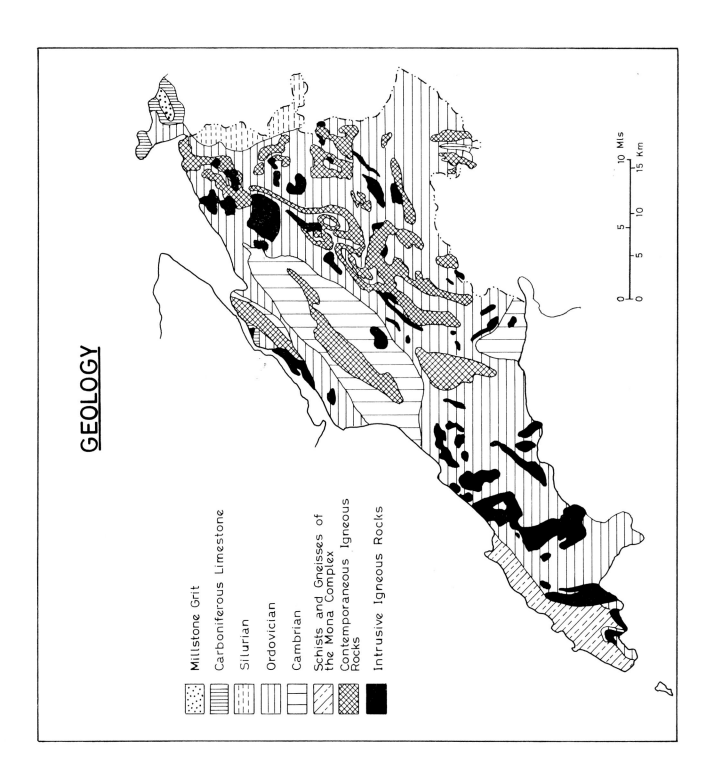

GEOLOGY

Millstone Grit

Carboniferous Limestone

Silurian

Ordovician

Cambrian

Schists and Gneisses of
the Mona Complex

Contemporaneous Igneous
Rocks

Intrusive Igneous Rocks

10 Mls

15 Km

10

5

5

0

0

Geology

Caernarvonshire is characterised not only by a marked diversity of relief but also by an equally varied range and distribution of rock outcrops. Within this small area there are representations of all systems from the Pre-Cambrian to the Carboniferous. Coupled with crumpled, fractured, cleaved and folded sediments are some of the finest examples of ancient volcanoes and records of several periods of major earth movements. A cursory study of rock types and surface features reveals a broad correlation, and some of the most rugged mountains of Snowdonia owe their outline to the resistance of their tough volcanic rocks to the severest agents of denudation. Snowdon with its surrounding upland provides a spectacular centrepiece to the scenic grandeur of North Wales, and the rock formations of practically the whole county and particularly of this central core are arranged in the form of a synclinorium with a general north-east to south-west fold alignment.

The generalised map of geological outcrops indicates the present limited extent of Pre-Cambrian rocks within the county. Schists and gneisses in the far tip of Llŷn extend from Bardsey Island along the northern coast as far east as Nefyn, and further east, Pre-Cambrian rocks are exposed in two narrow parallel ridges, the one extending from Caernarfon to Bangor (the Bangor Ridge) and the other from Llanllyfni to Bethesda (the Padarn Ridge). They comprise a vast thickness of highly varied sedimentary and igneous rocks, and bear record of at least two periods of intense mountain-building movements as well as extensive metamorphism.

Similarly, the extent of Cambrian outcrops is very limited. They are mainly found as an ellipse surrounding the Llanllyfni-Bethesda Ridge (Padarn Ridge), where the shales and mudstones between Nantlle and Bethesda in the Lower and Middle Cambrian rocks were metamorphosed into slates of excellent quality and gave rise to a very active slate-quarrying industry. A small, triangular outcrop of Upper Cambrian rocks, with its base along the rugged coastline between Cricieth and Porthmadog extends some five miles inland. Slate has also been extracted in this area, but the structure is partly concealed by glacial drift and alluvium in the Porthmadog area.

Ordovician rocks form the most extensive tracts within the county, and are contiguous with the complex syncline of Snowdonia which extends north-eastwards in the upland areas above Penmaen-mawr and Conwy, and westwards to form the greater part of the Llŷn peninsula. Apart from the Pre-Cambrian outcrops already mentioned in the extreme west, Llŷn is occupied almost entirely by such Ordovician rocks with igneous extrusions and intrusions. Volcanic activity was the outstanding feature of the Ordovician period in Snowdonia. These volcanic outbursts are nearly all sub-marine, localized in different parts of the district with centres near Capel Curig, Conwy, Snowdon and Llŷn. Lavas and coarse agglomerates are characteristic rocks in the vicinity of the old craters, and are largely responsible for the rugged nature of the Snowdonian landscape today, whilst the more extensive deposits of ashes and tuffs are further away. Associated with these extensive lavas and tuffs are many igneous intrusions (dykes and sills) which have cut through the Ordovician sediments, the larger of which often form the present day steep isolated hills and were probably in many cases the plugs of ancient volcanoes. In Llŷn, the correspondence between outcrop and topography could hardly be more perfect. The hard igneous rocks, particularly those of the intrusions, stand up above the surrounding country of less resistant sedimentary rocks. Igneous rocks are also responsible for the higher ground of the headlands, as at Mynydd Penarfynydd, Mynydd Rhiw, Llanbedrog and Cricieth. The igneous rocks of Llŷn have been extensively quarried, as at Trefor, and further east the large quarries of similar rocks at Penmaen-mawr still give a great output of crushed stone.

The Silurian rocks of the Conwy valley extend eastwards into the Denbigh Moors. They consist in the main of blue, black and mid-grey shales and mudstones, with occasional interbedded sandy and gritty bands. The Caledonian Orogeny at the end of the Silurian period not only led to considerable folding and fracturing of rocks but also imposed upon North Wales a general trend or strike of the axes of folding in a north-east to south-west direction. Subsequent erosion has enhanced this effect by etching out the hard bands so that the topographical 'grain' of the county follows this broad direction.

The outcrops of Carboniferous rocks in the county are confined to the south bank of the Strait west of Bangor, but more spectacularly in the Great and Little Orme of the Creuddyn Peninsula.

The Pleistocene period saw the onset of arctic conditions in Britain, and this, the Great Ice Age, was a time when much of the country was intermittently submerged beneath a blanket of ice. Within this area there were considerable formations of snow and ice in the upland areas, and ice flowed outwards in a general radial direction.

Contemporaneous with the glaciers of Snowdonia, ice sheets from the Clyde valley, the Southern Uplands of Scotland, the Lake District and north-eastern Ireland were moving southwards and in part thrusting against the land mass of North Wales. This Irish Sea ice, in meeting the northward-flowing ice from Snowdonia, was in part diverted westwards over Anglesey and the Llŷn peninsula. The extent of the incursion of Irish Sea ice is now indicated by the occurrence of rock derived from extra-Welsh sources. Rocks from the Lake District and pebbles from Ailsa Craig (Firth of Clyde) are common in the drift deposits of Llŷn. There also occur at various heights on the hill-slopes many patches of sand containing marine shells, and the great force of the movement of Irish Sea ice may be gauged by the fact that patches of such dredged-up marine sand occur at heights of nearly 1,400 feet on Moel Tryfan between Caernarfon and Snowdon, and at lower levels on Yr Eifl and the hills of Llŷn.

The close of the Ice Age revealed the extent of the massive erosion and deposition caused by the sheets and tongues of ice. The hills of Snowdonia were left deeply scarred with cwms, rock-basins, lakes, roches moutonnés, ice striations, over-deepened U-shaped valleys, hanging tributaries, pyramidical peaks and arêtes abounding everywhere.

On the lowlands, valleys, coastal plains and Llŷn were deposited vast thicknesses of drift and boulder clay, drumlins, eskers, moraines and outwashes of sand and gravel. These deposits changed the landscape and caused much diversion of drainage. At the end of the Great Ice Age, Caernarvonshire was very much as it is at present, and the principal changes since have been due to slight subsidence.

The geology and rock outcrops have greatly influenced man throughout the ages. Apart from the nature of the relief and the quality of the soil, man has extracted minerals and metals such as slate, granite, sand, gravel, copper, lead, iron ore, manganese, calcium, and pyrites wherever they were found in viable reserves.

BIBLIOGRAPHY

Bowen, E. G. (ed.), *Wales: A Physical, Historical and Regional Geography,* Methuen, 1957.

Smith, B. and George, T. N., *North Wales, British Regional Geology,* H.M.S.O., 1948.

Carr, H. R. C. and Lister, G. A., *The Mountains of Snowdonia,* Crosby Lockwood, 1948.

D. F. Ball, *The Soils and Land Use of the District around Bangor and Beaumaris,* London, 1963.

Condry, W. M., *The Snowdonia National Park,* The New Naturalist Series, London, 1966.

Embleton, C., *Snowdonia,* Sheffield, 1962.

Brown, E. H., *The Relief and Drainage of Wales,* Cardiff, 1960.

Trueman, A. E., *Geology and Scenery of England and Wales,* London, 1949.

Y Garn, Elidir Fawr and Foel Goch from Tryfan   *Copyright: Snowdon National Park Authority*

MEAN ANNUAL RAINFALL

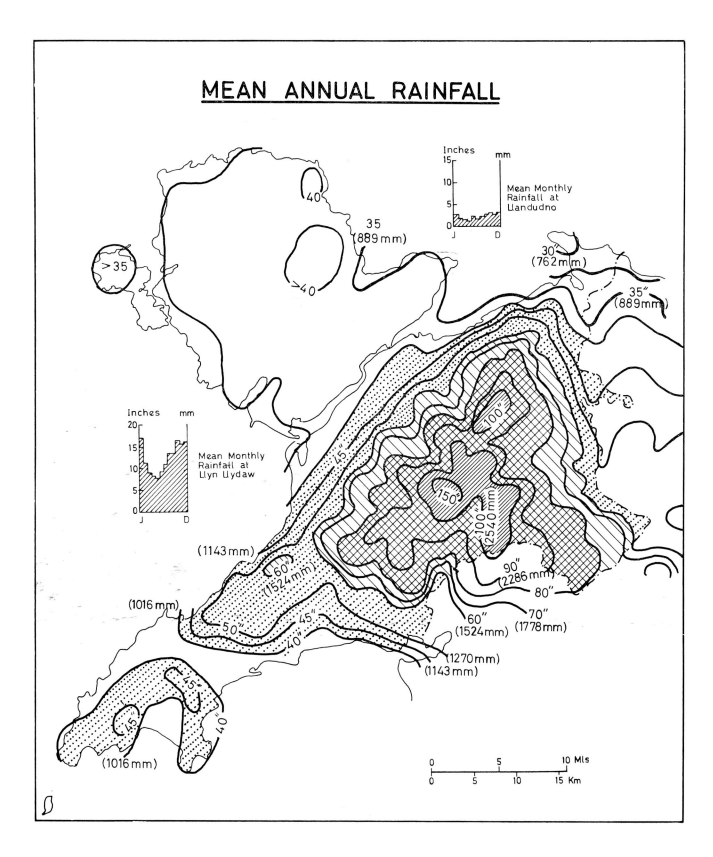

Rainfall

The correlation between the distribution of the annual rainfall and the relief of Caernarvonshire is very marked. The general elevation of Snowdonia is largely responsible for a very high rainfall; the configuration of the land is responsible for the great variation in the mean amounts of rainfall experienced. The passage of cyclonic storms and the moisture-laden prevailing south-westerlies drench the uplands of Snowdonia, but the Conwy valley and the Creuddyn peninsula to the lee of the mountains have much lower rainfall totals. The coastal lowlands everywhere, particularly in Llŷn and the lower Conwy valley, experience modest annual totals of between 30 and 40 inches a year. Inland on the lower hill slopes and moorlands, the annual totals increase to 80 or 90 inches, and on the upper slopes of Snowdonia, the yearly totals increase very rapidly, with Snowdon itself, one of the wettest areas in Britain, probably with over 200 inches a year. Llyn Glaslyn, within a few hundred yards of the summit of Snowdon, has an annual average of 198 inches, Crib Goch 171 inches and Llyn Llydaw 150 inches.

The seasonal distribution of rainfall is typical of western Europe with a decidedly wetter winter half year, the three wettest consecutive months almost everywhere being October, November and December. This winter rainfall to some extent replenishes the reserves of underground water and refills the lakes and reservoirs of the county. With water as one of the most coveted resources for industrial, agricultural, domestic and social purposes, this is most fortunate; yet a very high proportion of this valuable resource is lost in swollen rivers and in a very rapid surface run-off. In late spring and early summer, during the months of April, May and June, the county experiences its lowest rainfall, and in spite of the prevalence of April showers, that month can be minimally drier than May (Llandudno). Generally, though, the driest month of the year is either May or June. In an area so devoted to tourism, it is worth noting that May, June and July are usually far drier than the popular holiday month of August. Farmers throughout the lowlands and lower slopes do well to concentrate on their hay harvest in June and July and their corn harvests in late August and early September.

Whilst the mean monthly figures give a valuable indication of the rainfall distribution over the years, extremely wet as well as unusually dry seasons have been recorded. Any year may show surprising variations from the mean rainfall, and the vagaries of the weather, particularly in Snowdonia, are familiar to all. In 1926, 7.25 inches of rain were recorded at Llyn Llydaw in 24 hours.

Not surprisingly, the county must be classified as wet and damp, for most of the uplands record 225 rain days a year, although in Llŷn and the coastal lowlands the average is between 175 and 200. In addition, over most of the moorland and upland country prolonged periods of cloud, mist and drizzle are experienced which cause reduced sunshine and reduced evaporation.

The frequency of snow cover within the county is subject to great variation and is again closely related to altitude and to the nature of the relief. All the summits in Snowdonia are intermittently covered with snow from November to March each year, and are often clad with a scatter of snow before and after those months. Some of the gullies at high levels have an accumulation of snow during winter which may remain largely unmelted during the summer. Snow remains longest in hollows and gullies high up in slopes facing northwards where it is sheltered from the sun and from the south-westerly rains — as on the north-eastern face of Carnedd Llywelyn and on the north face of Crib y Ddysgl. Of these, the best known is Y Ffos Ddyfn, at 3,000 feet, north-north-west of the summit of Carnedd Llywelyn. The frequency of the snow cover, apart from altitude, is closely related to sea influences, and in North Wales snow cover generally increases from west to east. These contingencies demand the constant attention of upland farmers during the winter months. The mean annual number of days with snow or sleet cover is very low in Llŷn, and along the northern coastal plain it is usually fewer than five. It increases slightly eastwards along the northern coast and inland to more than a 100 on the highest slopes of Snowdonia. In general, the isopleths run parallel with the coast.

The high rainfall totals and the incidence of wet days, apart from factors of relief, have through the centuries favoured pastoral rather than arable farming. Less wet conditions would make tourism more attractive in summer, whilst heavier and longer snowfalls in the hills, although a great hazard to farmers, would make winter sport more feasible.

AVERAGE ANNUAL AND MONTHLY RAINFALL IN INCHES

Station and Altitude	J	F	M	A	M	J	Jly.	A	S	O	N	D	Year
Llandudno 13′	2.94	2.17	1.86	1.69	2.07	1.79	2.07	2.54	2.72	3.23	2.85	2.91	28.84
Llyn Llydaw 1,480′					7.80	9.51	11.89	13.41	13.46	16.41	15.35	15.86	150.75

AVERAGE ANNUAL AND MONTHLY RAINFALL IN MILLIMETERS

Station and Altitude	J	F	M	A	M	J	Jly.	A	S	O	N	D	Year
Botwnnog 180′	125	90	65	65	65	70	85	95	95	125	115	115	1,110
Cwm Ystradllyn 601′	205	145	105	105	105	110	135	150	155	200	195	185	1,780
Tryfan 1,100′	400	285	205	205	210	215	265	295	305	390	370	360	3,500

(Gwynedd River Board)

CONVERSION TABLE

Inches	Millimeters		Inches	Millimeters
1	25.4		70	1,778
10	254		80	2,032
20	508		90	2,286
30	762		100	2,540
40	1,016		150	3,810
50	1,270		200	5,080
60	1,524			

Y Garn, Foel Goch, Llyn Ogwen

MEAN MONTHLY TEMPERATURES

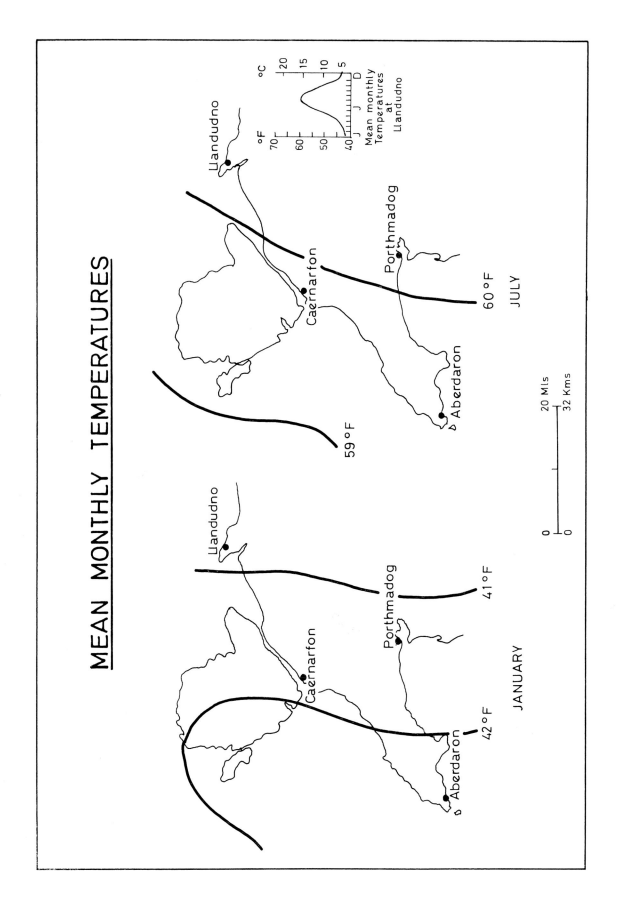

JANUARY

JULY

Llandudno

Caernarfon

Porthmadog

Aberdaron

41°F

42°F

Llandudno

Caernarfon

Porthmadog

Aberdaron

59°F

60°F

Mean monthly
Temperatures
at
Llandudno

20 Mls

32 Kms

Temperatures

Diurnal and seasonal temperatures in Caernarvonshire vary considerably in relation to altitude and increasing distance from the sea. Yet, as no place in the county can be more than 23 miles from the sea, the dominant factors influencing local changes of temperature are altitude, aspect and the nature of the relief. With such vast changes in altitude, the corresponding significant changes in actual and mean temperatures between the coastal plains and the Snowdonian ridges are inevitable. Similarly, whilst conditions along the coastal plains have been adequately recorded, such records in the upland areas are scant.

Along the coastal plains, January and February are the coldest months, with the mean monthly temperature for February being minimally lower than for January along the coasts of north-west Wales. The lowest mean monthly temperature for Aber is 42.2°F in February, and 41.2°F for the same month at Llandudno. Such conditions are also found at stations nearby outside the old county boundary, as at Holyhead with a February mean of 42°F and Colwyn Bay with a mean of 41.9°F. Inland, the mean temperatures drop perceptibly with increasing altitude in the moorlands and mountains. On Snowdon, the mean January temperature is given as 30°F.

The lowlands of the county are everywhere characterised by a very small annual range of temperature (as, for instance, Llandudno with 18.5°F), with a January mean of between 40 and 42°F and a July mean of between 58° and 60°F. The diurnal ranges of temperature are equally moderate.

The length of the frost-free season over most of the county has a close correlation with altitude. On the interior moorlands there is an average of 157 days free of frost, whilst on the coastal fringes there is at least an average of 240 days free of frost. The shorter frost-free conditions on high ground means a shorter growing season, and seriously limits agricultural activity. The frost-free period on the coastal lowlands lasts from mid-April to mid-October, but it would be considerably shorter inland.

The growing season for crop plants can be defined as the period during which the average temperatures are above 42°F, since plant growth generally begins at about this temperature, although some mountain species grow appreciably at mean monthly temperatures of 40°F. In general, lower temperatures are found with increasing distance from the sea and with increasing altitude. At Llandudno, the monthly average temperature does not fall below the threshold value of 42°F in any month, but at Betws-y-coed it is below 42°F from December to March inclusive. The duration of cold spells during winter increases inland, and unusual extremes which overlap critical values may have disastrous effects on plants, insects, animals, pests and man's activities. The effect of the mildness of the western lowlands, particularly in Llŷn, on plant growth has been recorded, and whilst the average flowering date of certain selected plants is earlier than May 4th in Llŷn and Anglesey, a short distance inland the average date is not until after May 11th.

Day-to-day temperatures are influenced by the direction from which the winds come, for those from the south and south-west are warmer than those from the north and north-east. High winds are frequent on the little-sheltered ridges of Arfon which are especially open to the prevailing westerly and south-westerly winds. However, these prevailing winds are responsible for milder winters compared with areas of prevailing easterlies. The distribution of the annual average number of days with gales varies considerably from about 30 in the extreme west of Llŷn to less than 10 over the Menai Strait. Within the mountainous region, the mountain slopes are cooler than the valleys which intersect them, except for brief intervals when clear sunny conditions prevail in the height of the summer.

In soil development, the most important climatic influence in a limited area is probably rainfall, and temperature more directly affects the kinds of crops that can be grown and ripened, although it may also affect the level of soil moisture.

The more eqable temperatures and the lower rainfall of the coastal plain make settlement more attractive, agricultural activity more profitable and all of man's pursuits more pleasant than on the moorland and upland interior.

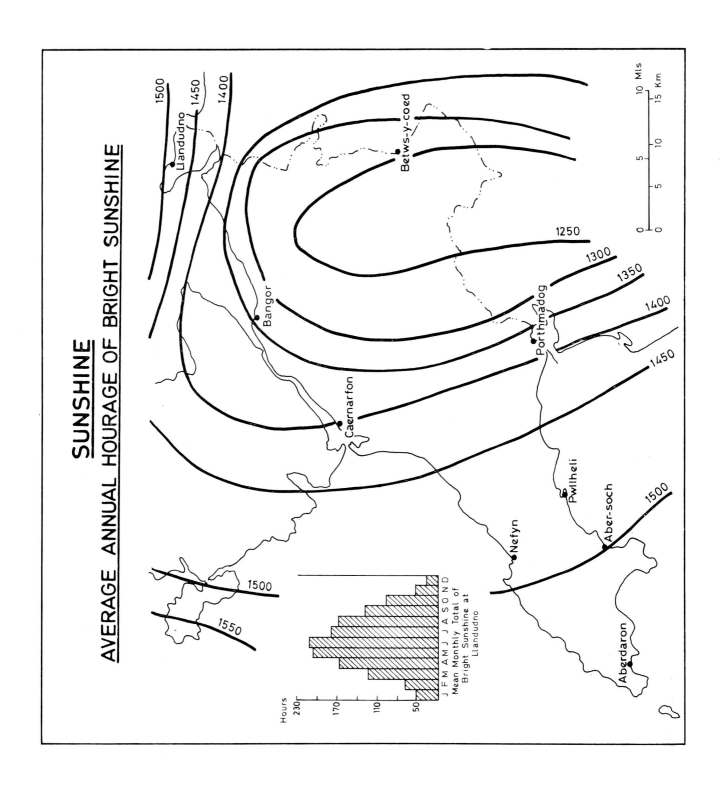

SUNSHINE
AVERAGE ANNUAL HOURAGE OF BRIGHT SUNSHINE

Sunshine

With the accentuated relief which characterises the county, sharp local variations are to be expected in the duration of sunshine. Local variations of aspect, slope, alignment and altitude of the relief will have a direct influence on this. Slopes receiving strong noonday sun and possessing the advantages of a general southern aspect are obviously favoured when compared with north-facing slopes and deep valley floors which are often without sunshine continuously for periods of many days, sometimes maybe weeks during the winter months.

The total time that the sun is above the horizon in Wales is about 4,463 hours a year, and the sunniest parts are along the south and south-western coasts of the country, which receive between 1,550 and 1,600 hours a year. The coasts of Caernarvonshire have over 100 hours less sunshine every year, e.g., Llandudno has 1,499 hours, while the upland interior, which has a cloud cover for days on end, may have up to 300 hours a year less sunshine than the coastal areas.

Llandudno has an average of 5.8 hours of sunshine per day from April to September. For most of the coastal stations of the county, the mean daily sunshine for the year is about 4.2 hours, which represents some 35% of the possible sunshine. This mean decreases away from the coast, and it is likely that the mean daily value for the year falls to 3.5 hours or less in Snowdonia. Since most bright sunshine is received in summer, the average graph shows a steep rise in spring and a steady fall in the autumn. During the summer the sunniest month, June, has about 7 hours sunshine daily in Llandudno, but Snowdonia only receives between 4 and 6 hours daily at this time.

In December, the mean values of 1.3 hours in the coastal areas are about 0.5 hours less than in the sunniest parts of Wales. Although the coastal margins have 10% more sun than the inland areas in summer, the difference in winter is less apparent. Whilst June is the sunniest month, December is the dullest. So apart from any other factor, the coastal regions have the least amount of cloud and most sunshine, and the upland areas have the greatest amount of cloud and the lowest sunshine totals.

MEAN MONTHLY TEMPERATURES (°F)

Station	J	F	M	A	M	J	Jly.	A	S	O	N	D	Year
Llandudno	42.7	42.1	44.4	47.6	52.1	57.2	60.5	60.6	57.6	52.4	46.7	43.7	50.6
Aber	42.9	42.2	44.6	47.5	51.9	56.9	60.1	60.1	57.2	52.1	46.6	44.0	50.5
Betws-y-coed	39.8	40.3	41.8	45.9	51.0	56.4	58.8	58.3	54.8	48.6	43.5	41.0	48.4

CONVERSION TABLE °F/°C

°C	...	—17.8	—10	0	5	10	15	20	25	30	35	37.8	100
°F	...	0	14	32	41	50	58	68	77	86	95	100	212

DAILY MEAN HOURAGE OF BRIGHT SUNSHINE AT LLANDUDNO

	J	F	M	A	M	J	Jly.	A	S	O	N	D	Year
Hours	1.66	2.45	3.95	5.95	6.66	7.10	5.81	5.39	4.38	3.18	1.83	1.26	4.10

MEAN MONTHLY TOTAL OF BRIGHT SUNSHINE AT LLANDUDNO

	J	F	M	A	M	J	Jly.	A	S	O	N	D	Year
Hours	52	69	123	165	206	213	180	167	131	99	55	39	1,499

STONE AGE IMPLEMENTS

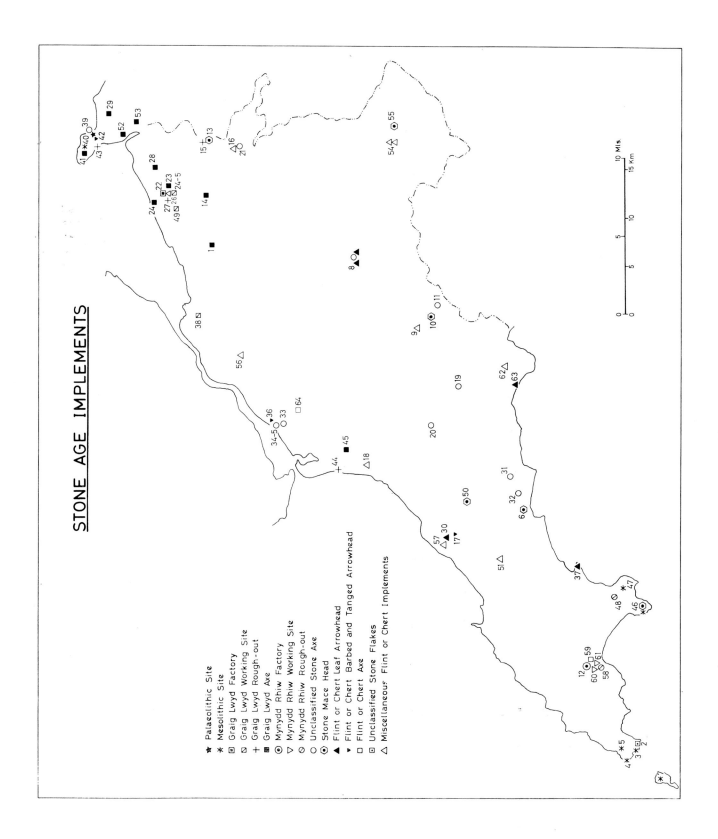

Palaeolithic Site ★
Mesolithic Site ✳
Graig Lwyd Factory ⊡
Graig Lwyd Working Site ⊠
Graig Lwyd Rough-out +
Graig Lwyd Axe ■
Mynydd Rhiw Factory ⊙
Mynydd Rhiw Working Site ▽
Mynydd Rhiw Rough-out ⊘
Unclassified Stone Axe ○
Stone Mace Head ⊙
Flint or Chert Leaf Arrowhead ▲
Flint or Chert Barbed and Tanged Arrowhead ▼
Flint or Chert Axe □
Unclassified Stone Flakes ⊡
Miscellaneous Flint or Chert Implements △

Stone Age Sites and Implements

Finds of stone implements provide the most comprehensive evidence for the activity of early man in Caernarvonshire. Stone implements cover a very long period of habitation. Finds of particular importance are the Gravettian occupation (c. 20,000 B.C.) of Kendrick's Cave, Llandudno, the Neolithic (c. 2,500 - 2,000 B.C.) axe factories at Graig Lwyd, Penmaen-mawr and Mynydd Rhiw, and the axe working site and habitations at Tynewydd, Llandygái.

The finds of flint implements are also noteworthy, as flint is not found naturally in the county. The various Mesolithic sites (8,000 - 4,000 B.C.) seem to represent inland penetrations by small groups of hunters who lived in areas now submerged by the Irish Sea and who were obtaining their flints from drift material. Finds of flints of later date (in particular, arrowheads and the hoard of flint flakes from Glasgwm, Penmachno) indicate the use of imported materials.

No.	N.G.R.	Parish	Site	Description
1	668700	Aber	Rhaeadr Fawr	Graig Lwyd Axe
2	154244	Aberdaron	Pared	5 Stone Flakes
3	147246	,,	Pared Llechymenyn	Mesolithic Flints
4	138252	,,	St. Mary's Church	Mesolithic Flints
5	161249	,,	Porth-y-pistyll	Flint and Stone Industry
6	397366	Aber-erch	Tŷ Gwyn	Mace Heads
7	119219	Bardsey	Carreg	Mesolithic Flints
8	654541	Beddgelert	Muriau'r Dre	4 Stone Axes; Flint Arrowheads
9	581479	,,	Cwm Cloch	Flint Flake
10	594461	,,	Aberglaslyn	Mace Head
11	605457	,,	Gardd Llygad-y-dydd	Stone Axe
12	234299	Bryncroes	Mynydd Rhiw	Stone Axe Factory
13	775703	Caerhun	Roman Fort	Mace Head
14	717706	,,	Bwlch y Ddeufaen	Graig Lwyd Axe
15	774705	,,	Caerhun Hall	Graig Lwyd Rough-out
16	765676	,,	Porthlwyd	Flint Flake
17	369439	Carnguwch	Cae'r Gribin	Barbed and Tanged Arrowhead
18	441534	Clynnog	Wern Bach	Flint Flake
19	523436	Dolbenmaen	Bryncir Old Hall	Stone Axe
20	483464	,,	Tafarn Faig	Stone Axe
21	7767	Dolgarrog	Valley Floor	Stone Axe
22	719752	Dwygyfylchi	Graig Llwyd	Axe Factory
23	725747	,,	Moel Lus	2 Graig Lwyd Axes
24	715763	,,	Penmaen-mawr	2 Graig Lwyd Axes
25	722746	,,	Druid's Circle	Flints and Flakes of Graig Lwyd Rock
26	721745	,,	Stone Circle	Flint Flakes
27	721746	,,	Stone Circle	Graig Lwyd Rough-out
28	747760	,,	Sychnant	Graig Lwyd Axe
29	803809	Eglwys-rhos	Cwm Howard	Graig Lwyd Axe
30	365447	Llanaelhaearn	Yr Eifl	Petit Tranchet Derivative Arrowhead
31	4338	Llanarmon	Chwilog	Stone Axe
32	412372	,,	Broom Hall	Stone Axe
33	485624	Llanbeblig	Segontium	3 Stone Axes
34	4863	,,	Caernarfon	Stone Axe (?)
35	,,	,,	,,	2 Stone Axes

No.	N.G.R.	Parish	Site	Description
36	4863	Llanbeblig	Caernarfon	Mace Head
37	337308	Llanbedrog	Trwyn Llanbedrog	Leaf-shaped Arrowhead
38	595712	Llandygái	Tynewydd	Graig Lwyd Axe-Working Site
39	778826	Llandudno	Kendrick's Cave	Upper Palaeolithic Occupation; Polished Stone Axe
40	762836	,,	Great Orme	Mesolithic Flints
41	,,	,,	,,	Graig Lwyd Axe
42	779826	,,	St. Tudno's Church	Barbed and Tanged Arrowhead
43	770821	,,	West Shore	Graig Lwyd Rough-out
44	437564	Llandwrog	Dinas Dinlle	Graig Lwyd Rough-out
45	457555	,,	Glynllifon	Graig Lwyd Axe
46	290238	Llanengan	Trwyn Cilan	Mesolithic Flints; Mace Head
47	321259	,,	Bryn'refail	Mesolithic Flints
48	305268	,,	Bodlondeb	Mynydd Rhiw Rough-out
49	704739	Llanfairfechan	Dinas	Graig Lwyd Axe-working Site
50	402426	Llangybi	Glasfryn	Mace Head
51	344390	Llannor	Tir-gwyn	Flint Scraper
52	780794	Llan-rhos	Gannock Park	Graig Lwyd Axe
53	779794	,,	Plas Mariandir	Graig Lwyd Axe
54	773506	Penmachno	Glasgwm	Hoard of Flint Flakes
55	7950	,,	Unknown	Mace Head
56	555699	Pentir	Goetre Uchaf	Flint Scraper
57	359450	Pistyll	Nant Gwrtheyrn	Flint Flake
58	235286	Rhiw	Church	Axe Rough-out and Scraper
59	239295	,,	Mynydd Rhiw	Flint Axe
60	238288	,,	Tan-y-muriau	Mynydd Rhiw Axe-working Site
61	2329	,,	Mynydd Rhiw	Mynydd Rhiw Axe-working Site
62	543384	Treflys	Cist Gerrig	2 Flint Flakes
63	524375	,,	Y Greigddu	Leaf-shaped Arrowhead
64	498606	Waunfawr	Castellmai	Chert Adze

BIBLIOGRAPHY

M. Herity, ' The Early Prehistoric Period around the Irish Sea ', in (ed.) D. Moore, *The Irish Sea Province in Archaeology and History* (Cardiff, 1970).

J. X. W. P. Corcoran, ' Multi-Period Construction and the Origins of the Chambered Long Cairn in Western Britain and Ireland ' in (ed.) F. M. Lynch and C. B. Burgess, *Prehistoric Man in Wales and the West* (Bath, 1972).

W. F. Grimes, *Guide to the Collections Illustrating the Prehistory of Wales in the National Museum of Wales* (Cardiff, 1951).

Royal Commission on Ancient and Historical Monuments in *Wales: Inventory of Caernarvonshire* (3 volumes, London, 1956-64).

(ed.) T. G. E. Powell, *Megalithic Enquiries in the West of Britain* (Liverpool, 1969).

K. Watson, *North Wales* (London, 1965).

C. H. Houlder, ' Stone Axes and Henge Monuments ', in (ed.) G. C. Boon and J. M. Lewis, *Welsh Antiquity* (Cardiff, 1976).

F. M. Lynch, ' Towards a Chronology of Megalithic Tombs in Wales ', in (ed.) G. C. Boon and J. M. Lewis, *Welsh Antiquity* (Cardiff, 1976).

W. F. Grimes, ' Neolithic Wales ', in (ed.) I. Ll. Foster and G. E. Daniel, *Prehistoric and Early Wales* (London, 1963).

G. de G. Sieveking, ' The Kendrick's Cave Mandible ', in *The British Museum Quarterly*, XXXV, 1-4.

R. G. Livens, ' The Irish Sea Element in the Welsh Mesolithic Cultures ' in (ed.) F. M. Lynch and C. B. Burgess, *Prehistoric Man in Wales and the West* (Bath, 1972).

Clynnog: Fach-wen Megalithic Grave

Photo: R.C.A.H.M., by permission of the Controller, H.M.S.O.

Dwygyfylchi: Druid Circle

Photo: R.C.A.H.M., by permission of the Controller, H.M.S.O.

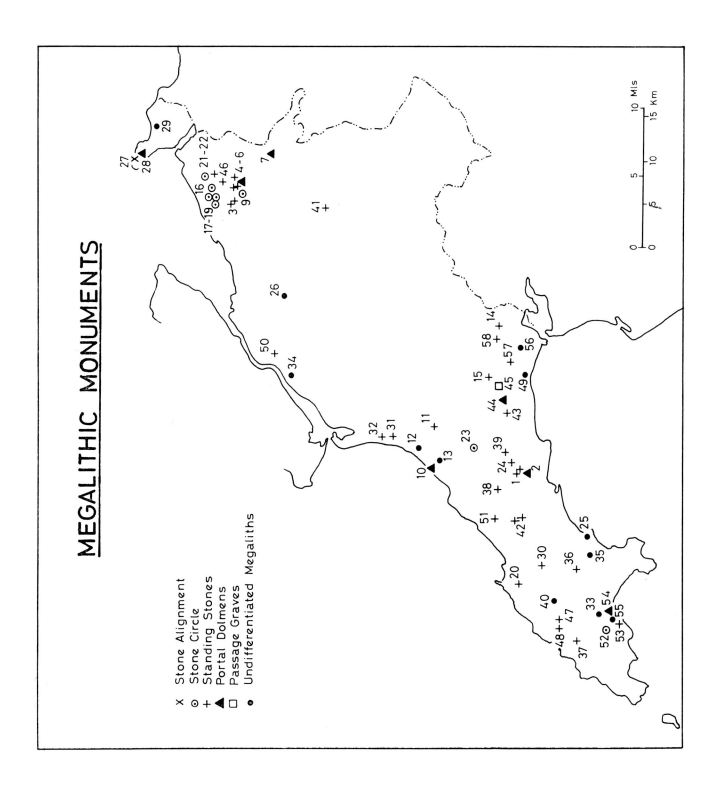

MEGALITHIC MONUMENTS

X   Stone Alignment
⊙   Stone Circle
+   Standing Stones
▲   Portal Dolmens
□   Passage Graves
●   Undifferentiated Megaliths

Megalithic Monuments

The Megalithic monuments of Caernarvonshire fall into two main categories:

1. *Standing Stones:* Many of these are undateable. Elsewhere (notably in Anglesey), some examples have been established as of Neolithic or Early Bronze Age date. A pot of indeterminate form — possibly Late Bronze Age — was found at the foot of the Maen Llwyd stone. Other stones, such as the Bwlch y Ddeufaen examples, may be route-markers, while others may be the remains of collapsed chambered tombs.

2. *Chambered Tombs:* Three types of monuments of this type can be distinguished.

   (a) Portal Dolmens, with a monumental facade at one end and the entrance blocked by a single large stone.

   (b) Passage Graves, with an approach passage to a burial chamber.

   (c) Undifferentiated types.

The Portal Dolmens have affinities in Ireland and elsewhere in Wales (notably the Ardudwy area of Merioneth) and are commonly regarded as of early Neolithic date (*c.* 3,000 B.C.). The Passage Grave type is represented by a single example, Coetan Arthur, Llanystumdwy, with parallels in Anglesey and Ireland. It is probably of later date.

None of the Caernarvonshire chambered tombs has been excavated recently. Although they are all presumably funereal monuments, they are held to reflect the pattern of settlement at this time, when the first agricultural communities were penetrating the area. Taken with the evidence of stone axes (Map 1), they suggest a coastal settlement with penetration into suitable areas, such as the hinterland of Eifionydd and Llŷn and the flanks of the Conwy Valley.

No.	N.G.R.	Parish	Site	Description
1	400389	Aber-erch	Four Crosses	To Standing Stones
2	399384	,,	,,	Portal Dolmen
3	714718	Caerhun	Bwlch y Ddeufaen	Two Large Stones
4	740717	,,	Maen y Bardd	Portal Dolmen
5	741718	,,	—	Two Standing Stones near Maen y Bardd
6	735716	,,	—	Standing Stone
7	770677	,,	Porth-llwyd	Portal Dolmen
8	738716	,,	Ffon y Cawr	Standing Stone
9	724713	,,	Cerrig Pryfed	Stone Circle and Outlier
10	407494	Clynnog	Y Fach-wen	Portal Dolmen
11	455491	,,	Cefngraenog	Standing Stone and Cairns
12	430510	,,	Pennarth	Undifferentiated
13	415486	,,	Pen-yr-allt Uchaf	Destroyed
14	568411	Dolbenmaen	Y Fach-goch	Standing Stone
15	507424	,,	Bryniau'r-tyddyn	Standing Stone
16	732749	Dwygyfylchi	—	Remains of Stone Circle
17	721745	,,	—	Stone Circle
18	718746	,,	Cors-y-carneddau	Stone Circle
19	721746	,,	—	Remains of Three Circles
20	270394	Edern	Nythfa	
21	747749	Gyffin	—	Standing Stone
22	747752	,,	—	Stone Circle
23	430444	Llanaelhaearn	Cae Maen-llwyd	Stone Circle

No.	N.G.R.	Parish	Site	Description
24	411402	Llanarmon	Plas-du	Standing Stone
25	325311	Llanbedrog	Bryn-parc	Undifferentiated
26	605688	Llandygái	Fron-deg	Undifferentiated
27	765840	Llandudno	Hwylfa'r-ceirw	Stone Alignment
28	772829	,,	Llety'r-filiast	Portal Dolmen
29	804814	,,	—	Undifferentiated
30	292364	Llandudwen	Garn Fadrun	Standing Stone
31	444541	Llandwrog	Maen-llwyd	Standing Stone
32	442553	Llandwrog	Bodfan	Standing Stone
33	300235	Llanengan	Trwyn Llech-y-ddôl	Undifferentiated
34	515660	Llanfair-is-gaer	Bryn	Dubious
35	303308	Llangïan	Yr Allor	Destroyed
36	287323	,,	Pandy	Standing Stone
37	208325	Llangwnnadl	—	Standing Stone
38	379416	Llangybi	Trallwyn	Standing Stone
39	421407	,,	Cae'r-fron	Standing Stone
40	251351	Llaniestyn	Tref-y-garnedd	Destroyed
41	705607	Llanllechid	Cwm y Bedol-arian	Standing Stone
42	344390	Llannor	Tir-gwyn	Two Standing Stones
43	464405	Llanystumdwy	Betws Fawr	Standing Stone
44	483408	,,	Rhos-lan	Portal Dolmen
45	498413	,,	Coetan Arthur	Passage Grave
46	739735	Liechwedd	Maenpenddu	Standing Stone
47	229345	Penllech	Mynydd Cefnamwlch	Undifferentiated
48	222345	,,	—	Standing Stone with Cup-marks
49	511382	Penllyn	Caerdyni	Undifferentiated
50	541682	Pentir	Cadair Elwa	Standing Stone
51	345420	Pistyll	Gwynnys	Standing Stone
52	219290	Rhiw	Meillionydd	Stone Circle
53	226276	,,	Capel Tan-y-foel	Standing Stone
54	237287	,,	Tan-y-muriau	Portal Dolmen
55	231281	,,	Bronheulog	Standing Stone
56	543384	Treflys	Cistgerrig	Undifferentiated
57	526398	,,	Pentre'r-felin	Undifferentiated
58	553414	Ynyscynhaearn	Cwm-mawr	Standing Stone

Maen-y-Bardd, Caerhun, Megalithic Grave   *Photo: R.C.A.H.M., by permission of the Controller, H.M.S.O.*

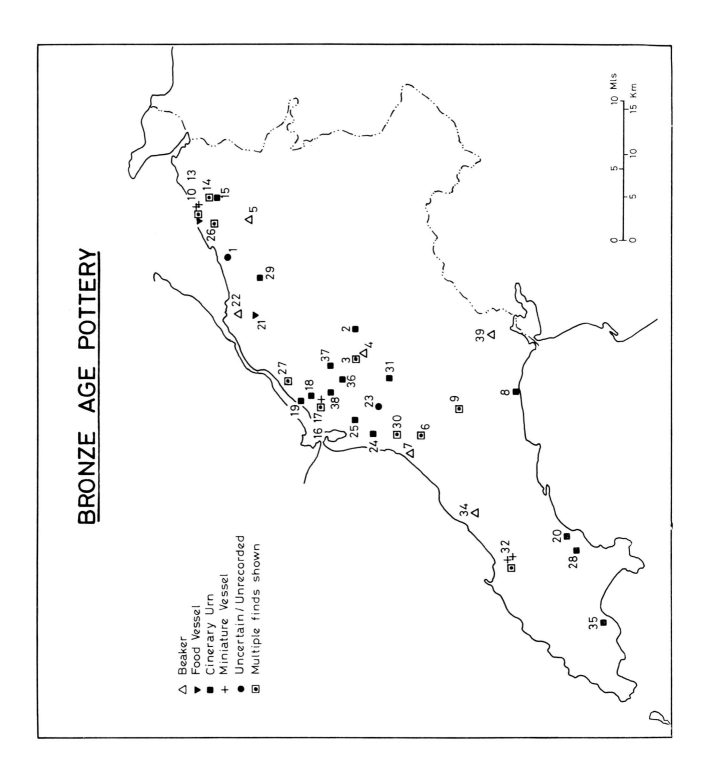

BRONZE AGE POTTERY

Beaker △

Food Vessel ▼

Cinerary Urn ■

Miniature Vessel +

Uncertain / Unrecorded ●

Multiple finds shown ▣

Bronze Age Pottery and Bronze Age Implements

The patterns of settlement and trade during the Bronze Age (1800 - 600 B.C.) are shown in these two maps. The first metal-users are thought to have been the makers of Beaker pottery (Map 3), whose origins can be traced back to the Rhineland and ultimately to Spain. The presence of metal ores in the area seems to have led to extensive activity within the Snowdonia massif, as well as a continuation of settlement in more favoured areas.

BRONZE AGE POTTERY

No.	N.G.R.	Parish	Site	Description
1	662729	Aber	Pen-y-bryn	Doubtful
2	572469	Beddgelert	Drws-y-coed	Urn
3	570540	,,	Glanrafon	' Urns '
4	565470	,,	Moel Hebog	Beaker
5	701694	Caerhun	Bwlchygwryd	Beaker
6	443492	Clynnog	Bryn Ifan	2 Cinerary Urns
7	426510	,,	Pennarth	Short-necked Beaker
8	499378	Cricieth	Castle	Urn
9	481449	Dolbenmaen	Pen Llystyn	10 Cinerary Urns
10	707759	Dwygyfylchi	Braich-lwyd	11 Cinerary Urns
11		,,	,,	2 Pigmy Cups
12		,,	Braich-lwyd ?	Food Vessel
13		,,	,,	Cinerary Urn
14	722746	,,	Druid Circle	3 Cinerary Urns
15	721745	,,	Stone Circle	Urn
16	482615	Llanbeblig	Bryn Saint	' Several ' Urns
17		,,	,,	Pigmy Cup
18	491625	,,	Maesybarcer	Enlarged Food Vessel
19	487641	,,	Waterloo Port	Cinerary Urn
20	330320	Llanbedrog	Tremvan	Cinerary Urn
21	592691	Llandygái	Carnedd Hywel	3 Food Vessels
22	594710	,,	Tynewydd	3 Beakers Assoc. W. Henges
23	486546	Llandwrog	Caeforgan	' Pottery '
24	444541	,,	Glynllifon	Enlarged Food Vessel
25	469572	,,	Penyboncyn	Urn
26	696740	Llanfairfechan	Tynyllwyfan	Urn + Fragments
27	509652	Llanfair-is-gaer	Bryn-crug	2 Cinerary Urns + Bronzes
28	3131	Llangïan	Pen-y-graig-wen	Urn + bones
29	635682	Llanllechid	Moel Faban	Cinerary Urn
30	443523	Llanllyfni	Eithinog-wen	2 + Cinerary Urns
31	510533	,,	Nantlle	Cinerary Urn
32	2939	Nefyn	Pen yr Orsedd	4 Cinerary Urns
33		,,	,,	Pigmy Cups (?)
34	356431	Pistyll	Llithfaen	Short-necked Beaker
35	228278	Rhiw	Rhiw	Urn with bronze awl and bronze pommel

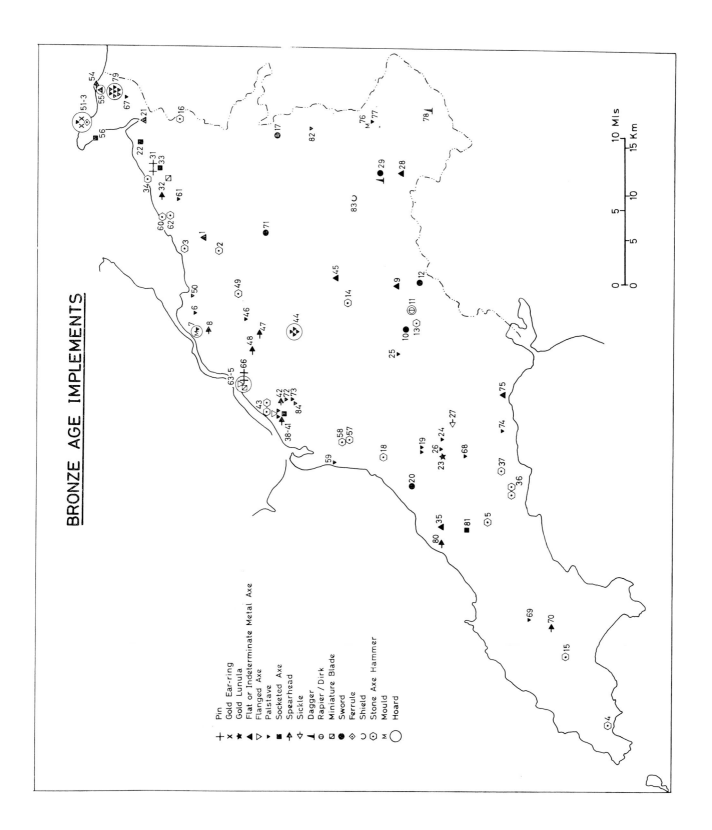

BRONZE AGE IMPLEMENTS

Pin

Gold Ear-ring

Gold Lunula

Flat or Indeterminate Metal Axe

Flanged Axe

Palstave

Socketed Axe

Spearhead

Sickle

Dagger

Rapier / Dirk

Miniature Blade

Sword

Ferrule

Shield

Stone Axe Hammer

Mould

Hoard

10 Mls

15 Km

No.	N.G.R.	Parish	Site	Description
36	509596	Waunfawr	Brynbeddau-isaf	Cinerary Urn
37	526605	,,	Garnedd-wen	Cinerary Urn
38	494605	,,	Rhos-bach	2 Cinerary Urns
39	565406	Ynyscynhaearn	Tanrallt	Long-necked Beaker

BRONZE AGE IMPLEMENTS

No.	N.G.R.	Parish	Site	Description	
1	665705	Aber	Wig Bach	' Bronze Celt '	
2	6569	,,	Moel Wnion	Axe-Hammer	
3	652727	,,	College Farm	Axe-Hammer	
4	174268	Aberdaron	Caerau	Axe-Hammer	
5	380399	Aber-erch	Crymllwyn	Axe-Hammer	
6	587715	Bangor	Maesgeirchen	Looped Palstave	
7	570711	,,	Cae Deon	Hoard of Mould-Valves & Palstave	
8	5770	,,	Unknown	Socketed Spearhead	
9	620500	Beddgelert	Llyn Dinas	' Axe Head '	
10	574488	,,	Meillionen	Sword	
11	594483	,,	Sygyn Bach	Hoard of 50 + ' rapiers '	
12	624476	,,	Buarthau	Sword	
13	581479	,,	Cwm Cloch	Axe-Hammer	
14	6053	,,	Snowdon	Axe-Hammer	
15	243313	Bryncroes	Trygarn	Axe-Hammer	
16	784735	Caerhun	Tremorfa	Axe-Hammer	
17	7763	,,	Craig Eigiau	Sword	
18	443510	Clynnog	Foel Dryll	Axe-Hammer	
19	4547	,,	Ynys-yr-arch	2 Palstaves	
20	414480	,,	Cwm Gwared	Sword	
21	784774	Conwy	Castle	Flat Axe	
22	760777	,.	Conwy Mountain	Socketed Axe	
23	447448	Dolbenmaen	Llecheiddior Uchaf	Gold Lunula	
24	464448	,,	Mynydd Cennin	Unlooped Palstave	
25	549497	,,	Cwm Trwsgl	Palstave	
26	455448	,,	Tuhwnt-i'r-mynydd	Unlooped Palstave	
27	480438	,,	Plas Llecheiddior	Sickle	
28	735498	Dolwyddelan	Tan-y-bwlch	Flat Axe	
29	7352	,,	Unknown	Sword and Dagger	
30	733756	Dwygyfylchi	Braich-lwyd	Socketed Axe	
31	,,	,,		2 Bronze Pins	
32	702754	,,	Braich y Dinas	Looped Spearhead	
33	722746	,,	Druid Circle	Bronze Blade (found in Urn)	
34	7277	,,	Penmaen-mawr	Axe-Hammer	
35	373446	Llanaelhaearn	Tre'r Ceiri	Flat Axe	
36	412372	Llanarmon	Broom Hall	2 Axe-Hammers	
37	433384	,,	Chwilog	Stone Hammer	
38	486624	Llanbeblig	Segontium	Flanged Axe	
39	,,	,,	,,	2 Palstaves	? Hoard
40	,,	,,	,,	Socketed Axe	
41	,,	,,	,,	Socketed Spearhead	
42	494622	,,	Brickworks	Spearhead	
43	4863	,,	Unknown	2 Axe-Hammers	
44	565608	Llanberis	Glyn Rhonwy	Hoard of 4 Palstaves	
45	626563	,,	Dinas Mot	Flat Axe	

No.	N.G.R.	Parish	Site	Description
46	582659	Llanddeiniolen	Carreg y Gath	Palstave
47	568644	,,	Fron-chwith	Socketed Spearhead
48	550653	,,	Dinas Dinorwig	Spearhead
49	606669	Llandygái	Pen-y-ffriddoedd	Axe-Hammer
50	603719	,,	Penrhyn	Unlooked Palstave
51	779839	Llandudno	Pigeon's Cave	2 Gold Ear-rings
52	,,	,,	,,	Looped Palstave — Hoard
53	,,	,,	,,	Ferrule
54	815827	,,	Creigiau Rhiwledin	Riveted Spearhead
55	8182	,,	Little Orme	Hoard of ' about 100 bronze celts '
56	762827	,,	Gogarth	Socketed Axe
57	4655	Llandwrog	Glynllifon	Axe-Hammer
58	457554	,,	,,	Axe-Hammer
59	436563	,,	Dinas Dinlle	Unlooped Palstave
60	685752	Lianfairfechan	Parc Nant	Axe-Hammer
61	701734	,,	Camarnaint	Axe-Hammer
62	685745	,,	Tyn-y-llwyfan	Axe-Hammer
63	515664	Llanfair-is-gaer	Bryn Crug	Double-looked Palstave
64	,,	,,	,,	Pin — Burial
65	,,	,,	,,	Blade — Group
66	,,	,,	,,	Pin (found in urn)
67	808797	Llangystennin	Cilmeityn-bach	Unlooped Palstave
68	447425	Llangybi	Ynys-y-creua	Unlooped Palstave
69	280352	Llaniestyn	Garn Fadrun	Looped Palstave
70	273329	,,	Ffridd-cefn-gaer	Socketed Spearhead
71	6764	Llanllechid	Carnedd Llywelyn	Sword
72	502620	Llanrug	Glangwna	Looped Palstave
73	5062	,,	Unknown	Unlooped Palstave
74	474386	Llanystumdwy	Churchyard	Looped Palstave
75	510385	Penllyn	Caerdyni	Flat Axe
76	783532	Penmachno	Bwlch-y-maen	Flat Axe Mould
77	,,	,,	,,	Unlooped Palstave
78	8047	,,	Eidda Boundary	Knife-Dagger
79	803806	Penrhyn	Gloddaeth	Hoard of 6 Palstaves
80	357447	Pistyll	Nant Gwrtheyrn	Spearhead
81	3742	,,	Carnguwch	Socketed Axe
82	778594	Trewydir	Nant Bwlch-yr-heyrn	Looped Palstave
83	705546	,,	Moel Siabod	Shield
84	498606	Waunfawr	Castellmai	Palstave

BIBLIOGRAPHY

H. N. Savory, ' The Later Prehistoric Migrations across the Irish Sea ', in (ed.) D. Moore, *The Irish Sea Province in Archaeology and History* (Cardiff, 1972).

W. F. Grimes, ' The Stone Circles and Related Monuments of Wales ', in (ed.) I. Ll. Foster and L. Alcock, *Culture and Environment* (London, 1963).

J. Evans, *The Ancient Bronze Implements, Weapons and Ornaments of Great Britain and Ireland* (London, 1881).

H. N. Savory, ' The Bronze Age ', in (ed.) I. Ll. Foster and G. E. Daniel, *Prehistoric and Early Wales* (London, 1965).

(ed.) R. G. Livens, *The Prehistoric Bronze Implements of Wales* (Cardiff, forthcoming).

Lunula of Irish origin, Llanllyfni.

Photo: National Museum of Wales

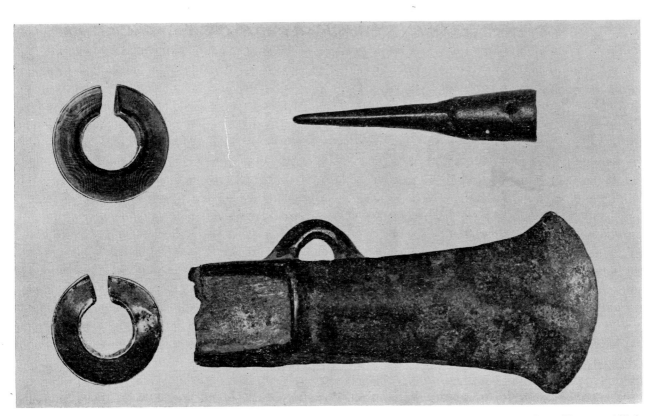

Bronze Hoard, Pigeon's Cave, Great Orme, Llandudno

Photo: National Museum of Wales

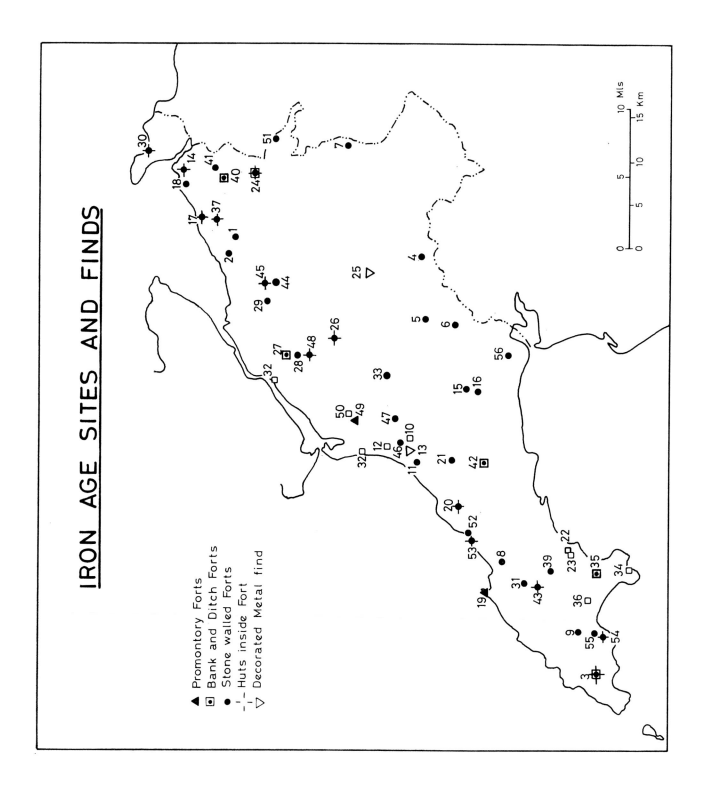

IRON AGE SITES AND FINDS

Promontory Forts
Bank and Ditch Forts
Stone walled Forts
Huts inside Fort
Decorated Metal find

10 Mls
15 Km

44

Iron Age Sites

The principal evidence for settlement during the Early Iron Age (600 B.C. - 100 A.D.) is the large number of defended hilltop enclosures (hillforts) which occur widely throughout the area. Some of these sites have huts within them and may have been permanently inhabited.

There are two principal types of hillfort which can be identified in Caernarvonshire:

(a) The Bank-and-Ditch type, which occurs mainly in coastal areas, is characterised by defences consisting of a large ditch, with the upcast heaped into a bank. This type of fort is common elsewhere in Britain, and the Caernarvonshire examples could have been introduced by immigrants from S.W. England.

(b) The Stone Walled type, with defences consisting simply of a massive dry-stone wall. This could well have been built by the native population.

The fact that both types of structure occur successively on the same site (e.g., Dinas Dinorwig) shows that there were two separate traditions.

The occasional finds of decorated metal-work are presumably imported: the Pen-y-Pass mount probably originated in S.W. England.

Some hillforts were certainly occupied into the Roman period (e.g., Braich y Dinas, Tre'r Ceiri, Dinas Emrys).

No.	N.G.R.	Parish	Site	Description
1	680717	Aber	Moel Dduarth	Stone Fort
2	663725	,,	Maes-y-gaer	Stone Fort
3	187284	Aberdaron	Castell Odo	Stone and B. & D. Fort + Huts
4	606492	Beddgelert	Dinas Emrys	Stone Fort
5	591488	,,	Dinas	Stone Fort
6	586457	,,	Pen-y-gaer	Stone Fort
7	786582	Betws-y-coed	Castell	Stone Fort + Huts
8	310393	Boduan	Garn Boduan	Stone Fort
9	232302	Bryncroes	Castell Caeron	Stone Fort
10	450507	Clynnog	Y Foel	B. & D. Fort
11	426497	,,	Penygarreg	Stone Fort (?)
12	441534	,,	Wern-fach	B. & D. Fort
13	439508	,,	Hendre-bach	Bronze Collar
14	760778	Conwy	Conwy Mountain	Stone Fort (2 phases) + Huts
15	509439	Dolbenmaen	Castell Caerau	Stone Fort
16	506427	,,	Craig-y-tyddyn	Stone Fort
17	701753	Dwygyfylchi	Braich y Dinas	Stone Fort + Huts
18	745773	,,	Allt-wen	Stone Fort
19	275416	Edern	Dinllaen	B. & D. Promontory Fort
20	373446	Llanaelhaearn	Tre'r Ceiri	Stone Fort + Huts
21	428455	,,	Pen-y-gaer	Stone Fort + Huts
22	323314	Llanbedrog	,,	B. & D. Fort
23	321314	,,	Nant-y-castell	B. & D. Fort
24	750693	Llanbedrycennin	Pen-y-gaer	Stone B. & D. Fort + Huts
25	6455	Llanberis	Pen y Pass	Enamelled bronze mount
26	566598	,,	Dinas Tŷ-du	Stone Fort and Huts
27	549653	Llanddeiniolen	Dinas Dinorwig	Stone and B. & D. Fort + Huts
28	547644	,,	Glasgoed	Stone Fort
29	610680	Llandygái	Pendinas	Stone Fort

No.	N.G.R.	Parish	Site	Description
30	779830	Llandudno	Pen-y-dinas	Stone Fort + Huts
31	286369	Llandudwen	Wyddgrug	Stone Fort
32	437563	Llandwrog	Dinas Dinlle	B. & D. Fort
33	526535	,,	Nantlle	Stone Wall
34	303246	Llanengan	Castell	B. & D. Fort
35	298282	,,	Pen-y-gaer	Stone and B. & D. Fort
36	292267	,,	Castell	B. & D. Fort
37	700738	Llanfairfechan	Dinas	Stone Fort + Huts
38	519671	Llanfair-is-gaer	,,	B. & D. Fort
39	298337	Llanfihangel Bachellaeth	Garn Saethon	Stone Fort
40	744729	Llangelynnin	Caer-bach	Stone and B. & D. Fort
41	754739	,,	Cerrig-y-dinas	Stone Fort
42	424417	Llangybi	Garn Pentyrch	Stone and B. & D. Fort
43	280352	Llaniestyn	Garn Fadrun	Stone Fort + Huts
44	628672	Llanllechid	Pen-y-gaer	Stone Fort
45	628679	,,	Rachub	Stone Fort and Huts
46	448520	Llanllyfni	Craig-y-dinas	Stone Fort
47	477526	,,	Caer Engan	Stone Fort
48	547627	Llanrug	Caer Carreg-y-frân	Stone Fort and Huts
49	471573	Llanwnda	Hen Gastell	B. & D. Promontory Fort
50	480579	,,	Gadlys	B. & D. Fort
51	793665	Maenan	Pen-y-castell	Stone Fort
52	342434	Pistyll	Ciliau-canol	Stone Fort
53	334436	,,	Carreg-y-llam	Stone Fort and Huts
54	228274	Rhiw	Creigiau Gwineu	Stone Fort and Huts
55	230283	,,	Conion	Stone Fort
56	549389	Ynyscynhaearn	Moel-y-Gest	Stone Fort

BIBLIOGRAPHY

A. H. A. Hogg, ' Early Iron Age Wales ', in (ed.) I. Ll. Foster and G. E. Daniel, *Prehistoric and Early Wales* (London, 1963).

H. N. Savory, *Guide Catalogue of the Early Iron Age Collections* (National Museum of Wales, Cardiff, 1976).

Ordnance Survey, *Map of Southern Britain in the Iron Age* (London, 1962).

A. H. A. Hogg, ' The Size-Distribution of Hill-forts in Wales and the Marches ', in (ed.) F. M. Lynch and C. B. Burgess, *Prehistoric Man in Wales and the West* (Bath, 1972).

H. N. Savory, ' The Later Prehistoric Migrations across the Irish Sea ', in (ed.) D. Moore, *The Irish Sea Province in Archaeology and History* (Cardiff, 1972).

A. H. A. Hogg, ' Hill-forts in the Coastal Area of Wales ', in (ed.) C. Thomas, *The Iron Age in the Irish Sea Province* (London, 1972).

Above (left):
Tŷ Newydd, Llandygái. Aerial photograph of the Neolithic/Early Bronze Age Henge Monuments.

Above (right):
Tre'r Ceiri, Llanaelhaearn. Aerial photograph of the Iron Age hill-fort.

Right:
Dinas Dinorwig, Llanddeiniolen. Aerial photograph of the Iron Age hill-fort.

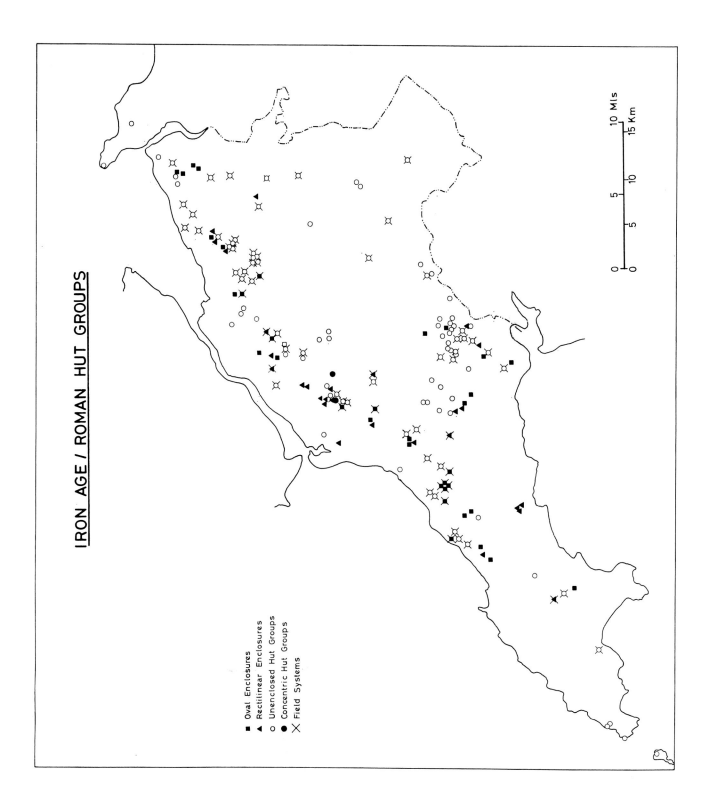

IRON AGE / ROMAN HUT GROUPS

■ Oval Enclosures
▲ Rectilinear Enclosures
o Unenclosed Hut Groups
● Concentric Hut Groups
X Field Systems

48

Iron Age and Roman Hut Groups

The most extensive evidence of settlement and land use is provided by the Hut Groups and Field Systems. Although these sites, where excavated, usually produced material of Roman date, it is possible that they reflect a pre-Roman pattern.

The most distinctive pattern of site is the Rectilinear Hut Group, where an enclosure made up of straight walls may contain up to a dozen huts of both circular and rectangular plans. These sites may be a native imitation of the Roman Villa. Finds usually indicate that they were occupied after 200 A.D.

The Oval Enclosures show less uniformity of pattern and date. The scattered huts occur mainly in upland areas, perhaps because similar sites have elsewhere been destroyed by later activity, and they may be associated with pastoral farming.

Many sites have adjacent tracts of ground which show traces of agricultural use. The areas of such field systems range from about 5 acres to about 15 acres per site. Traces of metalworking — principally ironwork — have been found on many sites (e.g., Hafod Wern-las, Cae Meta).

N.G.R.	Parish	Site	Details
673693	Aber	Afon Goch	Scattered Huts and Fields
671696	,,	,,	,,
667698	,,	Afon Rhaeadr-bach	,,
667697	,,	Aber Valley	,,
650715	,,	Ffridd Ddu	,,
665720	,,	,,	,,
657717	,,	,,	,,
658713	,,	,,	,,
674714	,,	Hafod Gelyn	Rectilinear Enclosure, scattered Huts and Fields
677716	,,	Moel Dduarth	Oval Hut Group
667703	,,	Rhaeadr Fawr	Oval Enclosure
667705	,,	,,	Rectilinear Hut Group
682719	,,	Moel Dduarth	,,
149276	Aberdaron	Mynydd Anelog	Scattered Huts
152277	,,	Anelog	,,
139256	,,	Mynydd Mawr	,,
386372	Aber-erch	Clogwyn Bach	Rectilinear Hut Group
385374	,,	,,	,,
383372	,,	Yoke House	,,
122218	Bardsey	Mynydd Enlli	Scattered Huts
654541	Beddgelert	Muriau'r Dre	Scattered Huts and Fields
638472	,,	Cwm Gelli-lago	Scattered Huts
636475	,,	,,	Scattered Huts and Fields
613450	,,	Bwlch Gwernog	Scattered Huts
655524	,,	Hafod Lwyfog	,,
579447	,,	Llyn Oerddwr	,,
647483	,,	Llyn Llagi	,,
588461	,,	Oerddwr Uchaf	,,
570478	,,	Llyn y Gadair	,,
570478	,,	Cwm Bleiddiad	Oval Hut Group
577448	,,	Cwm Ystradllyn	,,

N.G.R.	Parish	Site	Details
584448	Beddgelert	Hafod Gwyfil	Scattered Huts
590448	,,	Coed Oerddwr	,,
579453	,,	Pant Paladr	Oval Hut Group
582463	,,	Bwlch Golau	Scattered Huts
528582	Betws Garmon	Llwyn Bedw	Concentric Circle
515588	,,	Bryn Mair	Scattered Huts and Fields
708666	Caerhun	Pant-y-griafolen	,,
717668	,,	Cwm Dulyn	Rectilinear Hut Group
740719	,,	Maen y Bardd	Scattered Huts and Fields
243699	,,	Pen-y-gaer	,,
380428	Carnguwch	Carnguwch Mawr	Oval Hut Group
376435	,,	Tyddyn Cadwaladr	,,
373419	,,	Llech Engan	Scattered Huts
469488	Clynnog	Caerau	Oval Hut Group, Scattered Huts and Fields
455489	,,	Cefngraeanog	Rectilinear Hut Group
458493	,,	Graeanog	Oval Hut Group
455494	,,	,,	,,
430460	,,	Cwm	Scattered Huts and Fields
427508	,,	Pennarth	Scattered Huts
437476	,,	Cwm	Scattered Huts and Fields
464498	,,	Graeanfryn	,,
747757	Conwy	Llyn y Wrach	Scattered Huts
762778	,,	Mynydd y Dref	,,
505428	Dolbenmaen	Craig y Tyddyn	Oval Hut Group
499434	,,	Ty-newydd	,,
560418	,,	Moel yr Erw	Rectilinear Hut Group and Fields
492443	,,	Ty'n-y-caeau	Rectilinear Hut Group
487445	,,	Llystyn-ganol	,,
487449	,,	,,	Scattered Huts
579431	,,	Tai-Cochion	Rectilinear Hut Group
499477	,,	Mynydd Craig-Goch	Scattered Huts
501475	,,	,,	,,
498480	,,	,,	,,
552445	,,	Braich-y-gornel	Scattered Huts and Fields
548460	,,	Ceunant-y-ddôl	,,
556452	,,	Plas Llyn	,,
576437	,,	Moel Ddu	,,
568442	,,	Clogwyn y Gath	,,
567453	,,	Ffridd Isaf	,,
522472	,,	Gilfach	Scattered Huts
554448	,,	Tal-y-llyn	,,
574450	,,	Bwlch Cwm Ystradllyn	,,
551444	,,	Capel Saron	,,
489461	,,	Cefn Trefor-uchaf	,,
535430	,,	Cildrygwr	,,
516461	,,	Sulgwm	,,
581431	,,	Tai-cochion	,,
570458	,,	Yr Ogof	,,
565425	,,	Llyn Du	Scattered Huts and Fields
551407	,,	Ty'n-yr-Allt	,,
546447	,,	Caerfadog-uchaf	,,
739654	Dolgarrog	Moel Eilio	,,
695519	Dolwyddelan	Clogwyn Mawr	,,
713751	Dwygyfylchi	Graig Lwyd	,,
746758	,,	Pen y Ffordd-goch	Scattered Huts

N.G.R.	Parish	Site	Details
753768	Dwygyfylchi	Pen y Ffordd-goch	Oval Hut Group
753767	,,	,,	,,
404457	Llanaelhaearn	Cwm Corun	Oval Hut Groups and Fields
426451	,,	Tyddyn-Mawr	Rectilinear Hut Group and Fields
422451	,,	Cwmceiliog	Oval Hut Group and Fields
391457	,,	Maes-y-cwm	,,
397467	,,	Y Gurn Ddu	Scattered Huts and Fields
402471	,,	,,	,,
566598	Llanberis	Ty-du	Scattered Huts
576587	,,	Ceunant-bach	,,
569586	,,	Yr Aelgarth	,,
559634	Llanddeiniolen	Cae-coch	Oval Hut Group
572646	,,	Cae'r-mynydd	Oval Hut Group and Fields
574655	,,	Cefn-y-braich	,,
568652	,,	Castell	,,
547647	,,	Glasgoed	Oval Hut Group
535650	,,	Cae Meta	Rectilinear Hut Group and Fields
548650	,,	Pen-y-groes	Rectilinear Hut Group
552667	,,	Ty-mawr	Oval Hut Group
555636	,,	Caecorniog	Scattered Huts and Fields
550636	,,	Tan-y-coed	Scattered Huts
517645	,,	Aden	Scattered Huts and Fields
594685	Llandygái	Cororion	Scattered Huts
601684	,,	Parc Gelli	,,
588668	,,	Gerlan	,,
754841	Llandudno	Great Orme	,,
493572	Llandwrog	Coed-y-brain	Oval Hut Group and Fields
497571	,,	Hafoty Tynewydd	Oval Hut Group, Scattered Huts and Fields
521537	,,	Gelliffrydiau	Oval Hut Group and Fields
521537	,,	Geulan	Rectilinear Hut Group and Fields
528543	,,	Nantlle	Scattered Huts and Fields
683733	Llanfairfechan	Garreg-fawr	,,
686748	,,	Gwern-y-plas	,,
702740	,,	Dinas	,,
311356	Llanfihangel Bachellaeth	Carn-bach	Scattered Huts
286335	,,	Penbodlas	Rectilinear Hut Group with Fields
292323	Llangïan	Saethon	Oval Hut Group and Fields
297313	,,	Mynytho	Oval Hut Group
753741	Llangelynnin	Cerrig y Dinas	,,
751736	,,	Ffynnon Gelynnin	,,
657669	Llanllechid	Cwm Caseg	Scattered Huts and Fields
632684	,,	Llanllechid	,,
640690	,,	Llefn	,,
643684	,,	Cwm Ffrydlas	,,
637681	,,	Moel Faban	,,
629673	,,	Tyddyn Sabel	,,
636665	,,	Y Garth	Oval Hut Group and Fields
616684	,,	Coed-uchaf	,,
616693	,,	Rhiw-goch	Oval Hut Group
692607	,,	Lake Ogwen	Scattered Huts and Fields
491536	Llanllyfni	Hafodlas	Oval Hut Group and Fields
476540	,,	Tyddyn-bach	Rectilinear Hut Group and Fields
479539	,,	Llwyndu-bach	Oval Hut Group
743630	Llanrhychwyn	Gwydir Forest	Scattered Huts and Fields

N.G.R.	Parish	Site	Details
517617	Llanrug	Prysgol	Rectilinear Hut Group
517613	,,	Hafod Rug-isaf	,,
551615	,,	Gallt-y-celyn	Scattered Huts and Fields
547616	,,	Parciau Gleision	Scattered Huts
505579	Llanwnda	Gaerwen	Scattered Huts and Fields
500582	,,	Hafoty Wern-las	Rectilinear Hut Group, Concentric Circle, Scattered Huts and Fields
501585	,,	Cae Hen	Oval Hut Group
511584	,,	Pen y Bryn-bach	Rectilinear Hut Group
501583	,,	,,	Scattered Huts
506589	,,	Erw	Rectilinear Hut Group
464577	,,	Dinas y Pryf	Rectilinear Hut Group (?)
494590	,,	Brynbeddau	Rectilinear Hut Group and Fields
503595	,,	Gwredog-isaf	Rectilinear Hut Group
464591	,,	Pont-faen	Scattered Huts
755764	Llechwedd	Gwern Engan	Scattered Huts and Fields
760498	Penmachno	Glasgwm	
800809	Penrhyn	Gloddaeth	,,
583696	Pentir	Ty-coch	Scattered Huts
350450	Pistyll	Nant Gwrtheyrn	,,
359447	,,	Graig Ddu	Oval Hut Group and Fields
333414	,,	Ty-gwyn	Scattered Huts and Fields
346431	,,	Bwlch	Rectilinear Hut Group
351442	,,	Mount Pleasant	Scattered Huts and Fields
330405	,,	Bryn-dymchwyl	,,
343417	,,	Gwynnys	Oval Hut Group
232284	Rhiw	Rhiw	,,
541383	Treflys	Ty-mawr	Scattered Huts and Fields
537390	,,	Garth Morthin	Oval Hut Group
731550	Trewydir	Cefn Glas	Scattered Huts and Fields
736554	,,	,,	Scattered Huts
549413	Ynyscynhaearn	Cwm Mawr	,,
560412	,,	Cwm Bach	Oval Hut Group
			Scattered Huts

BIBLIOGRAPHY

M. G. Jarrett, ' The Military Occupation of Roman Wales ', *Bulletin of the Board of Celtic Studies,* XX, Pt. 2, 206-220.

V. E. Nash-Williams (ed. M. G. Jarrett), *The Roman Frontier in Wales* (2nd edn., Cardiff, 1969).

G. C. Boon, ' Segontium ', *Amgueddfa* 18 (1974).

A. H. A. Hogg, ' Pen Llystyn: A Roman Fort and other Remains ', *Archaeological Journal,* CXXV, 101-192).

A. H. A. Hogg, ' Native Settlement in Wales ', in (ed.) C. Thomas, *Rural Settlement in Roman Britain* (London, 1966).

C. A. Gresham, ' The Interpretation of Settlement Patterns in North-West Wales ', in (ed.) I. Ll. Foster and L. Alcock, *Culture and Environment* (London, 1963).

Roman Fort, Segontium

Photo: Ministry of the Environment

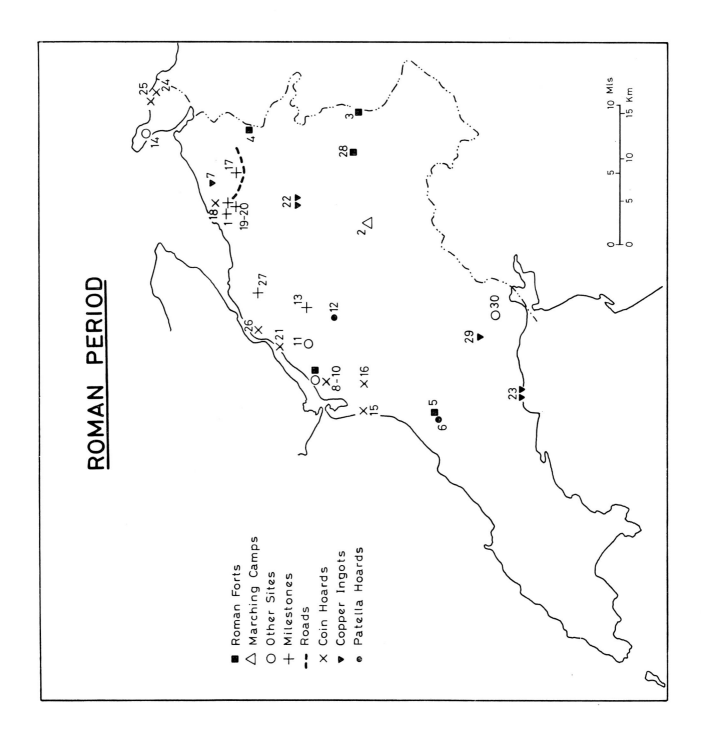

ROMAN PERIOD

25 24

14

4

3

17

7 28

18 1 19-20

22

2

27

13

12

26 21

11

30

29

8-10

16

23

15

5

6

Roman Forts

Marching Camps

Other Sites

Milestones

Roads

Coin Hoards

Copper Ingots

Patella Hoards

Roman Period

The distinctively Roman sites in the area are purely military, with the exception of the site at Tremadog, Ynyscynhaearn.

The majority of sites are forts, associated with the garrisoning and exploitation of the area, which commenced under Agricola in 78-80 A.D. There is little evidence of the course of Agricola's conquest, or of the campaign of Suetonius Paulinus in 60-61 A.D. The only marching-camp known (Penygwryd) is too small to accommodate a major expedition.

The pattern of occupation seems to have varied: Pen Llystyn was abandoned by 100 A.D. and Bryn y Gefeiliau was built at about this time. Both Segontium and Caerhun had extensive civil settlements outside the forts, and may well have remained in use until c. 100 A.D.

Finds of milestones give an indication of the extent and use of the road-system. The number of coin-hoards indicates a measure of native prosperity and finds of copper ingots suggest exploitation of the local ores.

No.	N.G.R.	Parish	Site	Description
1	665735	Aber	Madryn	Milestone of Postumus
2	660557	Beddgelert	Penygwryd	Marching Camp
3	795557	Betws-y-coed	Royal Oak	Fort?
4	775703	Caerhun	Caerhun	Fort
5	481449	Dolbenmaen	Pen Llystyn	Fort
6	484844	,,	,,	Hoard of Patellae
7	701753	Dwygyfylchi	Penmaen-mawr	Fragment of Copper Ingot
8	483624	Llanbeblig	Segontium	Fort
9	482624	,,	Hen Waliau	Walled Enclosure
10	483624	,,	Segontium	Coin Hoard
11	502634	,,	Bryn-glas	Defensive Earthwork
12	5660	Llanberis	?	Hoard of Patellae
13	566635	Llanddeiniolen	Cae'r-bythod	Milestone of Decius
14	775830	Llandudno	Great Orme	Copper Mines
15	437563	Llandwrog	Dinas Dinlle	Coin Hoard
16	474563	,,	Llwyn-y-gwalch	Coin Hoard
17	719716	Llanfairfechan	Cae-coch	Milestone of Constantine
18	683757	,,	Pinehurst	Coin Hoard
19	679727	,,	Rhiwiau	Milestone of Hadrian
20	,,	,,	,,	Milestone of Severi
21	520662	Llanfair-is-gaer	Cae'r-Brenin	Coin Hoard
22	685637	Llanllechid	Carnedd Llywelyn	Two copper ingots
23	457372	Llanystumdwy	Glanllynnau	Two copper ingots
24	825814	Penrhyn	Penrhyn Bay	Coin Hoard
25	807822	,,	Little Orme	Coin Hoard
26	537695	Pentir	Y Faenol	Coin Hoard
27	537696	,,	Ty-coch	Milestone of Severi
28	746572	Trewydir	Bryn y Gefeiliau	Fort
29	532424	Ynyscynhaearn	Clenennau	Copper Ingot
30	557401	,,	Tremadog	Building with Hypocaust

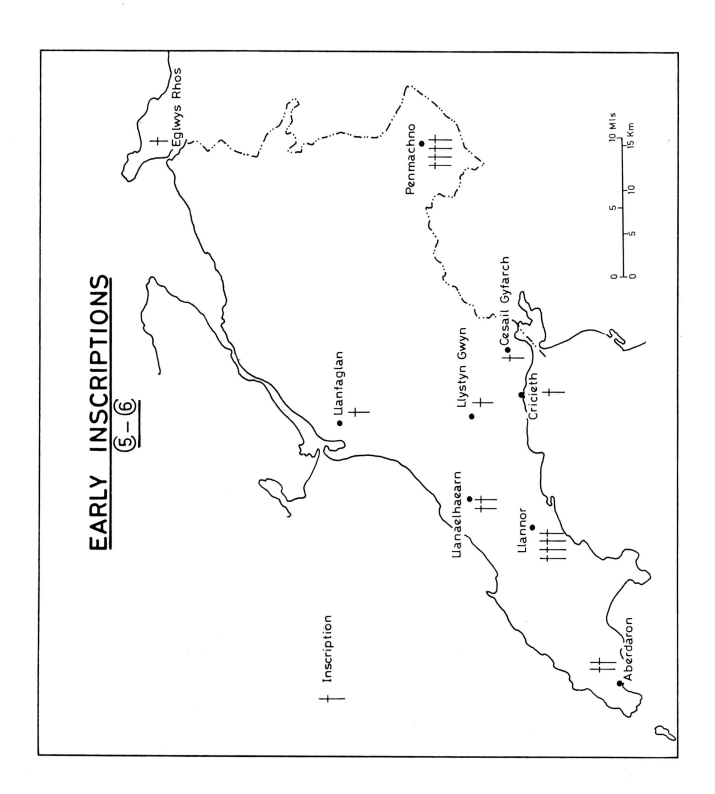

EARLY INSCRIPTIONS
⑤ – ⑥

Eglwys Rhos

Penmachno

Cesail Gyfarch

Llanfaglan

Llystyn Gwyn

Cricieth

Llanaelhaearn

Llannor

Aberdaron

┼ Inscription

10 Mls
15 Km

5

10

5

5

0
0

Early Inscriptions

Valuable information concerning some aspects of the early history of this part of Gwynedd from the end of the fifth to the end of the sixth centuries can be gathered from the inscriptions carved on memorial stones. The evidence of these inscriptions is also important for the study of the development of the Welsh language from its Brythonic antecedents as well as for the study of the forms of Latin used in Britain.

Seventeen inscriptions from Caernarvonshire have survived (it is known that one from Pen-prys, Llannor, has disappeared). The inscriptions are in Latin and the lettering is in the Latin alphabet, but the inscription at Llystyn Gwyn, Bryncir, is in Latin together with a name in Ogam characters. The Ogam 'alphabet' was a system of notches cut across the angle of the face and side of the stone (there are twenty 'characters' in the alphabet). Ogam developed in Ireland and there are inscriptions in Wales with Ogam alone as well as with Ogam and Latin together. The Llystyn Gwyn stone provides an example of a 'bilingual' inscription — Latin: ICORI FILIVS POTENTINI, Ogam: ICORIGAS. This, and a similar 'bilingual' inscription on the Clocaenog (Denbigh) stone, are the only two in North Wales with Ogam. The use of Ogam testifies to the persistence of Irish influence in Wales, but the significance of the Ogam on this stone in Eifionydd has not yet been fully explained (the Irish origin of the names *Llŷn* and *Portinllaen,* or *Porth Dinllaen,* is relevant in this context).

The inscriptions can be dated by reference to Latin epigraphic styles and also according to the formulae employed in them. It is possible to identify the influence of forms which are characteristic of Christian Latin monuments in Gaul on about twelve of the Caernarvonshire inscriptions. The formulae of Ogam inscriptions were different and their pattern can be discerned in some of the Latin inscriptions — for example, at Llanfaglan, Llannor (VENDESETLI), Eglwys Rhos, Llanaelhaearn, Llystyn Gwyn, and Penmachno (*]* FILI AVITORI). Another Latin inscription was added on the Penmachno stone. The words on it have been abbreviated and the interpretation is uncertain. According to one interpretation, a precise date is recorded, namely, 'in the time of the consul Justinus' (that is, A.D. 540); another reading has been suggested — '(the grave of) a most loving and righteous

husband'. In any case, it is not certain that the two inscriptions on this stone were carved at the same time.

It is most likely that these stones were set up to mark the burial places of notable Christian persons (men and women). The Eglwys Rhos inscription states that SANCTINVS was a SACER*[DOS]* 'bishop', probably. The Aberdaron inscriptions, which were at one time sited near Capel Anelog, name two priests (the term is *presbyter*): VERACIVS and SENACVS. *Senacus* is said to be resting with a multitude of brethren (CVM MVLTITUDNEM FRATRVM), and this suggests that there is reference here to a grave within the cemetery of an ecclesiastical community, the nucleus perhaps of the later *clas* at Aberdaron. Occasionally a formula was used which was not necessarily factually correct; for example, one of the Penmachno inscriptions, CARAVSIVS HIC IACIT IN HOC CONGERIES LAPIDVM ('Carausius lies here in this cairn of stones'). Both this stone and one at Treflys (Cricieth) have the *Chi-Rho* symbol — a monogram formed from the first two letters of the Greek form of the name of Christ: X(*chi*) and P(*rho*). There are no other examples of this symbol with an inscription in Wales.

Not every memorial stone was set up near an ecclesiastical foundation — for example, the inscribed stone at Cesail Gyfarch, Penmorfa, which names CVNACVS (corresponding to Welsh *Cynog*) and the stone at Llystyn Gwyn, Bryncir. The stones discovered at Llannor were used to provide two sides for a later grave (it is not known whether this was a Christian burial). The name VENDESETLI is recorded on one of these — it corresponds to the later Welsh form *Gwynhoedl*. Since the Llannor inscription is probably of fifth century date, it is difficult to establish that it commemorates Gwynhoedl the saint associated with Llangwnnadl whose period, according to the Welsh genealogies, seems to have been the sixth century. On the other hand, it is possible that the inscription may refer to the lay patron of a Christian foundation in the district. The early name of the district was Nant Gwnnadl (and this explains why the name of the parish is not 'Llanwnnadl').

The significance of two of the Penmachno stones has already been noted. On one of the others it is stated that CANTIORI*[X]* lies there, that he was

VENEDOTIS CIVE[S] and a close kinsman of *Maglos* who was *magistratus. Venedotis* is an adjectival form of the Brythonic name for Gwynedd (*Ueneda*); the corresponding Welsh form would be Gwyndod and there is a reference in the 'Stanzas of the Graves' to Gwrgi, '*Gwyndodydd lew*' — 'the hero of the men of Gwynedd'. Cantiori[x] was an important *Gwyndodwr* whose family shared his pride in the dignity implicit in the term *cives*, 'citizen'. The exact nature of the office of *magistratus* at this period is not clear, but the word suggests that there was a fairly well-established social organization in this part of Gwynedd. Taliesin, at the end of the sixth century, eulogizes Gwallawg who was *ygnat* (*ynad*) in Elfed — a district in Yorkshire which included Leeds — and it may be that *magistratus* and *ygnat* were synonymous terms for equivalent offices. It should be noticed that neither *cives* nor *magistratus* occurs on any other Christian inscription in Britain. Moreover, references to the professional occupations of laymen are extremely rare in the Christian inscriptions of Britain. The Llangïan inscription is therefore of particular interest: MELI MEDICI — '*Melus* the doctor', son of *Martinus.* The term *medicus* does not occur on any other monument in Britain.

A man who died far away from his native territory is commemorated on the Llanaelhaearn stone: ALIORTVS ELMETIACO. He was a stranger whose roots were in Elfed but he was neither the first nor the last to move 'from kingdom to kingdom' to serve a lord in his court or in his war-band.

The inscriptions from Caernarvonshire record 26 personal names. Ten of these are Latin names and there are Welsh derivatives of some of them. Thus, IOVENALI FILI ETERNI is named on one of the Llannor inscriptions; the first name is a form of *Juvenalis,* and *Iouanaul* occurs as the name of a cleric in the 'Book of Llandaff'; *Eternus* appears in Welsh as *Edyrn* and *Edern.* The name SANCTINVS in the Eglwys Rhos inscription corresponds to the Welsh form *Seithin.* Celtic elements can be identified in the other 16 personal names. For example, at Llanfaglan — FILI LOVERNII ANATEMORI, that is, '[the stone of] *Eneidfawr* (literally, 'Great Soul' or 'The magnanimous one') son of *Llywern*'; llywern is one of the Welsh names for 'fox' and it occurs as a personal name, *Louern,* in the 'Book of Llandaff' and in the place-name Llanfihangel Ystum Llywern in Gwent. LOVERNACI is named on an inscription at Merthyr, near Llannewydd (Newchurch), Carmarthenshire. Reference has been made to *Vendesetli/Gwynhoedl* (Llannor) and to *Maglos* (Penmachno): the Welsh form of *Maglos* is *mael,* 'prince, leader', and this element is found in the names of *Maelgwyn, Cynfael, Brochfael* and *Arthfael.* In *Cantiori[x]* (Penmachno) and *Icori[x]* (Llystyn Gwyn, Bryncir), the second element *-rix* corresponds to Welsh *rhi,* 'king'; forms corresponding to the first elements in these two names are found in personal names in Gaul, and *Cantiori[x]* probably meant 'king of hosts'.

BIBLIOGRAPHY

V. E. Nash-Williams, *The early Christian monuments of Wales* (Cardiff, 1950).

Kenneth Jackson, *Language and history in early Britain* (Edinburgh, 1953).

I. Ll. Foster and Glyn Daniel (ed.), *Prehistoric and early Wales,* Chapter VIII (London, 1965).

The Royal Commission on Ancient and Historical Monuments in Wales, *An inventory of the ancient monuments in Caernarvonshire,* 3 Cyfrol (H.M.S.O., London, 1956, 1960, 1964).

Archaeologia Cambrensis, CXIX (1970), t. 160.

Llanfaglan

Llanaelhaearn

Aberdaron

Penmachno

59

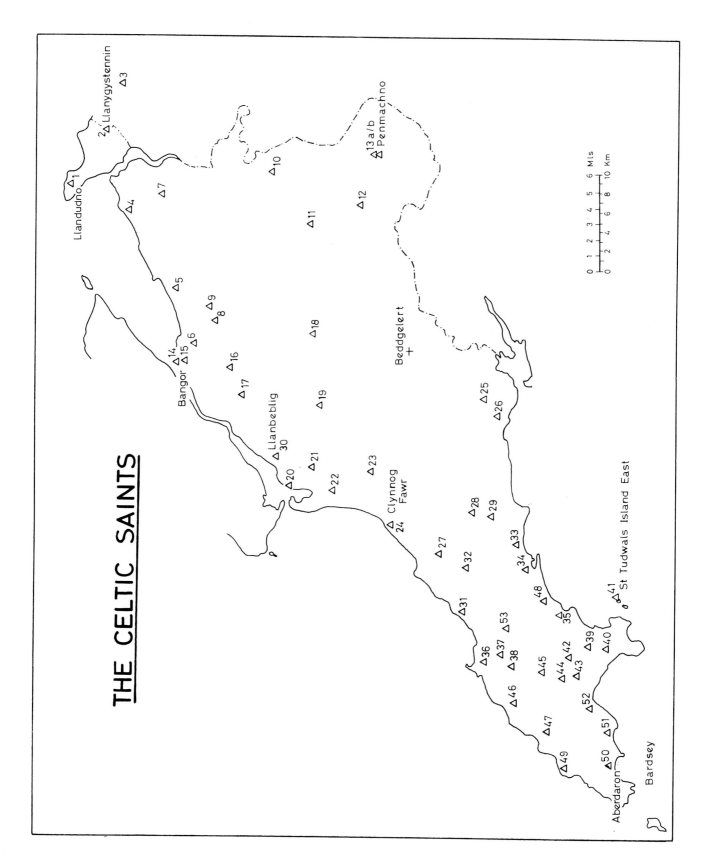

THE CELTIC SAINTS

Δ3

²Δ Llanygystennin

Δ1 Llandudno

Δ7

Δ4

Δ10

13a/b Δ Penmachno

Δ12

Δ11

Δ5

Δ9
Δ8

Δ18

Beddgelert
+

Δ14 Δ6
Δ15
Bangor

Δ16

Δ17

Δ19

Δ25
Δ26

Llanbeblig
30

Δ20 Δ21

Δ22

Δ23

Clynnog
Fawr
Δ24

Δ28
Δ29

Δ27

Δ32

Δ33
Δ34

St Tudwals Island East
Δ41

Δ31

Δ48
Δ35

Δ53
Δ37

Δ39

Δ40

Δ36

Δ38

Δ45

Δ44 Δ42
Δ43

Δ46

Δ52

Δ47

Δ51

Δ49

Δ50 Aberdaron

Bardsey

0 1 2 3 4 5 6 Mls
0 2 4 6 8 10 Km

The Celtic Saints

We know that there was some Christianity in Britain during the period of the Roman occupation, but there is little evidence of its presence in Wales, except possibly in the south-eastern corner. In the centuries following the withdrawal of the Roman troops, Wales was Christianised through the efforts of the Celtic saints. Celtic Christianity seems to have resulted from a fusion, which may have taken place in the Severn Sea area, between what remained of Christianity in Britain and incoming influences from Gaul. The latter were strongly influenced by the teaching of St. Martin of Tours and his followers, who had absorbed many of the ideas and practices of the Desert Fathers in Egypt.

It is probable that Roman government ceased in North Wales earlier than in the rest of Britain — a fact closely related to the withdrawal of troops by Maximus in 383 to support him in his bid for the Imperial Purple. Maximus seems to have had close associations with Caernarfon (Segontium), and is known to have had a Welsh wife — Helena. After crossing to the continent and being victorious in battle, the new Emperor set up his court at Treves in eastern Gaul. Here, he and his wife frequently entertained St. Martin, whom they counted among their personal friends. When, subsequently, Maximus was defeated and slain, it is said that his wife and her two sons, Constantine and Publicius, returned to Wales as 'Saints'. It is significant that Helena's sons are remembered in church dedications in Caernarvonshire; Constantine at Llangystennin (2), and Publicius at Llanbeblig (30). The archaeological evidence we possess in the form of Early Christian Inscribed Stones tends to confirm this early arrival of Christianity in Caernarvonshire from Gaulish sources.

As Celtic Christianity took root in the western lands, it would appear that three types of settlement developed: large monastic training schools; settlements resulting from the widespread missionary activity of the saints, usually containing a few bee-hive huts and a little church, and known as a LLAN; and, thirdly, tiny hermit cells. All three carried with them the name of the saint who founded them or, perhaps, that of his special patron. In time, some of the more important settlements developed into a CLAS, or mother church, becoming the centre of a family of saints who did further missionary work in the countryside around. The Celtic settlements at Bangor, Clynnog Fawr and Aberdaron belong to this class. Some, too, like St. Beuno's settlement (24), became places of popular pilgrimage. Centuries later, many of these primitive churches and cells were replaced by structures in wood and stone, surviving into our own time as parish churches, rebuilt, but still bearing the names of their original founders. Indeed, little is known of the Celtic saints in a strictly historical sense beyond their names, preserved in this way, and in various genealogies.

The most notable saint in Gwynedd was undoubtedly St. Beuno (24, 25, 31, 32, 34, 44), and closely associated with him in his work were SS. Aelhaearn (27), Cwyfan (46), Edern (36) and Twrog (22). The other great name is Deiniol, who is accredited with the foundation of the ecclesiastical centre at Bangor (14, 15). Likewise, in attempting to assess the contemporary picture, little help is obtained from archaeological sources. Few structural remains survive, apart, possibly, from the foundations of Celtic cells uncovered at Bangor in ground below the University College (14), and the foundations of earlier buildings (including, possibly, the original church of St. Beuno), discovered beneath and near the present chapel (24).

Altogether, the map shows the sites of 54 churches and chapels bearing the names of Celtic saints. In the past, there were many more of them, for quite a number of our present-day churches, now dedicated to Biblical saints, almost certainly originally had Celtic dedications, which were later substituted by those more fashionable with the Anglo-Norman invaders, who were zealous adherents of the Roman Church. This is well illustrated at Beddgelert (said to be one of the oldest Celtic settlements in Caernarvonshire). When Gerald visited it towards 1200, it was still unconnected with any regular order of Roman monks, but just afterwards it adopted the rule of Augustinian canons, and the church was rededicated at that time to St. Mary. This important feature of Caernarvonshire churches is well illustrated for the county as a whole when we consider that in the eastern section of the county, where Anglo-Norman influences were strongest, 59% of the present churches have a Celtic dedication. In central

Caernarvonshire the percentage rises to 64, while in Llŷn Celtic dedications reach 77%. In considering the western churches in Llŷn, we should not ignore two other important matters, namely, the extreme importance of movement by sea from peninsula to peninsula, and from headland to headland that characterised the travels of the Celtic saints, and here was Llŷn, a veritable pierhead jutting out into the western seas. Secondly, we must remember the predilection of the Celtic saints for island sites as places of retreat. Bardsey Island and St. Tudwal's Island East come immediately to mind. The fame of Bardsey as the burial-place of saints and a place of pilgrimage from early times is well known. On the island itself, it would appear that there existed from the sixth century an important Celtic settlement, founded by a saint whose name is now unknown. The Celtic settlement was replaced later by the Abbey of St. Mary, the ruins of which still survive. There is no doubt also that the island acted as a retreat for the saints dwelling in the ' Clas ' at Aberdaron in Celtic times. In these circumstances, no symbol is placed on Bardsey Island on the map, important as it was. This, and similar problems at other sites, determined that the most satisfactory procedure in preparing the map was to plot only the sites of those churches which still carry the name of a Celtic saint.

	Parish	
1	Llandudno	TUDNO
2	Llangystennin	CWSTENNIN
3	Llysfaen	CYNFRAN
4	Dwygyfylchi	GWYNAN
5	Aber	BODFAN
6	Llandygái	TEGAI
7	Llangelynnin	CELYNNIN
8	Llanllechid	LLECHID
9	Llanllechid	Llanerchyn now Llanylchi (Old Church)
10	Llanrhychwyn	RHYCHWYN
11	Llandygái	CURIG (Cyriacus now)
12	Dolwyddelan	GWYDDELAN
13a	Penmachno	TUDCLUD
13b	Penmachno	ENCLYDWYN (Ruins of early cells)
14	Bangor	DEINIOL
15	Bangor	DEINIOL (The Cathedral)
16	Pentir	CEDOL
17	Llanddeiniolen	DEINIOLEN
18	Llanberis	PERIS
19	Betws Garmon	GARMON
20	Llanfaglan	BAGLAN
21	Llanwnda	GWYNDAF
22	Llandwrog	TWROG
23	Llanllyfni	RHEDYW
24	Clynnog Fawr	BEUNO
25	Penmorfa	BEUNO
26	Treflys	CYNHAEARN (Previously the Parish Church of Ynyscynhaearn)

	Parish	
27	Llanaelhaearn	AELHAEARN
28	Llangybi	CYBI
29	Llanarmon	GARMON
30	Llanbeblig	PEBLIG
31	Pistyll	BEUNO
32	Carnguwch	BEUNO
33	Aber-erch	CAWRDAF
34	Deneio	BEUNO
35	Llanbedrog	PEDROG
36	Edern	EDERN
37	Ceidio	CEIDIO
38	Llandudwen	TUDWEN
39	Llangïan	CIAN
40	Llanengan	ENGAN
41	St. Tudwal's Island E.	TUDWAL
42	Llangïan	YNYR (Gwerthyr Chapel)
43	Llandygwnning	GWYNININ
44	Botwnnog	BEUNO
45	Llaniestyn	IESTYN
46	Tudweiliog	CWYFAN
47	Llangwnnadl	GWYNHOEDL
48	Penrhos	CYNFIL
49	Bodferin	MERIN
50	Aberdaron	HYWYN (possibly Lleuddad)
51	Rhiw	MAELRHYS (Formerly Llanfaelrhys Parish Church)
52	Rhiw	AELIW (or AELRHIW)
53	Boduan	BUAN

BIBLIOGRAPHY

Baring-Gould. S. and Fisher, *The Lives of the British Saints,* 4 Vols., London, 1907-13.

Bowen, E. G., *The Settlements of the Celtic Saints in Wales* (Cardiff, 1954).

Bowen, E. G., *Britain and the Western Seaways* (London, 1972).

Chadwick, N. K., *The Age of the Saints in the Early Celtic Church* (Oxford, 1961).

Bardsey from the mainland

Photo: Geoff. Charles

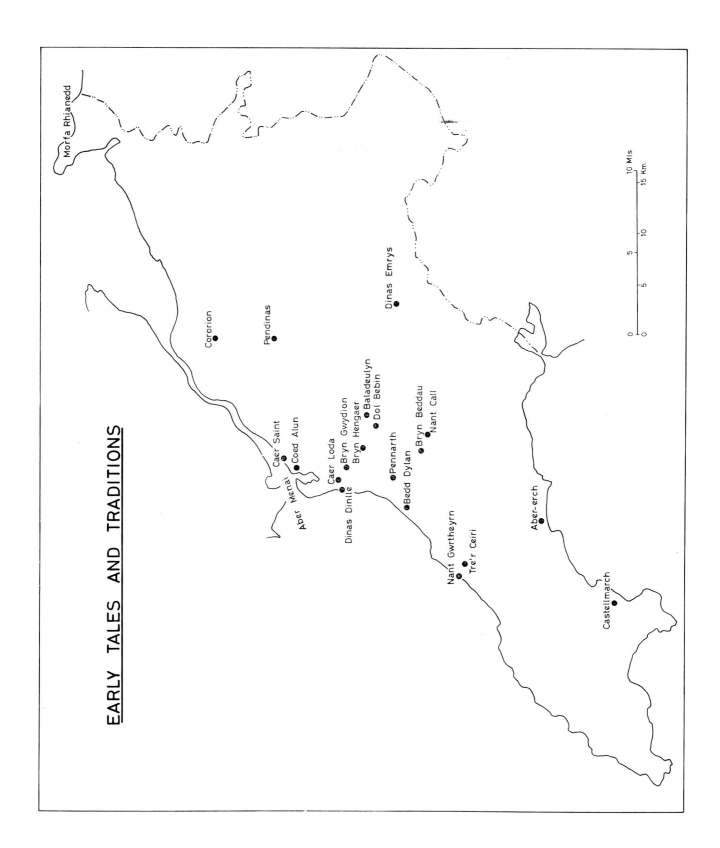

EARLY TALES AND TRADITIONS

Morfa Rhianedd

Cororion

Pendinas

Dinas Emrys

Caer Saint
Coed Alun
Aber Menai
Caer Loda
Bryn Gwydion
Bryn Hengaer
Baladeulyn
Dol Bebin
Dinas Dinlle
Pennarth
Bedd Dylan
Bryn Beddau
Nant Call

Nant Gwrtheyrn
Tre'r Ceiri
Aber-erch

Castellmarch

10 Mls
15 Km
10
5
5
0
0

Early Tales and Traditions

Many place-names in Caernarvonshire are associated with early tales and traditions, and there are occasional examples of tales composed to explain place-names.

In the *Historia Brittonum,* compiled by Nennius at the beginning of the ninth century, there is an account of Gwrtheyrn (Vortigern) coming to 'the region which is called Gwynedd' and discovering a suitable site on which to build a strong fort 'among the mountains of Eryri'. His 'magicians' or wise men (*magi*) inform him that the stronghold could not be constructed unless the blood of a child without a father is sprinkled over the foundations. Messengers find a child without a father, and the story relates how the boy explained the marvellous character of the foundations. A pool is discovered under the floor, with two vessels in it and a folded 'tent' or sheet within them, and two animals (*vermes*), one white and one red, within its folds. After they have been exposed, each animal pushes the other until eventually the red one drives the white one over the edge of the 'tent'. Then they pursue each other across the pool, 'and the tent vanished'. The meaning of all this is explained by the boy, who declares that his name is Emreis or Emrys (Latin, Ambrosius). Gwrtheyrn gave him the fort and all the kingdoms of western Britain, and then went away with his *magi* to the north where he built a fortress called Caer Gwrtheyrn.

There is another version of the episode of the two animals in the tale of *Lludd and Llefelys* (they are called 'dragons' here); this, too, occurred 'in the safest place . . . in Eryri' which was later known as 'Dinas Emreis' (its earlier name was 'Dinas Ffaraon Dandde').

The development of this fort — Dinas Emrys — can be traced from the Iron Age to the twelfth century. Excavation has revealed an artificial pool constructed during the first or second century A.D. to provide water for the inhabitants and their animals; it continued in use until the fifth century. According to one tradition, Gwrtheyrn died in Nant Gwrtheyrn, and Glasynys has reported that a cairn in the neighbourhood was called Bedd Gwrtheyrn ('Gwrtheyrn's Grave').

There are references to Caernarvonshire place-names in the 'Four Branches of the Mabinogi'. In the second branch, 'Branwen daughter of Llŷr', the thirteen ships which escorted Matholwch and Branwen to Ireland set out from Aber Menai. Bendigeidfran was at an assembly at Caer Saint in Arfon (that is, at Caernarfon) when the starling, with Branwen's letter under the roots of its wings, alighted on his shoulder. 'Aber Sein' and 'Caer Aber Sein' are mentioned in *Breuddwyd Macsen* ('The Dream of Macsen'): Elen's home was there. 'The highest stronghold in Arfon' is also mentioned in this tale, and it is likely that this is a reference to Dinas Emrys.

The local references are more frequent in the fourth branch, 'Math son of Mathonwy'. Here, in Arfon, was 'cadernid Gwynedd' ('the fastness of Gwynedd'). Math lived in 'Caer Dathyl in Arfon': this was probably Tre'r Ceiri; or, perhaps, Bryn Hengaer, between Pen-y-groes and Llanllyfni; or Pendinas, Llanddeiniolen. Math chose as his wife the daughter of Pebin 'of Dôl Bebin in Arfon': this is Dôl Bebin in the Nantlle Valley. On his way home from Dyfed with the pigs which he had obtained from Pryderi through his magic guile, Gwydion stays the night in several places 'which for that reason [are] still called Mochdref'. On the last night, in 'the highest township in Arllech-woedd' (Arllechwedd), a sty (creu) is made for the pigs, 'and for that reason was the name Creuwryon given to the township': namely, Creu-wrion or Cororion in Tre-garth. Later in the story two 'maenors' are mentioned — Maenor Bennardd (between Clynnog and Llanllyfni: the name is still preserved in that of the farm, Pennarth) and Maenor Coed Alun (across the river Saint, opposite Caernarfon). Pwyll and the men of the South retreated to Nant Call (Nancall, near Pant-glas), then as far as Dôl Benmaen. Gwydion and the un-named boy (he was later named Lleu) went to Caer Aranrhod — but this was not the 'caer' or fort marked on the maps about half a mile in the sea from Dinas Dinlle; this is a submerged reef visible at low water and the 'Caer Aranrhod' attribution dates from the sixteenth century. From Caer Aranrhod Gwydion and the boy proceeded towards Dinas Dinlleu. The name 'Lleu' is related

A page from the White Book of Rhydderch

By permission of the National Library of Wales

to that of one of the prominent gods of the Celts, and place-names corresponding to Dinlleu occur in other countries: for example, Lyons and Laon in France, Leiden in the Netherlands, Liegnitz in Poland. From Dinas Dinlleu they went towards 'Bryn Ayren' (probably Bryn Beddau, opposite Bryn Aerau) and Cefn Clun Tyno (near Bron-yr-erw, in upper Clynnog). In his search for Lleu, Gwydion followed the sow to Nantlleu (Nantlle), where there was an oak growing between two lakes (Baladeulyn). Other place-names around Dinas Dinlle evoke associations with this branch: for example, Maen Dylan, Bryn Gwydion, Caer Loda.

'Englynion y Beddau' or 'The Stanzas of the Graves', which refer to the graves of the 'warriors of Britain' (there is a copy of them in the 'Black Book of Carmarthen', *circa* 1250, but they were probably composed in the ninth century) mention Bedd Dylan in Llanfeuno (Clynnog); it is likely that there was formerly a complete story relating to Dylan 'eil Ton' ('son of Wave'), who is mentioned in the fourth branch. The grave of 'Tydai, tad awen' ('father of the muse') is said to be 'in the region of Bryn Aren'; that of Rhydderch Hael ('the Generous') at Aber-erch — although he was one of the heroes of north Britain; it has been suggested that the cromlech near Fourcrosses may have been the reason for this association. The grave of Lleu cannot be easily identified — it is 'under cover of the sea'. 'A well-built, tall man' had his grave in Eifionydd, 'Elwydd's land': the name has been preserved in Cadair Elwa (Elwydd), Clynnog. There is also a reference to 'the graves on the Morfa' — the graves of Sanant, Rhun, Garwen, Lledin and Llywy; and the Morfa is Morfa Rhianedd ('the Sea-strand of the Maidens') which lies between Great and Little Orme's Head, Llandudno.

The name Castellmarch in Llangïan suggests a connexion with a version of the history of Trystan and Esyllt.

ENGLYNION Y BEDDAU

Bet Tedei tad awen
yg godir Brin Aren
yn yd vna ton tolo
Bet Dilan Llan Beuno.

Bet mab Ossvran yg Camlan
gvydi llauer kywlavan
bet Bedwir in alld Tryvan.

Bet Owein ab Urien im pedrya[e]l bid,
    dan gverid Llan Morvael;
    in Abererch Riderch Hael.

Bet Llev Llaugyfes y dan achles mor,
    yn y bu y gywnes,
    gur guir y neb ny rodes.

En Eiwonit, Elvit tir,
Y mae [bet] gur hyduf hir:
lleas paup pan rydighir.

Y beddeu yn y Morua,
    ys bychan ay haelewy:
y mae Sanant, syberw vun,
    y mae Run ryuel afwy,
y mae Garrwen verch Hennin,
    y mae Lledin a Llywy.

BIBLIOGRAPHY

Rachel Bromwich, *Trioedd Ynys Prydein* (Cardiff, 1961).

Thomas Jones, 'The Black Book of Carmarthen, " Stanzas of the Graves "', *Proceedings of the British Academy*, LIII (1967), 97-137.

Ifor Williams, *Pedair Keinc y Mabinogi* (Cardiff, 1951).

Ifor Williams, 'Hen Chwedlau', *Transactions of the Honourable Society of Cymmrodorion*, 1946-7, 28-58.

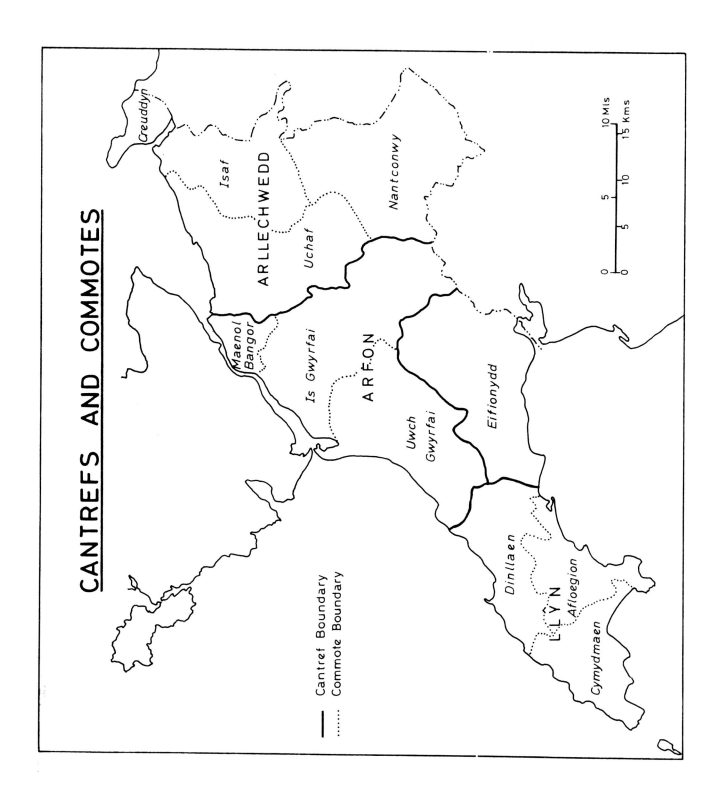

CANTREFS AND COMMOTES

Creuddyn

Isaf

ARLLECHWEDD

Uchaf

Nantconwy

Maenol Bangor

Is Gwyrfai

ARFON

Uwch Gwyrfai

Eifionydd

Dinllaen

LLŶN

Afloegion

Cymydmaen

Cantref Boundary
.... Commote Boundary

10 Mls
15 Kms

5   10

5

0   0

Medievel Administrative Divisions

The *gwledydd* or kingdoms of Wales were divided for administrative purposes into cantrefs or commotes, and a number of these were brought together by Edward I in 1284 to make the county of Caernarfon. The cantref, as the name indicates, may originally have comprised a hundred townships, and it was generally sub-divided into two or more commotes. Caernarvonshire consisted of three whole cantrefs, Archllechwedd, Arfon and Llŷn, and parts of two others, Rhos (the commote of Creuddyn) and Dunoding (the commote of Eifionydd), making ten commotes in all. Their names are often a reminder of our history; Llŷn, for example, takes its name from an Irish tribe, the Laigin, who are also remembered in the name of the Irish province of Leinster, and it therefore reflects early Irish settlement in Gwynedd. Dinllaen, one of the component commotes of Llŷn, contains the same element. According to tradition, Dunawd, the eponym of Dunoding, was one of the sons of Cunedda, and Eifion, from whom Eifionydd takes its name, was his son; this may suggest an early division of the cantref. Afloegion in Llŷn also bears the name of one of Cunedda's sons, Afloeg. Arfon included the Bishop of Bangor's lordship of Maenol Bangor, probably the earliest grant of lands to the church of Deiniol.

The basic unit of settlement was the township (*tref*), which might include several subsidiary hamlets. The main social division in early Wales was that between free and bond; these two classes held their land in different ways, and bond tenants owed a far heavier burden of rents and services than did the free. Townships were also either free or bond (although some were mixed); this meant that not only were they largely inhabited by freemen or bondmen, but also that they were held by free or bond tenure. As a rule, free townships consisted of a number of scattered homesteads, whereas in bond townships the houses were closer together and they might often resemble small villages. Bond townships might be granted in their entirety to ecclesiastical foundations or even to private individuals, and these grants might involve the delegation of some royal rights over the tenants; a number in Caernarvonshire were held by the churches of Bangor, Clynnog Fawr and Bardsey and the Cistercian abbey of Aberconwy (church

lands are shown on page 88). One township in each commote, the *maerdref,* was held directly by the lord, and was generally its administrative centre; some *maerdrefi,* like Nefyn and Pwllheli, had developed into trading centres or even boroughs before 1282, while Aber in Arllechwedd Uchaf was a favourite seat of Llywelyn ab Iorwerth. The distribution of townships on the map reflects the distribution of population in the medieval county.

Although territorial parishes were established in the twelfth and thirteenth centuries, the township was the more important unit until the time of the Tudors, when the Highway Act of 1555 and the Poor Law of 1601 made the parish the basic unit of local government; an inhabitant of the medieval county would describe himself as, for example, a free tenant of the prince in Cororion rather than in Llandygái, and both public and private documents refer invariably to the township rather than to the parish. The parish might often take the name of the township where the church was situated (as in Llanbedrog, Llanllyfni and Llanwnda), and in some cases parish and township might be coterminous; in other parishes the church might be isolated (e.g., Llandudwen, Llangelynnin). Many township names give some indication of their history or of the origins of rural settlement. The element *din,* denoting an early fortress, appears in Dinlle and Dinorwig, both adjacent to hill-forts, which may reflect an earlier pattern of rural organisation in Arfon. *Tref* (township) is very common, while sometimes the name illustrates the status as in Tregwyr-rhyddion (the township of the free men) in Maenol Bangor. Some are also connected with religious sites, e.g., Betws (-y-coed) in Nantconwy and Betws in Eifionydd (*betws:* oratory), Treferthyr in Eifionydd (*merthyr:* consecrated cemetery) and Treflan near the church of Betws Garmon in Is Gwyrfai. Many include personal names; the original form of Bodafon in Creuddyn, for example, was Bodfafon and the twelfth century ancestor of the adjacent family of Gloddaith was Mabon Glochydd. In some cases the same personal name may appear in the name of the township and of the church, as with Eleirnion and Llanaelhaearn. The names of many townships survive in later corrupt forms, one example being Bonyrafallen in

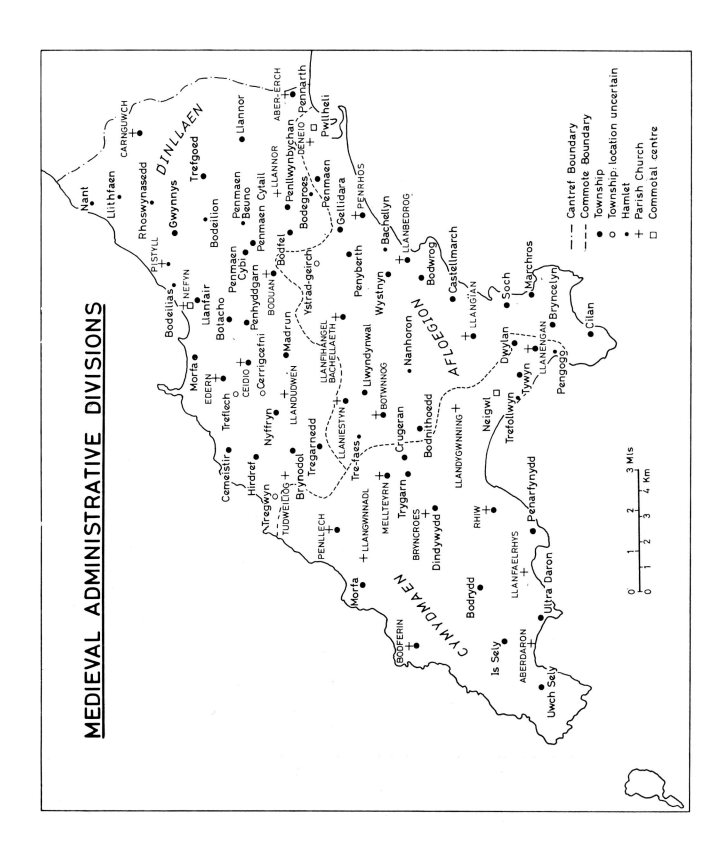

MEDIEVAL ADMINISTRATIVE DIVISIONS

CARNGUWCH
DINLLAEN
Nant
Llithfaen
Rhoswynasedd
Gwynnys
Bodeilion
Trefgoed
Llannor
Penmaen Beuno
Penmaen Cytail
LLANNOR
Penllwynbychan
Bodgroes
Penmaen
Gellidara
DENEIO Pennarth
ABER-ERCH
Pwllheli
PENRHOS
PISTYLL
Bodeilias
NEFYN
Llanfair
Botacho
Penmaen Cybi
Penhyddgarn
BODUAN
Bodfel
Bachellyn
LLANBEDROG
Bodwrog
Castellmarch
Marchros
Morfa
EDERN
CEIDIO
Cerrigcefni
Madrun
LLANFIHANGEL BACHELLAETH
Ystrad-geirch
Penyberth
Wystnyn
Bryncelyn
Cilan
Treflech
Nyffryn
LLANDUDWEN
Llwyndynwal
Nanhoron
AFLOEGION
LLANGIAN
Soch
Cemeistir
Hirdref
Brynodol
Tregarnedd
LLANIESTYN
Tre-faes
BOTWNNOG
LLANGIAN
Dwylan
Tywyn
LLANENGAN
Tregwyn
TUDWEILIOG
Crugeran
Bodnithoedd
LLANDYGWNNING
Neigwl
Trefollwyn
Pengogo
PENLLECH
LLANGWNNADL
MELLTEYRN
Trygarn
Penarfynydd
BRYNCROES
Dindywydd
RHIW
LLANFAELRHYS
Morfa
CYWYDMAEN
Bodrydd
Ultra Daron
BODFERIN
ABERDARON
Is Sely
Uwch Sely

Cantref Boundary
Commote Boundary
● Township
○ Township: location uncertain
● Hamlet
+ Parish Church
□ Commotal centre

3 Mls
4 Km
3
2
1
0

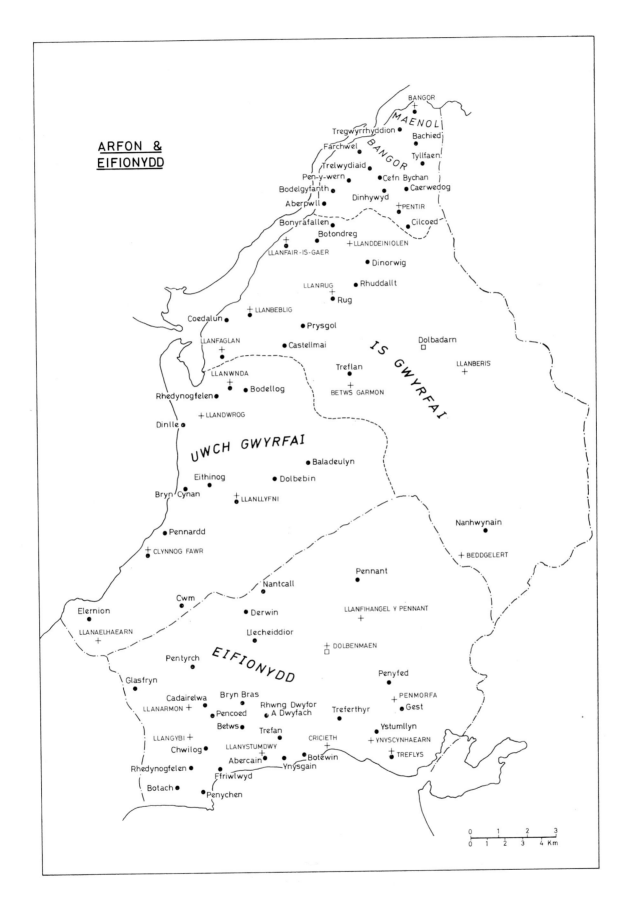

ARFON &
EIFIONYDD

BANGOR
MAENOL BANGOR
Tregwyrrhyddion
Bachied
Farchwel
Tyllfaen
Trelwydiaid
Pen-y-wern
Cefn Bychan
Bodelgyfarth
Caerwedog
Dinhywyd
Aberpwll
PENTIR
Cilcoed
Bonyrafallen
Botondreg
LLANDDEINIOLEN
LLANFAIR-IS-GAER
Dinorwig
Rhuddallt
LLANRUG
Rug
IS GWYRFAI
LLANBEBLIG
Coedalun
Prysgol
Dolbadarn
LLANFAGLAN
Castellmai
LLANBERIS
Treflan
LLANWNDA
BETWS GARMON
Bodellog
Rhedynogfelen
LLANDWROG
UWCH GWYRFAI
Dinlle
Baladeulyn
Eithinog
Dolbebin
Bryn Cynan
LLANLLYFNI
Nanhwynain
Pennardd
CLYNNOG FAWR
BEDDGELERT
Pennant
Nantcall
Cwm
LLANFIHANGEL Y PENNANT
Elernion
Derwin
LLANAELHAEARN
Llecheiddior
DOLBENMAEN
EIFIONYDD
Pentyrch
Penyfed
Glasfryn
PENMORFA
Cadairelwa
Bryn Bras
Gest
LLANARMON
Rhwng Dwyfor
Treferthyr
Pencoed
A Dwyfach
Ystumllyn
Betws
Trefan
YNYSCYNHAEARN
LLANGYBI
CRICIETH
Chwilog
LLANYSTUMDWY
TREFLYS
Rhedynogfelen
Abercain
Botewin
Ffriwlwyd
Ynysgain
Botach
Penychen

0   1   2   3
0   1   2   3   4 Km

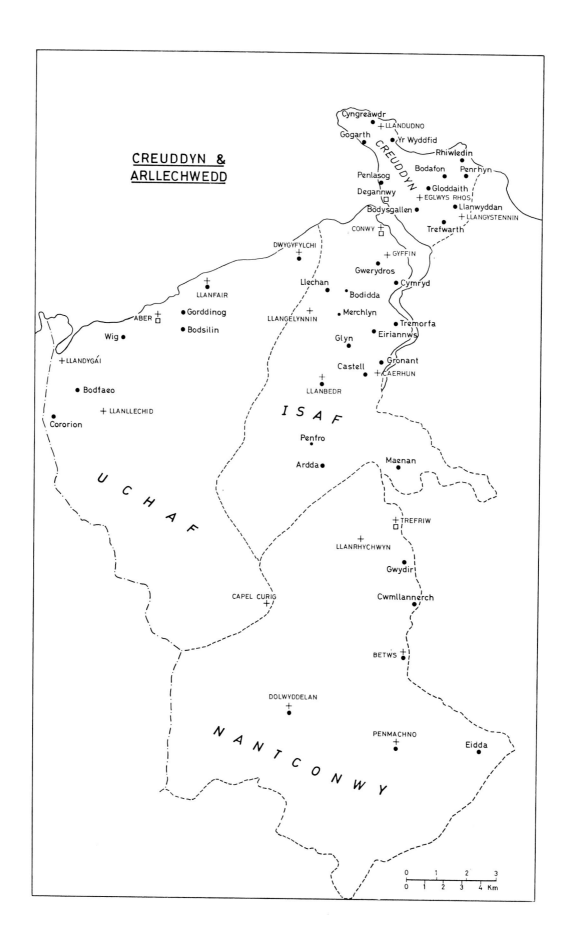

CREUDDYN &
ARLLECHWEDD

CREUDDYN

Cyngreawdr
+ LLANDUDNO
Gogarth
Yr Wyddfid
Rhiwledin
Bodafon
Penrhyn
Penlasog
Gloddaith
Degannwy
+ EGLWYS RHOS
Bodysgallen
Llanwyddan
+ LLANGYSTENNIN
CONWY
Trefwarth
DWYGYFYLCHI
+ GYFFIN
Gwerydros
Llechan
Cymryd
+
Bodidda
LLANFAIR
Merchlyn
LLANGELYNNIN
Tremorfa
ABER
Gorddinog
Glyn
Eiriannws
Wig
Bodsilin
Castell
Gronant
+ CAERHUN
+ LLANDYGAI
+
LLANBEDR
Bodfaeo
I S A F
+ LLANLLECHID
Penfro
Cororion
Ardda
Maenan

U C H A F

+ TREFRIW
+
LLANRHYCHWYN
Gwydir

Cwmllannerch
CAPEL CURIG
+

BETWS +

DOLWYDDELAN
+
N A N T C O N W Y
PENMACHNO
+
Eidda

0   1   2   3
0   1   2   3   4 Km

72

Is Gwyrfai which has become Pant-yr-afallen; others have disappeared completely.

This map makes no claim to be exhaustive. The location of some townships is uncertain, and some cannot be traced at all. A great deal more research is needed on such topics as township boundaries and on the relationship of township and parish; Dr. Gresham's splendid study of Eifionydd has shown the way to the historical topographers of the future.

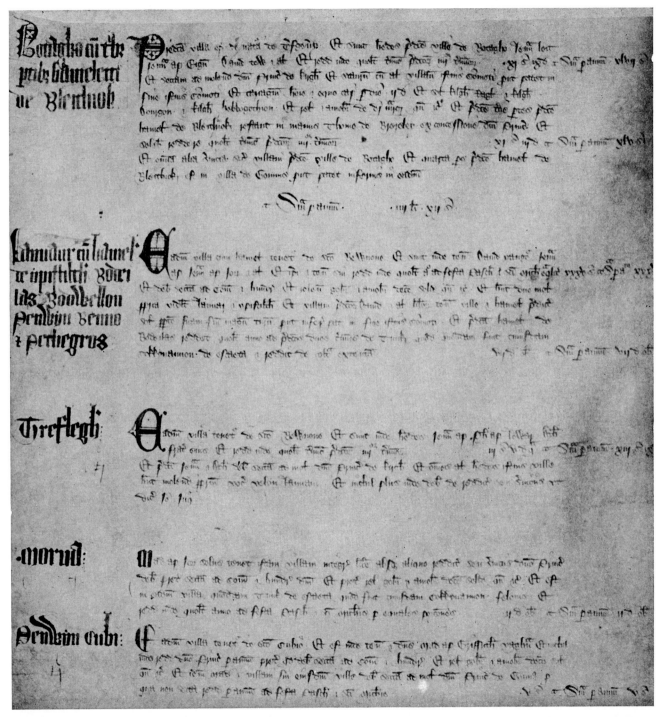

A page from the original Extent of Caernarvonshire, 1352, describing a part of the commote of Dinllaen, Llŷn.

By permission of the Librarian, U.C.N.W.

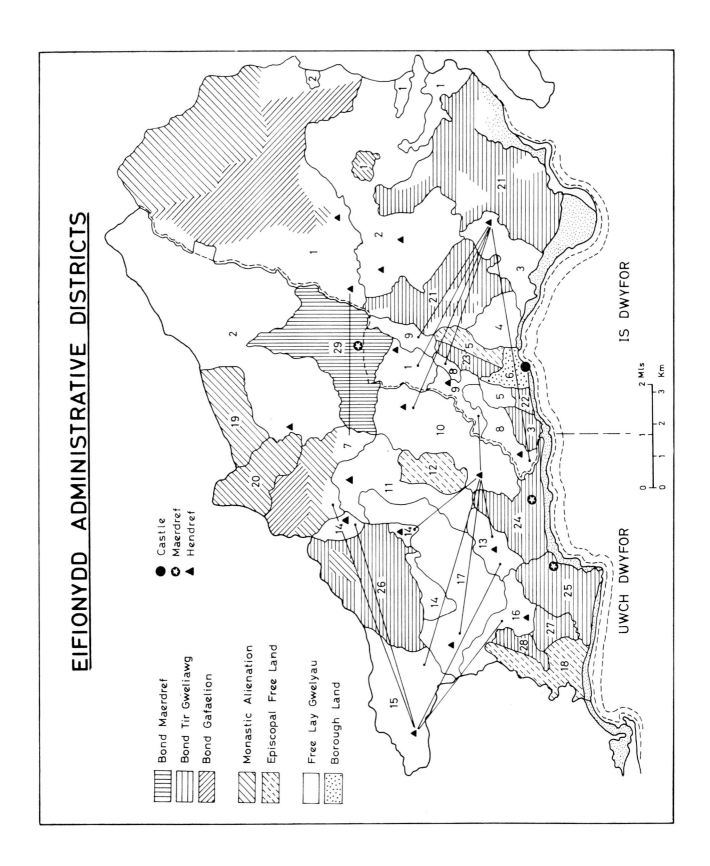

EIFIONYDD ADMINISTRATIVE DISTRICTS

Bond Maerdref

Bond Tir Gweliawg

Bond Gafaelion

Monastic Alienation

Episcopal Free Land

Free Lay Gwelyau

Borough Land

● Castle

✪ Maerdref

▲ Hendref

IS DWYFOR

UWCH DWYFOR

2 Mls

Km

74

Eifionydd Administrative Districts

Previous maps have shown the basic divisions of the county into Hundreds and Commotes with some indication of the subdivisions of ecclesiastical parishes and civil rural townships. This map of the single commote of Eifionydd shows in greater detail the complexity of the smaller subdivisions, which here lay in Is Dwyfor and Uwch Dwyfor — the two halves of the commote east and west of the Afon Dwyfor.

The boundaries of the commotes were laid down at an early period, possibly as far back as the sixth century A.D., and took little or no account of any existing settlements at that time; the boundaries are thus simple and straightforward, being based on the principal geographic features of the terrain and mostly following the natural divisions made by rivers and mountain ridges. The subdivisions were not made until the twelfth century, when they had to take into account the results of over five hundred years of expanding settlement, and this resulted in the intricate pattern of the boundaries and the existence of detached portions of several parishes and townships. This was particularly the case with regard to the free land, where originally only small numbers of persons had enjoyed a wide choice of sites on which to settle. As the free population increased and settlements were expanded by fresh intakes of land, which were made, as far as was possible, on the best soils available, this sporadic development resulted in the complexities round which the township boundaries had finally to be laid down.

The ecclesiastical parish boundaries (not shown on this map) were closely related to the civil township boundaries. Some of the parishes corresponded exactly to the townships, while the remainder enclosed within themselves several smaller townships. No township extended into more than one parish, but parishes could extend over the commote boundary; for instance, the parishes of Clynnog Fawr and Aber-erch extended over the boundary of Eifionydd from Arfon and Llŷn. This was doubtless due to the fact that the parish boundaries had to take into account the religious settlements which had been made at a very early period. The princes of Wales, particularly in the thirteenth century, were generous to religious houses in their gifts of land that had escheated to them for various reasons; thus in Eifionydd the priory of Beddgelert held land in the parish of Llanfihangel-y-Pennant, in the townships of Pennant and Llecheiddior, and the abbey of Enlli had a grange in the parish of Llangybi in the township of Pentyrch. The bishops of Bangor also had part of their Manor of Edern in the townships of Tre-ferthyr, Betws and Gogwmwd.

The bond townships, which were given their fixed boundaries in the twelfth century, must reflect some aspects of very early settlement patterns deriving from a time when the native population of the district was reduced to a servile status by small bands of intrusive Celtic overlords, but there was much reorganization during the course of later centuries, caused by changing administrative needs, and some evidence of this remains. By the thirteenth century, Dolbenmaen was the *Maerdref* and administrative centre of the commote, and its court was located where the principal road crossed Afon Dwyfor, the ford being guarded by an earth and timber castle. There is reason to suggest that there were similar early *tir-cyfrif* institutions in Pentyrch and Gest, and in the twelfth century local lords had manors in Penychen and Ffriwlwyd. By the time of the Conquest, all the bond townships, except Dolbenmaen, Penychen and Ffriwlwyd, were held under *tir-gwelyog* tenure, and after that the administrative centre was moved to Cricieth.

The free townships were apportioned out amongst a number of *gwelyau,* either one, two or three to each township. The principal landowner in the commote in the eleventh century was Collwyn ap Tangno, and several of the most important *gwely* founders in the twelfth century were his descendants. The Collwyn pedigree is not sufficiently full or accurate to reveal exactly how his land was shared out and inherited by his immediate descendants; however, we find Gwgan, a grandson with a *hendref* in Gwynfryn, extending his *gwely* lands from there into Trefan, Chwilog, Pencoed, Cadair Elwa and Glasfryn, and Gwyn ab Ednowain, a great-grandson with a *hendref* in Treflys, extending his *gwely* lands from there into Pennant, Trefan, Abercain and Rhwng Dwyfor a Dwyfach. It is possible that Dafydd was also a close descendant of Collwyn, and his grandsons had a *hendref* in Glasfryn with their *gwely* land extending into Cadair Elwa, Llecheiddior and Pennarth. These extensions of Collwyn land are shown by arrows linking the townships involved on the map. All the other free *gwelyau* were confined to their own townships, except for the Gwely Wyrion Cynan in Pennant, which had a small extension in Llecheiddior. This *gwely*, with Gwely Gwair, also in Pennant, and Gwely Wyrion Ithel and Gwely Wyrion Griffri, both in Penyfed, were all founded by persons not descended from Collwyn; this suggests that there was a difference in early settlements between the north-eastern and mountainous part of the commote and the remaining lowland part where Collwyn held sway.

There were only fourteen free *gwelyau* in Eifionydd, which indicates that there was a relatively small free population there in the late twelfth century. This was located in family groups on *rhandiroedd* in each township. The *rhandiroedd* were points of early settlement on good land, where *tyddynnod* were grouped round arable fields and surrounded by communal grazings on the township wastes. The devolution of these *gwely* holdings into separate estates is dealt with in a later section.

EIFIONYDD

FREE AND MIXED TOWNSHIPS

Map
No.

1 PENNANT
    Free (i) Gwely Wyrion Cynan, (ii) Gwely Gwair extending to Llecheiddior.
    Bond (i) Gafael Gwas Mihangel, (ii) Gafael Mab Bergam, (iii) Gafael Adda ap Dafydd.
    Monastic Priory of Beddgelert (i) Nant Colwyn, (ii) Braich-y-bib, (iii) Maes-y-llech.

2 PENYFED
    Free (i) Gwely Wyrion Ithel, (ii) Gwely Wyrion Griffri.

3 TREFLYS
    Free (i) Gwely Gwyn ab Ednowain. Extending into Pennant, Trefan, Abercain, Rhwng Dwyfor a Dwyfach.

4 YSTUMLLYN
    Free (i) Gwely Ithel Goch, (ii) Gwely Tegwared ap Robert.

5 TREFERTHYR
    Free (i) Manor of Edern, Land of the Bishop of Bangor, (ii) Borough of
6   Cricieth, Post-conquest Administrative Centre.

7 LLECHEIDDIOR
    Free (i) Parts of two gwelyau in Pennant, (ii) Part of Gwely Wyrion Dafydd.
    Bond (i) Gafael Tegerin.

Map
No.

    Monastic
    Free Clas of Clynnog Fawr, Two parts of Llecheiddior.
    Bond Priory of Beddgelert, Pant Ddreiniog, Bwlch Gwyn.

8 ABERCAIN
    Free (i) Gwely Seisyllt, (ii) Part of Gwely Gwyn ab Ednowain.

9 TREFAN
    Free (i) Part of Gwely Gwgan, (ii) Part of Gwely Gwyn ab Ednowain.

10 RHWNG DWYFOR A DWYFACH
    Free (i) Gwely Wyrion *ytot*, (ii) Gwely Gronw ap Tegwared, (iii) Gwely Gwgan, extending into Trefan, Chwilog, Pencoed, Cadair Elwa, Glasfryn, (iv) Part Gafael Tegwared ap Rhirid.

11 BRYN BRAS
    Free (i) Gwely Wyrion Ithel.

12 BETWS
    Free (i) Manor of Edern, Land of the Bishop of Bangor.

13 CHWILOG
    Free (i) Part Gwely Gwgan, (ii) Part Gwely Wyrion Dafydd.

14 CADAIR ELWA

Free (i) Part Gwely Wyrion Dafydd, (ii) Part Gwely Gwgan.

15 GLASFRYN

Free (i) Gwely Wyrion Dafydd, extending into Chwilog, Cadair Elwa, Llecheiddior, Pennarth, (ii) Part Gwely Gwgan.

16 PENNARTH

Free (i) Gafael Tegwared ap Rhirid, (ii) Part Gwely Wyrion Dafydd.

17 PENCOED

Free (i) Gwely Wyrion Caradog, (ii) Part Gwely Wyrion Dafydd, (iii) Part Gwely Gwgan.

18 GOGWMWD

Free (i) Manor of Edern, Land of the Bishop of Bangor.

MONASTIC TOWNSHIPS

19 NANCALL

The Abbey of Aberconwy.

20 DERWIN

The Clas of Clynnog Fawr.

BOND TOWNSHIPS

21 GEST

Bond Tir Welyog (? Formerly Tir Cyfrif)
(i) Gwely Prydyddion, (ii) Gwely Maer, (iii) Gwely Ednowain, (iv) Gwely Cellyn, (v) Gwely Heilyn.

Free 4 Bovates of Land.

22 BOTEWIN

Bond Tir Welyog
(i) Gwely Einion, (ii) Gwely Gethin.

23 YNYSGAIN
Bond Tir Welyog
(i) Gwely Selau, (ii) Gwely Rhingyll.

24 FFRIWLWYD

Bond Tir Welyog Manor and Township held by the Abbey of Aberconwy *c.* 1202 - 1350.

25 PENYCHEN

Bond Tir Welyog Manor and Township.
(i) Gwely Wyrion Madog, (ii) Gwely Wyrion Seisyllt.

26 PENTYRCH

Bond Tir Welyog (? Formerly Tir Cyfrif)
(i) Gwely Cynan, (ii) Gwely Iorwerth Ddu (*Coruerth oue*).

Monastic Bond
(i) Abbey of Ynys Enlli in Monachdy Biswail extending into Llecheiddior.

27 BOTACH

Bond Tir Welyog
(i) Gwely Iorwerth ap Maredudd (*M'with*).

28 RHEDYNOG FELEN

Bond Tir Welyog Escheat for lack of tenants.

29 DOLBENMAEN

Maerdref. Manor and Bond Tir Cyfrif Township. Pre-conquest Administrative Centre.

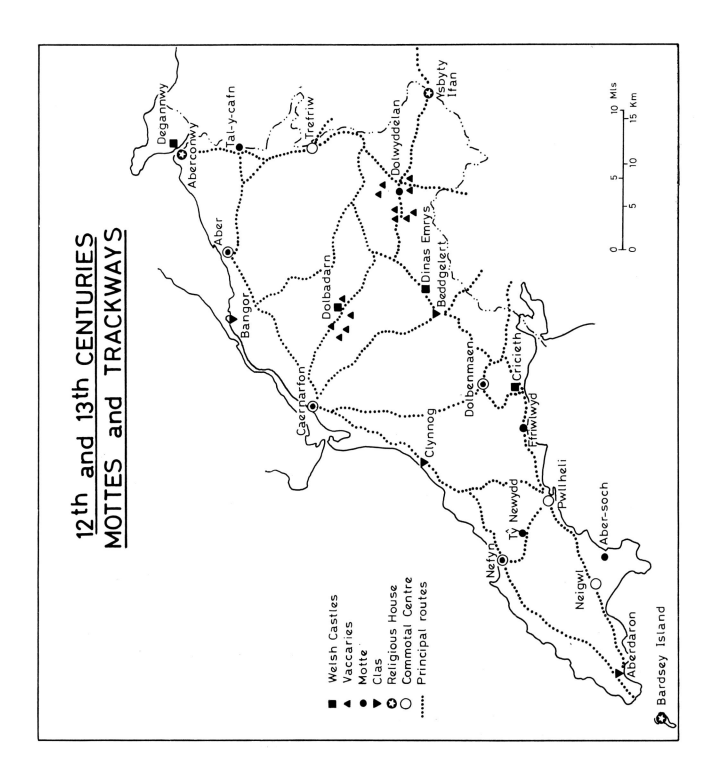

12th and 13th CENTURIES
MOTTES and TRACKWAYS

Degannwy
Aberconwy
Tal-y-cafn
Trefriw
Dolwyddelan
Ysbyty Ifan
Aber
Bangor
Dolbadarn
Dinas Emrys
Beddgelert
Caernarfon
Clynnog
Dolbenmaen
Cricieth
Ffriwlwyd
Nefyn
Tŷ Newydd
Pwllheli
Aber-soch
Neigwl
Aberdaron
Bardsey Island

10 Mls
15 Km

Welsh Castles
Vaccaries
Motte
Clas
Religious House
Commotal Centre
Principal routes

Twelfth and Thirteenth Century Mottes and Trackways

It was not long after the sweeping victory of the Norman in the Battle of Hastings in 1066 before Wales, too, felt the weight of his thrustful energy. The north, strangely enough, suffered considerably more than the south at first. Hugh the Fat, Earl of Chester, pushed his forces along the coast road and, for a period in the 1090s, made himself master of Anglesey and parts of Arfon. He, however, died in 1098, and the famous prince Gruffudd ap Cynan stepped into the breach to ensure the safety of Gwynedd for long years afterwards.

It is not easy to measure the influence of the Norman attacks on Arfon. It can be stated with confidence, however, that there was no true motte and bailey in these parts before their arrival. We know by now of a number of these in the old shire: there is Degannwy in the commote of Creuddyn, Abergwyngregyn in Arllechwedd Uchaf, Bryn Castell in Isaf, Tomen Castell in Nantconwy, Bangor as well as Caernarfon in Is-Gwyrfai, Tomen (Dolbenmaen) and Tomen Fawr (Penychen) in the commote of Eifionydd, Castell (Aber-soch) in the commote of Cafflogion and Nefyn in Dinllaen. These belonged to the lord or the prince of the commote; but there were others, such as Castell in Is-Gwyrfai and the Mwnt (Llannor) in Dinllaen, built, possibly, for the lesser lords. It is clear that there were trackways or 'roads' of some kind passing near to the earthwork castles and connecting many of them together. And, of course, the usual route in this period from the mainland to Anglesey was across Traeth Lafan from Abergwyngregyn.

There is no way of knowing exactly when these earthwork castles noted above were built, but those raised by the Normans can be ascribed to the years 1090 - 94 and the remainder, the Welsh ones, to the middle of the twelfth century and later. Whenever they were raised and whoever was responsible for building them, it is interesting to note that there was usually one motte in each commote, that they were located most often where the king (or lord or prince) of the commote had his *llys* (commote centre) and that they became therefore an integral part of the commote organisation which was already in existence.

In early days, the king went on circuit twice a year with his *teulu* (that is, his personal bodyguard or house host) and his officials, travelling from one commote to the other and staying, of course, in the commote *llys.* This practice allowed him to enjoy hunting while superintending the activities of the commote on the one hand and, on the other, claiming the *gwestfa* and the *dawnbwyd* which were due to him from his subjects, whether free or bond. The main constituents of *gwestfa* or *dawnbwyd* were bread, meat, butter and cheese to eat and mead or beer to drink. The king depended, too, on the service of his subjects to maintain himself and his whole retinue as well as their horses and hunting dogs. Most of the buildings of the *llys* were constructed of timber: the hall (the focal point of the life of the *llys*), the personal chamber of the king and his consort, gatehouse, barns and so forth. The bondsmen (*taeogion*) were responsible for erecting these and caring for them. The king's circuit was thus a heavy burden on the shoulders of his subjects, especially the unfree.

The queen, too, claimed a circuit once a year, but — owing to the special privileges extended to the men of Arfon — it is said that they were exempt from every other circuit — the circuit of the *penteulu* (leader of the bodyguard), of the chief huntsman and chief falconer among them. However, by the time of the princes of Gwynedd in the thirteenth century, the circuits as such had ceased and had been replaced by the payment of a fixed annual sum.

In the course of time, the stone castle evolved from the earthwork or motte and bailey — and that for sufficient reasons. For one thing, it was easy enough to destroy the wooden buildings of the earthwork castle with fire or to overturn them by mining beneath. Stone castles were much safer. Even so, if we except Dinas Emrys, only three stone castles were built within the limits of the shire by the princes of Gwynedd — although others, such as Degannwy, fell into their hands from time to time. The three castles were Dolwyddelan, Dolbadarn and Cricieth. Unlike the earthwork castles, these had little connection with the old commotal arrangements. They were not raised in exactly the same places as the old commotal centres, for their aim was mainly military rather than economic; their chief purpose was to strengthen the hold of the prince of Gwynedd against suspected enemies from within and without. Dolwyddelan and Dolbadarn stand guard over valleys which pierce Gwynedd, while the castle at Cricieth was built on a hillock beside the sea to stand watch over the road that leads into Llŷn. Strangely enough, the castle of Dolwyddelan (but not Dolbadarn) was retained in the English military pattern after the conquest of 1282-3, and it was strengthened by Edward I. The same happened to Cricieth; from the English point of view this made sense, for Edward demanded that each one of the new castles built by him in Gwynedd washed its feet in the sea.

Information about the Welsh stone castles before the conquest of 1282-3 is scarce. There is no certainty about the number of men kept to defend them — not more than 30 at most to judge by post-conquest evidence — but it is certain that the princes of Gwynedd used them as prisons; e.g., Llywelyn ein Llyw Olaf kept his brothers and others under lock and key for long years in the castles of Cricieth and Dolbadarn.

The three Welsh castles are connected more especially with Llywelyn the Great, prince of Gwynedd from *circa* 1200 to 1240. Tradition claims that he was born in Dolwyddelan, but this is difficult to reconcile with the belief that the castle was not built until the last years of the twelfth century; however, it was strengthened by Llywelyn the Great. Compared to the Edwardian castles, the plan of the Welsh castles is remarkably simple. The only comparatively complex one is Cricieth, the last to be built; there, in some places, the square tower (as in Dolwyddelan) is combined with the later round tower (as can be seen in Dolbadarn) to form special towers in the shape of a letter D.

The castles of Dolwyddelan and Dolbadarn are situated in the hinterland, and it is noteworthy that the princes established vaccaries around them to maintain a sufficient food supply for their garrison and others. Five farms on this pattern were set up around the castle of Dolbadarn; there were at least another eight near Dolwyddelan castle, and it is believed that they supported over 500 cattle from one year to the other.

A SELECTION OF THE ANCIENT LAWS

(With a modernized version)

Y gan y tayogeu y keiff y brenhin pynueirch yn y
Gan y taeogion y caiff y brenin y pynfeirch yn ei

luyd ac o bob tayawctref y keiff gwr a march a bwell y
luoedd ac o bob taeogdref y caiff ŵr a march a bwyeill i

wneuthur y gestyll, ac ar treul y brenhin y bydant.
wneuthur ei gestyll, ac ar draul y brenin y byddant.

Naw tei a dyly y bilaeneit eu hadeilat y'r brenhin:
Naw tŷ a ddylai'r bileiniaid eu hadeiladu i'r brenin:

neuad, ystauell, kegin, cappel, yscubawr, odynty, ystabyl,
neuadd, ystafell (gysgu), cegin, capel, ysgubor, odyndy, stabl,

kynhorty, peiryant.
porthordy (neu fragdy), tŷ-bach.

Kylch a geiff meirch y brenhin a'r vrenhines a'e
Cylch a geiff meirch y brenin a'r frenhines a'r

gwassanaethwyr y gayaf ar tayogeu y brenhin. Kerdoryon
gwasanaethwyr yn y gaeaf ymhlith taeogion y brenin. Cerddorion

gwlat arall a gahant gylch ar y bilaeneit tra uont yn arhos
gwlad arall cânt gylch ymhlith bileiniaid tra bônt yn aros

eu rodyon y gan y brenhin, os dyry.
eu rhoddion gan y brenin, os dyry.

BIBLIOGRAPHY

On the castles, refer, in particular, to the Royal Commission of Ancient Monuments: Inventory for Caernarvonshire, Vols. I and II, and Vol. III, for a general treatment of the early castles. For the Commotal System, read the classic work of J. E. Lloyd, *A History of Wales* (several editions), Chap. IX, and see also T. P. Ellis, *Welsh Tribal Law and Custom in the Middle Ages* (1926), Vol. I. For a general review of the content of the laws, read the useful booklet by Dafydd Jenkins, *Cyfraith Hywel* (1970).

Dolwyddelan Castle

Photo: By permission of Gwynedd Archives

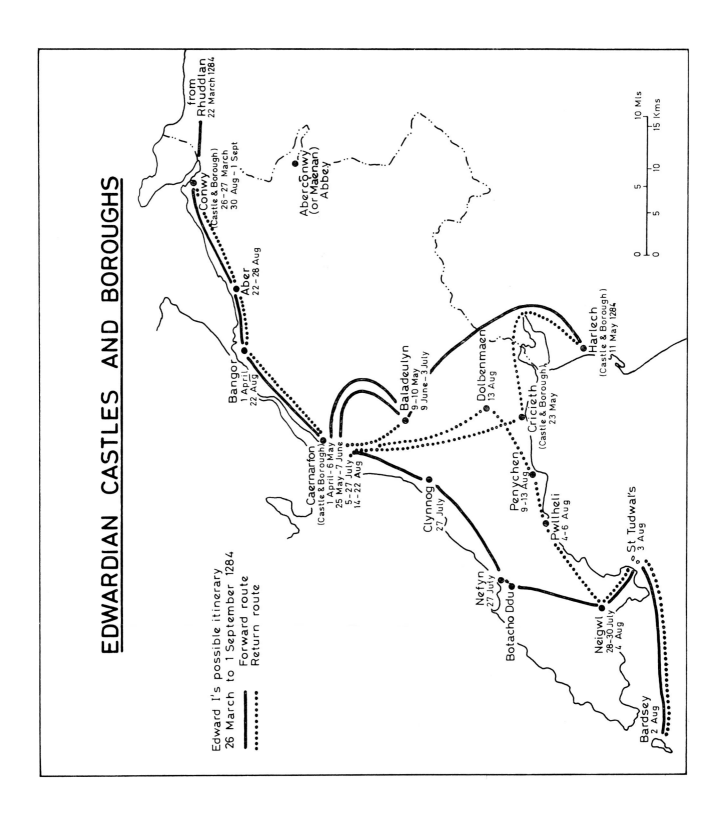

EDWARDIAN CASTLES AND BOROUGHS

Edward I's possible itinerary
26 March to 1 September 1284

▬▬▬▬ Forward route
•••••• Return route

from Rhuddlan
22 March 1284

Conwy
(Castle & Borough)
26-27 March
30 Aug - 1 Sept

Aberconwy
(or Maenan)
Abbey

Aber
22-28 Aug

Bangor
1 April
22 Aug

Baladeulyn
9-10 May
9 June-3 July

Dolbenmaen
13 Aug

Harlech
(Castle & Borough)
11 May 1284

Caernarfon
(Castle & Borough)
1 April-6 May
25 May-7 June
5-27 July
14-22 Aug

Cricieth
(Castle & Borough)
23 May

Penychen
9-13 Aug

Clynnog
27 July

Pwllheli
4-6 Aug

St Tudwal's
3 Aug

Nefyn
27 July

Botacho Ddu

Neigwl
28-30 July
4 Aug

Bardsey
2 Aug

10 Mls
15 Kms

Edwardian Castles and Boroughs

Late in 1282 the prince of Wales, Llywelyn II, was killed in a skirmish in mid-Wales, and in the following year, with the 'flower of his army dead', Welsh resistance crumbled altogether. Gwynedd, the last remnant of independent Wales, had succumbed at last. But Edward I's task was not yet done; he had to consolidate his victory. Clearly special precautions would have to be taken against an enemy who had resisted so resolutely the might of Anglo-Norman arms for over two centuries. The recent war had shown how easily a Welsh force had overcome the newly-built castle at Aberystwyth; more elaborate and more sophisticated defences were called for to hold the Welsh of Gwynedd in check.

Edward's solution was the string of well-nigh impregnable fortresses with which he encircled Snowdonia. Two of these, Conwy and Caernarfon, were sited in Caernarvonshire, in the very heart of Gwynedd. Even before the war of 1282-3 was over, work had already begun on the castle at Conwy, and soon afterwards work was in progress too at Caernarfon. At the same time, the old Welsh castle at Cricieth was taken over, added to and strengthened.

Castle-building went on apace in the 1280s. The magnificent castle at Conwy, the work of master English craftsmen, as were all the Edwardian castles, was erected and more or less completed in the five short seasons from 1283 to 1287. As defensive structures, the Edwardian castles, with their ultra-thick curtain walls, massive towers, and complicated system of gates and draw-bridges, were never surpassed. Garrisons of only 30-40 men sufficed to defend them — in the fourteenth century it was sometimes down to 8, hardly ever more than 16. The brain behind the castles was the Savoyard, Master James of St. George, a military engineer of genius, but careful thought must have been given to the siting of the castles in the first place. Caernarfon and Conwy, like most Edwardian castles, are near the coast, so that they could be supplied by sea in times of siege, or provided with an escape route if the siege went badly. Strategically, too, the site was important. Caernarfon, for example, effectively commanded one end of the Menai Strait. So highly thought of as a site was Conwy that the Cistercian abbey of Aberconwy was moved up-river and re-founded at Maenan to make room for the new town and castle Edward I had in mind.

Of all the Edwardian castles, one stands out supreme: Caernarfon. Its great size, its dignified proportions, its majestic design emphasise its uniqueness. In contrast to the others, its towers are multiangular, not rounded; polychrome stonework, too, has been incorporated into its building on the same pattern as at Constantinople. Legend connected that city with the Roman emperor Constantine, the son of Macsen Wledig, who, in the beautiful story in the *Mabinogion,* found his bride in a castle 'of various colours' at Segontium. In building Caernarfon castle in the way he did, Edward I was appealing to the Welshman's sense of history as well as defending his own conquest. He was doing more, for he intended it as the chief residence for a 'new line of Welsh princes of the royal blood', as the chief seat of government of the area he had conquered.

Closely connected from the beginning with the castle was the borough. Both formed part of what was essentially a unified system of defence. The building of the castle and of the town walls and gates began at the same time as part of a single operation. These plantation boroughs could not fail to be anything but garrison towns in those dangerous 'frontier' days. Their inhabitants were made up almost entirely of adventurous immigrant Englishmen — not a single Welshman is listed among the burgesses of Caernarfon in the late 1290s — and they were expected to man the walls at any time and provide for the maintenance of the castle.

For the risks they took, English burgesses were given special privileges. Nearly 700 acres were appropriated for the use of Conwy, nearly 1,500 acres for Caernarfon. In 1284, Caernarfon and Conwy — in 1285, Cricieth — were granted charters, giving them a fair measure of immunity from royal officials in municipal government, freedom from certain tolls and customs, and the right to hold markets and fairs. An attempt was made indeed to secure for them a complete monopoly of trade in their respective areas. They were to be in the van, fostering a money economy and taming a wild countryside. They clung tenaciously to their privileges throughout the Middle Ages and were despised for it; 'burgess' became synonymous with 'English'.

After conquering Gwynedd and 'settling' Wales, Edward I celebrated, in July 1284, by holding a famous tournament or round table at Nefyn, on fields belonging to Botacho Ddu. Knights from far and near gathered there to test their skill and strength at the 'games', before Edward moved on to Neigwl and Bardsey and began his first triumphant tour of Wales.

Caernarfon Castle

By permission of Gwynedd Archives

BIBLIOGRAPHY

Edwardian Castles and Boroughs: R. A. Brown, H. M. Colvin and A. J. Taylor, *The History of the King's Works* (1965), Vols. 1 and 2; *Royal Commission on Ancient Monuments, Inventory for Caernarvonshire*, Vols. I - II; E. A. Lewis, *The Medieval Boroughs of Snowdonia* (1912); C. A. Gresham, 'Tre Ferthyr and the Development of Criccieth', Caern. Hist. Soc., 27 (1966); N. Denholm-Young's article in *Studies in Medieval History presented to F. M. Powicke* (1948).

The Formation of the Shire: W. H. Waters, 'The Making of Caernarvonshire', Caern. Hist. Soc., 4 (1942-3): John Griffiths, 'The Revolt of Madog ap Llywelyn', in ibid., 16 (1955): A. H. Dodd, *A History of Caernarvonshire* (1968), Chap. 1, and W. H. Waters, *The Edwardian Settlement of North Wales* (1935).

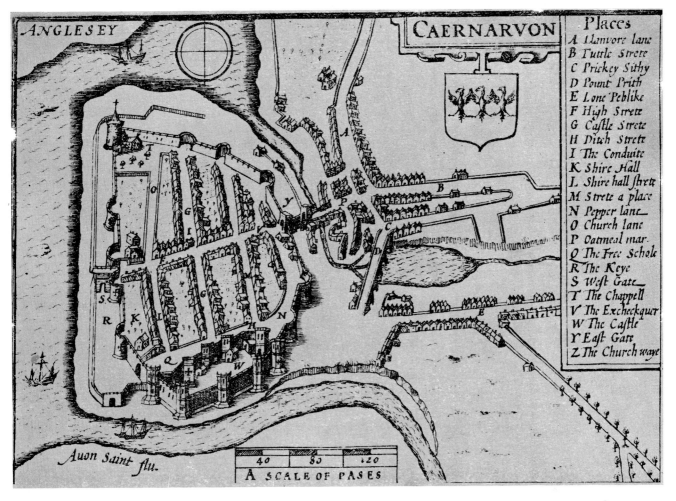

O FREUDDWYD MACSEN WLEDIG

Ac yny llog ua-
wr honno y kerdassant ar ymor
ac y doethant y ynys prydein,
ar ynys agerdassant hyny doethant y eryri. Llyman etwa
heb wy y tir amdyfrwys awelas
an harglwyd ni. Wynt adoethant
racdunt hyny welynt mon gy-
uarwyneb ac wynt. Ac hyny
welynt heuyt aruon. llyman
heb wynt y tir awelas yn harglwyd ni trwy y hun. Ac aber
feint awelynt ar gaer yn aber
yr auon. Porth ygaer awelynt yn agoret. yr gaer y doethant. Neuad awelsant y mywn
y gaer. llyman heb wynt ynev
ad awelas an harglwyd drwy
ehun.

Ac yn y llong fawr
honno y cerddasant ar y môr
ac y daethant i Ynys Prydain,
a'r ynys a gerddasant oni ddaethant i Eryri. Dyma eto
ebr hwy y tir amddyfrwys a welodd
ein harglwydd ni. Hwy a ddaethant
rhagddynt oni welent Fôn gyfar-
wyneb a hwy. Ac oni
welent hefyd Arfon. Dyma
ebr hwy y tir a welodd ein harglwydd ni trwy ei hun. Ac aber
Saint a welent a'r gaer yn aber
yr afon. Porth y gaer a welent
yn agored. I'r gaer y daethant.
Neuadd a welsant y tu mewn
i'r gaer. Dyma ebr hwy y neuadd
a welodd ein harglwydd drwy
ei hun.

From the White Book of Rhydderch.

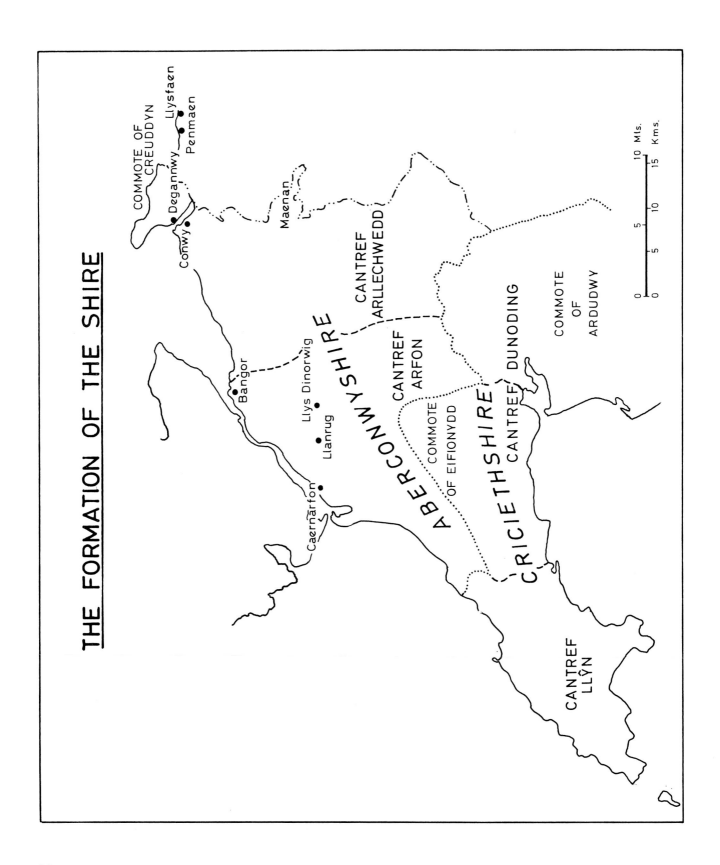

THE FORMATION OF THE SHIRE

COMMOTE OF
CREUDDYN

Llysfaen

Penmaen

Deganwy

Conwy

Maenan

CANTREF
ARLLECHWEDD

ABERCONWYSHIRE

CANTREF
ARFON

Bangor

Llys Dinorwig

Llanrug

Caernarfon

COMMOTE
OF EIFIONYDD

CRICIETHSHIRE

CANTREF DUNODING

COMMOTE
OF
ARDUDWY

CANTREF
LLŶN

10 Mls.
15 Kms.
5
5
0
0

The Formation of the Shire

The county of Caernarfon, like the counties of Anglesey and Merioneth, was the creation of the great Statute of Wales issued at Rhuddlan on 19 March 1284. After subduing Gwynedd in 1282-3, Edward I had been left to ponder the problem of how best to administer the land he had subjugated. It took him the greater part of a year to arrive at a satisfactory solution. The first matter that had to be determined was how to divide Gwynedd into shires. There was little difficulty about knowing what to do about Anglesey: since it was a fair-sized island its three *cantrefi* could be merged and administered as one unit, as one shire, without more ado. But the problem posed by the rest of Gwynedd, with its six *cantrefi* and fourteen commotes, could not so easily be resolved. The first solution that presented itself involved the creation of *three* other counties: an 'Aberconwy-shire', formed from the merger of the northern cantrefi of Arfon and Arllechwedd (and the commote of Creuddyn); a 'Cricieithshire', composed of the amalgamation of the southern *cantrefi* of Llŷn and Dunoding, and a 'Merionethshire' comprising the remainder of Gwynedd. But other counsels prevailed, for though the separation of the northern from the southern *cantrefi* made good sense geographically, economically it would have seriously weakened the projected county of Merioneth. Consequently, the commote of Eifionydd was detached from the cantref of Dunoding and merged with cantref Llŷn and the northern cantrefi of Arfon and Arllechwedd and the commote of Creuddyn to form one large unit, the new county of Caernarfon.

This was a conservative solution on the whole. Edward I had observed the ancient divisions; he made no attempt whatsoever to change their names. But by allotting one commote (Eifionydd) of the *cantref* of Dunoding to Caernarvonshire and another (Ardudwy) to Merioneth, Edward I effectively dealt a mortal blow to the *cantref* of Dunoding; it ceased entirely to exist and even its name faded into oblivion. Nor was the addition of lands east of the Conwy to Caernarvonshire exactly logical, but circumstances forced Edward's hand. The commote of Creuddyn was wrenched from the *cantref* of Rhos because of the ancient, strategic importance of Degannwy; the vills of Eirias, Penmaen, and Llysfaen became part of the royal lands of Caernarvonshire because of the accident of forfeiture, and so did Maenan because Aberconwy abbey had been re-founded there by Edward I

This, then, was the new county of Caernarvon. The chief official who was given the task of administering the shire was the sheriff, an ancient English office but entirely new in Wales in 1284. It was he who was responsible for all the financial and judicial affairs of the county, and for the first twenty years or so he was paid as much as £40 per annum for his pains because of 'the newness of his office'. Few Welshmen held the shrievalty in Caernarvonshire before 1485, but Gruffydd ap Rhys — Sir Gruffydd Llwyd, the lord of Dinorwig and the darling of the English establishment — carried out the duties of the office twice in the early fourteenth century, in 1302-05 and 1308-09.

The sheriff presided over the county court, the chief organ of administration introduced into the shire by Edward in 1284. It was held once a month, presumably always at Caernarfon, and all the important men of the county owed attendance there. Criminal matters were dealt with there; so, too, were matters such as the granting of brewing licences and the election of two county coroners (another new office in 1284). The law administered was a combination for the most part of English criminal law and Welsh civil law.

The system which Edward I imposed in 1284 survived unchanged until 1536. It was not to the liking of all. Nearly 700 Caernarvonshire people were fined in 1322 for not attending the courts as they were obliged to do. They were harassed by ruthless officials; called upon to pay new taxes — Caernarvonshire must have contributed at least £1,000 to the tax on movables imposed in the early 1290s, and castles, harsh symbols of their subjection, were going up all around them. It is not surprising that, despite Edward I's conservatism, they erupted in revolt in 1294-5. The unfinished castle at Caernarfon was taken; the town walls were destroyed, and Roger de Pulesdon, the sheriff of Anglesey, was killed in the assault. Conwy withstood attack. By Christmas 1294, Edward I was back again in Caernarvonshire. He was in danger of being caught between Bangor and Conwy in January 1295, but early in May he was able to set out from Bangor for another triumphant tour of Wales.

LANDS OF THE CHURCH AND MONASTERIES

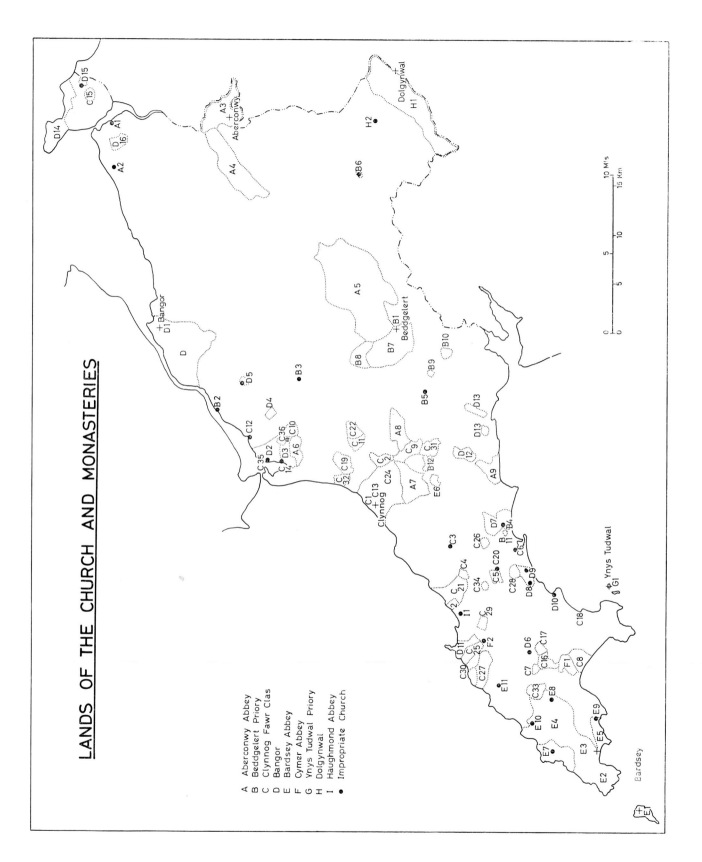

A Aberconwy Abbey
B Beddgelert Priory
C Clynnog Fawr Clas
D Bangor
E Bardsey Abbey
F Cymer Abbey
G Ynys Tudwal Priory
H Dolgynwal
I Haughmond Abbey
● Impropriate Church

Lands of the Church and Monasteries Early Fourteenth Century

The map shows the very large area of land which was owned by the Church in the first half of the fourteenth century, most of which was held until the Dissolution of the Monasteries in 1536-8 and a part much longer. The original settlements on which some of this land was based went back at that time some eight hundred years to the arrival of the first Christian missionaries in the sixth and seventh centuries. Over this long period, generous gifts of land were made by many of the local rulers in Gwynedd, and after the arrival in the late twelfth century of the continental monastic orders, some of which took over the primitive Celtic establishments, even larger grants of land were made by the Welsh princes. After the conquest of Wales, Edward I himself made further additions.

The lands of nine religious bodies are shown on the map. Of these, Bangor and Enlli were settlements of holy men made in the early sixth century under the leadership of Deiniol and Cadfan. The Clas of Clynnog Fawr was founded in the seventh century by Beuno, and Beddgelert is claimed to have been a very early hermitage, as may have been St. Tudwal's island. Bangor developed into the diocesan centre and was re-formed under Norman influence, when its lands became held jointly by the bishops and the Cathedral chapter; much of its land was granted later. By the same reforms, the Clasau of Clynnog and Aberdaron, the latter closely associated with Enlli, were abolished and became portionary churches. Their land consisted of early grants, but by the late fifteenth century Clynnog, by then a collegiate church, had parted with all its holdings in Arfon and Llŷn; they are thus not mentioned in the *Valor Ecclesiasticus* and other documents, and so it has not been possible to locate them and lay down their boundaries on the map as accurately as the other church lands.

The first grant to a monastic house outside Wales was that of Nefyn church to Haughmond Abbey, a house of Augustinian canons at Shrewsbury, by Cadwaladr ap Owain Gwynedd, who died in 1172. There was also a grant of land at Eidda to the Knights Hospitallers about 1190 to found a Hospital at Ysbyty Ifan, possibly by Ifan ap Rhys of Trebrys. In 1186 the Cistercians came first to Rhedynogfelen from Strata Florida, and soon after founded the Abbey of Aberconwy with grants of land from Gruffydd ap Cynan ap Owain Gwynedd. In 1198 Cymer Abbey was founded by the Cistercians in Ardudwy, and its land included a grant of part of Neigwl in Llŷn from Gruffydd's brother Maredudd ap Cynan. The land of these two foundations was confirmed and greatly increased a few years later by Llywelyn Fawr, and Edward I added Maenan to the former. About this time, Enlli, with its lands in Llŷn, St. Tudwal's island and Beddgelert, were placed under Augustinian rule, and the latter received land from Llywelyn ap Gruffydd.

All these church lands became crown property after the Dissolution of the Monasteries, except for those of Clynnog, which had already been disposed of, and those of the Bishops of Bangor; most of the latter were compulsorily sold in 1649 at the beginning of the Commonwealth. They were returned at the Restoration, but were finally disposed of when the Welsh church was disestablished in 1920.

(a) ABERCONWY

1 Aberconwy Church.
2 Dwygyfylchi Church.
3 Maenan.
4 Ardda and Dâr-las.
5 Nanhwynen
6 Rhedynogfelen.
7 Cwm.
8 Nancall.
9 Ffriwlwyd.

(b) BEDDGELERT

1 Beddgelert Priory Church.
2 Llanfair-is-gaer Church and Rectory.
3 Betws Garmon Church and Rectory.
4 Aber-erch Church and Rectory.
5 Llanfihangel y Pennant Church.
6 Dolwyddelan Church and land.

7 Tir y Prior in Nant Colwyn.
8 Cadair Wrychyn in Pennardd.
9 Tir y Prior in Braich-y-bib.
10 Maes-y-llech.
11 Prior in Aber-erch.
12 Pant Ddreiniog and Bwlch Gwyn in
   Llecheiddior.

(c) CLYNNOG FAWR

1 Clynnog Fawr.
2 Graeanog.
3 Carnguwch Church.
4 Bodfaelion in Llŷn.
5 Bodfel.
6 Deneio Church.
7 Part of Maesdref (?=Trefaes).
8 Part of Neigwl.
9 Derwin.
10 Bodellog.
11 Llanllyfni.
12 Gored Aber Saint.
13 Cilgoed (in Clynnog).
14 Gored Gwyrfai.
15 Ysgallen in Creuddyn.
16 Botwnnog.
17 Llwyndynwal.
18 Nant Soch in Llŷn.
19 Eithinog.
20 Llannor Church.
21 Bodelias in Llŷn.
22 Dôl Bebin.
23 Dolcoedog (in Clynnog).
24 Maesog (in Clynnog).
25 Llechedern in Llŷn.
26 Llan-fawr in Llŷn.
27 Hirdref in Llŷn.
28 Bodegroes.
29 Penhyddgen.
30 Treflech (?=Pentre Llech).
31 Part of Llecheiddior.
32 Bryn Cynan.
33 Mellteyrn.
34 Penmaen Beuno.
35 Llanfaglan Church.
36 Llanwnda Church.

(d) BANGOR

1 Maenol Bangor.
2 Llanfaglan.
3 Llanwnda.
4 Castellmai.
5 Rhuddallt.
6 Llaniestyn.
7 Aber-erch.
8 Llangynwyl.
9 Penrhos.
10 Llanbedrog.
11 Edern.
12 Betws.
13 Merthyr.
14 Manor of Gogarth.
15 Glanwydden.
16 Gwerydros.

(e) ENLLI

1 Bardsey
2 Uwch Sely.
3 Is Sely.
4 Tremorfa.
5 Ultradaron.
6 Mynachdy Biswail or Bach
   (part in Llecheiddior).
7 Bodferin Church.
8 Bryncroes Church.
9 Llanfaelrhys Church.
10 Llangwnnadl Church.
11 Tudweiliog Church.

(f) CYMER

1 Part of Neigwl.
2 Capel Ceidio.

(g) YNYS TUDWAL

1 Ynys Tudwal.

(h) YSBYTY IFAN (DOLGYNWAL)

1 Tir Eidda.
2 Penmachno Church.

(i) HAUGHMOND

1 Nefyn Church.

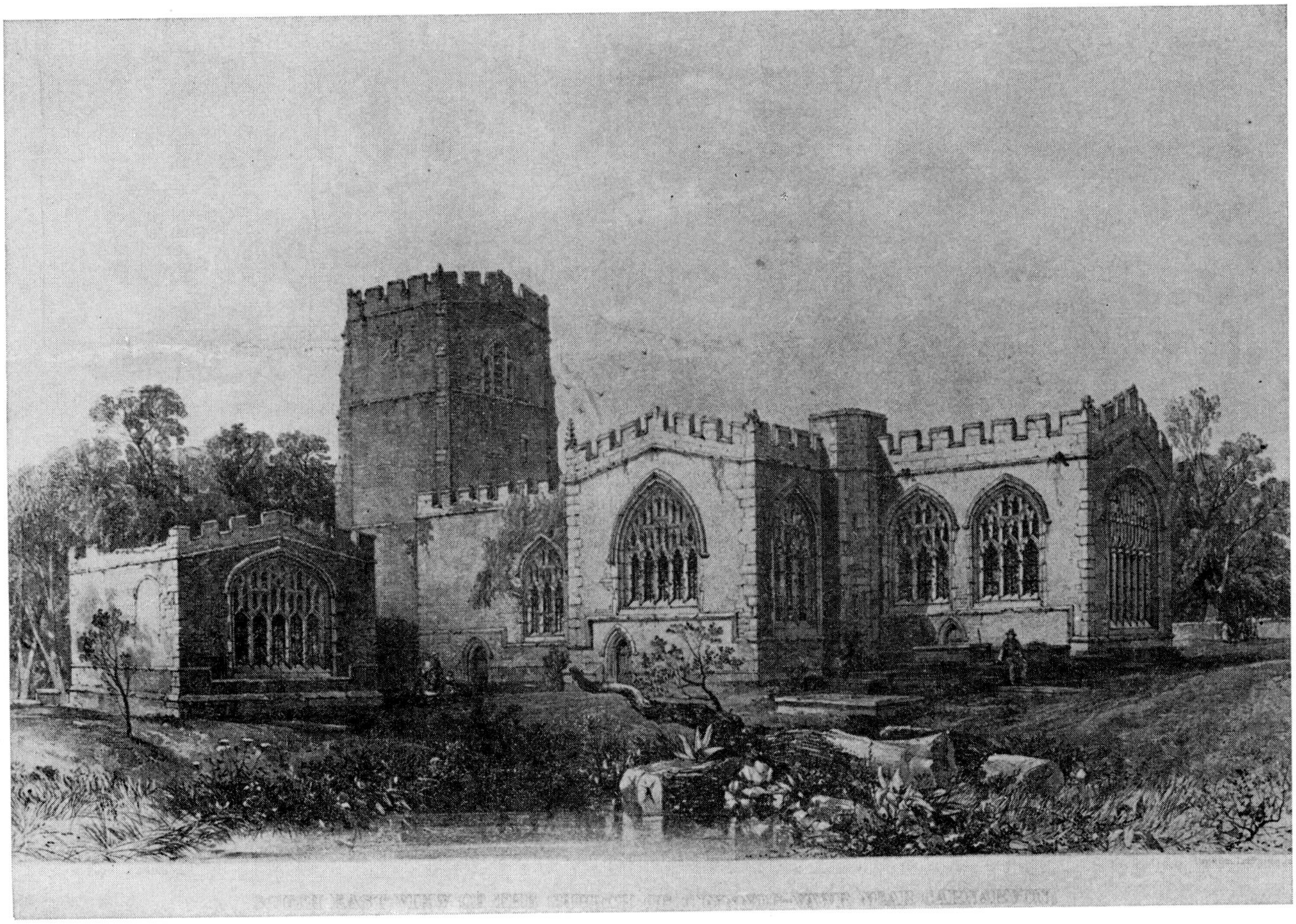

Clynnog Church

Photo: By permission of Gwynedd Archives

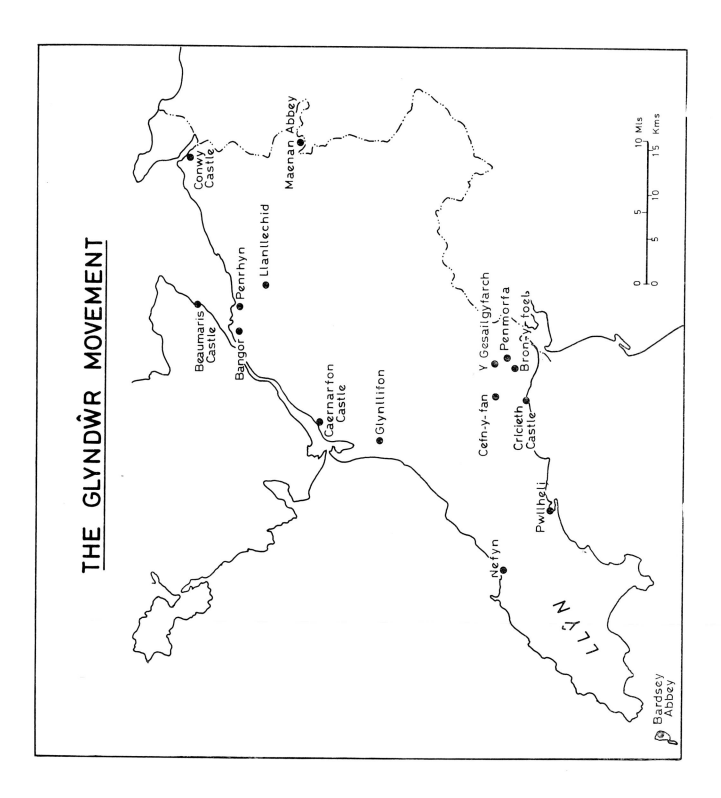

THE GLYNDŴR MOVEMENT

Conwy Castle
Maenan Abbey
Penrhyn
Llanllechid
Beaumaris Castle
Bangor
Caernarfon Castle
Glynllifon
Y Gesailgyfarch
Penmorfa
Bron-y-foel
Cefn-y-fan
Cricieth Castle
Pwllheli
Nefyn
LLŶN
Bardsey Abbey

10 Mls
15 Kms
10
5
5
0
0

The Glyndŵr Movement

Many factors — economic, social, political — led to the great national rebellion which broke out in 1400 and which is associated with the name of Glyndŵr. The first bold moves were taken on 16 September at Glyndyfrdwy when Glyndŵr was treasonably proclaimed Prince of Wales by his supporters. The scene then shifted swiftly to north-east Wales, where the 'English' boroughs of the area were attacked by a Welsh force under Glyndŵr's command. The revolt was barely a week old when the leader went to ground, not to reappear again till the following summer.

News of these dramatic events had caused the earth to tremble in north-west Wales, too. When Henry IV appeared, in a show of force, in North Wales in early October 1400, a number of Welshmen submitted and sought his peace, amongst them the abbots of Bardsey and Maenan and the rector of Llanllechid and his entire flock. Prominent churchmen in Caernarvonshire were clearly already implicated in the revolt. Heavy taxation, low morale and resentment of Englishmen holding high position in the Welsh Church had stirred rebellious thoughts in them.

The upper clergy played a constructive role in the movement. Lewis Byford, a man trained in the Papal curia, left Rome in 1404 to become Bishop of Bangor; he was an ardent supporter of Glyndŵr and served him well as a counsellor and ambassador. Gruffydd Young, Glyndŵr's chancellor, was also closely associated with Bangor. It was, too, in the archdeacon of Bangor's house early in 1405 that the 'Tripartite Indenture' was finally agreed upon, whereby the Earl of Northumberland, Edmund Mortimer, and Glyndŵr contracted to divide the kingdom into three portions, leaving Glyndŵr to rule over a Wales that included the western shires of England — a fantastic scheme which came to nothing.

Inevitably, the Caernarvonshire area, with its long memories of guerilla warfare, was the scene of much conflict. The report in early 1404 that the men of Caernarvonshire were preparing to go to Anglesey to bring all the men and cattle from there 'into the mowntens leste Englishmen should be refreshitte therwith' is a reminder of the tactics used in the days of independence. The castles of

the county were certain to attract attention, for whoever controlled them was ultimately master of Wales. On Good Friday, 1404, the Tudor brothers and 40 other Welshmen managed to seize the great castle of Conwy by a ruse, the 'wardens being slain by the craftiness of a certain carpenter who feigned to come to his accustomed work,' as Adam of Usk put it. Though Conwy had subsequently to be surrendered, this daring exploit re-lit the fires of rebellion in the land.

In the early years, the Welsh bent their energies to destroying or capturing castles. Caernarfon castle was, of course, a prime target. It was attacked by Glyndŵr in November 1401, and again with the assistance of a strong French force under Jean d'Espagne, in November 1403, but it held out. Glyndŵr was in complete command of the countryside — French ships were openly trading with the Welsh around the coast of Llŷn early in 1404 — but with the capture of Harlech and Aberystwyth castles in the spring of that year the centre of the stage moved to mid-Wales.

The rebellion divided families in Caernarvonshire as surely as in the rest of Wales. Two who died defending Caernarfon in November 1403 against the combined Franco-Welsh assault on the town and castle were Hwlcyn Lloyd, an ancestor of the Glyns of Glynllifon, and Ieuan ap Maredudd of Cefn-y-fan and Cesailgyfarch. In the opposing army was Ieuan's own brother, Robert, and his neighbour from Bron-y-foel; after the failure to capture Caernarfon, revenge was obtained by burning Cefn-y-fan and Cesailgyfarch to the ground; and Ieuan's body so it is said, had to be conveyed by sea, rather than by land, to its burial-place at Penmorfa.

Friends one moment might be enemies the next. One of the earliest to withdraw his support for Glyndŵr was Gwilym ap Gruffydd of Penrhyn. He made his peace with the crown in 1405 and was richly rewarded with many of the forfeited lands of his relations, the Tudors. Small wonder that the Penrhyn family was the most influential in the county in the fifteenth century. By removing 'rivals' and shattering the old social order beyond repair, the revolt effectively cleared the way for the rise of the 'gentry' of Tudor Wales.

The revolt left bitter memories. It was not a simple struggle between English and Welsh. The purely Welsh towns of Pwllheli and Nefyn were completely destroyed by the rebels and did not recover until the end of the century; like the hated English boroughs, they had claimed a monopoly of trading in their respective areas. The people of Caernarvonshire were heavily fined for their part in the rebellion, and the accounts of the county were in arrears for decades after the revolt. But all was not gloom; Conwy was as flourishing as ever by 1420, and Caernarfon shortly after.

Glyndŵr's Geat Seal

BIBLIOGRAPHY

Of particular value are J. E. Lloyd, *Owen Glendower* (1931); Glanmor Williams, *Owen Glendower* (1966). For a scintillating essay see Gwyn A. Williams, ' Owain Glyn Dŵr ', in A. J. Roderick, *Wales Through the Ages*, I (1959), 176-83. On Glyndŵr and the church, Glanmor Williams, *The Welsh Church from Conquest to Reformation* (1962), is indispensable; on economic aspects, E. A. Lewis, *The Mediaeval Boroughs of Snowdonia* (1912); and articles on Pwllheli and Nefyn by T. Jones Pierce in *Transactions of the Caernarvonshire Historical Society,* 4 ( )1942-3), 35-50, and Vol. 18 (1957), 36-53.

Plate III

FACSIMILE III (WELSH DOCUMENTS IN PARIS)

Owain Glyndŵr, appointing Doctor Gruffydd Young, his chancellor, and his brother-in-law, John Hanmer, as ambassadors to the court of Charles VI, King of France, May 10, 1404.

(The original document is in Latin, the international language of the Middle Ages. Note the beauty of the handwriting. The first sentence runs: Owynus dei gr[aci]a princeps Wallie universis has l[itte]ras

[nost]ras inspecturis salutem; that is, ' Owain, by the Grace of God, Prince of Wales, to everyone who sees these, our letters, Greetings.'

Note also the name of Charles VI (' Karolus ') in the second line, and the names of two ambassadors ' Griffinum Yonge ' and ' Johannem de Hangmer ' in the third line.)

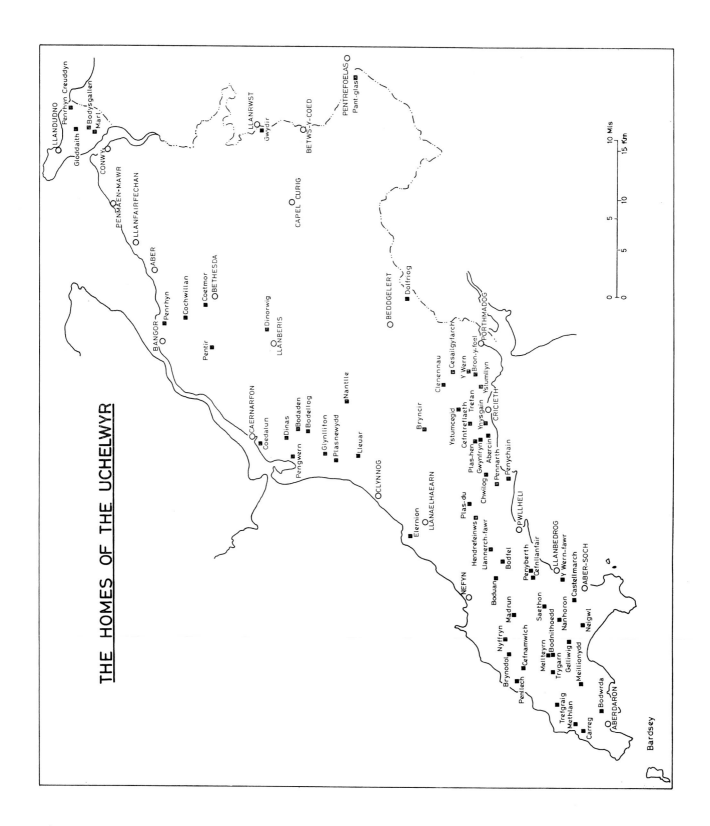

THE HOMES OF THE UCHELWYR

LLANDUDNO
Penrhyn Creuddyn
Gloddaith
Bodysgallen
Marl
CONWY
PENMAEN-MAWR
LLANFAIRFECHAN
ABER
BANGOR
Penrhyn
Cochwillan
Coetmor
BETHESDA
Pentir
Dinorwig
LLANBERIS
CAERNARFON
Coedalun
Dinas
Bodaden
Bodellog
Pengwern
Glynlliton
Plasnewydd
Llecuar
Nantlle
CLYNNOG
LLANRWST
Gwydir
BETWS-Y-COED
PENTREFOELAS
Pant-glas
CAPEL CURIG
BEDDGELERT
Dolfriog
PORTHMADOG
Cesailgyfarch
Y Wern
Bron-y-foel
Ystumllyn
CRICIETH
Clenennau
Bryncir
Ystumcegid
Ceintreflaeth
Tretan
Plas-hen
Gwynfryn
Abercin
Ynysgain
Pennarth
Penychain
Elernion
LLANAELHAEARN
Hendreteinws
Plas-du
PWLLHELI
LLANBEDROG
Y Wern-fawr
Castellmarch
ABER-SOCH
NEFYN
Llannerch-fawr
Bodfel
Penyberth
Cefnllanfair
Boduan
Madrun
Saethon
Nanhoron
Neigwl
Nyffryn
Cefnamwlch
Melltyarn
Bodnithoedd
Gelliwig
Meillionydd
Brynodol
Penllech
Trygarn
Tretfraig
Methlan
Carreg
Bodwrda
ABERDARON

Bardsey

10 Mls
15 Km
10
5
5
0

The Uchelwyr

For the period between 1300 and 1700 the uchelwyr formed the backbone of Welsh society. They were able to trace their ancestry for many generations, sometimes to the independent princes, and often, in Caenarvonshire, to Ednyfed Fychan, seneschal to Llywelyn the Great. They owned property, some on a bigger scale than others, and by purchase or discreet marriages or being on the right side on occasions such as the Glyndŵr rising or the Civil War, some of them had built up substantial estates, as the Gwydir and Penrhyn families did. Their life pattern was determined more by a regard for their own and their families' welfare than by lofty idealism. Rhys ap Gruffudd, grandson of Ednyfed Fychan, fought on the English side against Llywelyn ap Gruffudd, and it is said that Gruffudd Llwyd of Dinorwig was knighted for bringing news to King Edward of the birth of his son. At the time of the Glyndŵr rising, Gwilym ap Gruffudd of Penrhyn started off as one of the rebels, but changed sides before the end, to receive as his reward the lands of those of his own kinsmen who had adhered to Glyndŵr.

After the establishment of the shire system in Gwynedd in 1284, the uchelwyr of Caernarvonshire, like their counterparts elsewhere, were prepared to fill those offices which the English king had at his disposal, and in course of time they became justices of the peace and sheriffs and foresters, and occasionally constables of castles. As crown officers, they were responsible for the maintenance of law and order, though they themselves were often somewhat disorderly. They were notorious for their litigiousness, and there was very bad blood between them, particularly during Parliamentary elections, as was the case on more than one occasion between the Cefnamwlch and Gwydir families.

Their activities ranged far beyond Wales. Owen Gwynn of Berth-ddu became Master of St. John's College, Cambridge, in 1612. Uchelwyr's sons attended the London law schools and became prominent in legal circles, though few attained the eminence of Sir William Jones of Castellmarch, who was Chief Justice of the King's Bench. They were found in the English armies, in Ireland or on the Continent; William Thomas of Coedalun was killed in 1586 at the battle of Zutphen, where Philip Sidney also fell. The Church gave them ample opportunities for advancement. Morus Glyn of Glynllifon was archdeacon of Bangor, and his brother William archdeacon of Anglesey. Edmund Griffith of Cefnamwlch and Henry Rowland of Mellteyrn became bishops of Bangor; Humphrey Humphreys of the Cesailgyfarch family was bishop of Bangor and of Hereford; Richard Vaughan of Nyffryn was bishop of Bangor, Chester and London. The best known of them all was John Williams of the Cochwillan family, Lord Keeper of the Great Seal and Archbishop of York in the time of Charles I.

Not all the uchelwyr, however, were gainfully conformist. At great risk to life and limb, the Puw family of Penrhyn Creuddyn remained staunch Catholics for several generations. Robert Puw was one of those who, in 1587, were in hiding for months in Rhiwledin cave, engaged in printing a Catholic tract, *Y Drych Cristianogawl*. Then there were the two brothers from Plas-du in Eifionydd — Robert Owen, a Roman Catholic priest in exile in France, and Hugh, a diligent plotter against Elizabeth. Two brothers from Bodfel, Roger and Charles Gwynn, were also Catholic priests, and so was Robert Gwynn of Penyberth.

At the other extreme were the Puritan nonconformists, of whom the most prominent was Henry Maurice of Methlan in Llŷn, preacher and founder of churches. Bodfel house (strangely enough) was licensed for worship under the Toleration Act of 1672. The Nanhoron family had very definite Puritan leanings, and in the eighteenth century Cefnamwlch became a well-known name because of the association of Sidney Griffith and Howel Harris.

During the Civil War, John Owen of Clenennau was one of the king's most ardent supporters, while Thomas Madryn and Thomas and John Glyn of Glynllifon were prominent on the Parliamentary side.

One interesting feature of Caernarvonshire uchelwyr was the adoption by some of them of the names of their homes as personal surnames, such as Bodfel, Bodwrda, Carreg, Saethon, Coetmor, Madryn, Trygarn, and Glynllifon, abbreviated as

Glyn. These have virtually disappeared by now, unfortunately.

The greatest service which the uchelwyr gave to Wales was their patronage of poets. Up to about 1650, the poets of Wales were professional men, whose well-being depended on the welcome accorded to them in the homes of the uchelwyr. They sang eulogies and elegies to their patrons, and advised them on matters of behaviour, even administering a rebuke if necessary. They also provided mirth and entertainment. One of their most important functions was the tracing and recording of their patrons' pedigrees.

This relationship between the uchelwyr and the poets was an ancient one. At the beginning of the fourteenth century, Gwilym Ddu o Arfon sang the praises of Sir Gruffudd Llwyd of Dinorwig, and a little later Gruffudd Gryg sang to Einion ap Gruffudd of Chwilog, and Iolo Goch to Einion's son Ieuan. In the following century, Rhys Goch Eryri and Guto'r Glyn eulogised members of the Penrhyn

family. Throughout the period, scores of poems were composed in honour of Caernarvonshire families by such poets as Tudur Aled, Lewys Môn, Gutun Owain, Tudur Penllyn, William Llŷn, Morus Dwyfach and many others, until the time of Owen Griffith of Llanystumdwy at the beginning of the eighteenth century.

The uchelwyr did not confine themselves to patronage; some of them practised the art of poetry themselves. Three members of the Glynllifon family, for example, William Glyn, his son, Thomas Glyn, and his grandson, Sir William Glyn, were all poets. Richard Hughes of Cefnllanfair was an equerry at the court of Queen Elizabeth, and wrote some fine love poems in the free metres. About the middle of the seventeenth century, William Bodwrda was collecting and copying large numbers of the poems of the uchelwyr poets. The process of anglicisation was by then beginning to divert the interests of the uchelwyr from Welsh poetry to other pursuits.

Bodwrda

By permission of the Controller, H.M.S.O.

Gwydir

Mawl i Einion ap Gruffudd o Chwilog

Dewr a doeth benadur dawn
A diennig wyd, Einiawn,
A glain nod hael galon Nudd,
Brau faner bro Eifionydd.
A'th annedd berffaith hynod
Yn Chwilog, lys uchel glod,
Neuadd wen newydd annwyl,
I hon down bob hynod ŵyl.
Cwrt hir is llaw brodir Llŷn
Yno'n cynnal naw cannyn.
Llyna'r gaer lle llenwir gwin,
Llys agored, lles gwerin,
Lle'r oedd y tad llariaidd tau,
Waed dethol, lle'r wyt tithau
Yn rhannu, fy nêr hynod,
Yma i glêr aur am glod,
A diwarth roi da wrth raid
A hir gynnal rhai gweiniaid.

Gruffydd Gryg

(Second half of the 14th Century)

Mawl i Wiliam Gruffudd o Gochwillan

Mae da Wiliam i'm dwylaw,
Mae'n feistr im yn f'oes draw.
Gwely arras, goleurym,
A siambr deg sy'n barod ym.
Mae yno i ddyn mwyn a ddel
Fwrdd a chwpwrdd a chapel,
A gwych allor Gochwillan,
Ac aelwyd deg i gael tân.
Gwledd fraisg ac ymgeledd fry,
Gwin aml, a'i gywain ymy.
Ni châi Ddafydd, llywydd llwyd,
Gan Ifor ryw giniawfwyd.
Iolo Goch ni welai gael
Rhyw fwythau yn nhref Ithael.
Eiddil yw llu i ddal llys
Wrth enaid yr wyth ynys . . .
Fy nef, ei fro ef erioed,
Fu lan Ogwen flaeneugoed.
Mi af i'w lys, mwyfwy wledd,
Mal eidion moel i adwedd.
Ni ddof fyth o Wynedd fawr,
O dai Wiliam hyd elawr.

Guto'r Glyn
(Towards the end of the 15th Century)

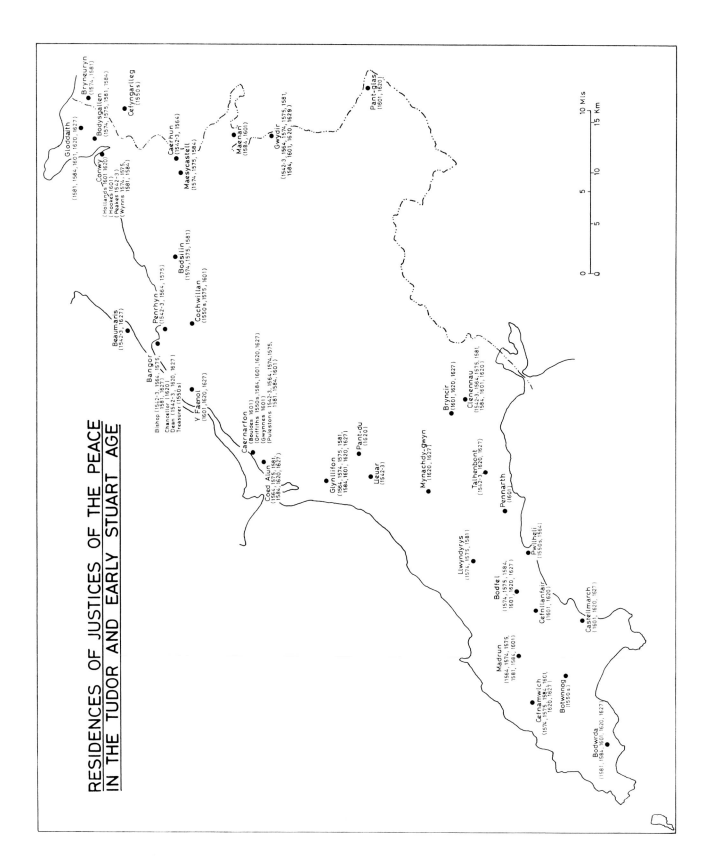

RESIDENCES OF JUSTICES OF THE PEACE
IN THE TUDOR AND EARLY STUART AGE

Bryneuryn
(1574, 1581)

Gloddaith
(1581, 1564, 1601, 1620, 1627)

Bodysgallen
(1574, 1575, 1581, 1584)

Cefyngarlleg
(1550s)

Conwy
(Hollands 1601 1620)
(Hookes 1620)
(Peakes 1542-3)
(Wynns 1581, 1584)

Caerhun
(1542-3, 1564)

Maesycastell
(1574, 1575, 1584)

Maenan
(1584, 1601)

Pant-glas
(1601, 1620)

Gwydir
(1542-3, 1564, 1574, 1575, 1581,
1584, 1601, 1620, 1629)

Bodsilin
(1574, 1575, 1581)

Beaumaris
(1542-3, 1627)

Penrhyn
(1542-3, 1564, 1575)

Cochwillan
(1550s, 1575, 1601)

Bangor
Bishop (1542-3, 1564, 1575,
1581, 1627)
Chancellor (1620)
Dean (1542-3, 1620, 1627)
Treasurer (1550s)

Y Faenol
(1601, 1620, 1627)

Caernarfon
(Bouldes 1601)
(Griffiths 1550s, 1584, 1601, 1620, 1627)
(Gwynnes 1601)
(Puleistons 1542-3, 1564, 1574, 1575,
1581, 1584, 1601)

Bryncir
(1601, 1620, 1627)

Clenennau
(1542-3, 1564, 1575, 1581,
1584, 1601, 1620)

Coed Alun
(1564, 1575, 1581,
1584, 1601, 1620, 1627)

Glynllifon
(1564, 1574, 1575, 1581,
1584, 1601, 1620, 1627)

Pant-du
(1620)

Lleuar
(1542-3)

Mynachdy-gwyn
(1620, 1627)

Talhenbont
(1542-3, 1620, 1627)

Pennarth
(1601)

Llwyndyrys
(1574, 1575, 1581)

Bodfel
(1574, 1575, 1584,
1601, 1620, 1627)

Cefnllanfair
(1601, 1620)

Pwllheli
(1550s, 1564)

Castellmarch
(1601, 1620, 1627)

Madrun
(1564, 1574, 1575,
1581, 1584, 1601)

Cefnamwlch
(1574, 1575, 1584, 1601,
1620, 1627)

Botwnnog
(1550s)

Botwrda
(1581, 1584, 1601, 1620, 1627)

10 Mls

15 Km

Justices of the Peace in the Tudor and Early Stuart Age

1536 has long been regarded as a turning-point in Welsh history. In that year, the 'Tudor union' of England and Wales was forged; in that year, too, the well-tried and uniquely English office of J.P. was introduced to Wales. The one measure was not unconnected with the other, for the success of the 'Union' depended upon laws and justice being 'ministered in Wales in like form' as in England. J.P.s were to be the midwives of change, the chief instrument whereby Wales was to be brought under the same system of local government as that of England. There were, however, to be no more than 8 J.P.s to each shire in Wales, and those were to be appointed by the Lord Chancellor on the advice of the President and Council in the Marches and the judges of Great Sessions. Furthermore, those admitted were to be simply of 'good name and fame' and not necessarily worth £20 a year in land, and all were to be conversant with the English language. They were to hold their sessions four times a year, and they were given the same extensive powers as their counterparts in England. As the main responsibility for the preservation of law and order in the Welsh counties was thenceforth to be in their hands, so, too, the main burden of local government was to fall on their shoulders until county councils took over their administrative duties in 1889.

Who were the men who were appointed to an office of such power and responsibility in Caernarvonshire after the 'Union'? They were, as the various lists for 1542-3, 1564, 1574, 1575, 1581, 1584, 1601, 1620, and 1627 indicate, the greater gentry for the most part, men who had already sufficient wealth and property to play a leading part in local affairs. Prominent amongst them were the Bulkeleys (Beaumaris), Griffiths (Penrhyn), Wynnes (Gwydir), Maurices (Clenennau), Glyns (Glynllifon), Bodfels (Bodfel), Madryns (Madrun), Griffiths (Cefnamwlch), Pulestons (Caernarfon) and Thomases (Coed Alun). Often enough, son followed father in office; e.g., Sir John Puleston was succeeded by his son Hugh and Sir Thomas Mostyn by his son Roger. So well-established was the succession principle that in 1610 Sir John Wynn of Gwydir claimed that it was usual for 'both father and son to be in the Commission' at the same time.

The greater gentry, many of whom were related by marriage, had thus a virtual monopoly of the office. Only rarely was a rich merchant like David Lloyd ap Thomas of Pwllheli admitted. Certainly, leading churchmen served the office, but they, too, had close links with the leading gentry: Arthur Bulkeley, bishop of Bangor 1541-52, was Sir Richard Bulkeley's brother; Edmund Griffith, dean and later (1633-7) bishop of Bangor, was a member of the influential Cefnamwlch family.

No family with any social pretensions could afford not to have a representative on the bench. Hence the tendency for numbers of J.P.s gradually to rise above 8 in defiance of statute. Adding fuel to this process was the patronage of a great magnate like the Earl of Leicester, who wanted to build up his family interest in North Wales and who was influential in Court circles. There was, too, the difficulty of administering an area like Caernarvonshire, which was experiencing a population explosion during this period. Eight J.P.s could not adequately minister to the needs of a county made up of ten hundreds, especially at a time when the duties of J.P.s were increasing. Even in 1575, when there were 19 J.P.s, the hundreds of Cafflogion, Eifionydd and Is Gwyrfai had to be content with the services of only one J.P. apiece. A fairly tight rein was, however, kept on numbers, and at no time before the Civil War did they exceed 30.

What success attended the efforts of the J.P.s? Their prime duty was the preservation of the peace, a very delicate plant indeed in the sixteenth century. The J.P.s themselves were not above flouting the law whenever their interests were threatened. They did not always 'set a good example to the inferior people'. The Clenennau family was involved in a murder in the early 1550s, the formidable Sir John Wynn in forcible entry into lands in 1615. Even the bishop of Bangor, Lewis Bayly, was accused of receiving bribes in his capacity as J.P. c. 1621. Nevertheless, respect for the rule of law grew in the sixteenth century, and J.P.s played no small part in its promotion.

As county administrators, too, they struggled manfully to cope with the maintenance of roads and bridges, with the care of 'poor aged and impotent persons', with the levying of rates and regulation of markets, and many other matters. Some of those appointed J.P.s at the 'Union' were not unfamiliar with holding local offices — as sheriffs or stewards or whatever — and all had had experience of local administration in the county court. But in the hundred years or so after the Union, under the watchful eye of the Council in the Marches, J.P.s gained enormously in confidence, served their apprenticeship well, and emerged as the natural 'governors of the county'.

FROM THE 'ORDER BOOK' OF SIR JOHN WYNN, 1618

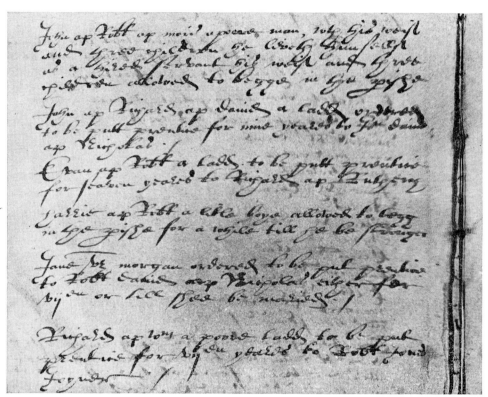

Gwynedd Archives

John ap Robert ap Moris a poore man, with his weif and three children he liveth himsellf as a hired servant his weif and three children allowed to begge in the parishe.

John ap Richard ap Dauid a ladd ordered to be putt prentice for nine yeares to Jon Dauid ap Nicholas.

Evan ap Robert a ladd to be putt prentice for seaven yeares to Richard ap Rutherch.

Harrie ap Robert a little boye allowed to begg in the parishe for a while till he be stronger.

Jane vch Morgan ordered to be put prentice to Robert Dauid ap Nicholas, either for vijen or till shee be maried.

Richard ap William a poore ladd to be put prentice for vijen yeares to Robert Jones joyner.

BIBLIOGRAPHY

Of fundamental importance is W. Ogwen Williams, *Calendar of the Caernarvonshire Quarter Sessions Record, I, 1541-1558* (1956). The introduction in part has been published separately as *Tudor Gwynedd*. For the seventeenth century there are two articles by Dr. J. Gwynfor Jones: 'Caernarvonshire Administration: the Activities of the Justices of the Peace, 1603 - 1660' in *Welsh History Review,* V (1970-1), 130-63; and 'Aspects of Local Government in Pre-Restoration Caernarvonshire' in *Transactions of the Caernarvonshire Historical Society,* 33 (1972), 7-32. To get the flavour of the period, one could not do better than browse in the printed *Calendar of Wynn Papers 1615 - 1690.*

Plas Mawr, Conwy

ROBERT WYNN, WHO BUILT PLAS MAWR

Robt Wynn born at Gweddr in ye said County third Son to John Wynn ap Meredith Serving Sr Philip Hobbie Knight in his Camber being one of ye councel of King Henry ye 8 and a great Commander of his Armie was with ye king and his Mr at ye Siege of Bullen where he received a Shott in his Legg whereof he was long lame notwithstanding all ye Surgery ye kings men could afford . . . he was at ye winninge and Burning of Edenborough and Leeth in Scotland and at ye Memorable Journeys mentioned in ye Chronikles in King Henrey ye 8: and Edward ye 6 tyme excepting Marloborow field in Scotland, whereat I did here him Say he was In ye Latter part of king Edward the 6th Raigne his Mr was sent Embasadoure to ye Emperour Charles ye 5th who was then in Hungary with the greatest Army yt the Christians ever had to Confront Solyman the Turke yt came with 5000000 Thousand Men to Conquer Christendome, at wch Service both his Mr and he was . . .

Robert Wynn his Servant returnd home and anone after married as afore Said, and he built a goodly house in ye town of Conway in this County; where he kept a worthy plenty full House all his time, & lieth buried in ye Church there . . .

From ' The History of the Gwydir Family ', by Sir John Wynn.

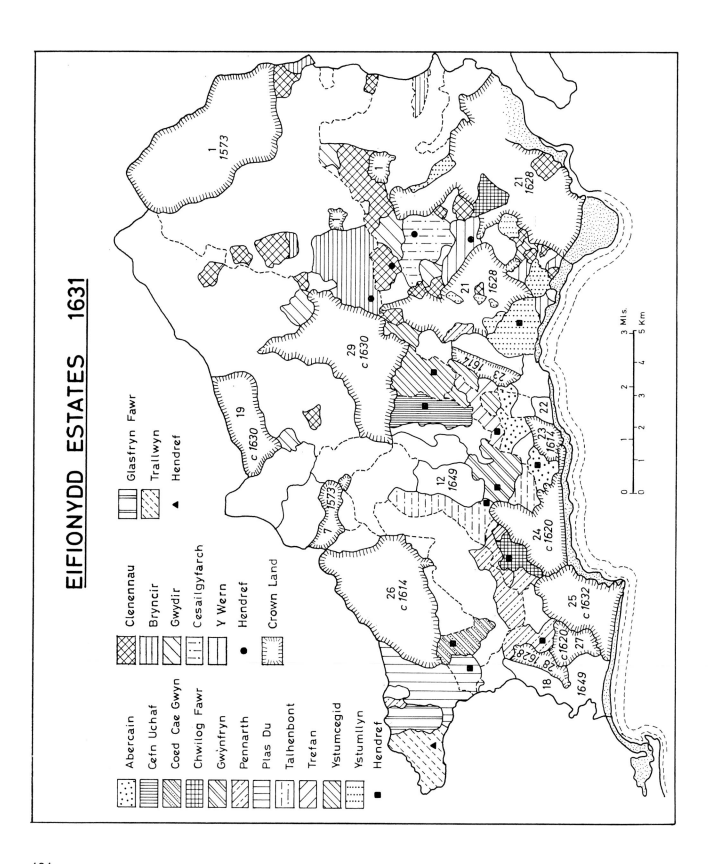

EIFIONYDD ESTATES 1631

Clenennau
Bryncir
Gwydir
Cesailgyfarch
Y Wern
Hendref •
Crown Land

Glasfryn Fawr
Trallwyn
Hendref ▲

Abercain
Cefn Uchaf
Coed Cae Gwyn
Chwilog Fawr
Gwynfryn
Pennarth
Plas Du
Talhenbont
Trefan
Ystumcegid
Ystumllyn
Hendref ■

3 Mls.
5 Km

Eifionydd Estates

A previous map has shown the boundaries of the free and bond townships in Eifionydd, with some indication of the principal *rhandiroedd* on which the descendants of Collwyn ap Tangno and other families were settled in the medieval period. After the conquest of Wales, the bond land became crown land held by the kings of England, but the freemen were permitted to continue holding their lands under the customary Welsh tenure, and to divide it between their descendants by *cyfran.*

There are hardly any records to show how the free lands were passed down from the twelfth century *gwely* founders to their descendants living in the fourteenth century, but the Extent of Caernarvonshire, drawn up in 1352, provides a basis from which the later devolution can be traced. The Extent and family pedigrees indicate that by that date the two principal Collwyn *gwelyau,* the Gwely Gwgan and the Gwely Gwyn ab Ednowain, were mostly in the possession of a Collwyn line descended from Gwgan himself through his great-grandson, Hywel ap Maredudd. There were other families holding some land with them, but these, being less distinguished, cannot be traced, except for one, the owner of Tŷ Mawr in Treflys, who was a great-grandson of Gwyn ab Ednowain.

As has been already explained in the previous section, these two Collwyn *gwelyau* had portions of their land in a number of the free townships of lowland Eifionydd, and it is in those particular townships that we naturally find the homes of the descendants of Hywel ap Maredudd mentioned above. The earliest houses were at Gwynfryn and Chwilog Fawr in the Gwely Gwgan, and at Bron-y-foel, Abercain, Cefn-y-fan and Cefn Uchaf in the Gwely Gwyn. There later appeared, by subsequent division of land, the houses of Talhenbont, Pennarth Fawr, Pencoed (Plas Du), and Coed Cae Gwyn. The last of this series to emerge was Trefan, but this was not until the sixteenth century, just after the abolition of *cyfran,* so there the younger son had to form his estate by purcnase and not inheritance as before.

In this way, the eleven Collwyn estates had come into existence by division by *gwely* land over a period of some two hundred years, and after about the middle of the fifteenth century, some small additions of purchased land had been made to them by their owners. As early as the fourteenth century, Cefn-y-fan (later Ystumcegid) and Cefn Uchaf (later Cefn Isaf) had passed through heiresses to families of other descent, but the rest remained in the hands of the direct descendants of Collwyn until the beginning of the seventeenth century, when Talhenbont passed to an heiress and Plas Du was sold. This resulted in the position revealed by a Rental of Eifionydd drawn up for the crown in 1631, and here shown on the map.

In a similar manner, estates had grown up in Is Dwyfor on the land of *gwely* founders not descended from Collwyn. These were the Gwely Wyrion Cynan in Pennant and the Gwely Wyrion Ithel and Gwely Wyrion Griffi in Penyfed. In the fourteenth century, this land had passed through heiresses to a family descended from Owain Gwynedd, which came to Eifionydd from Nant-conwy. By division between descendants and with a considerable amount of land purchased in the sixteenth century, the estates of Clenennau, Bryncir, Cesailgyfarch and land belonging to Gwydir had been formed.

By the time of the 1631 Rental, two other important estates had been formed through purchase of land by non-indigenous families, both in the township of Glasfryn on part of the land of the Gwely Wyrion Dafydd, which was probably original Collwyn land, and were Trallwyn and Glasfryn Mawr.

These eighteen indigenous estates are shown on the map. If we discount the areas of common land in Ffridd y Pennant, Llwytmor, Mynydd Cennin and Rhos-lan, it will be seen that they cover at least two-thirds of the original *gwely* land in the free townships. In the remaining free *gwely* land, left blank on the map, about ten estates centred outside Eifionydd had one or two holdings each, and the rest was held by an estimated thirty-six local small-holders. Many of these probably had inherited *gwely* land rather than made purchases, but in only a few cases can their pedigrees be traced to show this.

The map also shows the large blocks of crown land in Eifionydd; most of this represents the original bond townships, but some was former monastic land annexed after the dissolution of the monasteries in 1536-8. The land of the priory of Beddgelert in Pennant and Llecheiddior was sold by Queen Elizabeth I in 1576, and the grange of the Abbey of Enlli in Pentyrch was probably sold about the same time. The former bond lands were retained slightly longer and sold by James I and Charles I between 1614 and 1640. The bishops of Bangor also had land here, and their manor of Edern in Betws and Gogwmwd was sold in 1649. These large and compact blocks of land were purchased by local landowners and added to their estates, which were thereby greatly enlarged. As a result of this, the pattern of landownership, which up to then was still closely related to the scattered *gwely* holdings of the past, took on a new and different aspect.

During the next two hundred and fifty years, the estates grew by purchase of additional land, and some were merged together. In the nineteenth century, an entirely new estate, Broom Hall, was created by large purchases, and so grew to be the most extensive in Eifionydd. Then in the twentieth century, partly by failure to produce male heirs but mostly owing to the changed social conditions, all the old estates came to an end, the majority of the farms being sold to the tenants.

EIFIONYDD

ESTATES IN 1631 BASED ON ORIGINAL GWELY LAND
Inherited directly or through heiresses, with some purchases

1. GWELY FOUNDERS DESCENDED FROM COLLWYN AP TANGNO

    1   Abercain

Hywel Vaughan. Direct descendant.

In Gwely Gwyn ab Ednowain: Abercain, Bryndu, Cefn-y-maen, Cae-llobrith.

    2   Cefn Uchaf

John Owen. Direct descendant, through a former heiress.

In Gwely Gwyn ab Ednowain: Cefn Uchaf, Tŷ Cerrig, Tyddyn-y-felin. (*By purchase:* Cefn Isaf.)

    3   Coed Cae Gwyn

Hugh Gwyn. Direct Descendant.

In Gwely Gwgan: Coed cae gwyn, Talafon, Cae'r fron, Tyddyn Gwyn, Gelli'r gron.

    4   Chwilog Fawr

Maurice Lloyd. Direct descendant.

In Gwely Gwgan: Chwilog Fawr (including Chwilog Bach and Tŷ'n-y-coed), Pencarth Isaf.
Free land in Gest: Penamser.

    5   Gwynfryn

Owen Wynn. Direct descendant.

In Gwely Gwgan: Gwynfryn, Tyddyn Du, Tyddyn Madog Goch, Tyddyn Bach, Ty'n Llan.

    6   Pennarth Fawr

William Gwyn. Direct descendant.

In Gwely Wyrion Dafydd: Pennarth Fawr, Bryn-y-gwynt, Ty'n Rhos (in Chwilog), Tyddyn Heilyn, Y Ddôl-gam. (Also lands in Pencoed.)

    7   Plas Du (Pencoed)

Charles Jones. Purchaser (held by Hugh Owen, direct descendant until 1614).

In Gwely Gwgan: Plas Du (in Glasfryn), Castell Gwgan, Tyddyn Uchaf, Yr Orsedd, Pencaenewydd, Tan-y-bryn, Pen-y-bryn.

| 8 | Talhenbont | *William Vaughan.* Husband of direct heiress, Ann Vaughan. |

In Gwely Wyrion Ithel: Talhenbont, Llwyn y Forwyn, Beudy Mawr, Maes Gwyn, Y Gaerwen, Bryn Graeanog, (in Rhwng Dwyfor a Dwyfach): Glyn Dwyfach.

| 9 | Trefan | *Humphrey Jones.* Husband of the direct heiress, Elin Owen. |

In Gwely Gwgan: Trefan (in Chwilog), Pencarth Uchaf.

In Gwely Gwyn ab Ednowain: Tyddyn Morthwyl, Llwyn-y-bugeilydd.

| 10 | Ystumcegid | *Robert Wynn.* Husband of the direct heiress, Catherine Owen, who was descended from Owain Gwynedd but held her land from a former heiress of Collwyn. |

In Gwely Gwyn ab Ednowain: Ystumcegid (in Trefan), Cefn Ymwlch, Tyddyn Cethin, (in Abercain), Ynys Du, Y Gell, Cefn Collwyn. (In Pennant) Hafod Garregog, Dinas Du.

| 11 | Ystumllyn | *Owen Ellis.* Direct descendant. |

In Gwely Gwyn ab Ednowain (in Treflys): Bron-y-foel, Porth yr hirfaen.

In Gwely Tegwared ap Robert: Ystumllyn (purchased land).

Free land in Gest: Cwm Bach, Mynydd Du, Bron-y-gadair Bach, Tyddyn Ysguboriau, Nanhyra.

II. GWELY FOUNDERS NOT DESCENDED FROM COLLWYN AP TANGNO

| 12 | Clenennau | *Sir John Owen.* Inherited through heiresses, including much purchased land. |

Gwely Wyrion Ithel

Gwely Wyrion Griffri: Clenennau, Cefn Coch Uchaf, Ereiniog, Maes-y-llech, Ynys Wen, Pwll Budr, Bwlch-y-fedwen, Tŷ Cerrig, Tyddyn Mawr, Braich-y-ddinas, Blaen-y-cae.

Gwely Wyrion Cynan

Gwely Gwair: Cwrt Uchaf, Cwrt Isaf, Brithdir Mawr, Y Gyfyng, Oerddwr Uchaf, Cerrig y rhwydwyr.

Free land in Gest: Drwsdeugoed, Hendregadredd, Y Garreg Fawr, Moelfre, Tyddyn y Borth, Tyddyn Madyn.

| 13 | Bryncir | *James Brynker.* Descendant of Owain Gwynedd, inherited land through heiresses, some purchased land. |

Gwely Wyrion Cynan: Bryncir, Hendre Fechan, Isallt, Caer Fadog, Tyddyn y Waun, Aberdeunant, Prenteg.

| 14 | (Gwydir) | *Sir Richard Wynn.* Direct descendant of Owain Gwynedd. |

Gwely Wyrion Ithel

Gwely Wyrion Griffri: Cefn Coch Isa, Y Garnedd Hir, Y Fach, Cwm Fedw ddu, Moelfre, Llwyn-y-betws.

Gwely Gwyn ab Ednowain: Tyddyn Einion (in Treflys).

15	Cesailgyfarch	*Robert Wynn.* Direct descendant of Owain Gwynedd.

15 Cesailgyfarch   *Robert Wynn.* Direct descendant of Owain Gwynedd.

Gwely Wyrion Griffri: Cesailgyfarch, Cefn Perfedd, Bryn Coch.

16 Y Wern   *John Jones.* Direct descendant of Owen Gwynedd, holding most of his land by inheritance through heiresses.

Gwely Wyrion Griffri: Y Wern, Gwern Ddwyryd, Ty'n Llan, Y Wern Firagl.

Gwely Gwyn ab Ednowain: Coed-y-llyn, Penrhyn, Cefn Treflys, Cae Sion (in Treflys).

III. ESTATES CREATED OUT OF COLLWYN GWELY LAND BY OTHER FAMILIES

17 Trallwyn   *David Lloyd.* Descendant of Hywel Coetmor of Nant Conwy, possibly inheriting through a Collwyn heiress.

Gwely Wyrion Dafydd: Trallwyn, Coed-y-garth, Penfras, Ty'n-y-pant, Glasfryn Bach.

18 Glasfryn Fawr   *Cadwaladr ap Thomas.* Direct descendant of Owain Gwynedd. He, or his father, purchased the land.

Gwely Wyrion Dafydd: Glasfryn Mawr, Mur Cwymp.

CROWN LANDS — FORMER BOND LAND

21 Gest   *Sold* 1628 to the Mayor and Commonalty of the City of London. 1632 to Charles Jones. 1679 inherited by Col. William Price, Rhiwlas.

22 Botewin   *Sold c.* 1620, purchaser unknown.

23 Ynysygain   *Sold* 1614 to Hugh Richardson and Thomas Powel, who re-sold Ynysgain Uchaf to John Lloyd of Tŷ Mawr, Cricieth; Prystyfnog to Gruffydd ap Robert of Bach-y-saint, Cricieth; the remainder to Robert ap Elise.

24 Ffriwlwyd   *Sold c.* 1620, purchaser unknown; divided between Talhenbont and Glynllifon estates.

25 Penychen   *Sold c.* 1632, purchaser unknown; became part of the Glynllifon estate.

26 Pentyrch   *Sold c.* 1614 to Sir Thomas Middleton. 1626 sold to Charles Jones. 1679 inherited by Col. William Price, Rhiwlas.

27 Botach   *Sold c.* 1620 to Humphrey Jones of Y Ddôl and Craflwyn.

28 Rhedynog Felen   *Sold* 1628 to the Mayor and Commonalty of the City of London. 1632 to Charles Jones. 1679 inherited by Col. William Price, Rhiwlas.

29 Dolbenmaen   *Sold c.* 1630 to Sir Richard Trevor of Trefalun. 1637 inherited by John Griffith of Cefn Amwlch. 1721 sold to William Brynker of Bryncir. 1735 sold to William Owen of Clenennau, without Dolwgan.

CROWN LANDS FORMER MONASTIC LANDS

1	Pennant (part)	*Sold* 1573 to Lord Cheney. Sold by him — Meillionen and Hafod Ruffydd to Morris Wynn of Gwydir; Cwm Cloch unknown; Ty'n Llan to John Wyn Morris of Clenennau with Maes-y-llech; Braich-y-bib to Cadwaladr ap Maredudd of Y Wenallt. Priory of Beddgelert.
7	Llecheiddior (part)	*Sold* 1573 to Lord Cheney, being Pant Ddreiniog and Bwlch Gwyn, and by him to unknown purchasers. Priory of Beddgelert. (See also next entry.)
26	Pentyrch (part)	*Sold* 1566 to Sir Rowland Howard, being Mynachdy Biswail (Mynachdy Bach), a small part of which lay in Llecheiddior. Abbey of Enlli. (It became part of the land of Charles Jones and Col. William Price.)
19	Nancall	*Sold c.* 1630 to Hugh Hughes of Plas Coch, Anglesey. Land of the Abbey of Aberconwy.

FORMER EPISCOPAL LANDS

12	Betws	*Sold* 1649 to John Jones and George Twistleton of Lleuar. Betws became part of the Talhenbont estate, and Gogwmwd went into divided ownership. Part of the Manor of Edern, land of the Bishops of Bangor.
18	Gogwmwd	
5	Treferthyr (part)	Land of the Bishop of Bangor which appears to have been sold in the sixteenth century and later became the estate of Bach-y-saint with Mynydd Ednyfed.

FORMER CLAS LANDS

7	Llecheiddior (part)	The Clas of Clynnog Fawr held two parts of Llecheiddior (Ganol and Uchaf) and Derwin in the 15th century, when it was sold.
20	Derwin	

THE PROTESTANT REFORMATION

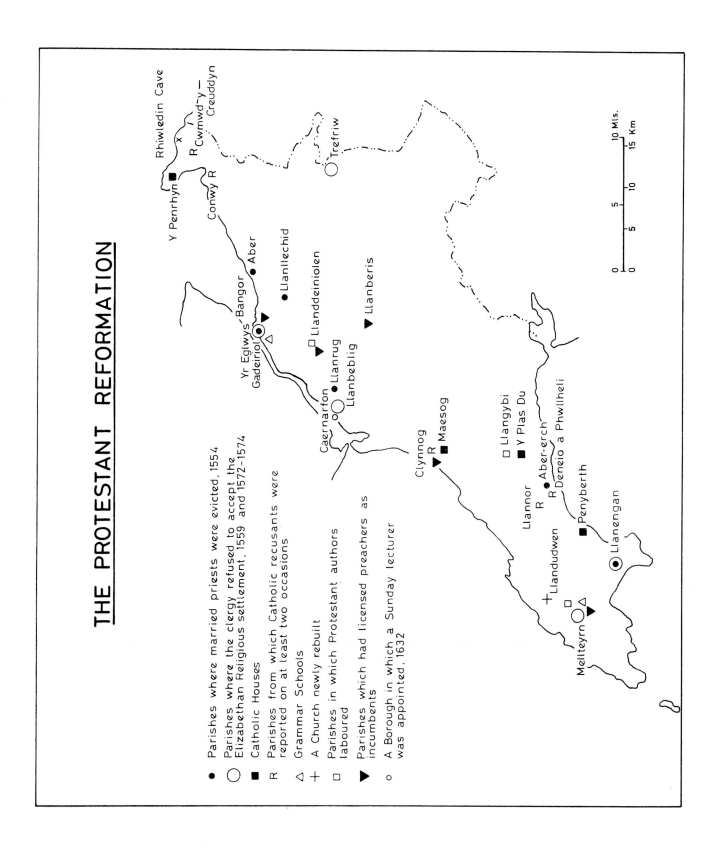

- **●** Parishes where married priests were evicted, 1554
- **○** Parishes where the clergy refused to accept the Elizabethan Religious settlement, 1559 and 1572–1574
- **■** Catholic Houses
- **R** Parishes from which Catholic recusants were reported on at least two occasions
- **△** Grammar Schools
- **+** A Church newly rebuilt
- **□** Parishes in which Protestant authors laboured
- **▶** Parishes which had licensed preachers as incumbents
- **○** A Borough in which a Sunday lecturer was appointed, 1632

The Protestant Reformation, c. 1547-1642

Like most of the ancient counties of Wales, Caernarvonshire accepted the numerous religious changes of the sixteenth century with equanimity. Nobody, as far as is known, protested when Henry VIII renounced the Papal supremacy and when he dissolved the religious houses of the county in 1536 and 1538. The same silence prevailed when the task of turning the kingdom Protestant was taken a broad step further by Henry's son, Edward VI, between 1547 and 1553. However, during the sharp Catholic reaction under Edward's sister, Mary, five married priests lost their livings, although two of these were reinstated when they agreed to put away their wives! Similarly, when Protestantism was finally re-established under Mary's sister, Elizabeth I, in 1558-9, a handful of committed Catholics refused to accept the new order: the bishop nominate of Bangor, Morus Clynnog, the Archdeacon of Anglesey, Gruffydd Robert (both of whom retired to the Continent and had distinguished careers there), and the parish priests or curates of Llanbeblig (although this case cannot be regarded as certain), Mellteyrn and Trefriw in the early fifteen seventies.

A remnant of Catholics persisted in the county throughout our period, although it should be stressed that their number was very small: no more than one out of every three hundred and fifty of the population, according to a report of 1603. They would not have existed at all had it not been for the efforts of the missionary priests from the Catholic seminaries on the Continent. Some twenty young men from Caernarvonshire joined those seminaries between 1570 and 1640, although only three certainly returned to proselytize in their native shire: Robert Owen of Plas Du (Llanarmon) — a brother of Hugh Owen 'the conspirator' — Robert Gwyn of Penyberth (Llanbedrog) and Blessed William Davies of Groesyneirias. Gwyn (c. 1546-93) was the first and most notable of these missionary priests, and he also wrote at least three (perhaps five) books in defence of the Old Faith. One of his books may have been *Y Drych Cristianogawl*, the first part of which was secretly printed in a cave in the Little Orme's Head (Llandudno), 1586-7. The patron of this enterprise was Robert Pugh of Penrhyn Creuddyn, and his house, like Plas Du and Penyberth, afforded from time to time a convenient refuge for the missionary priests. It was under the protection of such houses as these that recusancy flourished in the county; most of the recusants listed in the official records came either from Creuddyn and its vicinity or from Llŷn. It is the example of the Maesog family which accounts for the stubborn recusancy of Clynnog.

As has already been emphasised, the vast majority of the inhabitants of Caernarvonshire accepted the new order when Anglicanism became the state religion in 1558-9, although various customs highly repugnant to that order lingered for some time. The bishops of Bangor during this period were, on the whole, able and conscientious men, and four of them — Nicholas Robinson (1566-85), Richard Vaughan (1596-7), Henry Rowlands (1598-1616), and Edmund Griffith (1634-7) — were natives of Caernarvonshire. Gradually the clergy became better educated and non-residence less common. Grammar Schools were founded at Bangor (1558) and Botwnnog (1618), and it is certain that other humbler educational establishments were also active within the county; such are known to have existed at Caernarfon, Trewydir and Penllech, for example. The only parish church to be built anew was that of Llandudwen 1593; compare the *cywydd* in N.L.W. (MS. 16129, 86), but transepts or chapels were added to a number of others: Caerhun, Dolwyddelan, Gyffin, Llanaelhaearn, Llanbeblig, Llanbedrycennin, Llanberis, Llandygwnning, Llanfaglan, Llangelynnin and Llanrug. Two of the translators of the Bible into Welsh were born in Caernarvonshire — Bishop Richard Davies (Gyffin) and Bishop William Morgan (Penmachno) — but their contributions to this crucial task were made elsewhere. However, several clergymen in the county contributed to the body of Protestant literature in translation which appeared during this period: Huw Lewys of Llanddeiniolen (*Perl mewn adfyd*, 1595); John Pryse of Mellteyrn (part of Luis de Granada, *Of Prayer and Meditation* = N.L.W. Llanstephan MS. 187); Dafydd Rowlands of Llangybi (Christopher Sutton, *Disce Mori* = N.L.W. MS. 731). And priests who were also amateur poets, such as Morgan ap Huw Lewis of Llanwnda and Huw Roberts of Llandwrog (and Aberffro), produced a considerable amount of religious verse. Yet if religious literature was relatively plentiful, preaching appears to have been extremely difficult to come by; apart from the cathedral, only four parishes are known to have had licensed preachers as incumbents for some part of our period. It is certain that there was more preaching than the records suggest, but unlikely that it was ever readily available. In spite of their conformity, therefore, few of the inhabitants of Caernarvonshire could have had a firm grasp of the principles of Protestantism by the end of our period.

And yet, as far as can be seen, Puritanism never took root in the county before the beginning of the Civil War. It is known that the corporation of Caernarfon appointed a Sabbath lecturer, William Langford, in 1632 (N.L.W. MS. Llanfair-Brynodol 95), and corporation lecturers could be most effective purveyors of Puritan propaganda, but it is certain that Langford was no Puritan. However, there was in Caernarvonshire, particularly in Llŷn, a tradition of political inconformity which Parliament was able to exploit after coming to power, thus enabling the religious message of Puritanism to be heard at last in the land.

FROM DR. WILLIAM GRIFFITH AT CAERNARFON TO ARCHBISHOP JOHN WHITGIFT, 19 APRIL 1587

Most reuernde [sic] father in god & my very gratious good Lord my humble dewtye in most submisse manner to your grace remembred &c, your Grace shall vnderstande how that in the Counteye of Carnarvon in the Very poynte of the Sheire ther is a place called Gogarth that buttethe vpon Denbigh Sheire a twelue miles from Bangor yet I thinke it is in the Dioces of Saint Assapth [sic] & ther is a Cave bye the Sea side about 3 fadommes deepe the hante of the recusant[s] Seminaries & Jesuites in theise partes vnto me vnknowne till my last comminge to the Countrye yeat I knewe well ther weare notorius recusauntes in that hundreth of Crethen Alwayes & the xiiiith of this Apriell ther weare in the aforesaid Cave twelue or more Jesuites Seminaries & recusantes the which weare discovered by a neighbour therbye who sawe at the Caue mouth one or twoe of them with pistoles whom he spake with & fownd them strangers & such as cared not for officers wherfore he wente to the next Justice a great man in theise Countries Custos Rotulorum for the Sheire Signified to hime what he had seene the Justice which was nere was Master Thomas Mosten Raised people xl or ther aboutes came to the Caue mouth durst not or tooke on hime not to dare to enter the Cave the mouth therof was soe narrowe but lefte a Watch ther ouer nighte to the number of xxtie wherof some weare his owne men I wott not howe by the next morninge all weare suffered to escape & none of the wach is committyd the Justice dwelleth within

a myle Ther was fownde the next daye in the Cave Weapons Victualls & the Cave borded & their Alter Wainscotted as it was toulde me if my self had not bene trobled in the other end of the Sheire with Marine Causes I would have bene more privie to the qualitie of the persons & their doeinges & when I cann meete with anye of the watch I will learne and knowe more In th[e] meane tyme I thought it my bownden dewtie to aduertise your grace of what I kewe [sic] touchinge soe lewed a resorte and soe tollerated tha [sic] at your Graces good leysure you mighte redresse it In the meane tyme humblely Craueinge pardon for my bouldnes I commit your good Grace to god Who longe preserue you in all honour and happines. the xix th of Apriell Anno Domini 1587 Carnarvon in North-wales

Your Graces at commaundment

Wyllyam Gruffythe

And it shall please your Grace I haue mett with some Printtes of Leade & spaces as I take it to putt betwixt the prints the which the foresaide seminaries & recvsants vpon their flight did cast into the sea & I haue sent some of them vnto your grace by this messenger.

Journal of the Welsh Bibliographical Society, ix (1958 - 65), 1-23.

BIBLIOGRAPHY

In general, see Chapters III - V of A. H. Dodd, *A history of Caernarvonshire, 1284 - 1900* (Caernarfon, 1968); there is new light on Robert Gwyn in W. Gerallt Harries, ' Robert Gwyn: ei Deulu a'i Dylwyth ', *Bulletin of the Board of Celtic Studies*, XXV (1972-4), 425-38.

Caernarvonshire and the Civil War

When Charles I raised his standard at Nottingham on 22 August 1642, it was not to be expected that there would be sharp divisions on political grounds amongst the leading gentry of Caernarvonshire. It is true that Caernarvonshire men had not been 'blindly loyal' to Charles I and that they had occasionally voiced their discontent in the House of Commons. Charles Jones of Castellmarch, for instance, had helped to prepare the Petition of Right in 1628, whilst William Thomas of Aber, who represented Caernarfon boroughs, voted against Strafford and did not hesitate to attack some of the functions of bishops, deans and chapters. But a maritime county would be less resentful of the Ship Money impost than would an inland shire, and the levying of men for the Bishops' Wars aroused less antagonism here than in other areas. What opposition there was to the crown was represented by Thomas Glynne of Glynllifon, the brother of the more celebrated John, who later held high legal office, William Lloyd of Talhenbont (Llanystumdwy), mortally wounded by the royalists during the Second Civil War, and John Bodwrda of Bodwrda, who may have imbibed Puritan ideas at Cambridge. These three were arrested for a short time as 'disaffected' in 1642. During the first Civil War they were submerged by the prevailing loyalty of the county and were unable to surface until the tide of war turned decisively against the King.

Amongst royalists, the record of service was very varied. There were the unswervingly faithful, like Sir John Owen, who repeatedly faced death on behalf of his royal master, and realists like Archbishop John Williams, who returned to his native county at the outbreak of war to refortify Conwy and who came to terms with Parliament when further struggle seemed futile. Sir Richard Wynn of Gwydir, despite his long service in the royal household, was unable to give even lukewarm support to the crown in its hour of need. Feuds, too, injured the King's cause, and Archbishop Williams's unhappy relations with Sir John Owen reflected not only the antipathy between the civilian and the soldier, which was not uncommon, but also the distaste of a prince of the Church for the pretensions of a small Eifionydd squire.

The strategic significance of Caernarvonshire, which can only be understood within a wider background, was dominated by its links with Chester, Beaumaris and especially Ireland. Sir John Owen was unable to raise a regiment in time for the battle of Edgehill, as did Sir Thomas Salusbury in Denbighshire and Sir Edward Stradling in Glamorgan, but Caernarvonshire men were early sent to Chester, the first line of defence for North Wales. After Parliament had successfully enlisted the support of the Scots, Charles nursed the hope that he might land an army from Ireland which would tip the scales in his favour. Although Caernarvonshire had feared enemy invasion for generations, it was much more likely that an army would disembark in Beaumaris, which had a better harbour than anywhere else in North Wales (though it was by no means as splendid and spacious as Milford Haven). The long march over bad roads in a mountainous terrain would further deter an invader from landing in Caernarvonshire.

Archbishop John Williams corresponded regularly with Ormonde, the King's deputy in Ireland, and stores and passengers were landed in Beaumaris, despite increasing harassment by the parliamentary fleet after 1643. When Chester fell in February 1646, the end was in sight. The governor of the city was allowed to proceed to Caernarfon, and Parliament made a determined effort to capture Beaumaris, the only port where the dreaded troops from Ireland could land in strength in North Wales. Caernarfon and Beaumaris both fell in June, and Conwy, which had been by-passed, in August 1646. By March 1647 the last garrison in Wales had surrendered.

The fitful peace which followed was broken by the outbreak of the Second Civil War, and Y Dalar Hir, near the sea at Llandygái, was the scene of a vigorous, if confused, skirmish, where the minute army of Sir John Owen was scattered and its commander wounded and captured. (Sir John, after being sentenced to death in London, was finally reprieved and returned to honourable retirement at Clenennau.)

The castles of Caernarfon and Conwy were fortunately not 'slighted' or dismantled, and the ravages of peace proved more damaging than the assaults of war. Indeed, the repairs needed to make them reasonably habitable during the period of hostilities probably extended their days. A draft suggestion of 1644 that Caernarfon castle and town could be wholly encompassed by water came to nothing. Both castles dominated the surrounding countryside, but most of the soldiers locked within them were seldom gainfully employed. It appears that in Caernarfon the boredom of castle life was somewhat enlivened by the cumbersome frolics of a bear which, together with his ward, survived the seige. By 1644 Archbishop Williams considered that the counties of North Wales were 'utterlye eaten up with Castles and Governments' which never looked an enemy in the face, 'whilst these Governors drink their ale in these heaps of stones not permitinge any armye to quarter nere unto them (where they might doe service) for fear of hynderinge theyr contributions'.

Exactions of various kinds oppressed the country-side. Plundering raids, as at Gwydir, in order to feed the army naturally aroused hostility, and as early as April 1644 a number of the prominent gentry of Caernarvonshire listed their grievances in a petition to the King. Not the least of their complaints was that the sale of cattle, upon which they depended for their sustenance, was now no longer possible. But these economic wounds did not take long to heal when the war was over and a measure of prosperity returned by the middle years of the 1650s, which probably gave increasing stability to Cromwellian government throughout the country. Nor is it possible to attribute to the Civil

War and its aftermath any permanent change in social structure. Roundhead sympathisers were the backbone of the early committees appointed by parliament to govern the county, and the presence of military representatives was for a time increasingly apparent. But during the Protectorate the main traditional families came more and more to the fore, except for the brief unsettled months which followed Oliver's death. Puritanism, of which there were few portents in the county in 1642, grew during the next two decades and survived the Clarendon Code in small congregations of yeomen and of labourers which enjoyed the protection of the squires of Nanhoron, Madrun, Rhydolion and Lleuar.

The soldiers who really bore the scars of war emerge in the records of the county Quarter Sessions. As one might expect, there were more royalists than parliamentarians. In petitioning for pensions, only rarely do they speak of fighting within Caernarvonshire, and their references to the Thames Valley, Cheshire, Marston Moor, Scotland and Ireland are a reminder that the most savage conflicts took place beyond the borders of Wales. Some were sorely maimed. Rowland Hughes was so demented by his sufferings that he railed at the J.P.s who were to adjudicate upon his petition. Of these who fought and died in Sir John Owen's regiment we know nothing, and we can only surmise that, like many others, some of them were buried in the environs of Bristol and Newbury or in shallow graves in Naseby field where so many of our countrymen fought so bravely.

PETITION

To the Right Worshipfull the Justices of Peace now sitting at the Quarter Sessions in Carnarvon

The humble petition of Edward Ellis, late of Carnarvon, Tanner,

Humbly sheweth,

That your petitioner was severall times a souldier in his late Majestie's service King Charles the first in Ireland and England and at last he served as a souldier under the commaund of Captaine William Brynkir in England and since under his brother, Captaine John Brynkir, Sir John Owen beinge Colonell of the Regiment, and at Nasbie was cruelly wounded in 2 places of his body, viz., he was cutt onn the left shoulder and strucke with the stocke of a pistoll on his right arme soe that your petitioner is not able to worke by reason of the woundes he hath in his body.

Now your petitioner's humble request unto your Worships is that your Worships will be pleased to comiserate his condition and to allow him yearelie out of the maimed souldiers' mize what summe your Worships shall thinke fitt for his maintenance, he being but a poore man and not able to worke for his livinge.

And your petitioner shall ever pray etc.

Addition in same hand: Your pettitioner was imprested out of Carnarvon town to serve for his late Majestie.

Records of the Caernarvonshire Quarter Sessions, 1660.

Gwynedd Archives.

PETITION

To the Worshipfull the Justices of the Peace for this County of Carnarvon

The humble peticion of William Griffith of Llangïan in the County aforesaid

Humbly sheweth,

That your peticioner in the late warres did list himselfe in the parliament's service against the late king, wherein he continued for the space of 7 wholl yeares, dureing all which tyme your peticioner performed true and faithfull service to the said parliament, wherein your peticioner received diverse greivous wounds, to witt, your peticioner was shott thorough the necke with 3 shotts, 3 peics of his skull taken out being broken with a poleaxe, runned thorough the throat with a tucke, runned thorough the left side and thigh and left for dead in the feild and carried in a cart to Thame in Oxfordshire, besids many other wounds at other tymes, whereby your peticioner is disabled to doe or perform any manner of worke or labour for the maintenance of himselfe, wiefe and five small children, and being deprived of what debenters were due and owing to him.

Your peticioner therefore haveing noe other way to subsist humbly praieth that your worshipps would bee pleased to comiserate his sad condicion and to allowe him such a proporcion towards his owne, his wiefe and small children's maintenance out of the maimed souldiers' mize as to your worshipps shall seeme expedient.

And your peticioner (his wiefe and children) as in duty bound shall pray etc.

Court Order.
The peticioner is to be admitted as is desired by the Court. J. Hughes.

Records of the Caernarvonshire Quarter Sessions, 1657. Gwynedd Archives.

Sir John Owen, Clenennau (1600-1666)

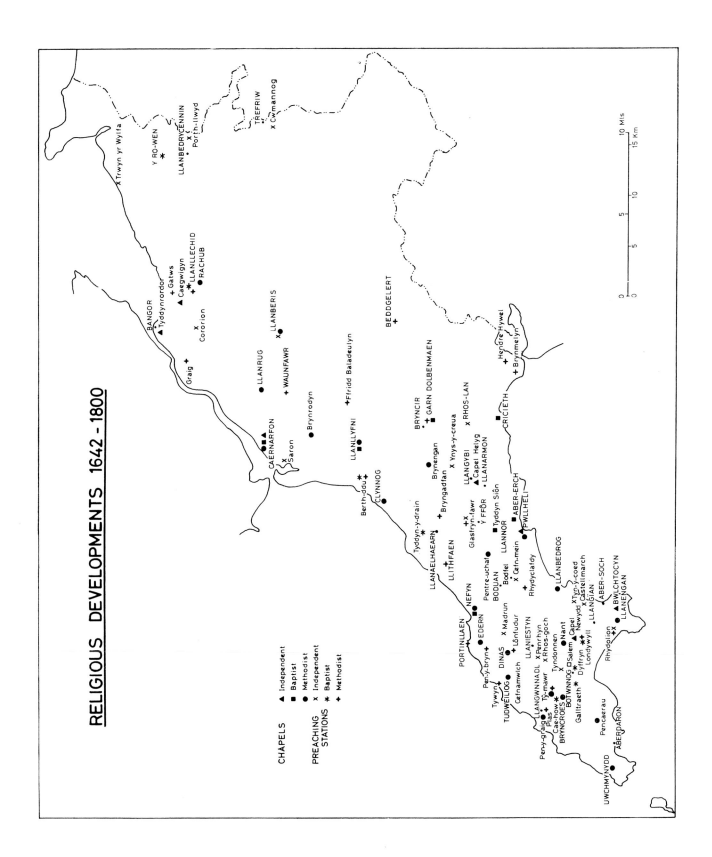

RELIGIOUS DEVELOPMENTS 1642 - 1800

CHAPELS
▲ Independent
■ Baptist
● Methodist

PREACHING
STATIONS
✕ Independent
✱ Baptist
✛ Methodist

✕ Trwyn yr Wylfa

Y RO-WEN
✱
LLANBEDRYCENNIN
✕ Porth-llwyd

TREFRIW
✕ Cwmmannog

▲ Tyddynrordor
BANGOR
✛ Gatws
✕ ▲ Caegwigyn
▲ LLANLLECHID
● RACHUB

✕ Cororion
● LLANBERIS
✕

● LLANRUG
✛ WAUNFAWR

Graig ✛

● Brynrodyn

▲▲ CAERNARFON
✕ Saron

+Ffridd Baladeulyn

BEDDGELERT
✛

Hendre Hywel
✛
✛ Brynmelyn

● LLANLLYFNI
■●

Berth-ddu ✱
✛ CLYNNOG

BRYNCIR
■ GARN DOLBENMAEN
● Brynengan
✕ Ynys-y-creua
✕ RHOS-LAN

Tyddyn-y-drain
✱
LLANAELHAEARN
✛ Bryngadfan
LLANGYBI ● LLANARMON
▲ Capel Helyg

● CRICIETH

Glasfryn-fawr
✕✕
LLITHFAEN   ✛ Ý FFÓR
● Tyddyn Siôn
✛ Cefn-mein
LLANNOR
ABER-ERCH
✛ PWLLHELI
●

PORTINLLAEN
■ NEFYN
Pentre-uchaf ●
● EDERN   BODUAN
✕ Madrun   Bodfel
✛ Rhydyclatdy

● LLANBEDROG
✕ Tyn-y-coed

Pen-y-bryn
✛
TUDWEILIOG ●
Cefnamwich ✕
Tywyn ●
DINAS
✛ Lônfudur
LLANIESTYN
✕ Penrhyn
✛ ✕ Rhos-goch
Plas ● LLANGWNNADL
Cae-how ✱ Tyndonnen
BRYNCROES ✱ Nant ▲ Capel
✕ Newydd
Galltraeth ✱ BOTWNNOG □ Salem
Dyffryn ✱✱ ▲ Castellmarch
Londywyll ✛ ● LLANGIAN
ABER-SOCH
▲ BWLCHTOCYN
▲ LLANENGAN

● Pencaerau
Rhydolion ✕
✕

UWCHMYNYDD
● ABERDARON

10 Mls
15 Km
10
5
5
0

116

Religious Developments 1642-1800

Llŷn during this period proved to be a remarkable source of religious energy. Puritanism found patrons amongst such gentry as Richard Edwards (Nanhoron), Jeffrey Parry (Rhydolion), Griffith Jones (Castellmarch), Hugh Lloyd (Trallwyn), Thomas Madryn (Madrun) and the ordained minister, John Williams (Ty'n-y-coed, Llangïan), in the years between 1642 and 1660. It was under such patronage that a gathered church of Congregationalists emerged in the area. In 1672 these Congregationalists took out licences under the Declaration of Indulgence to worship at Bodfel, at Ynys-y-creua, Llangybi, and the house of William Rowland at Pwllheli. Although they were scattered over a wide area, they were still considered to be members of one church, according to Henry Maurice in 1675. At Caernarfon, Ellis Rowlands, who was ejected from Clynnog in 1660, had secured a licence in 1672 and was still holding services and maintaining a school at his house in the town in 1689. In 1689, also, in virtue of the new freedom granted by the Act of Toleration, Nonconformist worship was 'recorded' — that is, licensed — at Ellis Owen's house at Llangybi, at William Thomas's house at Pwllheli, and at Lôndywyll, Llangïan. In the course of the eighteenth century, these worshippers were able to provide themselves with three meeting-houses, Capel Helyg in Llangybi, Capel Pen-lan in Pwllheli and Capel Newydd at Nanhoron (1769). The congregation at Caernarfon was a very small one, and by 1770 it had ceased to exist. But by then the Methodist Revival had brought new life to the older Dissenters and the consequences of this new inspiration were to be seen in new meeting-houses at Caernarfon (1780), Bwlchtocyn, Caegwigyn (Tal-y-bont, Bangor) and Tyddynrordor (Bangor), as well as in the cottage meetings initiated at such places as Rhos-goch and Penrhyn (Llaniestyn), Rhos-lan, Saron (Llanwnda), Trwyn-yr-wylfa (Dwygyfylchi), Porth-llwyd (Llanbedrycennin), Cwmannog (Trefriw) and Cororion in the Vale of Ogwen.

Howel Harris first visited Caernarvonshire in 1741 and preached at Glasfryn-fawr, Llangybi, at that time the home of William Pritchard (1702-73) and the place where Jenkin Morgan (died 1762) kept Rhydyclafdy; Tywyn, Tudweiliog; Rhydolion and school. He went on to preach at Tŷ'n Llanfihangel,

Portin-llaen. Methodism soon took root in Llŷn and the first society was organised at Plas, Llangwnnadl. The first Methodist chapel was built at Tŷ-mawr, Bryncroes, in 1752 and the second at Clynnog about 1764. One of the most active of the early societies was that at Brynengan, but there were others also at Lônfudr (Dinas), at Nant and Brynmelyn. These meetings were held in fairly substantial farmhouses and sometimes (as at Berth-ddu and Lôndywyll) preachers from the older denominations were welcomed.

The next step was to build a chapel. By 1800 there were chapels at Edern (1775), Uwchmynydd (1774), Pencaerau (1776), Y Nant (1782), Nefyn (1785), Pen-mownt, Pwllheli (1781), Brynengan (1777), Dinas (1794), and Beddgelert (1794).

In the Vale of Nantlle area, the societies sprang from that which was meeting by 1750 at Berth-ddu Bach in Clynnog. From there religious activity spread to Llanllyfni round about 1763 and a chapel was built there in 1771. By 1768 there was preaching at Ffridd, Baladeulyn, and from there sprang the churches at Brynrodyn (1777), Bwlan, Rhostryfan, Tal-y-sarn and Carmel.

The Society at Waunfawr began about 1747, but it was not until 1785 that the chapel was built there. This was to be the mother-church of Methodism in that area. Similarly at Llanberis, although there were society meetings there at an early date, Capel Coch was not built until 1777. The chapel at Llanrug was built in 1798. The Methodists found some difficulty in finding a foothold at Caernarfon, although David Jones of Llan-gan preached there in the early days of the Revival. The first Methodist chapel in the town was built in 1793. Arfon similarly proved a difficult area for the Methodists in the eighteenth century. But Rachub chapel in the Vale of Ogwen was built in 1793. One of the most effective means of propagating the principles of Nonconformity at the end of the century was the Sunday School. By 1811 there were 24 of them associated with societies in various parts of the counties, although several of them were 'non-denominational'.

The Baptists established their North Wales mission in 1776. In the August of that year, David Evans, Dolau (1740-90), visited the county and preached at Pen-lan (Pwllheli), Capel Newydd (Nanhoron)

and three unspecified places — Ro-wen in the Conwy Valley being possibly one of them. The first chapel was built at Aber-erch in 1784, but the cause there failed and the neighbourhood was later served by the Baptist church at Pwllheli. The congregation that built Salem Chapel in 1785 was the fruit of the preaching services held at Dyffryn. Other chapels were built at Nefyn (1785) and Garndolbenmaen (1786). Richard Michael dispensed the sacrament of Baptism by immersion for the first time in the county in 1783, and David Evans baptised 15 soon afterwards at Ro-wen and incorporated them into a church there. Chapels were built not long afterwards at Cricieth (1791), Llanllyfni (1787) and Tyddyn-Siôn. When the Baptist churches were convulsed by the controversy associated with the name of J. R. Jones, Ramoth (1765 - 1822), a church consisting of his supporters was formed at Cae-how, Bryncroes, and the congregation at Cricieth joined his movement in 1798. As was the case with the Congre-gationalists and the Methodists, the Baptists, too, held numerous cottage meetings at places like Lôndywyll, Ty'n-y-mur, Galltraeth, Tyddyn-y-drain and Berth-ddu. These groups depended much upon the services of ministers from South Wales. The most distinguished of these was Christmas Evans (1766 - 1838), who was ordained at Salem in 1789. He ministered to the Baptists of Llŷn until Christmas Day 1791 when he moved to Anglesey. There was preaching at the other end of the county as well. Since 1786 services had been held at Llwyncelyn, Llanberis and for a time at Cilfoden, Llanllechid. The church at Caernarfon was formed in 1799 and its members were drawn from a wide area extending from Llanllyfni to Cilfoden.

The eighteenth century in the county was the period when Nonconformists were laying the foundations. It was in the years immediately following the end of that century that the time of phenomenal increase occurred.

Capel Newydd Nanhoron

By permission of National Monuments Records

118

FROM THE DIARY OF HOWELL HARRIS

Glasfryn in Llangybi in Caernarvonshire North Wales 10 miles from the Great Trath Sunday (Feb. 1 1741) up 9 . . . I was in great strait where to go to hear today ye flesh fearg sore to go to hear this Minr he being a sad Persecutr & tandem seeing it answered no end I resolved to go to Llanfor Church (hearg he had preached well last Sunday) 3 miles . . . went towd Llanfor Church . . . tandm wn pt 12 I came near here I was set upon by slavish fear agn . . . before I go to Church — a large Congregation indeed . . . tandm he went to preach on 2 Cor. 11 13, 14, 15. I imediately found I was ye Text & dreadfull was ye way he treated me . . . he did so paint us out in such dreadfull Colours that no one wd hardly think it a sin to murther us I cd think of nothg but of ye Jesuits & cd not well expect to go from there witht being murtherd . . . came out abt 2 . . . ye People pointgg att me & . . . after buryg (there was a Buryal) I went aftr ye Minr to Church & askd if I shd speak to him He askd me whence I came I sd I was a Welsh man he askd me from whence I sd from So: Wales that I likd his Sermon very well agt such as it belong'd to but that I supposd he meant it agt him that taught a Welsh School in This he then sd if it was only a Welsh School there was no harm in that (Harris's offer to explain was refused, and he was followed by the mob & pelted Country but that he seemd to be misinform'd of him with stones) . . . wth much ado I got to my Horse in great Haste & most wonderfully they were as it were chaind & restraind till I mounted . . . went wth my Life in my hand to exhort to pt 7 expectg to be Mobbd to-night . . . discours'd on ye 2d Point in ye Chatechism & on ye 10 Commdmts practically . . . postea to Privt . . . to pt 1

Glasfryn (Caernarvonshire) Monday (Feb. 2, 1741) up before 9 Bro-Jenkn unwillg to stay here as starvg his own soul for want of any means & I advisd him to stay for others' sakes, it being much to have an opportunity of speakg to one here in this Uttr Darkness & he willg to go were it but to one House here . . . postea I felt a slavish fear on going near a great man's house . . . I heard of ye great men here favourable felt dr Love to God's people ye Dissrs here — our Church is all Darkness almt here came to Llanvih. (Bachellaeth) pt 3 & there as soon as I came among them I felt Love to them . . . discoursg on Our Father . . . postea in privt in ye house eatg &c. to pt 6 parted in great Love & Joy &c. went pt 6 towd Dollie in Llangian Psh. 4 miles . . . came there pt 8 & discours'd wth Power to pt 10 . . . (all These Parts is calld yr Llyn we are in Sight of Ireland)

. . . postea readg writg this &c. to pt 12 . . . here are calls for many Welsh Schools . . . to privt near 1 . . .

Dollie in Llangian Psh. Caernarvonshire — near the sea-side -20 miles in ye Country in sight of Ireland — Tuesday (Feb. 3 1741) up 9 ye People here are simple but in some most dreadfull fury & Rage The Minrs sadly oppose . . . ye Gent- are not so violent, more moderate here is 36 membrs of Diss — in ye country & one dr Soul a Minr Mr Thos an old man full of ye Love of God There is 3 Or 4 places he does preach in & some movg among ye dry bones in these Parts of late . . . postea went to eat ' shave &c. to 11 then exhorted to 1 wth an Incomon Power . . . on Jn 7.37 . . . aftr I had done I retird . . . readg Hanes y Byd &c. somethg abt ye Originl of our Annual Feasts, Wakes & Consecration of Churches &. . . . pt 1 towd Towyn (in this Nech of Land call'd ye Llyn encompassd as an Isthmus) 6 miles wth Bro-Jenkn . . . we came by Kefenamwlch ye seat of ye Latemembr for this County — a fine seat indeed but where is ye inhabitr for this County in a Moderate man I see where ye Tories are there is more persecution every where . . . I saw ye Isle of Man (alias Mon) in that county is not one Dissentr & no open Door for ant Thing thro' them ye Door is opend here and elsewhere — one of them is now guide . . . came there to ye Sea Side pt 3 & discours'd to 5 as soon as I came there (sure these are more noble than those att Llannor) they rec'd us kindly, some hundreds being met on short notice to-day . . . discours'd on Math. 1 28 . . . then publishd I wd discourse 2 hours hence agn in ye House . . . havg eat &c. to 7 discours'd agn to near 9 with more power than before to a Housefull . . . writg this &c. to pt 10 tis from hence home to us near 90 Computed miles & near 140 measurd ones I think little did I think to see this Place ever . . . writg a Lettr to &c. to near 2 . . .

Towyn Bedwelliog Psh in Llyn in Caernarvonshire Wednesday (Feb. 4 1741) Publick Fast slept before 3 up before 8 . . . went to discourse . . . on ye broken Heart on our originl sin Jn 3.3 & Depravity of Nature . . . I parted pt 9 (sure ye Ld sent me here -incitg them to Societies) near 10 towd Nefin Town . . . pt 11 it being too late to Nefin we went to Chappel Keidiog (fearg to go to discourse to Nefin as being not directly calld by any man — fearg least it was not a followg God then a man came to call me to the Trath to his House . . . in Church . . . postea I went to discurse wth ye Minr abt a Welsh School . . . & he wd not encourage it wthout a License from ye Chancellr that ye seemg Pretence was good but there may be somewt in ye bottom I reason'd wth him but in vain.

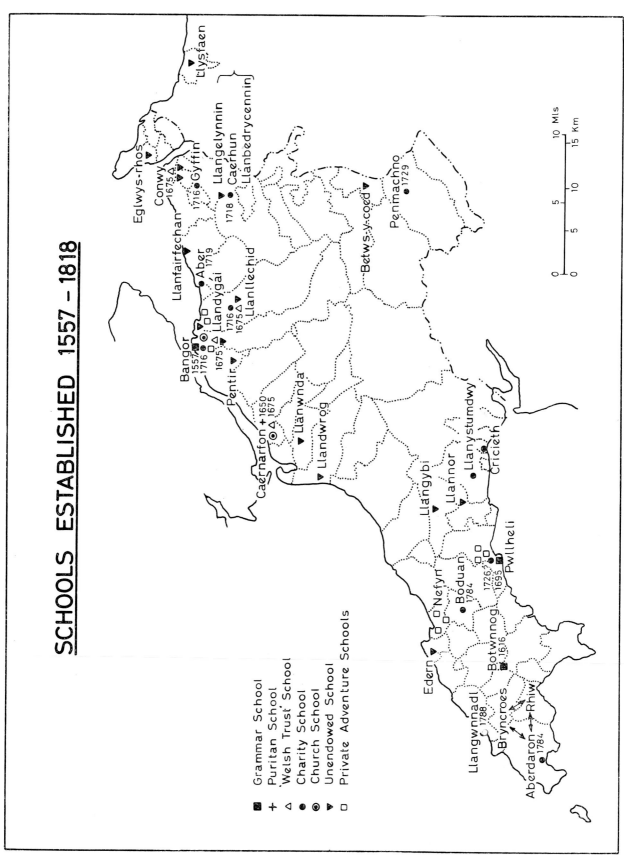

SCHOOLS ESTABLISHED 1557 – 1818

Tlysfaen

Eglwys-rhos

Conwy
1675

1716 ● Gyffin

Llangelynnin
1718 ▼ Caerhun

Llanbedrycennin

Penmachno
● 1729

Llanfairfechan

Aber
1719

Llandygái
1716 ●
1675 △ Llanllechid

Betws-y-coed

Bangor
1557
1716 ●
1675 ▼ Pentir

Caernarfon + 1650
⊙ △ 1675

Llanwnda

Llandwrog

Llangybi

Llannor

Llanystumdwy

Cricieth

Nefyn

Boduan
1784

1726
1695 Pwllheli

Edern

Llangwnnadl
c. 1788

Bryncroes

Botwnnog
16.16

Aberdaron
● 1784

Rhiw

10 Mls
15 Km
10
5
5
5
0
0

Grammar School
+ Puritan School
△ Welsh Trust School
● Charity School
⊙ Church School
▼ Unendowed School
□ Private Adventure Schools

120

Education before 1800

Sir John Wynn of Gwydir said that his great-grandfather had, about the end of the fifteenth century, attended a school at Caernarfon where he learnt to read and write English and Latin. Later, in the seventeenth century, a Clynnog schoolmaster was summoned on a charge of immorality. In the Bangor Diocesan Register there are references to Thomas Owen, licensed to keep school in Caernarfon in 1720, and to his successor, Jeremiah Griffiths, in 1742, and to William Tilsley, appointed as teacher in Llandygái in 1741. It seems then that the Established Church had not completely forgotten its task of educating.

The Renaissance and Protestant Reformation awakened a new interest in learning, reflected in the establishment of an Endowed Grammar School in Bangor in 1558 by Geoffrey Glyn, brother of the bishop. He left the old Dominican Priory, together with money, to endow a school 'for the better education and bringing up of poor men's children'. His example was followed by Henry Rowlands, Bishop of Bangor, who established a school in Botwnnog in 1618 with the proviso that the head-master had to be an M.A. of Cambridge and an Englishman. The third was founded in Pwllheli under the will (1695) of Hugh Jones, vicar of Llanystumdwy. Those schools were intended to provide a classical education, and that was so at The Friars until the eighteenth century, although subjects like arithmetic had been added to Greek and Latin. It appears, however, that the instruction provided for the majority of the pupils at Botwnnog and Pwllheli by 1800 was elementary. Glyn had provided for free places for ten poor children, but the school also attracted the sons of the small squires of Anglesey and Caernarvonshire and the merchants of Bangor. By 1721 there were 76 there. A somewhat similar number attended Pwllheli, and there were about 30 boys in Botwnnog in 1818, the earliest figure we have.

There was also a school in Caernarfon under an Act for the Better Propagation of the Gospel in Wales (1650), with Rowland Lloyd, the school-master, receiving £15 p.a. The school was short-lived, but it is interesting as the first venture of the state into education. This Puritan venture may have inspired later charitable movements. The first of these was Thomas Gouge's Welsh Trust. The object of the Trust was to found schools to teach poor children to read English and count so that they might be more useful members of society. The use of English as the teaching medium probably impaired their usefulness, but between 1672 - 1675 there were schools in Caernarfon, Conwy, Llanllechid and Llandygái, the last patronised by Sir Robert Williams of Penrhyn. Useful packets of religious books were also distributed in Caernarfon and Conwy and in the parishes of Llanllyfni, Llandwrog, Cricieth and Llanystumdwy.

Gouge died in 1681 and his Trust ended, but from 1699 the gap was filled by the Society for the Propagation of Christian Knowledge. Gouge, a Puritan himself, had received support from prominent Anglicans, but the new society was completely Anglican and intended to revive that Church. It strove to awaken the interest of local squires and clergymen, and country correspondents were chosen to keep in touch with the central committee in London. John Evans, Bishop of Bangor, showed considerable interest, but the chief patron in Anglesey and Caernarvonshire was John Jones, Dean of Bangor, 1699 - 1927. As early as 1699, he wrote, 'I have set up schools for the poorer sort at my own charge, but of late their poverty is so great that they cannot allow themselves to learn.' There is no certain evidence of S.P.C.K. schools in the county before 1716, but in that year three are referred to, established by John Jones in Bangor, Gyffin and Llanllechid. In his will, he left £100 to each, together with £100 for a school at Aber, with instructions that 10-15 poor children in each parish were to be taught to read Welsh and learn and understand the Catechism in Welsh and, if possible, a little writing and arithmetic. He found little support among the squirarchy apart from the Rev. Lancelot Bulkeley, who left £120 to clothe, teach and maintain six poor children from the parishes of Llangelynnin, Caerhun and Llanbedrycennin, and Roderick Lloyd, a London lawyer, who established a school in Penmachno where the children learnt to read and write English. Two Nonconformist schools, provided for under the will of Dr. Daniel Williams, were maintained at Caernarfon and Pwllheli.

THE SCHOOLS OF GRIFFITH JONES 1741-1777

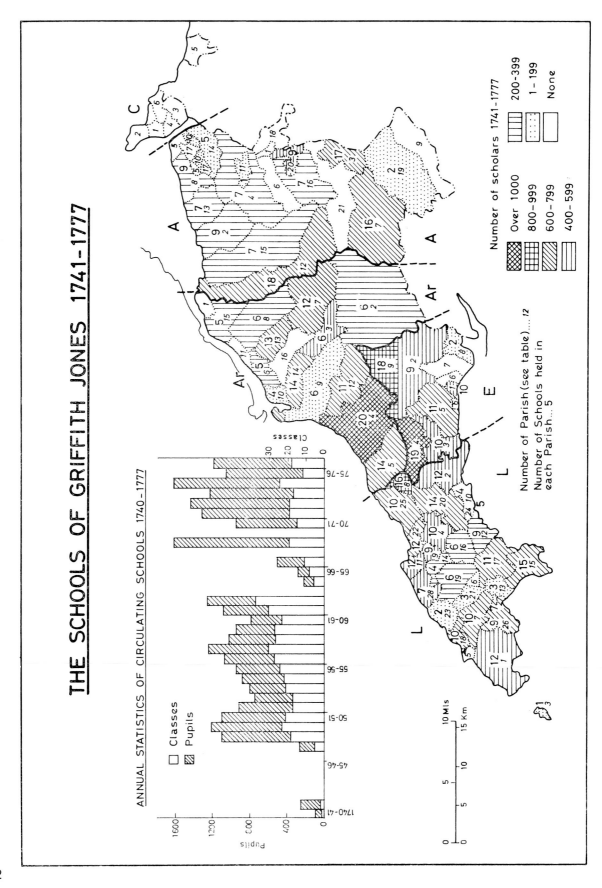

ANNUAL STATISTICS OF CIRCULATING SCHOOLS 1740-1777

Number of scholars 1741-1777

Over 1000
800-999
600-799
400-599
200-399
1-199
None

Number of Parish (see table)....12
Number of Schools held in
each Parish...5

The enthusiasm of the S.P.C.K. for establishing schools had cooled by 1720, but the gap was soon filled by the most successful educational experiment of the eighteenth century, the circulating schools of Griffith Jones of Llanddowror. His purpose was to deepen the spiritual and moral wellbeing of the peasantry of Wales by teaching them to read the Bible. He sent his teachers for periods of three months, usually on the invitation of the parish clergyman, to teach children during the day and older people sometimes in the evenings. He believed three months to be sufficient to teach the pupils to read the Welsh Bible.

According to *Welch Piety,* the annual report of the movement, the first school was established in the parish of Llangybi in 1740-1 by Jenkin Morgan, a South Walian and friend of Howell Harris. The following year there were flourishing schools in Tudweiliog and Llanengan. Howell Harris himself visited the area as representative of Griffith Jones, and the schools were suspected of being under Methodist influence and suffered a setback. There is no further reference to the county until 1747-8, when there were three schools in Llŷn and two in Arfon — in Llanberis and Llanrug. From then on, they made rapid progress. Between 1748-62, the number of schools varied between 17-37 yearly, and the number of pupils between 700 - 1,250. Apart from Creuddyn, where there is no reference to any school, and the towns of Conwy, Bangor and Caernarfon, where there may have been some provision already or where the church authorities were hostile, the circulating schools covered the county.

Griffith Jones died in 1761, and progress slowed down until 1766 when Robert Jones, Rhos-lan, succeeded in persuading Madame Bevan to take up the reins. From then on, the schools prospered exceedingly until her death in 1777, reaching a maximum of pupils (1,621) in 1774-5.

There is no question that this was the most successful educational effort up to that time among the Welsh peasantry. The curriculum may have been narrow, but a desire for learning was created and that did not die in 1777. Robert Jones continued his efforts, and generous men like Robert Evans stepped into the breach. He set aside £80 in 1784 to support a teacher circulating at yearly intervals between the parishes of Rhiw, Aberdaron and Bryncroes. In the same year, William Lloyd of Glanrafon left £100 to maintain a teacher in the parish of Boduan to teach children their Catechism and to read Welsh. In 1788, Robert Griffith of Bryn-yr-orsedd left £40 to teach the poor children of Llangwnnadl, and in 1795 Robert Ellis, rector of Cricieth, set aside £200 to be used after the death of his wife to endow a school in the town. She lived until 1817!

Although Griffith Jones himself denied it, there is a close connection between his schools and the development of Methodism, and it may be suggested that Welsh Methodism became most firmly rooted in those areas where the schools had flourished. This may have been their greatest influence.

THE SCHOOLS OF GRIFFITH JONES, 1741 - 1777

	Parish				Population 1749	Greatest No. of Pupils in one year	No. of School Sessions	Total of Pupils
A1	The Abbey	...	...	...				
A2	Aber	...	...	...		132	4	347
A3	Betws-y-coed	...	...	...	200	117	17	751
A4	Caerhun	...	...	...	200	145	7	336
A5	Conwy	...	...	...	700			
A6	Dolgarrog	...	...	...				
A7	Dolwyddelan	...	...	...	450	114	16	668
A8	Dwygyfylchi	...	...	...	180	82	9	349
A9	Eidda	...	...	...				
A10	Gyffin	...	...	...	450	46	5	185
A11	Llanbedrycennin	...	...	...	360	30	1	30
A12	Llandygái	...	...	...	795	150	18	765
A13	Llanfairfechan	...	...	...	480	100	7	275

	Parish				Population 1749	Greatest No. of Pupils in one year	No. of School Sessions	Total of Pupils
A14	Llangelynnin	...	...	...	175	73	5	181
A15	Llanllechid	...	...	...	530	156	7	326
A16	Llanrhychwyn	...	...	...		78	7	302
A17	Llechwedd ...	...	...	...				
A18	Maenan ...	...	...	...				
A19	Penmachno	...	...	...	620	41	2	82
A20	Trefriw ...	...	...	...	450	181	9	561
A21	Trewydir ...	...	...	...				
C1	Eglwys-yn-Rhos	...	...	...				
C2	Llandudno ...	...	...	...				
C3	Llangystennin	...	...	...				
C4	Llan-rhos ...	...	...	...				
C5	Llysfaen ...	...	...	...				
C6	Penrhyn ...	...	...	...				
Ar1	Bangor ...	...	...	...				
Ar2	Beddgelert	...	...	...	225	60	6	265
Ar3	Betws Garmon	...	...	...	250	159	6	428
Ar4	Clynnog ...	...	...	...	500	273	20	1,070
Ar5	Llanaelhaearn	...	...	...	265	155	14	646
Ar6	Llanbeblig ...	...	...	...		139	5	215
Ar7	Llanberis ...	...	...	...	120	97	12	627
Ar8	Llanddeiniolen	...	...	...	625	66	6	242
Ar9	Llandwrog ...	...	...	...	1,500	73	6	197
Ar10	Llanfaglan ...	...	...	...	150	40	4	146
Ar11	Llanfair-is-Gaer	...	...	...				
Ar12	Llanllyfni ...	...	...	...	450	215	11	699
Ar13	Llanrug ...	...	...	...	350	107	13	611
Ar14	Llanwnda ...	...	...	...	540	193	14	753
Ar15	Pentir ...	...	...	...		119	5	228
Ar16	Waunfawr ...	...	...	...				
E1	Cricieth ...	...	...	...	600	315	10	543
E2a	Dolbenmaen	...	...	...	690	125	9	472
E3	Llanarmon ...	...	...	...	550	72	10	427
E4	Llangybi ...	...	...	...		294	19	1,263
E5	Llanystumdwy	...	...	...	600	184	11	616
E6	Penllyn ...	...	...	...				
E7	Treflys ...	...	...	...				
E8	Ynyscynhaearn ...	...	...	...		33	2	60
E9	Llanfihangel-y-Pennant	...	...	...	250	274	18	954
L1	Aberdaron ...	...	...	...	1,020	210	12	597
L2	Aber-erch ...	...	...	...	700	169	12	594
L3	Enlli ...	...	...	...		20	1	20
L4	Boduan ...	...	...	...	200	351	10	569
L5	Bodferin ...	...	...	...				
L6	Botwnnog ...	...	...	...	120			
L7	Bryncroes ...	...	...	...	700	243	10	644
L8	Carnguwch ...	...	...	...		224	16	967
L9	Ceidio ...	...	...	...		283	9	505
L10	Deneio ...	...	...	...		43	4	122
L11	Edern ...	...	...	...	750	80	12	525
L12	Llanbedrog ...	...	...	...	295	120	9	376
L13	Llandygwnning	...	...	...		44	3	120
L14	Llandudwen	...	...	...		118	4	272

	Parish				Population 1749	Greatest No. of Pupils in one year	No. of School Sessions	Total of Pupils
L15	Llanengan	...	...	...	435	106	15	760
L16	Llanfihangel Bachellaeth	...	...	190	49	6	217
L17	Llangïan	...	...	...	755	141	11	613
L18	Llangwnnadl	...	...	...	300	203	10	702
L19	Llaniestyn	...	...	...		54	6	294
L20	Llannor	...	...	...		155	14	673
L21	Mellteyrn	...	...	...	140	40	3	108
L22	Nefyn	...	...	...		213	12	756
L23	Penllech	...	...	...		65	2	99
L24	Penrhos	...	...	...		40	5	146
L25	Pistyll	...	...	...		417	10	714
L26	Rhiw	...	...	...	150	56	9	393
L27	Llanfaelrhys	...	...	...	135	50	7	274
L28	Tudweiliog	...	...	...	400	176	7	434

Bettws y Coed in Carnarvonshire, May 13, 1757.

This is to certify, that *R— M—*, Master of the *Welch* Charity School in this Parish, hath behaved himself in a careful and diligent Manner, the Children under his Care daily improving in their Reading and Catechism. Though the Poverty of their Parents, and the Scarcity of Corn in these Parts, have lessened his daily Numbers, by their being obliged to beg from Door to Door most part of the Time. For this Reason, the Parishioners and myself humbly beg you would be so good as to leave him with us another Quarter, as he is so beneficial to the poor People. And may the Blessing of Almighty God accompany this Work of Charity, which He has put into the Hearts of his Servants, in behalf of these poor Children! That being trained up in the Way they should go, when they are old they may not depart from it. May He of his Mercy, keep them save amidst the Danger of this bad World through which they are to pass, and preserve them unto his heavenly Kingdom, is the sincere Prayer of, &c.

William Evans, Curate Ibidem.

(From Welch Piety, 1755-7.)

BIBLIOGRAPHY

A. I. Pryce, *The Diocese of Bangor during Three Centuries* (1929).

M. Clement, *The S.P.C.K. and Wales* (1954).

T. Richards, *The Puritan Movement in Wales* (1920).

M. Clement, *Correspondence and Minutes of the S.P.C.K. relating to Wales* (1952).

F. A. Cavanagh, *The Life and Work of Griffith Jones* (1938).

Selections from Welch Piety (ed. W. M. Williams, 1938).

Ysgrifau ar Addysg (gol. Williams, Cyf. IV, 1966).

The Dominican (ed. Jones and Haworth, Fourth Centenary Number, 1957).

Report of the Charities of the County of Caernarvon (H.M.S.O.).

Cylchgrawn Cymdeithas Hanes y Methodistiaid Calfinaidd Cyf. XXII, Rhifyn 1, Mawrth 1937.

Bulletin of the Board of Celtic Studies, Vol. IV, 1939; Vol. V, pt. Iv, 1931.

Transactions of the Honourable Society of Cymmrodorion (Hanes Ysgol Botwnnog, gan Gruffydd Parry, 1957).

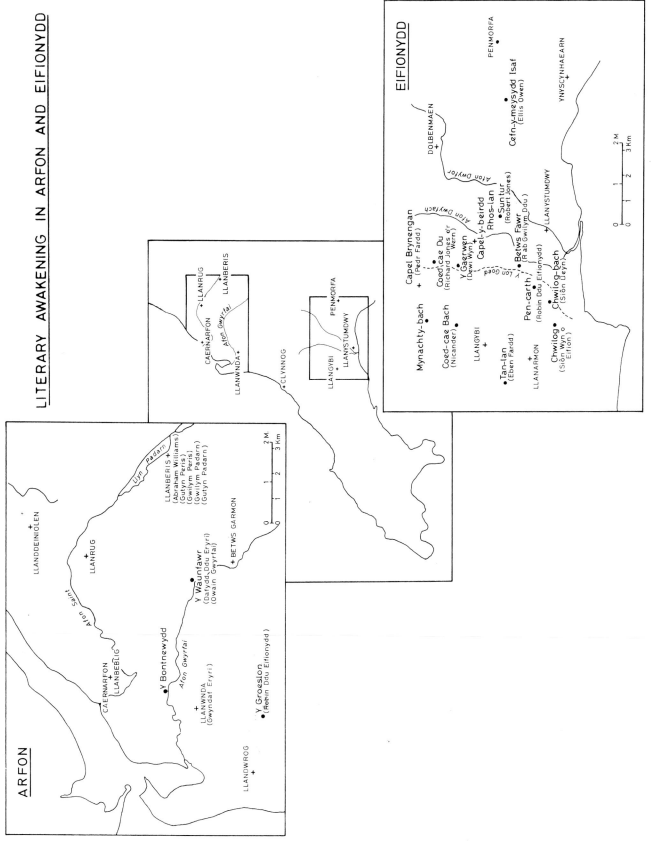

LITERARY AWAKENING IN ARFON AND EIFIONYDD

EIFIONYDD

PENMORFA

DOLBENMAEN +

Capel Brynengan +
(Pedr Fardd)

Coed-cae Du
(Richard Jones o'r Wern)

Y Gaerwen
(Dewi Wyn)

Capel-y-beirdd
Rhos-lan
Suntur
(Robert Jones)

Betws Fawr
(R ab Gwilym Ddu)

Mynachty-bach

Coed-cae Bach
(Nicander)

LLANGYBI
+

Tan-lan
(Eben Fardd)

LLANARMON
+

Pen-carth
(Robin Ddu Eifionydd)

Chwilog-bach
(Siôn Lleyn)

Chwilog
(Siôn Wyn o Eifion)

Cefn-y-meysydd Isaf
(Ellis Owen)

YNYSCYNHAEARN

Afon Dwyfor

Afon Dwyfach

Lôn Goed

LLANYSTUMDWY +

0   1   2   3 Km
0   1   2 M

CAERNARFON +
LLANBEBLIG

Afon Gwyrfai

LLANRUG +

LLANBERIS

LLANWNDA +

CLYNNOG +

PENMORFA +

LLANGYBI +

LLANYSTUMDWY +

ARFON

LLANDDEINIOLEN +

LLANRUG +

LLANBERIS +
(Abraham Williams)
(Gutyn Peris)
(Gwilym Peris)
(Gutyn Padarn)

Llyn Padarn

Afon Saint

CAERNARFON +
LLANBEBLIG

Y Bontnewydd •

LLANWNDA +
(Gwyndaf Eryri)

Afon Gwyrfai

Y Waunfawr •
(Dafydd Ddu Eryri)
(Owain Gwyrfai)

+ BETWS GARMON

Y Groeslon •
(Robin Ddu Eifionydd)

LLANDWROG +

0   1   2   3 Km
0   1   2 M

The Literary Awakening in Arfon and Eifionydd

Culturally, the eighteenth century in Caernarvonshire was an undistinguished period. But then, at the turn of the century — as a result of the spread of the evangelical and educational awakening which we call the Methodist Revival, and following the revival of the eisteddfod under the patronage of the London Gwyneddigion Society from 1789 onwards — there occurred in Arfon and in Eifionydd a notable literary awakening.

The leading figure in Arfon was David Thomas — *Dafydd Ddu Eryri* (1759 - 1822). He was born at Pen-y-bont, Waunfawr, the son of one of the early leaders of Methodism in that district. An elder brother, John, became a local Methodist preacher, but David Thomas was more attracted to literature. In the company of a slightly older companion, Abraham Williams — *Bardd Du Eryri* (1755 - 1828), a quarryman who emigrated to America in 1793, he began to interest himself in verse-making. He got to know the Rev. David Ellis, a collector and transcriber of manuscripts who had been curate of Llanberis from 1764 to 1767; he became acquainted with the Rev. Rice Jones, curate of Llanbeblig, the son of the poet Rhys Jones of Blaenau near Dolgellau, and himself a Welsh scholar and poet.

Such people provided for the young David Thomas a link with the Welsh poetic tradition. He mastered the rules of traditional Welsh metrics, he read the works of poets of old, and he made the acquaintance of a wider circle of contemporary men of letters. One of these was Robert Hughes — *Robin Ddu yr Ail* (1744-85), a native of Anglesey and a poet who, before moving to Caernarfon in 1783, had spent years in London where he had been a leading member of both the Cymmrodorion and Gwyneddigion societies. From him David Thomas heard of the monthly meetings of the London societies, of the literary ideas of Goronwy Owen, and of the projects discussed amongst London Welshmen to foster Welsh literature.

Throughout the eighteenth century a few Welsh poets had been meeting periodically, to compose extempore stanzas and complain about the passing of the old order, in tavern get-togethers which they called 'eisteddfodau'. In 1789 the London Gwyneddigion Society extended outside patronage to these meetings; it offered a prize for the best long poem on a topic announced publicly in advance. David Thomas submitted an ode to the first of the reformed eisteddfodau, at Bala in 1789, but the prize went to a young university educated clergyman, the Rev. Walter Davies. The following year at St. Asaph, and again at Llanrwst in 1791, the prize went to Thomas for his odes on 'Liberty' and on 'Truth'. His double success gave him status. The London Welshmen turned to him for assistance with their scholarly projects. Nearer home, younger poets turned to him for advice and instruction.

He responded with enthusiasm. He sold copies of the newly published edition of the poems of Dafydd ap Gwilym on behalf of the Gwyneddigion; in 1795 he organised an eisteddfod for the same society at Penmorfa. His main contribution, however, was in instructing younger poets. He took it upon himself to hand on to a new generation the knowledge which he had acquired of Welsh metrics and of the literary values of the eighteenth century neo-classicists. He wrote a treatise on 'The Rules of Welsh Prosody' which he hoped to have published; more importantly, he established literary circles in the Gwyrfai district. The best known of these was 'Cymdeithas yr Eryron' (the Society of Eagles), which for a time held its meetings at the Bull's Head at Bontnewydd. In this society, the members were required to compose exercise poems on set topics, not for the glory of winning a prize, but so that David Thomas could criticise them and point out their metrical failings. The society was in a real sense a bardic school and David Thomas was its master. In this way there gathered around Thomas a brotherhood of disciples, such as Robert Morris — *Robin Ddu Eifionydd* (c. 1767 - 1816), the miller of Melin Forgan near Groeslon and grandfather of Ellis Roberts — *Elis Wyn o Wyrfai* (1827 - 95); Griffith Williams — *Gutyn Peris* (1769 - 1838), and William Williams — *Gwilym Peris* (1769 - 1847), two quarrymen from Llanberis; Richard Jones — *Gwyndaf*

Eryri (1785 - 1848), a stone mason from Llanwnda; William Edwards — *Gwilym Padarn* (1786 - 1857), another Llanberis quarryman and the father of Griffith Edwards — *Gutyn Padarn* (1812 - 93); Owen Williams — *Owain Gwyrfai* (1790 - 1874), a cooper and manuscript collector from Waunfawr; and William Ellis Jones — *Cawrdaf* (1795 - 1848), who was a member of the circle while he served his apprenticeship as a printer at Caernarfon. Besides these local disciples, David Thomas instructed others, such as John Roberts — *Siôn Lleyn* (1749 - 1817) from Llanystumdwy, and Evan Pritchard — *Ieuan Lleyn* (1769 - 1832), from Bryncroes, by correspondence. It is to this circle of pupils that reference is made in a couplet carved on David Thomas's tombstone at Llanrug, where it is said of him:

> Poets looked upon him as their uncle, he was their teacher,
> He was a tower of strength encouraging them.

These poets wrote carols in the eighteenth century manner; they composed occasional pieces — *in memoriam* stanzas by them are to be seen in most graveyards in Gwyrfai; but it was on lengthy ambitious odes that they concentrated their talents. Very little of their work wins praise from modern critics. In assessing their contribution, however, we must remember that it was these local poets who in the first quarter of the last century maintained the *eisteddfod* and created that distinctive literate village culture which we today look back upon with admiration as we become increasingly aware of its passing.

In Eifionydd in the same period there was a similar cultural awakening. There something of the old medieval bardic tradition had persisted — in Owen Gruffydd (*c.* 1643 - 1730) of Llanystumdwy, a weaver who addressed praise poems to members of the gentry in the traditional manner, and in his disciple, William Elias (1708 - 87), a shoemaker from Clynnog. By the last quarter of the eighteenth century, however, this tradition of verse-making had run dry. In 1789 David Ellis became vicar of Cricieth; the following year David Thomas came to Llanystumdwy as a schoolmaster. An eisteddfod was held at Penmorfa. In a short while a whole group of poets are to be found in Eifionydd; Robert Williams — *Robert ab Gwilym Ddu* (1766 - 1850), the farmer of Betws Fawr, Llanystumdwy; Richard Jones (1772 - 1833) of the same parish and later of Wern, Llanfrothen; Peter Jones — *Pedr Fardd* (1775 - 1845), who as a young man emigrated to Liverpool; David Owen — *Dewi Wyn* (1784 - 1841), the farmer of Gaerwen, near Betws Fawr; John Thomas — *Siôn Wyn o Eifion* (1786 - 1859) from Llanarmon, who, we are told, was bed-ridden for a quarter of a century; Ellis Owen (1789 - 1868), farmer and antiquary, of Cefn-y-meysydd Isaf, Ynyscynhaearn; and two younger men from Llangybi, Ebenezer Thomas — *Eben Fardd* (1802 - 63) and Morris Williams — *Nicander* (1809 - 74). Robert Williams of Betws Fawr was their leader. He was the most senior member and the most thoroughly conversant in the rules of Welsh prosody, especially as David Thomas had left Llanystumdwy after a year and returned to Gwyrfai. The Eifionydd circle retained their links with their brothers in Arfon. They corresponded. They visited one another; we hear of poets from Arfon calling at Betws Fawr ' according to the custom of the Christmas holidays '. The tradition of meeting in cultural circles took root in Eifionydd; half a century later, in 1846, Ellis Owen established a well-known literary society at Cefn-y-meysydd.

The Eifionydd poets, like their comrades in Arfon, wrote for eisteddfodic competitions. The excitement of competing enlivened their society. When in 1819 Robert Williams failed to gain the prize for a stanza at the Carmarthen Eisteddfod and David Owen's ode to ' Charity ' was unsuccessful at an eisteddfod at Denbigh, the Eifionydd circle complained of the wrong they had suffered. Five years later they rejoiced when one of their youngest members, Ebenezer Thomas, won the chair at the Welshpool Eisteddfod for his ode on ' The Destruction of Jerusalem ' — the best eisteddfodic ode of its period.

Besides competition poems, the Eifionydd poets wrote occasional pieces of celebration and mourning. They also composed religious poems — carols, versifications of passages of the scriptures, and hymns. Hymns by Robert Williams, Robert Jones of Wern, Peter Jones, Ebenezer Thomas and the Rev. Morris Williams are to be found in the hymn-books used today in Welsh chapels and churches. These hymns, and the intense religious *englynion* of Robert Williams, are the masterpieces of the evangelical and literary revival which affected Eifionydd so deeply at the beginning of the last century. It is fitting that the building which remains as a link with this cultural activity is ' Capel y Beirdd ' (The Poets' Chapel), a small Baptist chapel that Robert Williams and David Owen had a part in erecting.

DAFYDD DDU ERYRI

Y BARDD YN EI HENAINT

Minnau'n hen mewn anhunedd
Yma'n byw ym min y bedd;
Gwyro mae fy moel gorun
At lawr gallt dan y gwallt gwyn;
Daw eraill feirdd awdurol
Yn fuan, fuan ar f'ôl.

ROBERT AB GWILYM DDU

ANNERCH YR AWEN
(ar lan Afon Dwyfach)

Mor fwyn, fy llawforwyn fach,
Yw dyfod at fin Dwyfach
I'th gwrdd unwaith, gerdd enwawg,—
Myfyrio a rhodio rhawg,
Mynnu eistedd, mwyn osteg,
Ar fin dŵr tir Eifion deg . . .

Cefais awr o ddistawrwydd
Uwch ei phen i'r awen rwydd,
Awr fach ymhlith oriau f'oes,
Fwynaf o oriau f'einioes.
Eilio, mân byncio mwyn bili
Dan lawen wybren Ebrill;
Egor llais, wrth gwr y llyn,
Digymell ar deg emyn,
Tan gysgodwydd, irwydd iach,
Mwyn dyfiant, ym min Dwyfach,
Ac ednaint gwâr, lafar lu,
Uwchben oedd yn chwibanu . .
Difyr cael dan dewfrig gwŷdd
Rhoi anadl i'r awenydd.

CRIST GERBRON PEILAT

Dros fai nas haeddai, mae'n syn — ei weled
Yn nwylaw Rhufeinddyn;
A'i brofi gan wael bryfyn,
A barnu Duw gerbron dyn.

ELLIS OWEN

BEDD-ARGRAFF GWRAIG GELWYDDOG

Dwedodd a fedrodd tra fu — o gelwydd.
Gwyliwch ei dadebru,
Neu hi ddywed, 'rwy'n credu,
I bawb mai'n y nef y bu.

PEDR FARDD

HIRAETH AM EIFIONYDD

Fy hen serchog fryniog fro,
Ni chaf ond prin ei chofio.
Aeth y Garn ymaith o gof,
Brynengan bron i angof,
Ac nid oes am oes i mi
Un gobaith am Langybi.
Fy enaid am Eifionydd
Mewn hiraeth ysywaeth sydd.

DEWI WYN

CYNI'R GWEITHIWR
(o awdl ' Elusengarwch ')

Aml y mae yn teimlo min
Yr awel ar ei ewin,
A llwm yw ei gotwm, gwêl,
Durfing i'w waed yw oerfel.
Noswylio yn iselaidd
A'i fynwes yn bres oer, braidd.
Ba helynt cael ei blant cu
Oll agos â llewygu.
Dwyn ei geiniog dan gwynaw,
Rhoi angen un rhwng y naw.

EBEN FARDD

DINISTR JERUSALEM

Ys anwar filwyr sy yn rhyfela,
Enillant, taniant Gastell Antonia.
Y gampus Deml a gwympa — cyn pen hir,
Ac O! malurir gem o liw eira.

Wele drwy wyll belydr allan, — fflamol,
A si annaturiol ail sŵn taran.
Mirain deml Moreia'n dân. — Try'n ulw.
Trwst hon, clyw acw'r trawstiau'n clecian.

Tewynion treiddiawl tân a ânt trwyddi;
Chwyda o'i mynwes ei choed a'i meini.
Uthr uchel oedd, eithr chwâl hi, — try'n llwch,
A drych o dristwch yw edrych drosti . . .

Llithrig yw'r palmant llathrwyn,
Môr gwaed ar y marmor gwyn.

BIBLIOGRAPHY

Thomas Parry, 'Sir Gaernarfon a llenyddiaeth Gymraeg', *Caern. Hist. Trans.,* 1941, 43-71, and 'Emynwyr Eifionydd', *Bwletin Cymd. Emynau Cymru,* 1967.
E. G. Millward, 'Eifionydd y beirdd', *Caern. Hist. Trans.,* 1964, 42-65, and 'Detholion o ddyddiadur Eben Fardd', 1968 (gol.), E. D. Rowlands, *Prif-feirdd Eifionydd,* 1914. William Rowland, *Gwŷr Eifionydd,* 1953. T. Lloyd Jones (gol.), *Coffa beirdd y Lôn Goed,* 1951. Cynan, 'Tad Beirdd Eryri', *Trans. Hon. Soc. Cymm., 1969.* Stephen J. Williams (gol.), *Robert ap Gwilym Ddu,* 1948, Llyfrau Deunaw. Derwyn Jones, 'Robert ap Gwilym Ddu', etc., *Caern. Hist. Trans.,* 1963.

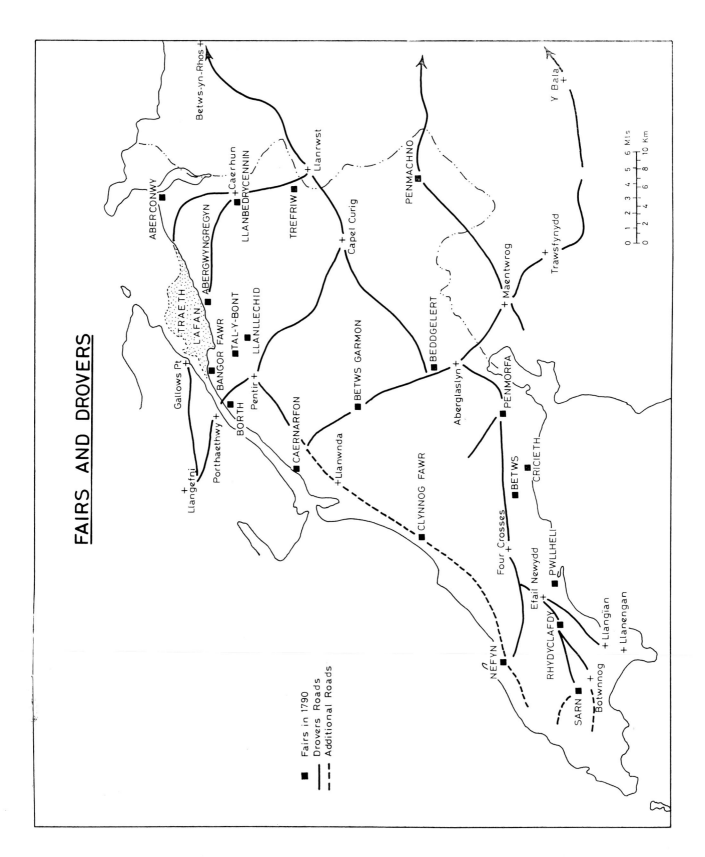

FAIRS AND DROVERS

ABERCONWY
Betws-yn-Rhos +
+ Caerhun
ABERGWYNGREGYN
LLANBEDRYCENNIN
TREFRIW +
Llanrwst +
PENMACHNO
Y Bala +
Capel Curig +
Maentwrog +
Trawsfynydd +
TRAE TH
L'AFAN
TAL-Y-BONT
LLANLLECHID
BANGOR FAWR
Pentir +
BETWS GARMON
BEDDGELERT
Gallows Pt +
BORTH
Porthaethwy +
CAERNARFON
+ Llanwnda
Aberglaslyn +
PENMORFA +
Llangefni +
CLYNNOG FAWR
CRICIETH
BETWS
Four Crosses +
Efail Newydd +
PWLLHELI
RHYDYCLAFDY
+ Llangian
+ Llanengan
NEFYN
SARN
+ Botwnnog

Fairs in 1790
Drovers Roads
Additional Roads

Fairs and Drovers

In the days before the Industrial Revolution, Wales had very little surplus for export, the only exception being herds of store cattle, which by the mid-seventeenth century represented one of the primary sources of Welsh revenue, thus justifying the famous analogy made by Archbishop John Williams at the time, when he compared the Welsh drovers bringing wealth to Wales with the Spanish galleons that brought gold from the New World to Spain.

The cattle in Wales were bought by dealers and drovers in the fairs or on the farms. They were driven to collecting centres where they were shod with little quarter-circle metal 'shoes' in order to protect their hooves on the long journey across the country to the English markets. These were located in the East Midlands, in East Anglia and in the London area, where the fairs at Barnet and Smithfield were well known. The droves that crossed the country varied in size from one hundred to four hundred cattle, attended by four to eight drovers with their dogs. The normal progress was about twenty miles a day, so that the journey from Llŷn to London occupied about two months. The bulk of the cattle exported consisted of the Welsh Blacks from the moorlands, but it was well known that the pastures of the lowland fringes of Snowdonia supplied a superior breed of black and white cattle that was greatly sought after by the English buyers. The cattle trade of Caernarvonshire was, therefore, of great importance. Sheep, pigs, and even ducks and geese were moved short distances, but this study is primarily concerned with the cattle trade.

The main sources of the cattle collected in and passing through Caernarvonshire were in Anglesey, Arfon and Llŷn. The cattle fairs were of the greatest importance, and were held on a vast scale at the turn of the eighteenth and nineteenth centuries. Cattle lined the streets, and the fields around the towns where the fairs were held were full of beasts for sale. Thus, Gwallter Mechain notes that in 1810 some 14,000 'Welsh Runts' were being sent to the Midlands annually from Llŷn and Anglesey alone.

The map indicates the location of the Caernarvonshire fairs in the period 1790-1799, when the cattle trade was at its height. The fairs and the dates on which they were held were always listed in the Welsh almanacs of the day. Those on the map are taken from *Yr Almanac Cymraeg* compiled by John Harris, a well-known 'teacher of arithmetic' at Cydweli in Carmarthenshire. On the other hand, we must not over-emphasise the fairs, for Hyde Hall tells us that at Beddgelert fair in 1809 'the show of animals was in general but trifling, as the drovers have for many years been accustomed to go about from house to house in order to make their private bargains with the farmers'.

The actual routes followed by the drovers avoided the roads. The herds were driven directly across the countryside, and whenever possible on the soft turf of the open moorlands. The Anglesey cattle were collected at Llangefni, and some were driven on to Porthaethwy, where they swam across the Strait. On the Caernarvonshire side, the drovers avoided Bangor, and moved the animals south-eastwards to Pentir, and then *via* the Nant Ffrancon Pass to Capel Curig. From here, they made for Llanrwst and over Mynydd Hiraethog to Betws-yn-Rhos. They then followed the Clwydian Hills to Rhuthun and Llandegla, which was the great meeting-place for cattle from many parts of North Wales before they entered England. Another route for the Anglesey cattle involved a collection at Gallows Point, near Beaumaris, and then over the Lafan Sands at low tide to Aber on the Caernarvonshire shores. They were then either driven directly over the hills, or *via* the Sychnant Pass towards Caerhun, and thence southwards to Llanrwst to follow the same route towards England.

Very much the same procedure was adopted in the case of the cattle collected on the Arfon sea-plain. They were driven southwards *via* Betws Garmon towards Aberglaslyn, turning eastwards before reaching the bridge, where they might have to pay tolls, and onwards to Capel Curig and Llanrwst as before. The Llŷn cattle were collected at Sarn Mellteyrn, Botwnnog, Llanengan and Llangïan, and moved eastwards, avoiding Pwllheli, and passing on through Rhydyclafdy and Efail-newydd to Four Crosses, where they might meet others coming from the Nefyn area. From Four

Crosses, the cattle passed near to Llanystumdwy, making contact with the great marshy tract (as it was before it was drained early in the nineteenth century by W. A. Madocks) of the Traeth Mawr at Penmorfa. The drovers kept well to the northward and westward of this difficult area, and made for Aberglaslyn. They avoided the marsh by passing on *via* Llanfrothen to Maentwrog, where a choice of routes was available to the eastern Borderlands, either through Penmachno, Cerrig-y-drudion to Corwen and Llandegla, or by way of Trawsfynydd and Bala to Corwen and Llangollen. To complete the story of the Llŷn cattle, we need to return to Nefyn, where an alternative or 'switch route' followed north-western Llŷn *via* Clynnog Fawr and Llanwnda into Arfon, where several of the routes along the foothills and passes of Snowdonia, already described, were available to them.

The drovers made a great contribution to the social life of the countryside, as well as following their own trade. They brought back news of current events from London, and particularly of what had been said in Parliament. They introduced new fashions in dress, particularly in ladies' dress. They returned with cuttings of fruit-trees, and the seeds of special field crops which were subsequently cultivated by the Welsh farmers. They frequently acted as agents and carriers for shopping transactions, and with the ready money which they brought back to Wales they not only acted as bankers to farmers and squires but even pioneered their own private banks and printed their own banknotes for general circulation. It was the coming of the railways that finally put an end to this long-distance droving, as the railways offered such obvious advantages for transporting the animals.

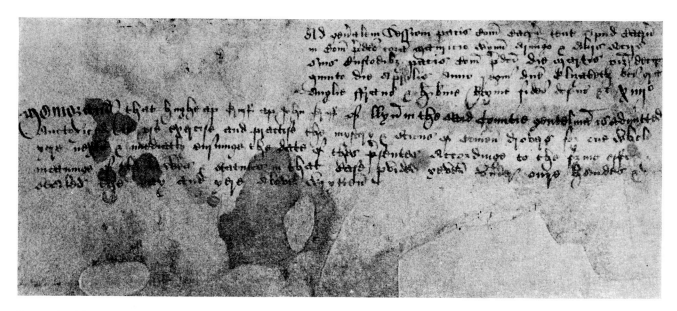

Drover's Licence, 1572

Gwynedd Archives

Ad generalem sessic[ne]m pacis comitatus Caern' tentam apud Caern' in comitatu predicto coram Mauricio Wynn armigero et aliis sociis suis custodibus pacis comitatus predicti die Martis videlicet decimo quinto die Aprilis anno regni domine Elizabeth dei gracia Anglie Francie et Hibernie regine fidei defensoris etcetera xiiii°

Memorandum that Hughe ap Gruffy*dd* ap John Gruffy*dd* of Llyn in the said countie gentelman is admitted and auctoriced to use exercise and practise the mystery and sciens of commen drovers for one whole yere nexte and imediatly ensuinge the date of thes presentes accordinge to the forme effect and meaninge of the lawes and statutes in that case provided. Yeven under oure handes and seales the day and yere above wrytten.

132

The Drovers

Rowlandson

CATTLE CROSSING THE MENAI STRAITS

' They are urged in a body by loud shoutings and blows into the water, and as they swim well and fast, usually make their way for the opposite shore: the whole troop proceeds pretty regularly till it arrives within about a hundred and fifty yards of the landing place, when, meeting with a very rapid current formed by the tide, eddying, and rushing with great violence between the rocks that encroach far into the channel, the herd is thrown into the utmost confusion. Some of the boldest and strongest push directly across, and presently reach the land, the more timorous immediately turn round, and endeavour to gain the place from which they set off; but the greater part, borne down by the force of the stream, are carried towards Beaumaris bay, and frequently float to a great distance before they are able to reach the Caernarvonshire shore. To prevent accidents a number of boats well manned attend, who row after the stragglers to force them to join the main body; and if they are very obstinate, the boatmen throw ropes about their horns, and fairly tow them to the shore, which resounds with the loud bellowings of those that are landed, and are shaking their wet sides. Notwithstanding the great number of cattle that annually pass the Strait, an instance seldom, if ever, occurs of any being lost.'

Arthur Aikin, *A Tour through North Wales* (1797).

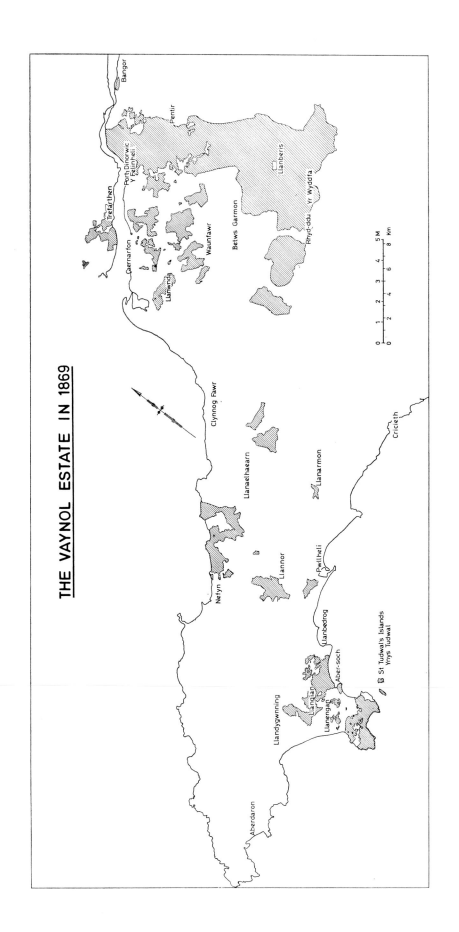

THE VAYNOL ESTATE IN 1869

Bangor
Pentir
Porth Dinorwic
Y Felinheli
Trefarthen
Llanberis
Yr Wyddfa
Caernarfon
Betws Garmon
Waunfawr
Rhyd-ddu
Llanwnda
Clynnog Fawr
Llanaelhaearn
Llanarmon
Cricieth
Nefyn
Llannor
Pwllheli
Llanbedrog
Aber-soch
St Tudwal's Islands
Llandygwnning
Llangian
Ynys Tudwal
Llanengan
Aberdaron

5 M
Km
8
0 1 2 3 4 5
0 2 4 6 8

The Vaynol Estate

The Vaynol Estate follows quite closely a general pattern of development shown by many other landed estates in Great Britain over the past two hundred years.

In 1696, Sir William Williams, owner of the Vaynol Estate and the last of his line, died childless. He left an unusual will, bequeathing a life interest in the estate to two friends, Sir Bourchier Wrey, a most unsavoury character from all reports, and his brother, the Rev. Chichester Wrey. On their death the estate was to revert to the Crown. In anticipation of this event, the Crown granted the estate to John Smith, the Speaker of the House of Commons, and his heirs, though John Smith himself did not live long enough to enjoy the fruits of this gift. It was not until 1756, when the Rev. Chichester Wrey died, that the estate finally passed into the hands of the Smith family. The condition of the estate in 1756 was not encouraging. The Wreys had exploited the estate to the utmost during their tenure of it, putting out the holdings at rack rent and carrying out no repairs or improvements. We know from a local observer in 1725 that they sold off even the young trees — 'they grubb up small oake that are not 6 inches round all growinge timber.' A valuation of 1799 paints a sorry picture of the poor condition of the estate, the result of years of neglect:

> On most of Mr. Smith's estates in the counties of Caernarvon and Anglesey the buildings are very old and poor and not proper for the occupation of them and most of his present tenants appear to be very indifferent farmers and do not attend to the proper cultivation of their farms . . .

The Smiths began the task of remodelling the tenancies as they fell vacant. In leases issued after 1778 clauses were inserted outlining the manner in which the land was to be farmed. The tenants had to undertake:

> To keep premises and all buildings, gates, stiles, plats, walls, hedges, ditches and banks in good and sufficient tenantable repair . . .

> Not to push plow or pare any part of the land without leave . . .

> Not to keep goats . . .

> To use hay and straw on the said premises and not to sell any muck the last year nor plow in any year more than a proportionable share of the whole arable land . . .

> To leave muck on the premises at the end of the term for succeeding tenant . . .

Under the Assheton-Smiths, the estate enjoyed considerable expansion. Even in 1696 it covered a considerable area of land in the parishes of Llanddeiniolen, Bangor, Llanberis, Llanfairisgaer, Llanrug, Llanbeblig, Llanllyfni, Clynnog, Beddgelert, Llandwrog, Llanwnda, Llanfihangel-y-Pennant, Llanaelhaearn, Llangïan, Llanengan and Caerhun in the county of Caernarvon, and Llanidan, Llangeinwen and Tregaean in the county of Anglesey. By 1799 it had spread over the parishes of Deneio, Llannor, Llanbedrog, Betws Garmon, Llanbedr, Llangelynnin and Gyffin. The acquisition of the Bodvel Estate in the early nineteenth century brought additional lands in the parishes of Llannor, Pistyll, Carnguwch, Llanarmon and Llanfaglan and Llaneugrad in Anglesey under its control. It benefited, too, from the enclosures of common lands taking place at this time. In 1843 the estate lent money to the Corporation of Caernarfon, then in embarrassed financial circumstances, and became the mortgagee of the Corporation's extensive estates in Caernarfon town. From the 1850s onwards considerable sums were spent on estate improvements and plantations, and the great wall surrounding Vaynol was constructed at this time.

The Assheton-Smiths developed the industrial potential of their estate. In the late eighteenth century Dinorwig quarry had been leased to a group of adventurers, but in 1809 Thomas Assheton Smith took the quarry under his own management. He developed Y Felinheli, later renamed Port Dinorwic, as a slate exporting port, and it was considerably enlarged in 1829 by his son. A tramroad was constructed between the quarry and the port of shipment and later in 1843 the Padarn Railway line built. The reduction of duties on slate in 1831 led to a period of steady expansion in the slate industry during the next fifty years. Other industrial developments were encouraged. Limestone quarries at Brynadda and Nantporth were opened, while copper mines at Clogwyn-coch,

Nantperis and Drws-y-coed, and lead mines at Penrhyn Du were leased to developers.

By 1869, when the new heir, George William Duff Assheton-Smith, took control, the estate was almost at the height of its power and was the second largest and most powerful estate in the county, covering over 33,000 acres, with a rental of over £42,000 from urban, industrial and agricultural properties.

The old order was to change, however. Perhaps the first hint came during the election of 1868 when the Vaynol Estate threw all its influence behind the Tory candidate and expected the tenants and quarrymen to follow its lead. The county, however, voted against the wishes of the great landowners, and the Liberal candidate, Love Jones Parry, was elected. Amongst Parry's most prominent supporters was John Owen of Tŷ'n-llwyn, a tenant of the Vaynol Estate, who ignored the estate's threat to evict him from his farm. The resultant eviction caused a storm of protest and bitterness and the memory of this endured years after the event.

From the late 1870s, the county suffered a severe agricultural depression, due mainly to the fall in prices caused by foreign competition. By 1887, the arrears of rent reached £2,000. Rent rebates had to be allowed to the struggling tenants during the late 1880s and 90s and the Estate's receipts from agricultural rents suffered in consequence. The slate trade in the 1880s suffered its first serious depression after fifty years of continuous expansion. Though trade recovered in the 1890s, sales and production slumped again after 1900 as a result of foreign competition, and the slate trade went into a long, slow decline exacerbated by the effects of two world wars.

Relations between landlord and tenant and between employer and employee were altering, too. The majority of the Dinorwig quarrymen in 1874 joined the North Wales Quarrymen's Union. The strike of 1874 which followed their action caused bitterness on both sides. In correspondence of 1876 between the Vaynol Estate agent and a group of quarrymen wanting greater security of tenure over their cottages this embittering of relations is clearly shown. Captain Steward wrote:

You refer in glowing terms to the administration of this estate in the days of the late Mr. Assheton-Smith and the sad contrast these present times present. You seem to forget, however, that great changes have occurred since those paling days and that the memorialists themselves with their unions and strikes have been mainly instru-

mental in bringing about those changes. We must therefore keep pace with the times in which we live, but should the memorialists be pleased to give their servitude *now* on the same terms as then, I am sure Mr. Assheton Smith will be only too delighted to revive and continue the same privileges and terms of tenure as was granted by his late uncle.

There was an increasing feeling among the quarrymen that the quarry owner was showing favouritism towards Churchmen and Conservatives — feelings which contributed to the prolonged and bitter strike of 1885-6.

The agricultural depression and the distress it brought to the farmers on the estate to a certain extent caused an embittering of relations between the landlord and tenant. Again there were suspicions of discrimination against Nonconformist and Liberal tenants on the estate. A new critical, radical Welsh press gave voice to this discontent in the quarry and on the land, and the Estate was subject to a barrage of criticism in the *Werin* and *Genedl* newspapers. It was frequently forced to justify its actions publicly to the press and, later, to the Royal Commission on Welsh Land which investigated the land question in 1893. It is important not to over-emphasise these new influences and attitudes, however, for in many respects the old order continued undisturbed to the end of the century.

It was the twentieth century that brought significant changes. After 1900 the Estate began to contract. In 1907 the owner sold off outlying parts in Llŷn in the area of Deneio, Llangïan and Llanengan. Over 3,600 acres were disposed of in 1907. In 1919 a further 4,000 acres in the parishes of Llanbeblig, Llanrug, Llanwnda, Waunfawr, Llanfair-is-gaer, Llanbedrog, Llangïan, Llanidan and Llangeinwen were sold. Economic conditions had altered and income tax, super tax besides death duties fell heavily on the owners of landed estates, and land brought in a lower return on the capital tied up in it than many other types of investment. The Vaynol Estate survived longer than many other great estates. In its contracted form it was kept together until 1967 when 21,560 acres were put under the auctioneer's hammer. Lands in the areas of Caernarfon, Llanfair-is-gaer, Bangor, Port Dinorwic, Pentir, Deiniolen, Llanberis, Nantperis, Rhyd-ddu, Nantlle and Trefarthen in Anglesey were finally sold. In 1969, Dinorwig Quarries, formerly one of the largest slate enterprises in the world, closed down. Only a small area around Vaynol Hall and Home Farm remains to remind us of what was once one of the largest and most powerful estates in Caernarvonshire.

THE VAYNOL HOUSEHOLD IN 1871

1871 Census	YEAR AND MONTH OF CENSUS					SHEET/FRAME NO.	

Parish or Township of BANGOR	Ecclesiastical District of BANGOR		City or Borough of			Town of	Village of

No. of House Holders Schedule	Name of Street, Place or Road and Name or No. of House	Name and Surname of each person who abode in the house on the night of	Relation to head of the family	Condition	Age of Males	Females	Rank, Profession or occupation	Where born
1	Vaenol	G. W. A. Smith, Esq.	Head	Unmar.	22		Landowner/ Magistrate, Deputy Lieut. of Carnarvonsh.	London
		Wm. J. Clampitt	Servant	Unmar.	39		House steward	Exeter, Devon
		Ann Hughes	Servant	Unmar.		37	Cook	Corwen, Mer.
		Betty Beddoes	Servant	Unmar.		24	Still room maid	Llandrillo, Mon.
		Cathrine Darrel	Servant	Unmar.		25	Kitchenmaid	Little Dawley, Salop.
		Elizabeth Davies	Servant	Unmar.		24	Upper house maid	Bangor, Carns.
		Mary Williams	Servant	Unmar.		28	2nd house maid	Bangor, Carns.
		Mary Jane Morgan	Servant	Unmar.		20	3rd house maid	Frampton, Glos.
		Jane Hughes	Servant	Widow		49	Upper laundry maid	Llanidan, Anglesey
		Jane Jones	Servant	Unmar.		29	Under laundry maid	Bangor, Carns.
		Mary Stephens	Servant	Unmar.		80	Upper nurse	Winchelsea, Essex
		James Perkinns	Servant	Unmar.	22		Footman	Llythwood, Salop
		Wm. Strickland	Servant	Unmar.	19		Footman	Youghel, Cork, Ire
		Pryce Thomas	Servant	Unmar.	17		Hallboy	Lythill, Corndown, Salop
		Cathrine A. Ross	Servant	Unmar.		20	Scullerymaid	Aberdeen

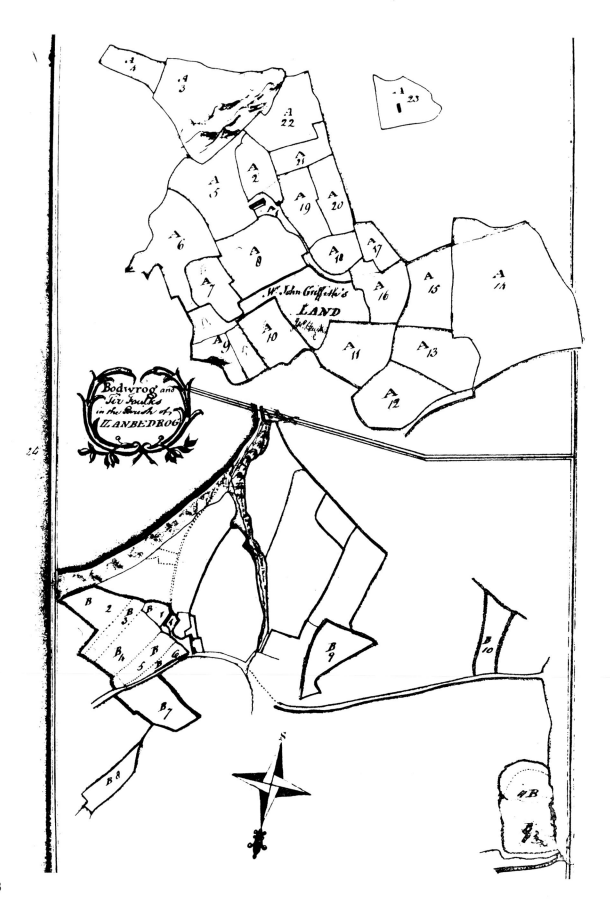

Bodwrog and
Tir Foulks
in the Parish of
LLANBEDROG

LLANBEDROG Parish			
BODWROG mark'd A			
A.1 House yards and Garden	.	2	30
2 yr Hdd	1	1	7
3 yr Allt fftt	5	.	28
4 Y Weirglodd	1	.	3
5 Llain y Weirglodd	3	.	24
6 Cae Nant	3	1	7
7 Bryn y ddwy Craig	1	2	1
8 Cae'r Hdd yr Ydd	2	1	30
9 Dwy Craig	1	3	14
10 Chwe Llathen	1	3	4
11 Cae'r hir ysgubor	2	1	36
12 Cae bihin	2	2	21
13 Cae Mawr	2	2	16
14 Cae Mynydd	10	.	15
15 Buarthau	2	1	9
16 Cae talcen y Buarthau	1	3	2
17 Gadlas y Cae hir	.	3	14
18 Cae'r Odyn	.	3	31
19 Cae'r Beudy	1	2	.
20 Cae'r Bryn	1	1	28
21 Cae'r Gamfa	1	.	15
22 Cae'r Allt	2	1	24
23 Cae Llwyd at distance	1	2	24
Tot.	54	1	23
TIR FOULKS marked B			
B.1 House Garden and half the Toft	.	1	32
2			
3			
4	4	2	16
5			
6			
7 Cae'r Drex	1	2	13
8	.	3	14
9 Llain ysgeiriad	1	1	28
10 Llain bol y Mynydd	1	.	15
11 Pen yr Hengarn	1	3	10
Tot.	11	3	8

Much information about the geography of farms and smallholdings and some glimpses of the farming methods and ways of life of the people may be obtained from estate maps and the related lists produced in recent centuries. An excellent collection of Vaynol Estate surveys has been deposited in the Gwynedd Record Office, and here a map of Bodwrog and Tir Foulks in the parish of Llanbedrog is reproduced, from the Survey dated 1777 (Vaynol Papers, 4055-6), as an example of the contents. The schedule accompanying the map shows that Bodwrog two hundred years ago was a farm of a little over 54 acres, and Tir Foulks a holding of above 11 acres. Bodwrog appears to be the site of a medieval *hendref*.

It will be seen that a field belonging to Bodwrog (A23 on the map, and named 'Cae Llwyd' according to the schedule) and three others belonging to Tir Foulks (B9, B10 and B11, being 'Llain ysgeiriad', 'Llain bol y Mynydd' and 'Pen yr Hengarn') were separated from their respective holdings. In many districts such fields 'at a distance' were not unusual, some of them being remnants of dispersed holdings in the Middle Ages, and others probably the result of later enclosure of the more promising parts of the open commons. It may be noted that a field owned by a certain John Griffith was surrounded by Bodwrog property — a small example of the interspersion of land ownership and tenure which caused considerable inconvenience and occasional disputation.

One of the fields of Tir Foulks (B2-6: the name is not given) is shown by broken lines to be divided into five parts, and such lines are also used to indicate the separation of three pieces of land west of the path leading northwards to the homestead. It is possible that these broken lines denote baulks of unploughed land serving as boundaries between strips and other patches held and cultivated by different people.

The most interesting and informative feature of the schedule accompany the maps is their record of field names. In the list relating to this map of Bodwrog and Tir Foulks, there are some common names like 'Cae'r Beudy', 'Cae'r Allt', 'Cae'r Gamfa', 'Buarthau', 'Cae Eithin' and 'Cae'r Odyn', and these give some information. 'Yr Ardd' (A2) and 'Cae'r Ardd yr Ŷd' (A5) recall the cultivation of those fields when they were so named, while 'Cae'r hen ysgubor' (A11) refers to the garnering of corn and/or hay to the 'old barn' long before 1777. It is possible that the yard known as 'Cadlais y Cae hir' (A17) continued to have a stack of hay or corn on it in that year; and although the 'Cae Hir' (Long Field) itself does not appear in the list, it may be guessed that it had been A20 'Cae'r Bryn' with an extension to the corner of A3, 'Yr Allt-Gyll'.

A notable feature of a number of the field names is that they include words that had definite meaning as descriptions of small areas of land in the Middle Ages — terms like ' erw', 'llain', 'llathan', and ' dryll'. In the list with this map, there is 'Llain y Weirglodd' (A5) and the previously mentioned 'Llain Ysgeiriad' (B9) and 'Llain bol y Mynydd' (B10) — such *lleiniau* being common in various schedules, especially perhaps in those relating to lowland holdings. 'Llain' was the term used in the medieval period for a strip of land held in an open field, and it has been suggested above that the old system of holding arable land in interspersed strips and patches may have persisted at Tir Foulks on the field B2-6 at the time when this map was drawn. The practice has continued until the present time in some seven places in Britain, one of them — the 'Vile' in Rhosili, Gower — being in Wales, and it lasted at Llanynys, Dyffryn Clwyd, until 1971. This system of tenure was also the source of the field name 'Chwe Llathan' (A10) in Bodwrog — as of 'Saith Llathan' in Ynysycheuryn, Llanddeiniolen, in the same period. These '*llathenni*' (yards) originally were definite measurements of the strips in the open fields.

The second example chosen from the Faenol Survey of 1777 is the map and schedule of Y Ffridd, Baladeulyn, in Llanllyfni parish. Comparison of this map with the contours of recent surveys shows that, even by the 1770s, land in the area had been enclosed up to altitudes of about 300 metres. The field names are not particularly distinctive. 'Y Ffridd Arw' (17), 'Cae Caled' (14) and 'Corsydd' (13) are inherited descriptions of rough uplands; and there is an interesting reference to an old 'hafod' (summer dwelling) in 'Cae Hafod Dafydd' (15). 'Y Fawnog' (2) was undoubtedly a source of the peat used in the district. Fairly near the houses and gardens (1) there were fields called 'Buarth Gwinau' (3), 'Y Fron' (6) and 'Cae'r Lloiau' (7 and 11), suggesting that they

were a little more tractable than the uplands. The 'Ungwys' had been divided and the name implies that its two parts (4 and 5) were ploughed, alternately, perhaps, only from one direction, downwards.

It is of considerable interest that the area shown in this map of Y Ffridd is the subject of a large contemporary painting called 'Llyn Nantle' (*sic*) by an Irish artist, George Barret, R.A. (1728? - 1784), who came to Britain in 1764. The painting can be seen in the City of Exeter Museum. It shows the two Nantlle lakes, Snowdon (probably) in the background, and a number of cottages — almost certainly those marked on the map, and another on the strip by the outflow (or *bala*) from one lake to the other. In the foreground there are a man with a plough, horses and a man mounted on one of them, and cattle at the edge of the lake. The Gwynedd Archives Service has recently obtained a copy of this painting.

Though the archaic term '*dryll*', from a piece of land, does not appear in the list accompanying this map, it seems worth referring to it as another example of a word that survived through the centuries and that is recorded in some of the Vaynol Estate documents. In Llanddeiniolen parish in 1777, 'Drylliau' was a field name in Erw-goch (alias Tros-y-waun); there were 'Dryll y tarw', 'Dryll y tarw isaf', 'Dryll yr haidd' and 'Dryll glan y gors' in Tan-y-dderwen; 'Drylliau' and 'Dryll Ysgawen' in Tyddyn Badin; 'Dryll y Fwyall' in Castell, and especially interesting as probably denoting portions of the headland of a ploughed area, 'Dryll Talerau' at Bryn Madog, Bryn'refail. 'Dryll y garnedd' has been noted in the list for Tŷ'n-llwyn, in that part of Bangor parish which, in 1888, became the parish of Pentir; and 'Dryll y Tŷ', in Drws-y-Coed, in the parish of Beddgelert. Dr. Colin A. Gresham, in his book on *Eifionydd,* refers to five farms or holdings with 'dryll' as part of their name.

Space does not allow more than mere reference to other interesting field names which appear in the Vaynol Estate documents — names like 'Cae'r brasgeirch', 'Dôl yr haidd', 'Buarth gwenith', 'Gwaith pladyr', 'Llain delyn', 'Llain pen yr henborth', 'Pigin ystwyth', 'Grappach' and 'Yr Ardd Gŵn'.

In addition to that of 1777, similar surveys of the Vaynol Estate were made in 1799, 1832 and 1869; and additional descriptions and lists were compiled in other years. One of the manuscript volumes has been published as *Farming in Caernarvonshire around 1800* (ed. R. O. Roberts, Caernarvonshire Record Society, 1973) — a short book which contains a description of Bodwrog and Tir Foulks, a photograph of old buildings at Bodwrog, and reproductions of maps and lists from the Survey of 1777. Many details may be found in E. Hyde Hall, *A Description of Caernarvonshire, 1809 - 1811* (ed.

E. Gwynn Jones, Caernarfon, 1952). For the earlier historical background, see *Medieval Welsh Society: Selected Essays by T. Jones Pierce* (ed. J. Beverley Smith, University of Wales Press, 1972); Colin A. Gresham, *Eifionydd: a Study in Landownership* (University of Wales Press, 1973); Glanville R. J. Jones, ' Field Systems of North Wales ' in *Studies of Field Systems in the British Isles* (ed. Alan R. H. Baker and R. A. Butlin, Cambridge University Press, 1973), pp. 430-479. See also the papers by C. A. Gresham, Glanville R. J. Jones and T. Jones Pierce in the *Transactions of the Caernarvonshire Historical Society,* Volumes 1, 2, 17, 18, 24 and 34. There is a useful discussion on the value of estate maps as historical sources in J. B. Harley, *Maps for the Local Historian* (London, 1972).

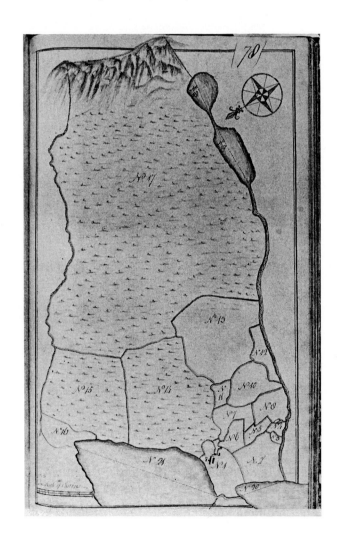

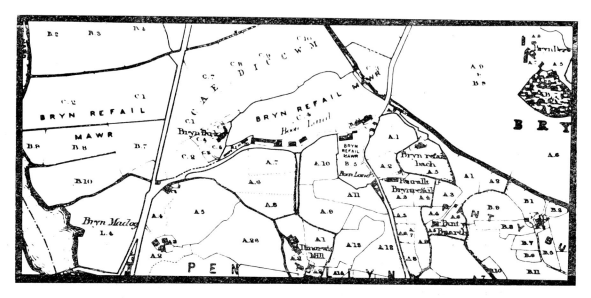

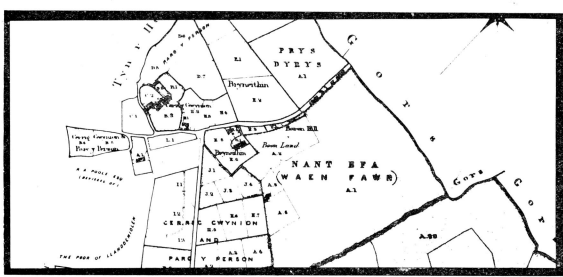

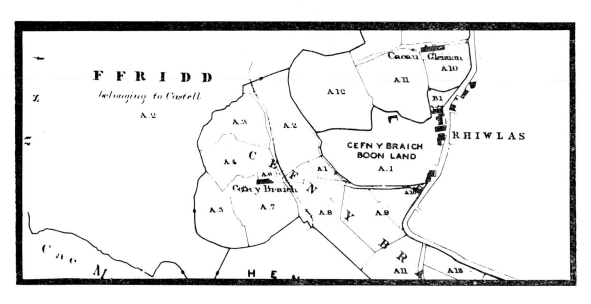

142

Boon Land: An Uncommon Type of Land Tenure

The reproductions opposite are of parts of maps contained in the Survey of the Vaynol Estate dated 1869 (Gwynedd Record Office, Vaynol Papers, 4194, Vol. 2, maps 7.28, 7.36 and 7.43). In each section there appears the phrase 'boon land', which refers to land held under a very unusual arrangement. The expression was first seen in the Tithe Apportionment Schedule for the parish of Llanddeiniolen, dated 1839, where it is used to describe certain lands at Bryn'refail, Rhiwlas and 'pen isaf o'r Waun'. For some years the meaning of the phrase could only be guessed.

As is well known, the term 'boon work' denotes the special services given by serfs to their lord in the Middle Ages — services like ploughing, sowing or reaping on the lord's land or shearing his sheep. Despite numerous enquiries, however, no one has been found who has seen elsewhere the phrase 'boon land', and it may be that it only appears in documents relating to the area of the old commote of Is Gwyrfai. As far as is known, there was no counterpart of the term in Welsh. It was surmised that it was used to describe land held by people who were obliged to render only special services (boon-work) to the lord of their manor, and some support to the supposition was given by the tradition that quarrymen from the Bethel and Deiniolen districts were required, during the last century, to work a certain number of days annually on the Vaynol home farm.

The survey of the estate made in 1777 (Vaynol Papers, 4055-6) contains a map and a list of 'cottages and gardens' in the Rhiwlas district, and another map of land nearby which shows a field of about fifteen acres marked 'Demesne'. This field was in a comparatively level and fertile area, but it was some three miles south-east of Vaynol's main farm or demesne near the Menai Strait. It seemed reasonable to suppose that the main reason for maintaining a small demesne at such a distance was that labour in the form of 'boon-work' was supplied by the cottagers of Waunbawgwydda nearby (the later Waunbentir) and Rhiwlas. It was wondered whether the cottages in those places were on 'boon land' — and so, too, the 'cottages and gardens' of Waunfawr and Waunwina, in the Penisa'r-waun district, which are grouped with those of the Rhiwlas locality in the index of the same survey volume of 1777. In the latter there is also a similar map of houses, cottages and gardens in Bryn'refail Bach and Bryn'refail Mawr.

It may be added that Vaynol had about 300 acres of land in Llanwnda parish which was described in 1777 as 'Dinas Demesne' — and about which it was stated in the next survey, in 1799, that 'This Estate ought to be divided into 4 or 5 small ffarms besides the Hall farm' (Vaynol Papers, 4060).

In the maps and schedules of 1799, information is given about dwellings and land at Bryn'refail, Penisa'r-waun and Rhiwlas, but there is no mention of 'boon land'. This survey, however, does refer to 'Boon Cottages' at Carreg-y-gath Uchaf, Rhiwlas, and to 'Booners' at Rhiwlas and Waunbawgwydda; and it was concluded that the 'booners' from both places would have worked at certain times, such as the harvest season, on the demesne nearby. (It is interesting that the same survey of 1799 refers to a 'Ffynnon & Pool now let to the Tenants of Dyffryn Mymbur & the Boon Cottagers'; it is therefore possible that the estate also had demesne land near Capel Curig.) In a manuscript volume which describes many of the farms and holdings of the estate in the same period (Vaynol 4057 — which has been published as a short book entitled *Farming in Caernarvonshire around 1800*) there appears the following revealing statement about the smallholding of Cae'r Llel: 'Most part of this is surrounded by the Common called Gwaen Baw Gwydda (on which sevl. cottages have been built who do Boonwork to Vaynol) . . . ' The reference in this excerpt to 'the Common' is significant.

'Boon land' is mentioned in a schedule (Vaynol Papers, 4202) prepared after 1825 — perhaps in the early 1830s. The term is there used for areas at Bryn'refail and Waunfawr (near Penisa'r-waun), and also for land at Carreg-y-gath and Rhiwlas for

Ffynnon Cegin Arthur

which there were references in earlier documents to 'Boon Cottages', 'Booners' and/or 'Boon-work'. Again, in a survey dated 1832 (Vaynol Papers, 4067-4072) the phrase 'boon land' similarly describes areas in the Bryn'refail, Penisa'r-waun and Rhiwlas districts; and as previously mentioned it appears in 1839 in the Tithe Apportionment Schedule for the parish of Llanddeiniolen.

The evidence taken together confirms the original supposition that 'boon land' — some if not all of it being common land — was an area for whose tenure 'acknowledgement' was given to the lord or the manor only in occasional labour services, i.e., in 'boon-work'.

In the maps reproduced on page 142, 'boon land' is shown to have persisted in the three districts as late as 1869. In the upper section it is denoted in two places (B5 and C4) in Bryn'refail Mawr. Part of the well-known bridge of Pen-llyn appears at the bottom left corner and to its right a straight double line depicting the railway from the Dinorwig quarry. There is shown also the flour mill remembered by a few until very recently. In the middle of the second section, 'Boon Land' is marked on an area adjoining Waunfawr. A part of the map showing a field similarly denoted had to be omitted in order to fit the three map sections on one plate; this field was across the road from Caecorniog Bach and shown on the map below the area interestingly labelled 'The Poor of Llanddeiniolen'. In the bottom section, the phrase 'Cefn Braich Boon Land' (A1) describes the exact area where the main group of houses of the village of Rhiwlas was built.

These map sections of 1869 confirm that feudal practices persisted until a very late period in the area of the old manor of Dinorwig.

For the background of the above account, see W. J. Gruffydd, *Hen Atgofion* (1936), Chapters 6 and 7; David Thomas, *Cau'r Tiroedd Comin* (1953), Chapters 4 and 5; E. H. Hyde Hall, *A Description of Caernarvonshire, 1809 - 1811* (ed. E. Gwynne Jones, 1952) and *Farming in Caernarvonshire* (ed. R. O. Roberts, 1973). Some additional detail is given in R. O. Roberts, 'Boon Land: an unusual form of tenure', *Folk Life,* Vol. 12 (1974), 104-106.

The engraving reproduced on the opposite page shows one of the 'boon land' districts — the one near Penisa'r-waun — as it appeared around the middle of the last century. It has been taken from the short book, *King Arthur's Well* (Caernarfon, 1858), by A. Wynn Williams, M.D., M.R.C.S., Tan-y-graig, Caernarfon. The sketch for the engraving was made by a certain W. Smith Davids, at a spot (map ref. about 555654) near Pen Dinas, or Dinas Dinorwig, Llanddeiniolen — a place from which excellent views can be seen, as described in Alun Llywelyn-Williams's *Crwydro Arfon* (Llandybïe, 1959), pp. 158-9.

In the left foreground of the picture the buildings of the medicinal springs of Ffynnon Cegin Arthur are shown, and it is interesting to find that the largest building was surrounded by a verandah as was common around the pump houses of contemporary spas. It will be noted that the land in the district had been enclosed, apart from the Waunfawr surrounding the Ffynnon: of course the mountains in the background, including Snowdon, were largely enclosed. The picture may be related to the middle map on page 142, for immediately beyond Ffynnon Cegin in the direction of the quarry there are shown the houses of Baron Hill, and behind them a piece of 'boon land' marked on the map. The engraving also indicates the size of the quarry by the middle of the nineteenth century, and the isolated rubble-heaps show how the workings were being extended up the slopes of Elidir Fach in the district known as 'Garret'. Below the quarry are the cottages of Gallt y Foel and of Llanbabo or Ebenezer — now, and for some decades, called Deiniolen — and to their right the 'Incline' of the tramway that in the early nineteenth century brought the slate through Clwt-y-bont, Efail Castell and Nant-y-Garth to Felin Heli or Port Dinorwic.

ENCLOSURES OF COMMON LAND

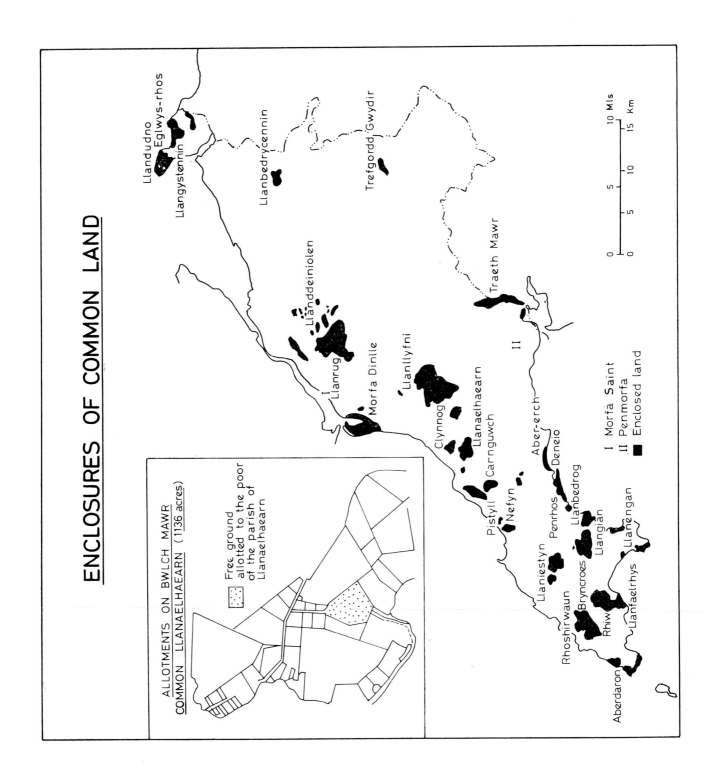

Llandudno
Eglwys-rhos
Llangystennin
Llanbedrycennin
Trefgordd Gwydir

Llanddeiniolen
Llanrug
Morfa Dinlle
Llanllyfni
Clynnog
Llanaelhaearn
Carnguwch
Pistyll
Nefyn
Aber-erch
Deneio
Penrhos
Llanbedrog
Llaniestyn
Llangian
Llanengan
Bryncroes
Rhoshirwaun
Rhiw
Llanfaelrhys
Aberdaron

Traeth Mawr

I Morfa Saint
II Penmorfa
■ Enclosed land

I
II

ALLOTMENTS ON BWLCH MAWR
COMMON · LLANAELHAEARN (1136 acres)

Free ground
allotted to the poor
of the parish of
Llanaelhaearn

10 Mls
15 Km

Enclosures of Common Land

It was the spirit of 'improvement' of the Agricultural Revolution, the high price of farm produce during the wars with France (1793 - 1815), together with the demand for metals and slates for the Industrial Revolution which inspired the movement to enclose the wastes and the sea marshes of the county. Most of the enclosing took place during the wars referred to. The initial steps were taken, almost without exception, by the landowners, men such as Assheton-Smith of Faenol, Sir Thomas Mostyn, and Sir Watkin Williams-Wynn, whose ancestors, generations earlier, had 'stolen from the mountain a slice of the parish', according to Ellis Wynne. The first formal enclosure was the enclosing and draining of Morfa Saint by the Corporation of Caernarfon in 1781 to provide better pasture for sheep and cattle. Before the end of the century, W. G. Oakley of Tan-y-bwlch had enclosed and drained over 1,000 acres of Penmorfa marsh near Tanrallt. These two enclosures took place by local private agreements. The majority of the others were authorised by private Acts of Parliament. The first step was a formal Petition to Parliament. Friends of the promoters usually sat on the Select Committee which guided the Act through Parliament, men like William Baldwyn, Member for Westbury, a Parliamentary neighbour of Thomas Assheton-Smith, or Rice Thomas of Coed Alun in the case of the Llanddeiniolen enclosure. On the average, twelve years passed between the initial Petition and the final award by the commissioner. It was the estate agents and lawyers of the landowners who also administered the Act. Walter Jones of Cefn Rug, Corwen, steward to Robert Williams Vaughan, Nannau, acted as agent for as many as nine enclosure acts in North Wales, and Thomas Roberts of Corwen was chosen as surveyor for the Llanddeiniolen act.

In no case was all the land petitioned for enclosed; even so, one-third to one-eighth of the wastes and commons was enclosed by private acts before the General Enclosure Act of 1845 provided some protection for the peasant. In all, 27,000 acres were enclosed. Some of the land was sold to meet administrative costs, and a proportion was set aside for roads and ditches; quarries were also ear-marked for repairing the new roads. Here and there, turbaries were provided for the poor to gather peat and furze for firing; 300 acres were set aside for that purpose by the Rhoshirwaun Act; 89 acres in the parish of Llanddeiniolen and 42 acres of free land were allocated on Bwlch Mawr for the poor of the parish of Llanaelhaearn. Even so, enclosure was without exception a loss to the poor. Squatters lost traditional rights to their 'tŷ unos' and the strip of land around it. There were as many as thirty-five of these on Maenor Dinorwig in 1809, but little notice was taken of the claims of such as Ffowc Ifan and Gryffudd the mole-catcher and the fishermen of Llŷn.

The fierce resistance of the fishermen of Rhoshirwaun was to be expected, nor should there be any surprise at the disturbances in Llaniestyn in 1810 and the pelting of John Ellis, the clerk, and his brother with stones and clods as they tried to administer the Act in the parishes of Nefyn, Pistyll and Llithfaen in September 1812. A number were thrown into prison after this incident, including women such as Margaret Rowlands and Ann Humphreys, and two were condemned to death, David Rowlands the shoemaker and Robert William Hughes, described as the 'captain of the mob'. In the event, Rowlands received a lesser punishment and the death sentence on Hughes was commuted to transportation. The help of the army had to be sought in Llanllyfni, and the Riot Act was read in Llanddeiniolen. The inhabitants of Llanwnda and Llandwrog, many of them working in Cilgwyn quarry, were fortunate enough to enlist the aid of Griffith Jones, the accountant, and John Lloyd, teacher and poet, of Anglesey. These succeeded in getting backing in Parliament to oppose the scheme of Lord Newborough and other landowners in 1806 to enclose 2,560 acres. Even so, 2,000 acres of Morfa Dinlle were enclosed.

The Rhoshirwaun Act specified that at least four crops of corn were to be raised on the enclosed land during the first seven years, but for the most part the land enclosed was high moorland, sandhills and marshes, and little could have been added to the arable acreage of the county. On the other hand, the enclosure did add to and help to improve pasturage. The most important result of the Llanddeiniolen enclosure was to make it easier for the squire of Vaynol to open up Dinorwig quarry.

The most important enclosure was probably the final enclosure of Traeth Mawr by Alexander Madocks. Apart from the extension of agricultural land, Caernarvonshire was linked to Merioneth by the new cob, and the small harbour nestling at one end of the cob in Porthmadog, gave a considerable impetus to the development of slate-quarrying in Ffestiniog.

THE ENCLOSURE ACTS

Year of Act	District/Parish	Date of Award	Acreage enclosed
1802	Rhoshirwaun, Bryncroes, Aberdaron, Llanfaelrhys	27.7.1814	1,414
1806, 1808	Llanddeiniolen	25.3.1814	3,346
1806	Llanrug, Llanbeblig	23.5.1820	2,257
1806	Morfa Dinlle		2,069
1807	Traeth Mawr	11.9.1823	1,046
1808	Llanbedrog, Llanfihangel Bachellaeth, Llangïan, Llaniestyn	12.8.1830	2,150
1811	Aberdaron, Llanfaelrhys, Rhiw, Bryncroes, Llanengan, Deneio, Penrhos, Aber-erch, Trefgordd Gwydir		2,789
1812	Nefyn, Pistyll, Carnguwch, Llanaelhaearn, Clynnog, Llanllyfni	8.3.1821	6,548
1812	Penmorfa, Dolbenmaen, Llanfihangel-y-Pennant		no map
1843	Eglwys-rhos, Llandudno	25.4.1848	4,820
By general Act, 1836	Llangystennin		
1850 By Commissioners under 1845 Act	Llanbedrycennin	25.10.1858	327

BIBLIOGRAPHY

Bowen, Ifor, The Great Enclosure of Common Lands in Wales (Chiswick Press, London, 1914).

Chaloner, W. H., Bibliography of recent work on inclosure, the open field and related topics (Agricultural History Review, 11, 1954).

Chambers, J.D. and Mingay, G. E., The Agricultural Revolution, 1750 - 1880 (Batsford, 1966).

Davies, W., A View of the Agriculture and Domestic Economy of North Wales (1811).

Dodd, A. H., The Industrial Revolution in North Wales (Welsh University Press, 1933).

Dodd, A. H., The enclosure movement in North Wales, Bulletin of the Board of Celtic Studies, 3, iii, 1926.

Jones, D. J. V., Before Rebecca — Popular Protests in Wales, 1793 - 1835 (Lane, London, 1973).

Kay, George, General View of the Agriculture of Caernarvonshire (1814).

Morgan, Colin, The effect of parliamentary enclosure on the landscape of Caernarvonshire and Merionethshire (Unpublished thesis, Aberystwyth, 1959).

Parker, R. A., Enclosure in the eighteenth century, Historical Association, 1960.

Plume, G. A., The enclosure movement in Caernarvonshire, with special reference to the Porth-yr-aur papers (Unpublished thesis, Bangor, 1935).

Thomas, David, Cau'r Tiroedd Comin (Hugh Evans, Liverpool, 1953).

ENCLOSURE TUMULT IN LLANDDEINIOLEN

In the beginning of the Month of September 1809 a person built the Walls of an intended Cottage upon a Common within the Manor of D(inorwig) in the parish of L(landdeiniolen) without the consent of the Lord of the Manor or his Agent — The Sollicitor of the Lord of the Manor threw down a part of such Walls and the Masons then promised not to rebuild them — In a Day and Night the walls were risen and green Sods thrown over as a Roof — The Sollicitor of the Lord of the Manor, his Agent, several Tenants and a Magistrate and Constables attended in order to take down the Walls of the Cottage, the person who had built it and several others being aware of an Intention to take down the Walls got into it, put a door upon it, no windows, had fire lighted, heated Water in order to throw over the persons who attended to take down the Walls: when the Magistrate and the other persons before mentd. attended at the Cottage there appeared a great Number of Men and Women who in a very violent manner declared that no person should take down the Incroachment — they were addressed by the Solicr. for the Lord of the Manor in a peaceable manner and informed that they were doing wrong and that they had no right to Incroach upon the common and that the Walls of the House would be taken down, they declared that they should not and would lose their lives in Opposition, they were informed that a Proclamation under the Riot Act wd. be made and that if they did not disperse within one Houre they would commit a capital Offence and that they would be liable to be hanged, they persisted in their Opposition and the Sollicitor of the Lord of the Manor attempted to take down the walls when he was attacked by a great Number of Men and Women some of them throwing Stones, Mud, Hot Water and others assaulting him and the Constables who were sworn upon the spot before the Mob to Keep the Peace — Then the Proclamation by virtue of the Riot Act was made by the Magistrate and the Mob to the number of 50 or 60 were requested to disperse and to return in a peaceable manner to their respective Dwellings and the Sollicitor of the Lord of the Manor attempted to take down the said Walls, he and some of the Constables were violently opposed, pelted with mud, Hot Water thrown over the Sollicitor and otherwise assaulted, Men and Women considerably above Twelve in Number continued upon the Spot above an Hour after the Proclamation was made and absolutely refused to depart but continued in a tumultuous manner to oppose the removal of the Incroachment and committing violent assaults, though repeatedly requested to disperse.

(U.C.N.W., Porth yr Aur 13035)

Mr. John Evans to Lord Bulkeley

My Lord,

I may now say as to the Llanddeiniolen Rioters that I fought and conquered. I went up yesterday with the Revd. Mr. Williams of Llanrug and eight Constables and took three of the Rioters without any resistance and conveyed them to the Goal where they now are, I expect to take two or three more tomorrow, I have compleately tamed the Tigers, they are Truly sensible of their Error. I do not expect any further opposition, they have offered to give up all their incroachment — I have written to Mr. A. Smith upon the Subject. It is very unpleasant to have Military brought into a County, unless absolutely necessary — I now think that I can manage all the encroachers in a peaceable manner. If your Lordship shd. not have written to the Earl of Liverpool before you receive this I would beg of your Lordship not to do so until I see you.

Carn. 22 Sept. 1809.

(U.C.N.W., Porth yr Aur 13034)

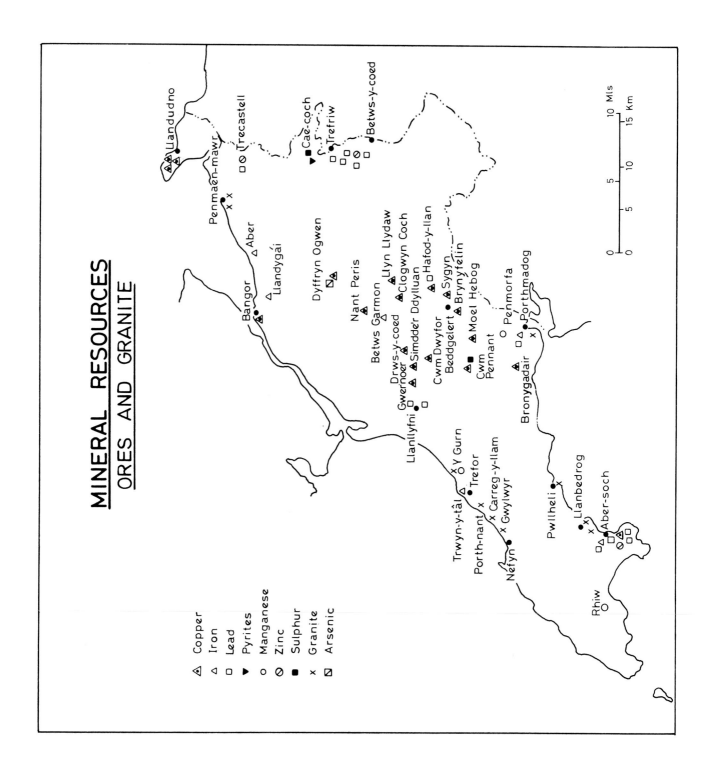

MINERAL RESOURCES
ORES AND GRANITE

Copper ⟁
Iron △
Lead □
Pyrites ▼
Manganese ○
Zinc ⊘
Sulphur ■
Granite ×
Arsenic ⌷

Llandudno

Trecastell

Caé-coch
Trefriw
Betws-y-coed

Penmaen-mawr

Aber
Llandygái

Bangor

Dyffryn Ogwen

Nant Peris

Llyn Llydaw
Clogwyn Coch
Hafod-y-llan
Sygyn
Brynyfelin
Moel Hebog

Betws Garmon
Drws-y-coed
Gwernoer
Simdde'r Ddylluan
Cwm Dwyfor
Beddgelert
Cwm Pennant

Penmorfa
Porthmadog

Bronygadair

Llanllyfni

Y Gurn
Trefor
Trwyn-y-tâl
Carreg-y-llam
Porth-nant
Gwylwyr
Nefyn

Pwllheli
Llanbedrog
Aber-soch

Rhiw

10 Mls
15 Km

150

Mineral Resources, Ores and Granite

There is evidence of mining in the county from the end of the Tudor period, and of greater efforts from about 1760 onwards. Copper was mined in the Ogwen Valley, in Nant Peris, in Drws-y-coed in Nantlle, on the Orme in Llandudno and from Pont Aberglaslyn to Beddgelert, and lead was mined at Penrhyn-du in Llŷn and in the Conwy Valley. Amounts of copper, calamine, sulphur and pyrites were also recovered in the latter area. The eighteenth-century adventurers formed a mixed group. Here and there local landowners tried their hand, and squires from outside the county, such as John Lloyd of Wickwar and Edward Lloyd of Cefn, played a leading part in Llandudno. There were clergymen among them, such as John Ellis, vicar of Bangor, and Richard Farington, who became Chancellor of the diocese. Others, such as Richard Richardson and the Smedleys, were already active in smelting in Flintshire. It is strange, considering the importance of the area in metal-working, that the only South Walian to take part was James Griffith of Swansea. The most powerful group attracted into the county in the eighteenth century was the partnership centred on Charles Roe of Macclesfield. They soon gave up mining in Penrhyn-du, but when their lease ran out in Mynydd Parys, prospected in several areas in Caernarvonshire. Some of the partners retained an interest in Llandudno, but their main effort went into Brynyfelin in Aberglaslyn and Nant Peris.

Miners moved in from Flintshire and Cardiganshire, but there were Cornishmen in the Ogwen Valley and Aberglaslyn by 1760, and Irishmen and Scots in Drws-y-coed. Others came from Derbyshire and Staffordshire. Surnames like Closs, Paynter, Roose, Wheldon and Fraser are still common enough and may be traced back to 1760 and beyond. Labourers, smiths, carpenters and masons were paid day rates, but the miners when they were opening up a mine were paid by piece work, so much a cubic yard. They might also be paid so much a ton for raising ore, the price varying with the state of the seam and the assay of the ore. But given their choice, they preferred to work as tributors, paying the adventurers a tribute of ore much as they themselves paid a royalty to the landowner.

A steam engine was introduced early to Penrhyn-du, but the usual power used for pumping and driving the stamps was water. A water wheel with accessory pipes and pumps could cost £800-£900 in 1800.

The lead was usually sent to the furnaces in Flintshire, the calamine to Bristol, the copper to South Wales and the pyrites to chemical works in the Liverpool area. By the turn of the century, work had started near Llyn Llydaw and soon afterwards in Cwm Pennant, and the Bronygadair mine was also active at one time. In the Conwy Valley, there were as many as 14 small undertakings in 1826, employing some 70 men. From 1829 the owners of the Faenol estate made a determined effort to exploit the ores on the estate at Drws-y-coed, Nantperis and Clogwyn-coch. There were 104 men and 4 boys, together with daymen, working in Drws-y-coed in 1833, and 87 miners with 7 boys in Nantperis and Clogwyn-coch in 1834. The most persistent mining, however, took place in Llandudno, where a number of small undertakings were grouped into the New Mine, the Old Mine and Tŷ-gwyn Mine. When Samuel Worthington gave up the Old Mine in 1846 about 100 miners with 20 daymen were employed there. It was bought in 1853 by John and Richard Taylor for £8,500, but mining had ceased in Llandudno by the late sixties.

In 1870, a local miner, E. Lloyd Roberts, struck a rich pocket of ore in Llanengan parish and sold his rights for £5,200. Soon there were eight undertakings in the area, employing at their busiest about 200 men, but the excitement was all over by 1895. Success here had drawn attention to the Conwy valley, and the small undertakings there were bought up by joint stock companies with attractive names such as Pandora and New Pandora.

Near Aberglaslyn, the old Moel Hebog mine was re-named Glistening Valley Mine, and the Great Snowdon Mountain Copper Mine Company was launched. As many as five separate companies worked Drws-y-coed between 1895-1914. By that time, apart from Cae Coch in the Conwy valley, where pyrites was still mined, working had practically ceased, and one is left with an impression that, whereas smaller undertakings might have succeeded, there was never sufficient ore to justify larger undertakings.

Manganese was exported from Conwy in 1808. By 1827, manganese had been found in Rhiw, and there were 50 employed there by 1840. It was sent to Liverpool. Small quantities of ore from Llanllyfni and Y Gurn Ddu, near Llanaelhaearn, went there also. During the two World Wars, there was much mining at Rhiw, and some 196,770 tons were raised between 1894 - 1945.

Iron ore was also mined in several parts of the county. In 1835 John Greaves and Samuel Holland worked the ironstone near Aber-soch and sent it to Cardiff; they had little success. Iron ore was also worked in the Tremadog area about 1840 by a man named Cooper. The Penmorfa Ironstone Quarries were offered for sale in 1841 and may have been purchased by a Mr. Heyward. This ore also went to Cardiff. There was a more persistent effort in Betws Garmon from the middle of the century, and efforts were made in the sixties to develop the deposits on Trwyn y Tâl on Yr Eifl. Later still, the deposits at Aber and Llandygái were worked and the ore sent to Brymbo and Swansea.

Granite quarrying was more important than any of these efforts. As transport developed around the factories and docks of the larger towns, the need was felt for a durable road surface. So a market was found for the granite pebbles on the beach at Penmaen-mawr. Much better than these pebbles were the setts made from quarried stone and shaped by skilful craftsmen into square and rectangular blocks. Some progress had been made in preparing setts in Penmaen-mawr in the twenties and the business started to develop on a greater scale from the thirties. The Gwylwyr quarry near Nefyn was opened for the same purpose, and by 1835 was being developed by Samuel Holland, who also succeeded in bringing a number of small enterprises in the Trefor area together as the Welsh Granite Company in 1844. Granite quarries were also worked in Llanbedrog, at Y Gest near Porth-madog and on Carreg yr Imbill, Pwllheli. The quarries were near the sea and so convenient for shipping the setts to England. There was some call for setts throughout the nineteenth century, but demand began to fall off after that and there was more demand for macadam. The first crushing mill was set up in Penmaen-mawr in 1888, and the demand for crushed stone increased during the following years for road-making, railway ballast and as concrete aggregate. Granite quarrying practically created the village of Llithfaen and Trefor, and when one remembers that the Penmaen quarry employed 510 men and the Graig-lwyd quarry 400 in 1894, the importance of quarrying to the development of Penmaen-mawr and Llanfair-fechan is obvious.

THE WEALTH OF MYNYDD MAWR AND CWM DU

Proposals laid by Griffith Pryse to J. Probert 4 August 1770 respecting sundry mine works of the Earl of Powis in Caernarvonshire in the manors of (blank) consisting as he says two veins of copper ore one yellow the other blue and green in the last of which are several pieces of gold ore from the size of a pin's head to that of a pullett's egg. And another vein of Gold out of which he says he raised a lump of malleable gold in weight 17 ozs — and besides these there is a vein of lead ore from 4-6 feet wide. All of which are unknown to any man living but himself . . .

National Library of Wales,
Powys Documents 3606

Henry Ellis a drover says that they (Griffith Pryse and John Powel) were the most notorious imposters that ever lived (ibid., 3210).

BIBLIOGRAPHY

For the general picture, A. H. Dodd, *The Industrial Revolution in North Wales* (1951); for leadmining, W. J. Lewis, *Lead Mining in Wales* (1967). See, too, various articles in *The Transactions of the Caernarvonshire Historical Society*; N. C. Black, ' A Brief Account of Copper Mining in Cwm Dyli, Snowdonia ', 31 (1970); C. J. Williams, ' The Llandudno Copper Mines ', 33 (1972); T. M. Bassett, ' Diwydiant yn Nyffryn Ogwen ', 35 (1974), and ' A Note on Penrhyn-du ', 34 (1974); Ivor E. Davies, ' A History of the Penmaenmawr Quarries ', 35 (1974). Also, Gwilym Owen, *Pentref Trefor a Chwarel yr Eifl* (1972).

Henryd Lead Mine

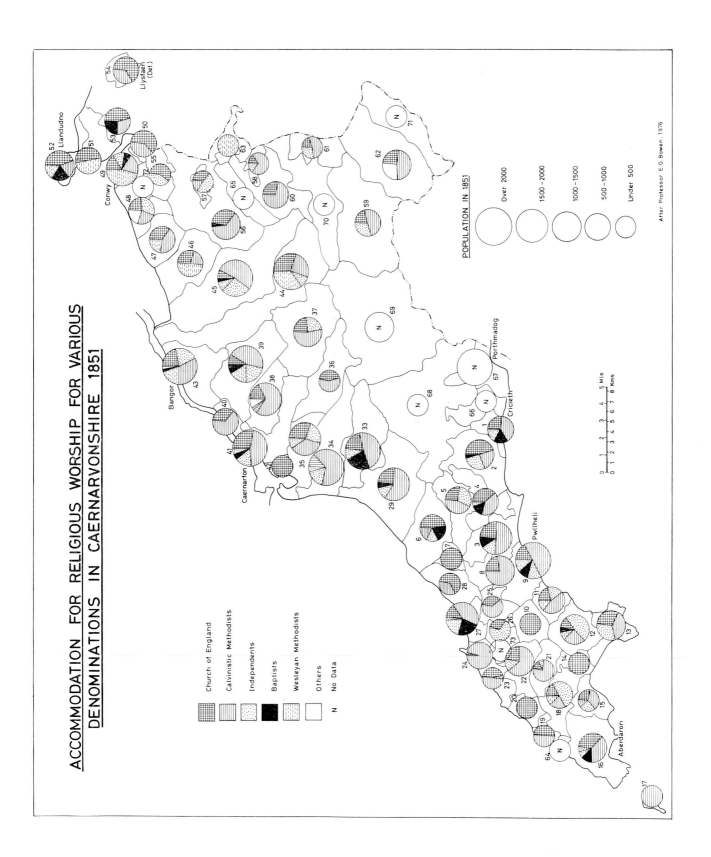

ACCOMMODATION FOR RELIGIOUS WORSHIP FOR VARIOUS DENOMINATIONS IN CAERNARVONSHIRE 1851

Church of England
Calvinistic Methodists
Independents
Baptists
Wesleyan Methodists
Others
N   No Data

POPULATION IN 1851

Over 2000
1500 - 2000
1000 - 1500
500 - 1000
Under 500

After Professor E.G. Bowen. 1976

0 1 2 3 4 5 Mls
0 1 2 3 4 5 6 7 8 Kms

Llandudno
Conwy
Bangor
Caernarfon
Porthmadog
Cricieth
Pwllheli
Aberdaron
Llysfaen (Det.)

Denominationalism in 1801 and in 1851

At the end of the eighteenth century the pattern of religious worship, as measured by the provision of churches and chapels, appeared to be simple and uncomplicated, and but little changed from what it had been for many generations in the past. The Church of England seemed secure in its traditional supremacy. It maintained at least one place of worship in each parish, and its leaders seemed justified in believing, despite the ruinous condition of some of its buildings, that its accommodation and manpower were sufficient to satisfy the needs of the inhabitants of the county. Congregations of dissenters were few, confined to the two denominations of Independents and Baptists, and located for the most part in the old boroughs and small towns of Llŷn. Only two of their chapels dated from the seventeenth century (Llangybi and Deneio), and all the others were of very recent foundations. More symptomatic of the changes about to take place in the religious life of the county were the Calvinistic Methodist societies. These were more ubiquitous, though mainly located in Llŷn, which was the region most worked over by the early Methodists. But only a minority of these had as yet built themselves chapels: they did not think of themselves as a movement distinct from the Church, nor were they organized as a separate denomination. That was not to come until 1811, and when it did so, to spark off a tremendous upsurge in chapel building. Nor had the Wesleyan missions to the county yet begun, and the complete absence of Roman Catholic congregations testified to the overwhelming Protestant orthodoxy of the county at large.

Fifty years later, a revolutionary transformation had taken place. The map shows the distribution of churches and chapels, and the relative strength of the individual denominations. There were now about 313 places of worship within the county — three times as many as in 1800 — and no less than 237 of these belonged to Nonconformist bodies. The Church of England had been displaced from its supremacy by the Calvinistic Methodists: indeed, *Yr Hen Gorff* had almost as many chapels as the other Nonconformist denominations put together and these included the Wesleyan Methodists who had only begun to build chapels in the first decade of the century. The Dissenting denominations, though much smaller than the Methodists in absolute terms, had grown at a higher relative rate in the course of the half century, their main areas of strength being in the commercial and industrial regions of the county.

The religious bodies altogether provided accommodation for more than 88 per cent of the total population of the county, and of this total, the Calvinistic Methodists provided about 43 *per cent,* the Anglican Church 24 *per cent,* the Independents 17 *per cent,* the Wesleyans 10 *per cent,* and the Baptists 5 *per cent.* In addition, there was a Roman Catholic church in Caernarfon and two very recently established congregations of Mormons, one at Caernarfon and the other in Bethesda. The little that can be discovered about actual attendances at the services provided by the various bodies suggests that the Calvinistic Methodists were by far the most popular denomination, followed by the Independents, the Wesleyans, the Anglicans, and the Baptists, in that order. Thus, by the mid-century the pattern of denominationalism in Caernarvonshire had been firmly established, and with only slight modifications this was to remain the pattern for the remainder of the century and to constitute a determining influence in the cultural and political life of the county thereafter.

PLACES OF RELIGIOUS WORSHIP PROVIDED BY VARIOUS DENOMINATIONS

Map No.	Parish	1800							1851						
		C. of E.	Ind.	Bapt.	C.M.	W.M.	Other	Total	C. of E.	Ind.	Bapt.	C.M.	W.M.	Other	Total
1	Cricieth	1	1					2	1		1	1	1		4
2	Llanystumdwy	1		1				2	1	2	1	1			5
3	Aber-erch	1						1	1	1	1	3			6
4	Llanarmon	1						1	1		1	2	1		5

155

| | | 1800 | | | | | | | 1851 | | | | | | |
Map No.	Parish	C. of E.	Ind.	Bapt.	C.M.	W.M.	Other	Total	C. of E.	Ind.	Bapt.	C.M.	W.M.	Other	Total
5	Llangybi	1	1		1			3	1	2		2			5
6	Llanaelhaearn	1			1			2	1	1	1	1			4
7	Carnguwch	1						1	1						1
8	Llannor	1			2			3	1			3			4
9	Penrhos with Pwllheli	1	1		1			3	2	1	1	2	1		7
10	Llanfihangel Bachellaeth	1						1	1						1
11	Llanbedrog	1	1		1			3	1	1		1	1		4
12	Llangïan	1		1	1			3	1	2	1	1	1		6
13	Llanengan	1	2	1				4	1	2		2			5
14	Llandygwnning	1						1	1						1
15	Rhiw with Llanfaelrhys	2						2	2	1		1	1		5
16	Aberdaron	1			3			4	1	1	2	3	1		8
17	Bardsey Isle	—						—				1			1
18	Bryncroes	1			1			2	1	1	1	1	1		5
19	Llangwnnadl	1			1			2	1			1			2
20	Penllech	1						1	1						1
21	Botwnnog with Mellteyrn	2		1	1			4	2		1	1			4
22	Llaniestyn	1	1		1			3	1	1		3			5
23	Tudweiliog	1			1			2	1	1		1			3
24	Edeyrn	1			1			2	1			1			2
25	Boduan	1						1	1			1			2
26	Ceidio	1						1	1			1			2
27	Nefyn	1		1	1			3	1	1	2	1	1		6
28	Pistyll	1			1			2	1			2			3
29	Clynnog	1			1			2	1	2	1	6			10
33	Llanllyíni	1		2				3	1	1	3	3			8
34	Llandwrog	1						1	1	4		5	1		11
35	Llanwnda	1				1		2	1	2		1	1		5
36	Betws Garmon	1				1		2	1			1			2
37	Llanberis	1				1		2	1	1		2			4
38	Llanrug	1				1		2	1	1		4	1	1	8
39	Llanddeiniolen	1						1	1	4	1	5	3		14
40	Llanfair-is-gaer	1						1	1			1			2
41	Llanbeblig with Caernarfon Borough	2	1		2			5	4	3	1	4	2		14
42	Llanfaglan	1						1	1						1
43	Bangor	2						2	2	6	1	6	4	1	20
44	Llandygái	2						2	3	2		2	2		9
45	Llanllechid	1			1			2	1	4	2	5	2		14
46	Aber	1						1	1			1	1		3
47	Llanfairfechan	1			1			2	1			1	1		3
48	Dwygyfylchi	1						1	1	1		1	1		4
49	Conwy	1			1			2	1	1		1	1		4
50	Gyffin	1						1	1	1	1	1	1		5
51	Eglwys-rhos	1						1	1			1			2
52	Llandudno	1						1	1			1	1	1	4
53	Llangystennin	1						1	1		1	2			4
54	Llysfaen			No data					1			1			2
55	Llangelynnin	1						1	1	1					2
56	Caerhun	1		1				2	1		1	3			5
57	Llanbedrycennin	1						1	1	2		1			4
58	Trefriw	1						1	1	1		2			4
59	Dolwyddelan	1						1	1	1		2			4
60	Llanrhychwyn	1						1	1			1			2
61	Betws-y-coed	1						1	1	1		1			3
62	Penmachno	1						2	1			2	1		4
63	Maenan (Township)												1		1

NOTES: (1) The numbers 30, 31 and 32 are not used for parish indication on the 1851 map.

(2) No data is available for the following parishes in the 1851 Census returns: Bodferin (64), Dolgarrog (65), Treflys (66), Ynyscynhaearn (67), Dolbenmaen (68), Beddgelert (69), Trewydir (70), Eidda (71), Llechwedd (72), Llandudwen (73).

The Established Church (1850-1900)

The Church in Caernarvonshire, through leaders like Nicander ('The Keble of Wales'), Philip Constable Ellis, Evan Lewis, Glasynys, William Hughes and Henry Thomas Edwards came under the influence of the Oxford Movement. Some of these men suffered for their espousal of the movement, as High Church tendencies were suspect. It was lamented, for instance, that Llanbeblig Church had become a Roman temple, with a cold, classic service and the people in the nave worshipping by proxy. Bishop Campbell, in his visitation charge in 1878, inveighed against sacramental confession as the appointed remedy for post-baptismal sin.

Basically, the movement gave new prominence to creed and rite, to history and tradition; it also gave fresh impetus to sacred music. To its credit, it must be said that, whereas the Church in Caernarvonshire at mid-century had been moribund, before the end of the century is showed a new intensity of life and much spiritual quickening. Retreats had become an acceptable feature of church life.

One of the most significant indications that the Church was aware of its mission was the establishment of the Diocesan Church Extension Society in 1869. The Society aimed to erect and endow churches as needed in populous areas, to provide halls for Sunday School and lecture purposes where the population was distant from the parish church, to increase the supply of curates and to create a class of Scripture readers to help the clergy. The Society worked with marked effect in Caernarvonshire.

The Bangor Lay Association was formed in the 1850s and had Glasynys and 'Y Sgolor Mawr' as its first secretaries. It aimed to band Churchmen together to rectify what was amiss in Church life, and to arrest the further Anglicisation of the Church. They were to press for more frequent Church services in the native tongue, greater efficiency in the Sunday Schools and the promotion of communicants' guilds. The licensing of lay readers became a mark of extended lay activity; laymen were encouraged to be Scripture readers, to minister in unconsecrated churches, to visit the sick and in other ways to promote godliness.

Church building went on apace, especially during the third quarter of the century, and the achievements in this direction were noted in the bishop's charge at every triennial visitation. District chapelries were created to serve new needs, and new ecclesiastical entities, including St. Thomas (Groeslon), Dewi Sant (Bangor), St. Ann (Bethesda), Pentir, Glanogwen, Llandinorwig and Waunfawr came into being. The Church Extension Society helped with curates' grants.

The cathedral, mother church of the diocese, was restored during 1868 - 1884 at a total cost of nearly £48,000. It was then that huge pillars were introduced into the crossing, and the base of a tower erected above.

The cathedral served many purposes. Dean Edwards held a Saturday morning school there, with 500 children, on average, attending. The mother church was noted, as always, for its fine music: classical works were performed periodically and greatly extolled. Many of the cathedral's lay clerks advanced to greater opportunities in England, notably at St. Paul's Cathedral.

Good music was not confined to the cathedral. Many Welsh hymn books were provided, and the then vicar of Pwllheli published a book of tunes for psalms and hymns in 1859. Choral unions were formed here and there in the county, especially in the rural deanery of Arllechwedd, where the influence of Eos Llechid proved to be outstanding.

Turning to education, the pioneer work of Dean Cotton (d. 1862) was furthered by the building of more Church schools, and a system of regular inspection was devised. Occasionally, where it was found difficult to maintain Church schools, some of them became Board schools.

An institution for the training of Church schoolmasters was established in Caernarvon in 1849. It assumed the status of a college, under the auspices of both northern dioceses, in 1856. Destroyed by fire in 1891, it was rebuilt in Bangor in 1893. It became known as St. Mary's College, and was given to the training of schoolmistresses. The college received consistently good reports from government inspectors.

The college was essentially Christian in character, with students cultivating a life of simple piety and attending the appointed means of grace. A chapel was first provided in 1871, free from the influence of the Oxford Movement, the bishop of Bangor insisting there should be ' no candles '!

The opening of the University College of North Wales at Bangor in 1884 marked an advance in the field of higher education. Dean Edwards was involved in the venture. He favoured a secular University College as a medium of higher education notwithstanding his keen advocacy of Church schools for less mature minds.

In 1871 the Bangor Diocesan Clerical Education Society was formed, and exhibitions were founded to help ordination candidates with their training. In 1885 steps were taken jointly by the dioceses of Bangor and St. Asaph to establish a Church Hostel at Bangor for the benefit of candidates for holy orders.

Church patronage exercised from without the diocese caused much unrest inasmuch as it delayed preferment from within the diocese. The bishop of Llandaff nominated to the Caernarvonshire parishes of Betws Garmon, Llandwrog, Llanengan, Llanrug and Trefriw, while the patronage of Clynnog Fawr, Llanwnda and Aberdaron belonged to Jesus College, Oxford. The situation was not resolved until the advent of disestablishment.

The question of language vexed the Church as essentially a bilingual society. It was a living issue, affecting the Church not only at parochial level, where often the only Sunday service would be in English, but also in her schools. English-speaking schoolmasters, out of touch with the local ethos, were known to express a sense of frustration that they could not get knowledge across to their monoglot Welsh pupils. The fact that this occurred betimes in British Schools — the school at Bethel aimed in 1865 to give children ' an English education ' — did not ease the misgivings of parents that children in Church schools did not receive their education in their first, and very often only, language.

One of the most marked projects connected with the Welsh language was associated with Patagonia, for in 1883 Hugh Davies, a clergyman, of Glasinfryn, near Bangor, was commissioned to go to the Chubut colony to minister to the Welsh inhabitants in their mother tongue. Voluntary financial aid to support him came from Bangor and district.

Turning to the realm of controversy, note must be taken of the rector of Llanfrothen's defiance of the provisions of the Burial Act of 1880. In 1888 he disallowed a Nonconformist burial, locking his churchyard gates. The gates were broken open at the instigation of David Lloyd George, the funeral was held and legal proceedings ensued. In the event, the action defying the rector's ban was sustained.

Let it be said, the clergy were unhappy about the Burial Act insofar as they were required to bury bodies that their Nonconformist brethren refused to bury. They were under legal compunction to do so. This made the Arllechwedd clergy very unhappy.

The burial issue was only one of many disestablishment issues arousing bitterness in the county. The conflict over tithes, the State connexion of the Church, the language problem and the deepening national consciousness of the Welsh people fostered the impatience of Nonconformists. The sectarian conflicts of the times were echoed in politics and industry, with ill-effects throughout the county. Anglican industrialists brought inordinate pressure to bear on their employees, forbidding them in some cases to attend meetings called to further the cause of disestablishment. This was particularly evident in quarrying districts.

The conflict between the local representatives of the Liberation Society and those of the Society for Church Defence reached extremes of acerbity and bitterness, and much that was said and done in the heat of controversy is best forgotten. Dean Edwards waged a vigorous campaign against the disestablishment of the Church, but it must be said, in fairness to him, that he also laid bare many of its weaknesses. Observers of a later date, reviewing especially his speech at the Swansea Church Congress in 1879, have tended to think that he exaggerated the failures of the Church.

Across the sectarian divide, which was so marked in the period under consideration, there was shed an occasional ray of hope. Dean Edwards, for example, pronounced Churchman though he was, longed for the reunion of his countrymen, and pleaded for the cessation of the abuse of Nonconformity matched by a genuine attempt to absorb its virtues. While he held tenaciously to his own cherished convictions, he nevertheless thought that a satisfactory *modus vivendi* could be achieved if Nonconformists would frequent Church altars three times a year, and Churchmen were permitted to hear sermons in chapel. Had such a practice prevailed, as it does as occasion demands in our day, a great deal of bitterness could have been avoided.

The Cathedral, early nineteenth century, before
restoration by Scott

The Cathedral after restoration by Scott

THE SLATE QUARRYING DISTRICTS

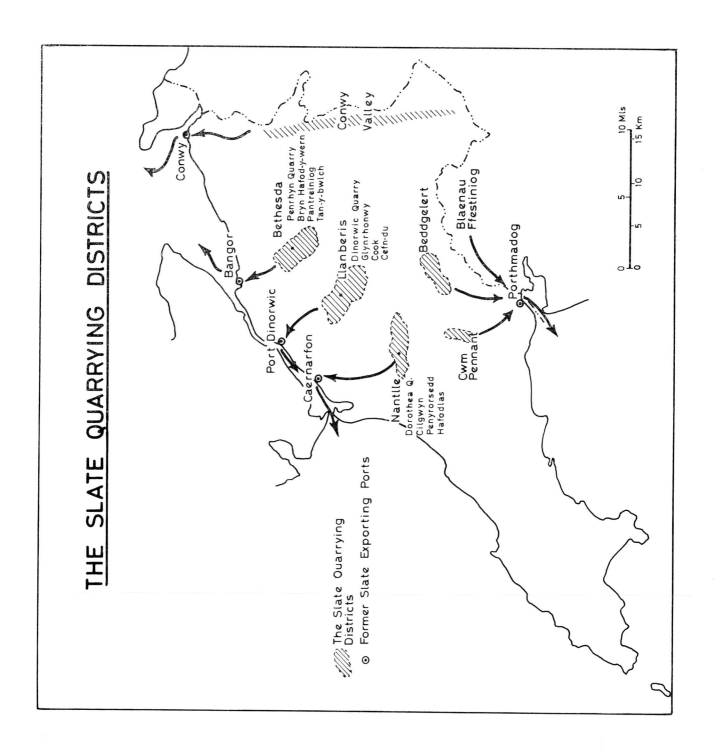

Conwy

Conwy Valley

Bethesda
Penrhyn Quarry
Bryn Hafod-y-wern
Pantreiniog
Tan-y-bwlch

Bangor

Port Dinorwic

Llanberis
Dinorwic Quarry
Glynrhonwy
Cook
Cefn-du

Beddgelert

Blaenau
Ffestiniog

Porthmadog

Caernarfon

Nantlle
Dorothea Q.
Cilgwyn
Penyorsedd
Hafodlas

Cwm
Pennant

The Slate Quarrying
Districts

⊙ Former Slate Exporting Ports

10 Mls
15 Km

The Slate Industry

Slate quarrying was the dominant industry in this county throughout the nineteenth century, and continued to be so up to the Second World War. Sporadic quarrying had existed for many centuries, but most quarries had been small, shallow excavations worked by local farmer-quarrymen, primarily for their own needs and for any local demand. Indeed, wherever metamorphosed Cambrian rocks with a characteristic cleavage outcropped within the county, slate had been extracted.

Although the industry began to develop as an organised concern in the second half of the eighteenth century, the main era of expansion came in the next century from about 1832 to 1882. During these years, the industry developed with considerable speed, but, sadly, declined at a surprising rate towards the end of the century. The map indicates a concentration of the industry in and around Bethesda, Llanberis, Betws Garmon, Nantlle, Cwm Pennant, Beddgelert and the Conwy valley. Of these, the three great centres were Bethesda, Llanberis and Nantlle.

The commercial development of the industry owed a great deal to pioneers such as Lord Penrhyn (1737 - 1808). In 1782, he not only took charge of the numerous small quarries in the Bethesda district but in 1790 he also constructed a small quay at the mouth of the Cegin near Bangor. A roadway was made to link the quay with his quarries, but with further development, Port Penrhyn was constructed in 1801, and a tramway was laid down between port and quarry which greatly facilitated the export of slate. The merging of several small workings into one large productive unit, together with improved transport, led to a considerable increase in the output of slates from less than 2,000 tons in 1782 to 24,418 tons in 1819, to 40,200 tons in 1829, to 73,700 tons in 1836 and to a record output of 130,017 tons in 1862. In that year, 3,285 men were employed at the quarry.

On the western slopes of the Elidir range above Llyn Peris, the equally famous Dinorwic Quarry developed in 1787 from a number of old excavations under the control of a business partnership with a lease of twenty-one years. On the expiry of this lease in 1809, a new partnership was formed which included the landowner — Assheton Smith. The remoteness and inaccessibility of the district handicapped the development of this quarry, too, in its initial stages, but in 1824 a horse-tramway was constructed from the quarries to Port Dinorwig, and greatly helped the export of slate. In 1826, the quarry produced 20,000 tons, but by the 1860s the output exceeded 100,000 tons a year.

In the Nantlle district, such well-known quarries as the Dorothea, Cilgwyn and Pen-y-bryn developed, but here the growth was somewhat slower, largely on account of the lack of capital and the high transport costs. However, matters improved with the opening of a railway track between the quarries and Caernarfon quay in 1828, but many of the smaller quarrying units of the district did not really expand until the 1860s.

The many smaller quarries in the Cwm Pennant, Cwm Ystradllyn and Beddgelert area were linked with the harbour at Porthmadog in 1863, which also dealt with slates from the Croesor and Blaenau Ffestiniog quarries (outside the county). Slates from small, scattered quarries in the Conwy valley were exported through Conwy harbour. Each little port was the scene of considerable bustle during these years.

In developing their quarries, these pioneers were responsible for the improvement of communications within the county. In the initial stages, slates were labouriously carried in panniers by horses until the coming of broad-wheeled carts. These were followed by horse-drawn wagons on narrow-gauge tramways until such time as steam locomotives were introduced. Slate from each district was exported by sea to all parts of Britain, to the countries of Western Europe and across the Atlantic to North America. Later, these rail tracks joined the main railway line which took the slates to all parts of Britain and to the larger ports of England. Later, the motor-lorry took the slates from quarry head to the building site.

The demand for slates both at home and abroad was enormous during the mid-decades of the last century; the large industrial towns and ports of British grew at an alarming rate, and the need for roofing slates was enormous. Slates were in demand for a multiplicity of other uses, from head-stones and monumental work to billiard tables and school slates. In these years there was no serious competition from clay tiles and other roofing materials, and foreign competition in supplying slate did not appear until 1895.

As more and more men were employed, labour was attracted to the slate districts and led to the rapid growth of the slate villages, many significantly with such Biblical names as Bethesda, Bethel, Ebenezer, Nazareth or Cesarea. In a few of the quarries, some of the men lived in what were known as the 'barracks' during the week, and only went home at weekends. Most of the labour was fairly local in origin, mainly from the agricultural parishes of Caernarvonshire and Anglesey, which meant that the industry remained singularly Welsh in character.

In spite of the harsh climatic conditions in these wide-open quarries, the arduous nature of the work at the rock face, the unhealthy conditions in the slate-dressing sheds, the large number of accidents — many of them fatal — the low wages, the spartan standards of living and the denominational rivalry, the communal life of these villages was flourishing and spirited. Few communities in Wales equalled the range or quality of the cultural interests of such a close-knit society.

Since the end of the last century, however, there has been a drastic contraction in the industry. The export trade reached its highest point in 1889 when 80,000 tons of slate were shipped from Caernarvonshire. Between 1897 and 1937, the number of operating quarries in the county fell from 45 to

14. The causes of the decline were many and varied. The declining home market, the loss of so many foreign markets, the importation of foreign slate, prolonged industrial disputes, increasing competition from other roofing materials, internecine price-cutting, the inability to mechanize the industry, the improved educational facilities which led to more remunerative posts elsewhere, the coming of public transport and the motor-car, which led to a greater mobility of labour, all contributed to the decline of the industry.

During the Second World War, the number of quarrymen employed in Snowdonia fell from 5,581 in 1937 to 2,955 in 1946. In the latter year, the Penrhyn and Dinorwic Quarries employed more men and produced more slate than all other quarries put together. The Penrhyn quarry in that year employed 1,065 men and produced 20,745 tons of slate, whilst the Dinorwic quarry employed 1,360 men and produced 30,975 tons. After years of chequered fortunes, the Dinorwic quarries closed down in 1969, the Dorothea quarries in 1970, and the last of the Blaenau Ffestiniog quarries in 1971. The Penrhyn quarry, employing no more than 300 men, is the only quarry of any size still functioning in the district.

The industry has all but disappeared, but the unsightly mounds of quarry waste still rear their ugly heads; the hewn terraces of former quarries still scar the hillsides; the villages are now dormitory settlements with their people employed elsewhere; some of the narrow-gauge railways have been adapted for tourism, and the slate ports are now the haunts of fishing and pleasure craft. The bustle of yester-year is no more.

BIBLIOGRAPHY

Dodd, A. H., *The Industrial Revolution in North Wales,* University of Wales Press, 1951.

Dodd, A. H., *A History of Caernarvonshire,* 1282 - 1900 (Caernarvonshire Historical Society, 1968).

North, F. J., *The Slates of Wales* (Natural Museum of Wales), Cardiff, 1925.

Parry, W. J., *Chwareli a Chwarelwyr,* Caernarfon, 1897.

Carr, H. R. C. and Lister, G. A., *The Industrial Activities of Snowdonia,* Chap. 12, by D. Dylan Pritchard in *Mountains of Snowdonia,* Crosby Lockwood, 1948.

Pritchard, D. Dylan, *The Slate Industry of North Wales: a study of changes in economic organisation from 1780 to the present day* (Unpublished M.A. thesis, University of Wales, 1935).

Ellis, Gweirydd, *A History of the slate quarryman in Caernarvonshire in the nineteenth century* (Unpublished M.A. thesis, University of Wales, 1931).

Richards, W. M. A., *A General Survey of the Slate Industry of Caernarvonshire and Merionethshire* (Unpublished M.A. thesis, Liverpool, 1933).

Griffith, J., *Chwarelau Dyffryn Nantlle a Chymdogaeth Moel Tryfan* (Conway, 1934).

Lindsay, J., *A History of the North Wales Slate Industry,* London, 1974.

Davies, D. C., *Slate and Slate Quarrying,* London, 1878.

Richards, W. M., ' Some Aspects of the Industrial Revolution in South-East Caernarvonshire ', *Trans. Caerns. Hist. Soc.,* 1944.

Erratum — Page 162 — Fourth Paragraph, Line 12 — *delete* " and the last of the Blaenau Ffestiniog Quarries closed in 1971 ".

Quarrymen on the rock face

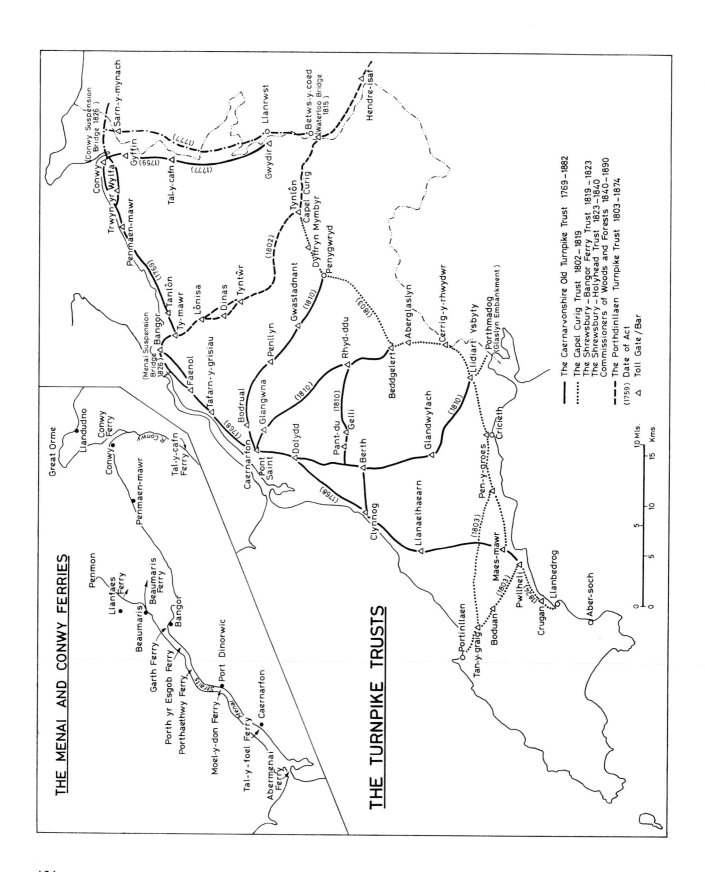

THE MENAI AND CONWY FERRIES

Great Orme

Llandudno

Conwy Ferry

Penmaen-mawr

Tal-y-cafn Ferry

Penmon

Llanfaes Ferry

Beaumaris Ferry

Beaumaris

Bangor

Garth Ferry

Porth yr Esgob Ferry

Porthaethwy Ferry

Port Dinorwic

Moel-y-don Ferry

Tal-y-foel Ferry

Abermenai Ferry

Caernarfon

R. Conwy

Menai Straits

THE TURNPIKE TRUSTS

The Caernarvonshire Old Turnpike Trust 1769–1882

The Capel Curig Trust 1802–1819

The Shrewsbury – Bangor Ferry Trust 1819–1823

The Shrewsbury – Holyhead Trust 1823–1840
Commissioners of Woods and Forests 1840–1890

The Porthdinllaen Turnpike Trust 1803–1874

(1759) Date of Act

△ Toll Gate / Bar

10 Mls.

15 Kms.

Communications: Roads

The first real roads in the county were constructed by the Romans, and thereafter no serious attention was given to road construction until the middle of the eighteenth century. Man, in the meantime, on foot or on horseback, moved along trackways and bridlepaths. Apart from traversing inhospitable moorlands and difficult upland areas, the crossing of such wide rivers as the Conwy or Glaslyn was also most hazardous. The crossing of the Menai Strait into Anglesey was an even greater hazard — particularly to the travellers en route from London to Holyhead and Dublin.

For centuries before the coming of bridges, regular ferries functioned at selected crossing points over the Conwy and the Strait. Passengers, goods, coaches and horses were precariously transported across the waters, and at times so were cattle, sheep and pigs. With the construction of bridges during the nineteenth century, to the great relief of harassed travellers, most of the ferries ceased to function altogether as in the case of Conwy (1826), Porthaethwy (1826), Beaumaris (1830), Abermenai (1840s), Porth-yr-Esgob (1852) and Tal-y-cafn (1897). A very colourful chapter in the history of communications was thus brought to a close. Other ferries lingered into the present century, but with the coming of the motor car they, too, ceased to function, as in the case of Tal-y-Foel (1929), Moel-y-Don (1935) and the Garth ferries from 1938 onwards.

Some of the earliest regular travellers to cross the country were the ' post boys ' who carried the mail from London to Dublin via Holyhead, and this crossing of the county to and from Ireland became one of the most important factors in the development of communications in the area. The postal service, which began in 1561, became a regular routine from 1599 onwards, but the county even in 1595 is described as ' the most rugged, impassable, barren county in Wales '. These ' post boys ', with a fresh horse every twenty miles, covered about a hundred miles a day, and followed a route from Chester through Denbigh to Conwy, and from near Penmaen-mawr or Aber faced the hazards of the Lafan Sands in crossing to Beaumaris. In 1623, the postmaster at Beaumaris requested that posts be placed across the Lafan

Sands ' to help when sudden mists and fogs do fall, for the danger is very great and ye kinges packets and subjects are likely to perish.' As late as 1750, the trackways in the mountainous areas of the county were so poor that sledges without wheels had to be used to carry peat, minerals and slates.

During the eighteenth century, however, people of diverse interests — local landlords, quarry owners, hotel proprietors, the owners of the Dublin Packet and, most important of all, the Turnpike Trusts — became directly interested in and concerned with the state of the roads of North Wales. More serious attention was then given to road building and maintenance than was ever given by the parishes.

The first Turnpike Trust in the county, formed in 1759, was to manage the road from Tal-y-cafn along the western side of the valley as far as Conwy town. A few years later, in 1777, a road was turn-piked from Shrewsbury to Llanrwst on the Denbighshire side of the river Conwy to join the turnpike road between St. Asaph and Conwy at a place called Sarn-y-mynach.

Of even greater importance to the county was the formation of the Old Turnpike Trust in 1769, which was given power to maintain the road from Tal-y-cafn through Conwy, Penmaen-mawr, Bangor and Caernarfon to Pwllheli. This, for the first time, opened up the remoter regions of Llŷn ' to itinerant trade, and so roused the long-dormant spirit of local amelioration '. Many difficulties, such as constructing a road over Penmaen-mawr, caused much concern, but a grant of £2,000 was secured from Parliament to complete this task. It was the first serious attempt to open up a coastal routeway since Roman times, and soon there was evidence that wheeled vehicles were making use of this route. Travellers to Ireland could then come from Chester or Shrewsbury to Conwy, and along the coast road to Bangor before crossing the Strait.

The upland country of the interior was still difficult to penetrate, and Thomas Pennant, late in the eighteenth century, referred to Nant Ffrancon as ' the most dreadful horse-path in Wales, worked in the rudest manner with steps for a great length.' Lord Penrhyn, in 1792, was the first to open up

Nant Ffrancon. He constructed a road along the western side of the valley to Lake Ogwen and continued with it as far as Capel Curig, and there built the Royal Hotel. It was a good enough road for wheeled vehicles, but was still not a through-road as it did not go any further than Capel Curig.

The Capel Curig Trust, formed in 1802, was bent on improving lines of communication from the coast through the hill country of the interior. A road which started at Llandygái was constructed along the eastern side of Nant Ffrancon and went on to Pentrefoelas. This was the first through road to penetrate the mountains, and four tollgates were placed on it. During ensuing years it was extended from Capel Curig, along the Penygwryd Pass, northwards to Llanberis and Caernarfon. The coastal route from Conwy (now the A55) and the Shrewsbury route via Capel Curig and Nant Ffrancon (now the A5) became the most important in the county.

The Portin-llaen Turnpike Trust, formed in 1803, was committed to the opening of roads in Llŷn and Eifionydd. This comprehensive Act secured a network of cross-country roads which was completed during the next six years or so between Portin-llaen, Pwllheli, Llanystumdwy and Cricieth, with links with Merioneth on the one hand and with Beddgelert, Nant Gwynant and Capel Curig on the other.

In 1811, William Alexander Madocks completed the embankment across the estuary of the Glaslyn, which improved the link between the southern reaches of the county and Merioneth. At the time, a sector of the community hoped that Portin-llaen would become a packet port for Ireland and that a roadway would be developed from mid-Wales, crossing the Glaslyn and on to Portin-llaen. So by the third decade of the nineteenth century, a fair network of roads had been established throughout the county, and whilst the condition of some of them left much to be desired, most villages and towns had been made reasonably accessible.

Wheeled vehicles appeared in the county from the middle of the eighteenth century, and apart from contending with indifferent roads, they had to face the hazardous ferries across the Conwy and the Strait. Nevertheless, in 1776 the landlord of the White Lion in Chester began to carry passengers every weekday to Holyhead by a 'flying post chaise' for two guineas. The landlord of the Raven & Bell, Shrewsbury, not to be outdone, followed immediately with a similar service via Wrexham, Mold and St. Asaph to Conwy. Great rivalry prevailed between the Chester and Shrewsbury routes for the next century or so. However, following these developments, the postal authorities in 1785 began a coach service with the mails from Chester, Conwy and Bangor to Holyhead. The stage-coach era was thus well and truly established in the district, and this particular service on the Chester-Holyhead route continued until 1808.

With improvements in the Shrewsbury route, which was shorter, the mail coach was transferred to that route via Llangollen, Pentrefoelas, Capel Curig and Bangor in 1808. The road was further improved in ensuing years, and the opening of the Menai Suspension Bridge in 1826 greatly facilitated the traffic on this route. In 1784, it had taken the stage coach 48 hours on the journey from London to Holyhead, but by 1836 it took only 36 hours. This was the hey-day of the stage coach — roads had improved, bridges had been built, roadways were better maintained and the well-known coaching inns on these routes catered for the needs of coachmen and passengers. Not all people approved of the charges made by the Turnpike Trusts at their tollgates, and there were reports of the destruction of gates, and of Rebecca-type disturbances in the county during the 1840s.

After the coming of the main railway line to the county in 1848, the golden era of the stage-coach declined, except in areas not served by railways. Although most of the Turnpike Trusts expired in the 1860s and 1870s, some continued to exist into the 1880s. Ultimately, the care of the roads passed into the hands of the new County Council. Naturally, horse-drawn vehicles continued on all highways until the coming of the motor-car in the third decade of this century.

BIBLIOGRAPHY

Dodd, A. H., The Industrial Revolution in North Wales, University of Wales Press, 1951.

Dodd, A. H., A History of Caernarvonshire, 1284 - 1900, Caernarvonshire Historical Society, 1968.

Davies, H. R., The Conway and the Menai Ferries, University of Wales Press, 1966.

Harper, C. G., The Holyhead Road, Vol. 2, 1902.

Dodd, A. H., The Roads of North Wales, 1750 - 1850, Arch. Cambs., 1925.

Pritchard, R. T., 'The Post Road in Caernarvonshire', Trans. Caerns. Hist. Soc., 1952.

Pritchard, R. T., 'Caernarvonshire Turnpike Trust', Trans. Caerns. Hist. Soc., 1956.

Vale, Edmund, The Mail Coach Men. London, 1960.

A Coach   *Gwynedd Archives*

Tollgate, Dinas (Tre-garth)   *Gwynedd Archives*

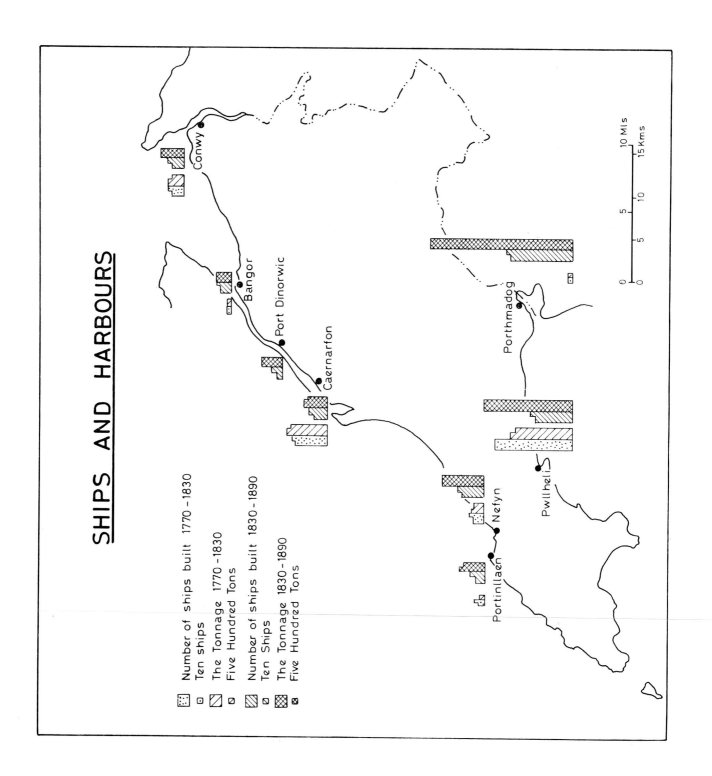

SHIPS AND HARBOURS

Number of ships built 1770 - 1830
☐ Ten ships

The Tonnage 1770 - 1830
◪ Five Hundred Tons

Number of ships built 1830 - 1890
◪ Ten Ships

The Tonnage 1830 - 1890
⬚ Five Hundred Tons

Conwy

Bangor

Port Dinorwic

Caernarfon

Porthmadog

Pwllheli

Nefyn

Portinllaen

10 Mls
15 Kms

Ships and Harbours

When a survey was made in the days of Henry VIII of all the havens, creeks and roads where 'any shippe . . . or any other vessel may enter or land' in the County of Caernarvonshire, twenty-three places were identified from 'Aber Kerrik Gwynion in Cruthyn' to the 'haven of pullele'. For centuries, as indicated in the preceding essays, men of different nationalities had landed on the shores of Caernarvonshire, some to settle, some to ravage, raid and destroy. The vessels of the Welsh princes had sailed from the Menai Strait for Ireland, the great Edwardian castles at Conwy and Caernarfon had been built in strategic positions with sea power as a prime consideration; foreign vessels had made brief visits, bringing wine and corn, but apart from fishing boats, there is scant evidence of local shipping until the sixteenth century.

The Elizabeth Port Books provide information regarding the cargoes imported and exported, mainly in foreign vessels, and it is evident that slate, butter and cheese were all exported from the local ports as well as occasional heavy catches of herring from Nefyn and Pwllheli. The sixteenth and early seventeenth centuries saw pirates of many nationalities making frequent visits to the coasts of Caernarvonshire, particularly to Bardsey and St. Tudwal's Roads. As in the case of other off-shore islands, such as Lundy and the Isle of Man, the pirates found Bardsey a convenient base from which to operate and distribute their pirated goods; the lonely beaches of South Caernarvonshire were convenient for landing unhindered by large naval ships which did not wish to be embayed, cast away on Sarn Badrig or caught in the steep, unpleasant seas off Porth Neigwl.

The proximity of the county to Ireland brought naval ships to these waters in the Civil War and during the troubled years of the Commonwealth and the later Stuarts. The new-found confidence in naval protection from pirates and enemies, the growth of the great port of Liverpool which coincided with the development of the Caernarvonshire slate and the Anglesey copper industries, all led to prolific shipbuilding on open beaches, in fields and sheltered coves, as well as small ports from the Mawddach to the Conwy estuaries. These vessels,

built in the late eighteenth and early nineteenth centuries, were for the most part small sloops and brigs: the table indicates the approximate number of vessels built, together with their tonnage, in the years 1770 - 1830 and 1830 - 1890.

	1770 - 1830		1830 - 1890	
	No. of Vessels	Tonnage	No. of Vessels	Tonnage
Conwy	51	2,677	56	4,056
Bangor	17	904	47	3,213
Port Dinorwic	—	—	29	4,122
Caernarfon	130	7,802	73	4,873
Nefyn	46	2,183	86	7,977
Portin-llaen	13	567	45	4,403
Pwllheli	300	13,415	146	17,080
Porthmadog and Borth-y-gest	8	446	245	26,992

A number of small vessels were also built at Trefriw, Llanaelhaearn, Porth Colmon, Aberdaron, Rhiw, Aber-soch, Llanbedrog, Cricieth, Towyn and Traeth Mawr; the late David Thomas estimated that, in all, 463 vessels were built in the Pwllheli area, amounting to a tonnage of 31,415 tons, and 303 in the Porthmadog area, amounting to 30,483 tons. Pwllheli built far more ships in the early years, the vast majority of them small sloops, and a number of brigs and barques in mid-century.

The larger vessels were obviously intended for the oceanic trades, but the cheapness and adaptability of large North American vessels, particularly those built in Prince Edward Island, New Brunswick and Nova Scotia, attracted many ship-owners from Gwynedd who saw their potential in the rapidly developing emigrant trades. In the late 1840s, when thousands of Caernarvonshire and Anglesey emigrants sailed from the Menai Strait for North America, they were packed in among the slate cargoes in vessels like the *Swallow, Hindoo* and the *Higginson,* owned by Humphrey Owen, a Caernarfon shipowner, and the *Chieftain, Northumberland, Tamarac, Peltonia, Oregon* and others of the rapidly expanding fleet owned by the Davies brothers of Menai Bridge. These wooden ships and barques brought cargoes of timber from Quebec to the Menai Strait; timber was much in demand by quarries, shipbuilders and the rapidly developing seaside resorts. Balks of timber were towed by small steamers to the beach at Llandudno for the building of the houses on the new promenade. The masters (and most of the crews in the early years) of the North American vessels were local men. Some of them achieved a considerable reputation; one example must suffice. Captain William Williams of Rhiw in Llŷn, who had served in Porthmadog ships in the 1840s, commanded the emigrant vessels of the Davies brothers in the 1850s and later himself owned the American clipper ships *Donald Mackay* and the *Light Brigade.*

The temporary boom in sailing-ship building in 1875 coincided with a prosperous period for the Caernarvonshire slate quarries. Their new-found affluence inspired quarrymen, shopkeepers, inn-keepers, ministers of religion and school teachers to try to emulate the most successful shipowners by forming companies such as the *Arvon, Gwynedd* and *North Wales Shipping* companies which bought a number of iron sister-ships built on Merseyside or North-east England, vessels like the *Moel Eilian, Moel Tryfan, Glanperis, Glandinorwig* and *Gwynedd,* destined for the Cape Horn and Far East trades. W. E. Jones, a Port Dinorwic shipbuilder, who designed the models for several of the vessels built at Sunderland and Liverpool for Welsh owners, played a major role in forming these companies, and himself built the *Ordovic* in 1877, the largest wooden barque built in Caernarvonshire. Other successful shipowners included Robert Thomas of Cricieth, a former schoolmaster at Nefyn: Hugh Roberts, who moved from Edern to Newcastle to form a thriving steamship company; the Williams Pwll Parc family and Captain Thomas Williams of Cricieth, owner of the *Cambrian* ships. It was widely believed that the large iron ships would rapidly bring higher profits than the locally built wooden ships in which the community had traditionally invested. This heavy involvement in 'foreign' ships and the recession in both the slate quarrying and shipping industries in the late 1870s led to a cessation of local shipbuilding. The last vessels were built at Pwllheli in 1878, Bangor in 1879, Nefyn in 1880, and Caernarfon in 1884. The exception was Porthmadog.

The demand for slate for Hamburg and the Baltic ports, and subsequently the well-developed trade of Porthmadog schooners which sailed regularly on annual voyages to Hamburg with slate, general cargo to Cadiz, salt from Cadiz to Newfoundland and Labrador, thence to the Mediterranean or Brazil with salt fish, and home with general cargoes, provided Porthmadog shipbuilders with the opportunity to develop the very beautiful schooners, which have been described as 'the ultimate development of the small wooden merchant sailing ship in Britain'. Contemporaries called them the 'Western Ocean Yachts'. These vessels brought together the accumulated experience of ship-builders in North Wales and in the wide range of ports in Europe and North America visited by Porthmadog seamen during the preceding seventy or more years. From 1895 to 1913, David Jones and David Williams completed approximately one vessel a year in their busy yards in Porthmadog; their own considerable rivalry, and that of groups of mariners and tradesmen who invested in their ships, and the masters who sailed them, added much to the achievements of Porthmadog during these years.

Shipbuilding continued in Porthmadog until the outbreak of the 1914 War, which brought an end to the German slate trade, and led to the sinking of many fine Porthmadog vessels. The railways had already made deep inroads into the county's seaborne trade and soon even the little steamers like the *Rebecca,* the *Prince Ja-Ja, Telephone* and *Dora* no longer plied between Liverpool and the small Caernarvonshire ports. The seamen had long since moved easily from the coastal trade to serve in the large Liverpool and London based full-rigged ships, four-masted barques and, of course, steamships.

The decline of the slate industry inevitably saw the once thriving ports with their busy wharves and shipyards fall into decay, and the maritime communities dwindle. Yachtsmen and tourists, however welcome for their contribution to the county's economy, now inhabit harbours whose greatest days, albeit harsh and costly in so many ways, are long since over.

BIBLIOGRAPHY

Thomas, David, *Hen Longau Sir Gaernarfon,* 1952.

Hughes, H., *Immortal Sails,* 1946.

Davies, H. R., *Menai and Conway Ferries,* 1942.

Eames, Aled, *Llongau a Llongwyr Gwynedd,* 1976.

Eames, Aled and Hughes, Emrys, *Porthmadog Ships,* 1975.

Unloading on Aber-erch beach

Shipbuilding at Porthmadog

RAILWAYS PAST AND PRESENT

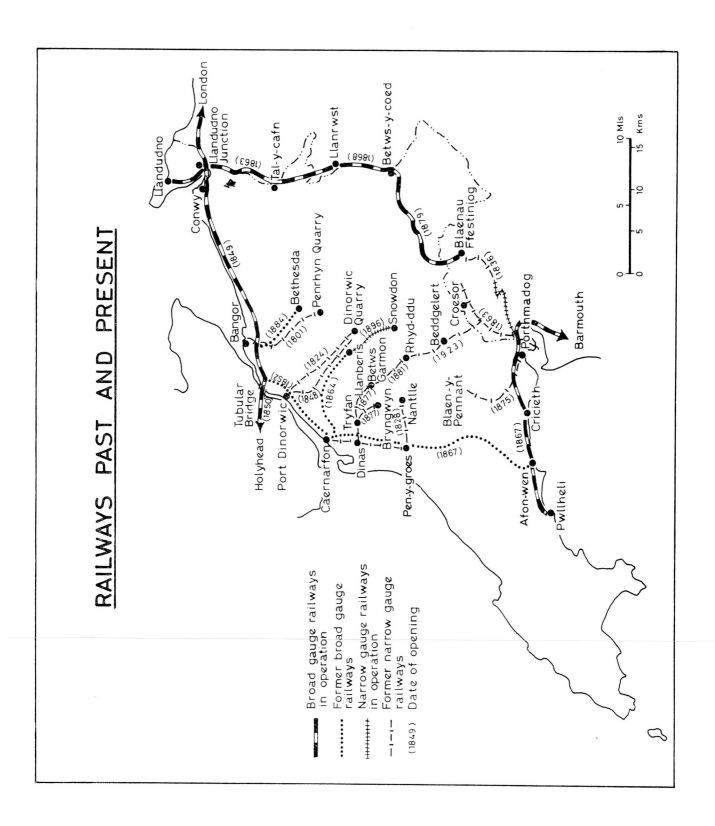

Broad gauge railways in operation

Former broad gauge railways

Narrow gauge railways in operation

Former narrow gauge railways

(1849) Date of opening

Communications: Railways

Whilst road development grew apace during the early years of the nineteenth century, several narrow-gauge railways were also constructed within the county at the same time. These were of particular significance in the opening up of Snowdonia, for, in turn, a narrow-gauge railway linked each of the slate quarrying districts with a nearby port. These not only facilitated the development of the slate trade, but also linked the whole interior with the coast.

From the Penrhyn quarry, Bethesda, a narrow-gauge track of six and a half miles was constructed to Port Penrhyn, Bangor, in 1801. Of course, it was horse-drawn wagons that plied between the quarry and the port until the coming of steam locomotives in the 1840s. A new narrow-gauge railway replaced the older one in 1874. The Dinorwic quarry, Llanberis, was linked with the harbour at Port Dinorwic by a track of seven miles in 1824. Here, too, the wagons were horse-drawn at first, but in 1843 the route was re-aligned with the construction of the Padarn railway, and in 1848 two steam engines — the *Fire Queen* and the *Jenny Lind* — were brought into commission. As from 1828, the quarries of the Nantlle valley were served by a narrow-gauge track to the port at Caernarfon. It greatly stimulated the export trade, and, as elsewhere, steam locomotion was adopted in 1848.

The quarries at Blaenau Ffestiniog, although outside the confines of the county, came to export the bulk of their slates through Porthmadog during the mid-nineteenth century. When the embankment across the Glaslyn was completed in 1811, a narrow-gauge track was laid down, but the railway between Porthmadog and Blaenau Ffestiniog was not completed until 1836. It was interesting to note that on the way down from the quarries, the wagons ran by gravity all the way from Blaenau to the embankment. On the down-run the horses travelled at the end of the train in special horse-boxes, and usually spent their time feeding. On the ten-mile return journey, the horses had to pull the empty wagons up to the quarries. Locomotive traction was introduced in 1863, and the line was opened for passenger traffic in 1865.

To the west and south-west of Snowdonia, several other sections of narrow-gauge railways were constructed during the second half of the nineteenth century. In 1863, a line joined the quarries of the Cwm Ystradllyn area with Porthmadog, and in the same year a line linked the Croesor quarries with the same port.

It was in the 1870s that short sections of the line were constructed from the village of Dinas, south of Caernarfon, to Bryn Gwyn and Llyn Cwellyn and on to Rhyd-ddu. As late as 1923, however, this line was extended southwards to Beddgelert and thence to join the Croesor-Porthmadog line. The through route of some 21 miles was given the grand title of the Welsh Highland Railway. Unfortunately, though, it only functioned for 14 years. Although constructed chiefly for the transport of goods, sections were also used for passenger transport. With the passing of time, all these narrow-gauge lines were linked not only to the little ports but to the main railway lines as well, and this enabled such commodities as slate to be transported to all parts of Britain by rail. Such a development seriously undermined the importance of coastal shipping.

The most remarkable narrow-gauge railway within the county, of course, is the Snowdon Mountain Railway of the rack and pinion type, built in 1896 solely as a scenic route for the tourist trade. Another short section of mountain railway was built on the Great Orme in 1902 for similar purposes. Today, sections of the Ffestiniog and the Llanberis narrow-gauge lines are used to serve the needs of tourists.

With the coming of the main railway lines in the 1830s and 1840s, considerable discussion ensued over the alignment of the railway route from London to Holyhead. Some advocated a route through mid-Wales via Dolgellau and Porthmadog to Portin-llaen, with the idea of making Portin-llaen the packet station for Dublin. Some even advocated the development of Llandudno for this purpose, but the supporters of Holyhead were eventually triumphant. The main railway line from Chester reached Bangor in 1848 — before the Tubular Bridge over the Strait had been completed. Difficult problems such as the building of tubular bridges across the Conwy (1848), and afterwards the Strait (1850) were solved by Robert Stephenson. Similarly, the tunnelling of the high cliffs at Penmaen-mawr and on either side of Bangor proved to be costly undertakings. It was, however, a most significant development, and the opening of the main line heralded a new era. Many of the functions of the stage-coach were immediately usurped. In turn, many of the hazards and much of the colour associated with the Royal Mail and the coaching days disappeared for ever. For over sixty years the stage-coaches had given valiant service, but with fast trains, however, goods could also be dispatched with speed and facility on the main lines to all parts of the country. Travellers and holidaymakers descended upon North Wales in vast numbers; tourism and the seaside resorts grew apace.

Link-lines were added in every direction. The line was extended to Caernarfon in 1852, and continued as far as Afon Wen in 1867. In that year, too, the Cambrian Coast Railway reached Porthmadog, Cricieth, Afon-wen and Pwllheli. Other inland towns were, in turn, connected with this coastal route, as in the case of Llanberis (1862), Betws-y-coed (1868) (with an extension later to Blaenau Ffestiniog in 1879), Nantlle (1872), and Bethesda (1884). The whole county was opened up as never before, but, alas, these railways slowly but surely usurped the functions of the little ships and ports. For a century (and up to the Second World War) the railways played a significant role in the life of the community, but with the coming of the buses, motor car and motor lorry during the inter-war period, the importance of the railways, in turn, suffered a sharp decline. Road transport of all kinds dominates today. Apart from the main London-Holyhead line, the only branch lines now remaining are those from Llandudno Junction to Betws-y-coed, and the section of the Cambrian Coast Railway from Pwllheli into Merioneth.

The modes of transport, and the lines of communication have changed greatly over the last two centuries. One mode of transport displaced another, and the speed of all means of communication has increased appreciably during the last half century.

BIBLIOGRAPHY

Dodd, A. H., *The Industrial Revolution in North Wales*, University of Wales Press, 1951.

Dodd, A. H., *A History of Caernarvonshire, 1284 - 1900*, Caernarvonshire Historical Society, 1968.

Lee, Charles E., *Narrow-gauge Railways in Wales*, 1945.

Boyd, J. I. C., *Narrow-gauge Railways in South Caernarvonshire* (Lingfield, 1972).

Lee, Charles E., *The Penrhyn Railway* (Welsh Highland Light Railway Ltd., 1972).

Lee, Charles E., *The Welsh Highland Railway* (The Welsh Highland Railway Society and David and Charles, 1962).

Davies, H. R., *The Conway and Menai Ferries*, Cardiff, 1966.

Dempsey, G. Drysdale, *Tubular Bridges*, London, 1864.

Baughan, P. E., *The Chester and Holyhead Railway*, Vol. 1, Newton Abbot, 1972.

Morris, O. J., *The Snowdon Mountain Railway*, London.

Clark, Edwin, *The Britannia and Conway Tubular Bridges*, London, 1850.

Dunn, John Maxwell, *The Chester and Holyhead Railway*, South Godstone, 1948.

Gibb, A., *The Story of Telford*, London, 1935.

The first train in the new Pwllheli Station, 1909

Sunday School Outing (about 1929)

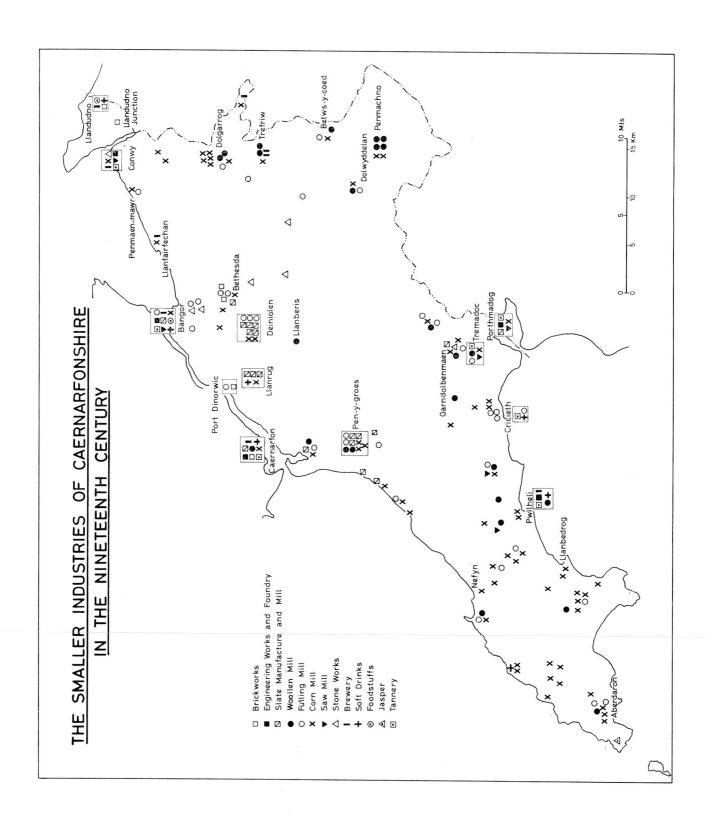

THE SMALLER INDUSTRIES OF CAERNARFONSHIRE
IN THE NINETEENTH CENTURY

Llandudno
Llandudno Junction
Conwy
Penmaen-mawr
Llanfairfechan
Bangor
Port Dinorwic
Caernarfon
Dolgarrog
Trefriw
Bethesda
Deiniolen
Llanberis
Llanrug
Pen-y-groes
Betws-y-coed
Dolwyddelan
Penmachno
Garndolbenmaen
Tremadoc
Porthmadog
Criccieth
Pwllheli
Llanbedrog
Nefyn
Aberdaron

Brickworks
Engineering Works and Foundry
Slate Manufacture and Mill
Woollen Mill
Fulling Mill
Corn Mill
Saw Mill
Stone Works
Brewery
Soft Drinks
Foodstuffs
Jasper
Tannery

10 Mls
15 Km
10
5
5
0
0

The Smaller Industries in the XIXth Century

The county's economy depended on many small industries which, in the pre-railway era, contributed essential goods and services to a relatively isolated and largely self-sufficient economy: with some exceptions, these relatively small units catered exclusively for local markets and many had close links with agriculture. Hyde Hall, in 1811, compiled an extensive parish by parish list of the county's many corn and fulling mills — the majority being family concerns, employing a few workers and using the fast-flowing streams and rivers of the county to turn their relatively unsophisticated machinery. The fulling mills, depending on wool which had been, in the main, manually processed — carded, spun, woven and dyed by domestic producers — flourished in the early decades up to mid-century, by which time they had been replaced by more comprehensive and, therefore, fewer factory based units. Their end product, homespun (y brethyn cartref), was marketed locally, as was the flour ground by the corn mills.

Hyde Hall also noted the existence of small hone-stone quarries in the county, particularly in the Dyffryn Ogwen area, at Blaen-y-nant, Nant-y-benglog and, possibly, at Marchlyn and Pant-y-darren on the slopes of Carnedd Llywelyn. The quarried stone was shaped and polished from 1801 - 1829 at Felin-isa, Llandygái, then owned by Samuel Worthington. About mid century a mill was set up for the same purpose near the quarry itself at Nant-y-benglog. Meanwhile, Worthington was also operating in 1800 a powerful mill at Llandygái for grinding imported flint and soapstones into powder which was sent to the Herculaneum delft potteries at Toxteth Park, Liverpool, in which he had an interest. At Conwy, too, the quarrying and preparation of millstones had developed by 1840 into an extensive undertaking. Paper was also being produced locally in this period by water-driven mills on the Saint at Pont-rug and at Pont-porth-lwyd in the Conwy valley. Breweries and canneries were also established in several market towns, producing entirely for local consumption. The oak bark used in the tanning process was partly collected in the county and partly imported from Merioneth, providing work for many on the poverty line. This reminds us of the indigent poor who scraped an existence during the early years of the century burning kelp and fern for use in the soap and glass making centres of England, of the lichen painfully scraped for a penny a pound for dye-making, and of the mussel-pearl collectors of Conwy who sold them to a middleman at 1s. 6d. - 3s. an ounce in the thirties.

However, these small early industries began to decline as the railway era brought external competition. Yet this was a gradual process because the relatively remote geographical location of the county enabled the more efficient of those industries to continue as viable units for a longer period. Indeed, as late as the eighties a moderate expansion occurred in brewing and tanning, while surviving corn mills, such as the complex owned by the Lewis family of Belmont and Caederwen, Bangor, were flourishing concerns in the late Victorian period. Railway development moreover, in boosting tourism, impelling the growth of commerce in the boroughs and in stimulating major industrial expansion by cheapening, for example, the internal transport costs of the slate industry, resulted in the emergence of new small-scale industries.

In the expanding tourist resorts, the manufacturing of soft drinks and foodstuffs was undertaken. At Llandudno, in 1886, Thomas Williams was in business as a manufacturer of the 'Celebrated Llandudno Sauce', and another company produced and bottled pickles under the appealing brand name of 'The Orme's Head Samphire'. Three breweries and two soda-water manufacturers quenched the thirst of Llandudno holidaymakers, while similar establishments prospered in other developing resorts, such as Pwllheli, Cricieth and Llanfairfechan and in the important commercial and railway stops of Caernarfon and Bangor. Caernarfon, too, had a single tobacco manufacturer in 1889.

Large-scale hotel and housing developments in expanding tourist and commercial centres and quarrying areas stimulated the establishment of eight brickworks. There were three in Caernarfon, two at Bethesda and one each at Conwy, Llandudno

Junction and Llandudno. Some of these developed into prosperous businesses: the Llandudno Brick, Lime and Stone Company in 1878, for example, producing 432,375 bricks, as well as other materials such as lime and cement for the building trade. They also manufactured earthenware tiles.

Slate manufacturing works were also developed apace in the quarrying areas and their proximal commercial centres. Lintels, plain and enamelled mantelpieces, door panels, plinths, dining-table tops and washstands were skilfully turned out. Writing slates and inkstands for the expanding educational market of the post-Forster era were produced and billiard-table tops as the demand for recreational activities in the expanding industrial areas soared, while gravestones were an ever present requirement. While these concerns were, on the whole, relatively small, the Penlon Works at Bangor employed nearly 100 at the turn of the century.

The first two important slate works begun in the county were probably those at Port Penrhyn which Hyde Hall described as ' an establishment for polishing and framing school slates, of which a number unaccountably great were exported ' and the Elidir Fach slate mill, erected in 1801 on the banks of the Caledffrwd river close to the Penrhyn quarry — ' For sawing blocks of slate into slabs for mantelpieces and tombstones and for dividing them into laminae for roofing.' By the eighties, a spate of similar works had developed in the quarry-port towns of Caernarfon (5), Bangor (4) and Porthmadog (2). Furthermore, in close proximity to the quarries of Nantlle, Ogwen and Llanberis, a cluster of slate works had emerged around the villages of Pen-y-groes, Llanllyfni, Llanrug and Deiniolen. Indeed, in the Deiniolen area there were five slate works in 1871, including Samuel Jones's Glan Dinorwig works which employed 33 men and 19 boys.

By the seventies, eleven steam sawmills had also emerged to cater principally for the housing boom and shipbuilding, the majority situated in or near the port towns, since they were dependent mainly on imported timber. At Pwllheli, Porthmadog, Bangor and Caernarfon several small engineering concerns and foundries also flourished as suppliers of engineering parts for agricultural machinery and ships, for quarry railways and quarrying equipment.

They also produced household fixtures ranging from lavatory equipment to boilers. The most notable of these concerns was the De Winton works at Caernarfon, employing between 200-250 workers in the eighties. It produced a vast range of products, including girders, punching machines, turntables, wagons, steam engines, marine engines and boilers. It specialized in engineering production for the quarrying industry.

By mid-century the woollen industry was involved primarily in the production of clothing for quarry-men. By 1850, the once numerous fulling-mills, depending on domestic spinning and weaving, had been largely replaced by fewer but more sophisticated comprehensive mills, where all the stages of production were organized under one roof. This process had begun in 1805, with the establishment of the first sophisticated comprehensive mill at Tremaoog by Alexander Madocks. By 1851 there were over twenty such mills in production, located in the traditional wool producing areas such as Penmachno with its four mills, which found a ready market for its products in the populous Blaenau Ffestiniog quarrying area. Though the industry benefited in the short term from quarrying expansion and to a lesser extent from the tourist industry, it could hardly compete with cheaper and less coarse English textiles. It was not a large industry in the fifties, and by 1881 only 101 people were working in it.

Gas and electricity works were also established in this expansionary period of urban and industrial development, but only in the towns and large quarrying areas. Caernarfon was the first town to embark on such a venture, in 1833, and by 1895, when the Llanberis gasworks were completed, eleven towns had their own works: their primary function was to provide street and shop lighting. Electricity came later. It was not until shortly after 1905 that these new sources of power began to be applied to industrial purposes.

The map shows the location of the various pre and post railway age smaller industries. The new emergent industries which flourished in the post-railway era were located primarily in the expanding urban centres of the county, the seaside resorts, commercial towns and in and around the booming quarrying villages. On the other hand, in the rural areas, particularly the fertile agricultural districts of Llŷn, Eifionydd and the Conwy valley, the more traditional agriculturally based industries, which flourished in the early decades were located — often dispersed throughout the countryside or established in the market towns.

The map does not reveal the vital contribution made to the economy, particularly in the early part of the century, by the craftsmen — the smiths, tinmen, saddlers, shoemakers, nailers, coach-builders, wheelwrights, limekiln workers, etc., in their small workshops, which are far too numerous and scattered to be mapped with accuracy. By the end of the century, although their number had been reduced by external competition from mass produced techniques, they still retained some importance. The Caernarvonshire Census of 1891, for example, showed there were still 559 black-smiths and 579 shoe-makers in the county. Because of its diversified nature, the important building industry has also been omitted from the map. In 1891 it employed 2,836 craftsmen, who represented a substantial proportion of the county's workforce (5.5%). The craftsmen confirmed further the diverse industrial pattern of the county during the period. Within this pattern, the smaller industries, though subordinate in manpower, capital expenditure and production to the dominant industries, nevertheless contributed, in no small way, to the impressive growth of Caernarvonshire in the nineteenth century.

Cae'r Gors, Rhosgadfan

Tŷ'r Ysgol, Rhyd-ddu

Writers of the Slate-quarrying Areas

The three slate-quarrying districts of Arfon — Bethesda, Llanberis and the Nantlle valley — are found within an area covering hardly more than a quarter of the former county of Caernarfon; they may be comfortably enclosed in a semicircle of some ten miles radius, centred on Caernarfon town. The contribution made to modern Welsh writing by men and women brought up in this small area is a matter of some justifiable pride. R. Williams Parry and T. H. Parry-Williams, two cousins, belong among a small handful of major Welsh poets of the present century; the latter was also the most accomplished practitioner of the modern literary essay in Welsh. W. J. Gruffydd was a poet, an inspired editor of a literary journal and a master of prose style. Richard Hughes Williams (Dic Tryfan) was the leading pioneer of the Welsh short story. Ifor Williams and Thomas Parry are two scholars who have tackled some of the most basic tasks in the field of Welsh learning. T. Rowland Hughes was the first Welsh novelist, properly so-called, after Daniel Owen. John Gwilym Jones is one of the two best contemporary Welsh dramatists. There are other names which would have to be included in any comprehensive survey of twentieth-century Welsh writing: from Bethesda come Caradog Pritchard, a poet and novelist of un-doubted talent and unique sensibility, and J. O. Williams, essayist, story-writer and co-author with Miss Jennie Thomas, also of Bethesda, of the most successful children's book ever to appear in Welsh. From Deiniolen comes Gwenlyn Parry, and from Penisa'r-waun Huw Lloyd Edwards, both dramatists. From Waunfawr come the philosopher Hywel D. Lewis and his brother, Alun T. Lewis, a writer of short stories. From the Nantlle valley come R. Silyn Roberts, poet and educationist; Gwilym R. Jones and Mathonwy Hughes, both poets, prose writers and journalists. The list is far from complete.

Although literary activity was but one aspect of the remarkable democratic culture which flourished in these communities following the rise of the slate industry, it is likely that the work of its writers will be its most lasting memorial. It is true of almost all of them that they were, first and foremost, 'local writers', drawing their inspiration from the life of the community around them, but their detailed observation of their own square mile detracts in no way from the wider truth of their testimony about man's condition. The village of Rhosgadfan may be clearly recognized in the stories of Kate Roberts, and Y Groeslon in the plays of John Gwilym Jones, but the experiences with which they are concerned are universal ones. No one was more of a 'local writer' than T. H. Parry-Williams. Rhyd-ddu and Drws-y-Coed, Afon Gwyrfai and Llyn y Gadair have all been possessed by his imagination and made part of his personal mythology; he has determined for all time the way in which the Welsh reader will see them; at the same time, he has given voice to a dilemma found in all the significant literature of the twentieth century, throughout the western world. R. Williams Parry was a 'local writer' in a somewhat different sense, responding not so much to the landscape of his locality as to its people, as individuals. Although he, too, voiced the terror of existence and the crises of civilization, he succeeded at the same time, through his many poems of greeting and tribute to friends and acquaintances in the Nantlle valley, in fulfilling part of the traditional function of the *bardd gwlad* or 'community poet'.

Williams Parry was a poet who profited much from the companionship and example of local verse-makers — Annant, Hywel Cefni and G. W. Francis. A fair account of this culture in its literary aspect cannot be given, nor, indeed, can the nationally known writers named earlier be understood, without bearing in mind the contribution made by the host of local writers — poets of local *eisteddfodau*, devotees of newspaper bardic columns, and makers of rhymes and ditties with a local appeal, many of them not even published, but read for amusement to a small circle of friends. The number of such writers would probably run into scores. Even if we restrict ourselves to those who have published volumes of their work, we must be content with three or four to represent the many. Some of the best of the tradition is to be found in such books as *Byr a Phert* (1928) by William Griffith, Hen Barc, Llanllechid, and *Telyn Eryri* (1932) by G. W. Francis of Nantlle. Two more recent volumes, containing strict-metre verse of notable skill, are *Caniadau Llyfni* (1968) by Llyfni

Hughes of Pen-y-Groes and *Swper Chwarel* (1974) by Lisi Jones of Cesarea.

Enough names have already been listed to suggest that not all of the writers brought up in the quarrying areas are 'quarry writers'. In the work of Parry-Williams or John Gwilym Jones, for example, the quarry as such hardly figures at all. In the work of Caradog Pritchard or J. O. Williams, it comes into greater prominence. To Kate Roberts and T. Rowland Hughes it is all-important. It should also be noted that only comparatively recently did the quarry itself become a subject for creative writing. It is little mentioned by the numerous nineteenth-century versifiers who actually worked in it, men like Griffith Williams (Gutyn Peris), William Edwards (Gwilym Padarn), J. O. Griffith (Ioan Arfon), O. G. Owen (Alafon) and John Owen (Ap Glaslyn). The prose writer, Owen Wynne Jones (Glasynys), likewise ignored it completely, although he had been a quarryman for a short time. The first writer of real note to take the quarry as his main inspiration was R. Hughes Williams,

whose first collection, *Straeon y Chwarel,* appeared *circa* 1915. From then on, that is during the years which saw the contraction and decline of the industry, there appears a body of writing in which the life of the quarryman is recalled, interpreted and celebrated. It is probably Kate Roberts in her short stories and T. Rowland Hughes in his novels who have done most to introduce the Arfon quarryman, his character, his values and the quality of his life, to the whole of Wales.

This short survey should not be brought to a close without mentioning some factual books which record history and reminiscences of the quarry and the society around it. One of the earliest volumes of this kind is *Chwareli a Chwarelwyr* (1897) by the Quarrymen's Union leader, W. J. Parry, Coetmor. Three recent books which are well worth reading for their interesting content and their literary quality are *Y Chwarel a'i Phobl* (1960) by H. D. Hughes; *Canrif y Chwarelwr* (1963) by Emyr Jones; and *Bargen Bywyd fy Nhaid* (1963) by Ernest Roberts.

Robert Williams Parry, *Cerddi'r Gaeaf*

Y DDÔL A AETH O'R GOLWG

(Dôl Pebin y Mabinogion)

Yn Nhal-y-sarn ystalwm
    Fe welem Lyfni lân,
A'r ddôl hynafol honno
    A gymell hyn o gân;
Ac megis gwyrth y gwelem
    Ar lan hen afon hud
Y ddôl a ddaliai Pebin
    Yn sblander bore'r byd.

Yn Nhal-y-sarn ysywaeth
    Ni welwn Lyfni mwy,
Na gwartheg gwyrthiol Pebin
    Yn eu cynefin hwy.
Buan y'n dysgodd bywyd
    Athrawiaeth llanw a thrai:
Rhyngom a'r ddôl ddihalog
    Daeth chwydfa'r Gloddfa Glai.

W. J. Gruffydd, *Hen Atgofion*

Byddaf yn caru cofio am yr hen ardal ar ddwy adeg — ar brynhawn Sul braf ym Mehefin pan fydd y werin a fagwyd yn y fro yn rhodianna yn ei dillad gorau ar hyd y llwybrau caregog — y mae'r wlad a'r werin mor debyg i'w gilydd ac yn cynganeddu

mor berffaith, y ddau, yn hardd ac esmwyth yn eu tlodi cynnes urddasol; ac ar brynhawn cuchiog yn yr hydref, pan fydd y gwynt o'r Eifl yn chwipio'r glaw ar draws y wlad, a phob lliw a ffurf wedi ymdoddi yn un düwch gwastad, a thoc dyma hi'n hindda godro ac ennyd o oleuni a thawelwch yn yr hwyr, a phelydrau llesg o'r haul gaerau dros Fôn yn dangos twr eglwys Llangaffo ac ystum cochddu eglwys Brynsiencyn. Mi welais y ddwy olwg hyn ar Landdeiniolen gannoedd o weithiau yn f'oes — yn Rhydychen, ym Morgannwg, yn yr Aifft, ac y mae'n ddigon tebyg mai ar y rhain y caea f' amrantau pan fyddant yn rhy flin i agor mwy, ymha le bynnag y bydd hynny.

Kate Roberts, *Traed Mewn Cyffion*

Cyraeddasant y ffordd drol a arweiniai i'r mynydd, yr un mynydd yr aethant drosto wrth fyned i dŷ Nain Ifan. Yr oedd y ffordd yn gul ac yn galed dan draed. O boptu yr oedd y grug a'r eithin, y mwsogl llaith a'r tir mawn. Yr oedd yr eithin yn fân ac ystwyth a'i flodau o'r melyn gwannaf megis lliw briallu, a'r grug cwta'n gyferbyniad iddo ef a'r tir tywyll oedd o'i gwmpas. Rhedai ffrydiau bychain o'r mynydd i'r ffordd, a llifent ymlaen wedyn yn ddŵr gloyw hyd y graean ar ei hochr. Weithiau rhedai'r ffrwd i bwll ac arhosai felly. Croesai llwybrau'r defaid y mynydd yn groes ymgroes ymhob man, a phorai defaid a merlod mynydd llaes eu cynffonnau hyd-ddo. Yr oedd popeth a gysylltid â'r mynydd yn fychan — yr eithin, y mwsogl, y defaid, y merlod. Torrid ar y tawelwch gan lef y gornchwiglen a hedai ar ei rhawd ac a ddisgynnai'n sydyn ar y mynydd ac wedyn rhedeg at ei nyth mewn twll — ôl pedol ceffyl, efallai.

Edrychai ar y pentref draw yn gorwedd yn llonydd-wch y prynhawn. I fyny ar y chwith yr oedd y chwarel a'i thomen yn estyn ei phig i lawr y mynydd fel neidr. O bell, edrychai'r cerrig rwbel yn dda, a disgleirient yng ngoleuni'r haul. Dyma'r chwarel lle y lladdwyd tad Ifan. Pwy, tybed, a wagiodd y wagen rwbel gyntaf o dan y domen acw? Yr oedd yn ei fedd erbyn hyn, yn sicr. A phwy a fyddai'r olaf i daflu ei lwyth rwbel o'i thop? I beth yr oedd hi, Jane Gruffydd, yn wraig ifanc o Lŷn, yn da yn y fan yma? Ond wedi'r cwbl, nid oedd yn waeth iddi yn y fan yma mwy nag yn Llŷn. Yr oedd yn rhaid iddi fod yn rhywle. Ac i beth y breudd-wydiai fel hyn?

Yr oedd rhywbeth prudd yn yr holl olygfa, y chwarel, y pentref a'r mynydd oedd ynghlwm wrth ei gilydd. Ond y munud nesaf wedyn yr oedd Jane yn hapus, hi a'i phlant, yn hapusach efallai nag y byddai y rhawg eto.

T. Rowland Hughes, *Y Cychwyn*

I'r Twll â hwy, i dyllu yng ngwaelod y fargen. Curai Huw Jones ac Owen bob yn ail, â morthwyl ' dwbwl-hand ' bob un, a throai Elias Thomas yr ebill rhwng pob trawiad. Cymerai yntau forthwyl pan flinent hwy, troai un o'r lleill iddo ef, a châi'r trydydd orffwyso. Ond gan wybod bod troi i ddau yn waith a oedd bron mor galed â tharo, gofalai Owen fod yr hen flaenor yn cymryd ' pum munud bach ' yn weddol aml. Yr oedd ei egni'n rhyfeddol, meddyliodd, ond grym ewyllys oedd dwy ran o dair ohono, ac wrth wrando ar ei anadl cyflym a'i frest wichlyd, gwyddai fod yr ymdrech yn fawr. Er hynny, doeth fu peidio â'i adael yn y wal yn eistedd drwy'r bore oer ar y blocyn hollti neu wrth y drafael: buasai wedi rhynnu yno.

Cyrhaeddodd Elias Thomas cyn hir, ac wedi iddynt guro'u breichiau am eu cyrff i gynhesu, dechreuodd y tri chwarelwr ar eu gwaith. A hwythau ar eu heistedd, heb symud fawr, ac wyneb eang y wal yn agored i'r tywydd, yr oedd eu traed bron â fferu cyn pen hanner awr. Gwelai Owen y cŷn yn llithro weithiau o law Elias Thomas, a'r hen flaenor yn ailgydio ynddo mor ddisylw ag y gallai, heb dddywedyd gair. Ond Huw Jones oedd y cyntaf i godi.

' Yr argian, mae hi'n annioddefol hiddiw, ond ydi? ' meddai, gan wasgu'i ddwylo dan ei geseiliau a dawnsio o gwmpas congl y wal. ' Y diwrnod oera' ers oesoedd. Ne' ydw' i'n gofio, beth bynnag. 'Dydach chi ddim bron â rhewi, deudwch, Lias Thomas? '

' Ydw, wir, fachgan. Ac mae'r clytia' 'ma'n anodd 'u trin, yn rhyw fân blicio fel ar dywydd poeth.'
' Wedi'u sychu gan y rhew, wchi.'
' Ia, ac yn 'cau'n glir â hollti'n deg. Dyna ti'r clwt dwytha' 'na holltis i. Mi ddylai hwn'na ildio pum crawan, chwech efalla', i'r fodfadd. Ond dim ond tair ges i bob tro, ac mi fûm i'n ffodus i gael cymaint â hynny o'i groen o. Mae'r cerrig gora' yn sâl hiddiw, ac am y rhai gwael, mae'r rheini'n . . . '

' Ddigon gwael i rywun fod ar 'i draed y nos efo nhw,' chwadal Robin Ifans.

' Ydyn', fachgan. Neu, fel y clywis i un hen frawd yn deud, " fel bara ceirch ". Go anodd fydd gwneud cyflog y mis yma, mae arna'i i ofn. 'Wn i ddim pryd y cawn ni fynd i fras-hollti'r plygion eraill a dŵad â'r cerrig o'r Twll.' Llithrodd y cŷn plygion eto i'r llawr, a chaeodd ac agorodd yr hen ŵr ei law chwith yn gyflym droeon. ' Mae'r cŷn 'na fel petai o'n serio 'nghnawd i un funud, a'r eiliad nesa' 'dydi o ddim yn fy llaw i.' Cododd oddi ar ei flocyn. ' Mi a' i at dân y caban am funud i roi clwt neu ddau ar fy llaw. Gobeithio bod rhywun wedi cynna' siwin o dân yno, yntê? '

T. Rowland Hughes, *Chwalfa*

Tawodd, a'i lygaid hen yn cau gan flinder. Agorodd hwy eto ymhen ennyd, a disgleiriai hyder ynddynt yn awr.

' Ond yn ystod y dyddia' dwytha' 'ma, fel yr on i'n deud neithiwr wrth Mr. Edwards y gwnidog, mae'r chwerwder wedi mynd bron i gyd, fachgan. Yr hyn sy'n aros yn fy meddwl i ydi ein bod ni, chwarelwyr syml, cyffredin, wedi meiddio sefyll am dair blynadd dros ein hiawndera', wedi ymladd ac aberthu mor hir dros egwyddor. 'Fasa' fy nhad ddim yn credu bod y peth yn bosib', a phrin y medrai'i dad o ddych-mygu'r fath haerllugrwydd. Colli'r frwydyr ddaru ni, ac erbyn y diwedd yr oedd afiechyd ac anobaith ac ofn wedi dryllio'r rhenga' a gwneud llawer ohono' ni'n llai na ni'n hunain. Dynion gwan a gwael yn gorfforol oeddan ni erbyn hynny, a Duw yn unig a ŵyr be' ydi dylanwad y corff ar y meddwl a'r ewyllys. Ond mi ddaru ni ymladd yn hir ac ymladd yn ddewr — hynny sy'n bwysig, Edward, hynny sy'n bwysig.'

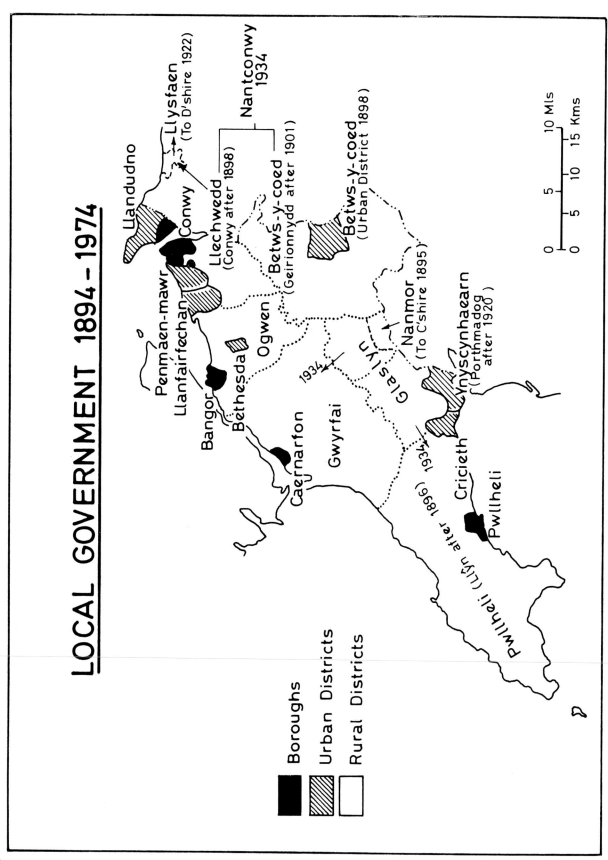

LOCAL GOVERNMENT 1894 – 1974

Llandudno

Conwy

Llysfaen
(To D'shire 1922)

Llechwedd
(Conwy after 1898)

Nantconwy
1934

Betws-y-coed
(Geirionnydd after 1901)

Betws-y-coed
(Urban District 1898)

Penmaen-mawr

Llanfairfechan

Ogwen

Bangor

Bethesda

Nanmor
(To C'shire 1895)

Caernarfon

Gwyrfai

Glaslyn

1934

Ynyscynhaearn
(Porthmadog
after 1920)

Criccieth

1934

Pwllheli (Llŷn after 1896)

Pwllheli

10 Mls

15 Kms

Boroughs

Urban Districts

Rural Districts

Local Government from 1834

Since Tudor times, county affairs had been run by the shire's magistrates sitting in Quarter Sessions, while more local matters were dealt with by parish officers responsible to parish vestry meetings.

By the nineteenth century, however, the old rural order was changing, and the old method of local government with restricted powers and weak authority could no longer cope with the pressures of a new industrialized age, even in a rural county such as Caernarvonshire. Single parishes in particular could not hope to tackle the problems of poor relief and sanitation, and the Industrial Revolution, with its new class of landless labourers moving from their family homes to centres of employment, inevitably led to an increase in the number of paupers.

By the 1834 Poor Law Amendment Act, parishes were compelled to join together into 'unions' for the exercise of their functions in this field. There were to be six unions in Caernarvonshire, five of which, however, straddled the county's boundaries. They were governed by a committee of elected Guardians, who were responsible for establishing workhouses and also giving out-relief to people in need of temporary assistance. The unions continued virtually unchanged until 1929, and also functioned, outside the towns, as 'Rural Sanitary Authorities' from 1872 to 1894.

In 1835, urban government was partially re-formed by the Municipal Corporations Act, which established democratically elected town councils in boroughs previously ruled by a corporation run by a handful of burgesses who could be easily influenced by a locally powerful personality. Caernarfon (Borough 1284 - 1834) and Pwllheli (Borough 1355 - 1834) became Reformed Boroughs and obtained modern councils under this Act, but only in 1876 did Conwy (Borough 1284 - 1870) adopt the provisions of the Act and become a Reformed Borough. In Bangor — for long governed by the ineffectual manor court of the bishop — a Local Board was set up in 1855, and it gained its charter as a borough, and thus a town council, in 1883. Cricieth (Borough 1285 - 1873) and Nefyn (1355 - 1882) both ceased to be boroughs during this period, however, having become commercially insignificant, with small populations. Nefyn reverted to parish status in 1882, and a Local Board was set up in Cricieth in 1873.

The problems of smaller or newer urban areas, without a borough tradition, likewise called for a more modern system of government for the efficient provision of such facilities as water supply, street paving, cleaning and lighting and so on. By the Public Health Act, 1848, the ratepayers of any town could petition for the establishment of a Local Board of Health, while elsewhere towns opted for the appointment of Improvement Commissioners, whose functions were similar to those of a Local Board. In all, seven such bodies were established in Caernarvonshire.

Ynyscynhaearn, Local Board (1858 - 1894).
Cricieth, Local Board (1873 - 1894).
Bangor, Local Board (1855 - 1883).
Bethesda, Improvement Commissioners (1854 - 1863), Local Board (1863 - 1875), Improvement Commissioners (1875 - 1894).
Llanfairfechan, Local Board (1872 - 1894).
Penmaen-mawr, Dwygyfylchi, Local Board (1866 - 1890), Penmaen-mawr, Local Board (1890 - 1894).
Llandudno, Improvement Commissioners (1854 - 1894).

Other local bodies were set up on an *ad hoc* basis to deal with various aspects of local government, such as a Highways Board set up by the various townships of Llanbeblig; a number of Turnpike Trusts to improve the county's roads; Burial Boards, in such places as Bangor, Cricieth and Penllyn and Llanfairfechan; School Boards in most parishes; Harbour Trusts at Caernarfon and Portin-llaen, and so on. Each body was empowered to raise money in its individual area.

While these bodies were a great improvement on the old order, their very variety led to problems. As a prominent advocate of reform stated in Parliament, there was 'a chaos as regards authorities, a chaos as regards rates, and a worse chaos than all as regards areas'.

The first step to reform in 1889 was the establishment of an elected county council to run the county

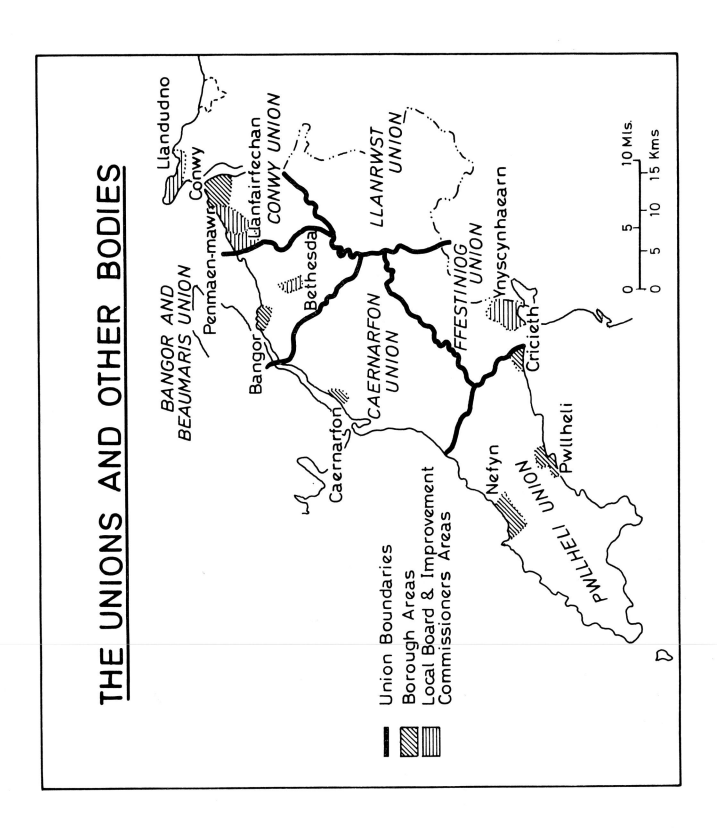

THE UNIONS AND OTHER BODIES

Llandudno

Conwy

Llanfairfechan

Penmaen-mawr

CONWY UNION

BANGOR AND BEAUMARIS UNION

LLANRWST UNION

Bethesda

Bangor

CAERNARFON UNION

Caernarfon

FFESTINIOG UNION

Ynyscynhaearn

Cricieth

Nefyn

Pwllheli

PWLLHELI UNION

Union Boundaries
Borough Areas
Local Board & Improvement
Commisioners Areas

10 Mls.
15 Kms
5
10
5
5
0
0

in place of the gentry who, as magistrates, had previously performed this function. Initially with little authority other than for roads, bridges, weights and measures, county property and joint control of the police, it took over responsibility for education in 1902 and for poor relief in 1929.

In 1894, a second Local Government Act was passed, setting up elected councils called Urban District Councils to take over from the Local Board in the towns, while in rural areas Rural District Councils took over public health functions from the Poor Law Unions. All but the smallest parishes gained elected parish councils to deal with local matters.

Thus the pattern of Local Government was established basically as it remained until 1974. There have been, however, numerous minor changes in boundaries over the years, to do away with awkward inconsistencies, many of them survivals from medieval times. For example, the old township of Eirias, where Colwyn Bay now stands, was mainly in Denbighshire, but some ten acres were in Caernarvonshire and thus became a separate civil parish under the 1894 Act; these ten acres were joined to Llysfaen in 1895. Similarly, the township of Nanmor in Beddgelert parish had been part of Merioneth, but in the same year was transferred to Caernarvonshire. In 1922, Llysfaen (the detached portion of Caernarvonshire) was transferred to Denbighshire.

Inside the county there have likewise been changes over the years; for example, the creation of a U.D.C. for Betws-y-coed in 1898. In 1934, many small parishes were amalgamated, especially in Llŷn, as were Conwy and Geirionnydd R.D.C.s In the same year, Glaslyn R.D.C., a small council with only five members, was dissolved. A number of councils, such as Criccieth and Porthmadog, extended their areas over the years as they grew in size. The most important of these changes are shown on the map, but the various County Council orders must be consulted for fuller details.

The old pattern of local government thus remained basically the same for nearly a century until 1974, when three new district councils replaced sixteen borough, urban and rural councils. The boundaries of 'communities', as the civil parishes are now called, are at present being examined prior to what promises to be a radical reorganisation aimed at establishing areas which have economic and social ties in the changed circumstances of the late twentieth century.

Below are to be seen some extracts from the minute books of a number of local authorities, which bear evidence to the essential part played by these bodies in the organisation and development of the towns and villages of the county.

'The Bailiffs gave permission to Owen Lewis to take in and enclose the waste before the House called Penpalad isa to the Road, he agreeing to pay annually . . . the sum of One Shilling.'

Criccieth Borough Court, 1839.

'The Bailiffs are desired immediately to give Notice to parties having Sea Weed and other Rubbish by the Turnpike Road to remove them in one Month's time from this day.'

Criccieth Borough Court, 1848.

'The site for a Pinfold having been discussed, it was decided to change it from Maes-y-facrell . . . to the space of ground immediately under the Wall in front of Rofft bâch — the latter site being considered more central and convenient.'

Llandudno Improvement Commissioners, 1854.

'The Town Hall has been let to Daniel Hughes to keep School for the sum of 1s. Yearly.'

Criccieth Borough Court, 1854.

'Complaint having been made of the bad state of repair of Mostyn Street, it was referred to the Finance Committee with a view to its being repaired.'

Llandudno Improvement Commissioners, 1855.

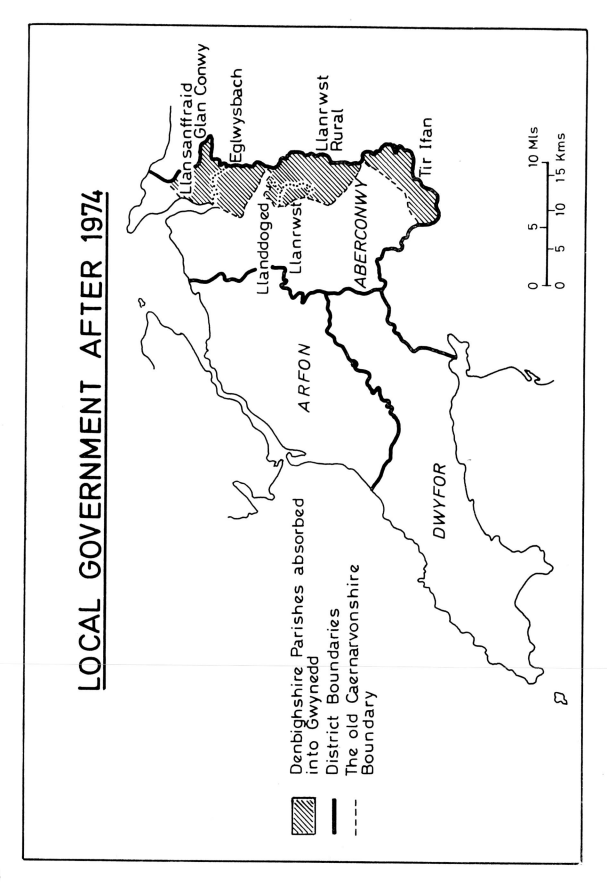

LOCAL GOVERNMENT AFTER 1974

Llansanffraid Glan Conwy

Eglwysbach

Llanrwst Rural

Tir Ifan

Llanddoged

Llanrwst

ABERCONWY

ARFON

DWYFOR

Denbighshire Parishes absorbed into Gwynedd

District Boundaries

The old Caernarvonshire Boundary

0   5   10 Mls

0   5   10   15 Kms

'Resolved that a respectful application . . . be made to the Magistrates . . . to examine and confirm the several Byelaws for the Regulation of Hackney Coaches, Horses & Donkeys, Pleasure Boats and Bathing Machines within the District.'

Llandudno Improvement Commissioners, 1855.

'Cricieth Fairs will be held as usual on the 23rd of May, 29th of June and the 22 of October.'

Cricieth Borough Court, 1857.

'Application having been made to this Board for the Town lamps to be lighted on the Quarry Pay & following night — It was resolved.'

Bethesda Local Board of Health, 1860.

'A complaint . . . laid respecting a prevalent nuisance in Bangor that of setting fire to Chimneys in lieu of Sweeping.'

Bangor Local Board of Health, 1861.

'Mr. G. W. Wallace, Band Master, Birmingham, applied for permission for his Band to play on the Promenade and in the Town during the Summer Season.'

Llandudno Improvement Commissioners, 1863.

Mr. Thos. Parry called attention to heaps of manure lying in the Street at the back of the Baptist Chapel . . . a similar Complaint of Slaughter House refuse being placed on the Road to the Gas Works. Ordered to be removed.'

Llandudno Improvement Commissioners, 1863.

'The Sanitary Committee was requested to visit and report upon the sanitary state of No. 44 Cilfodan Street.'

Bethesda Local Board of Health, 1867.

'Building plans . . . of a shed proposed to be erected on Lot No. 72 Gerlan for Owen Williams, approved.'

Bethesda Local Board of Health, 1867.

'The Inspector having, owing to the crowded state of the Nevin Churchyard or Burial-ground . . . recommended that the same be closed against future interment, it was Resolved that . . . immediate steps be taken in the matter.'

*Pwllheli Board of Guardians
(Rural Sanitary Authority), 1875.*

'Wm. Thomas of Madoc Street asked permission to have a Badge to act as Town Porter. Permission granted.'

Llandudno Improvement Commissioners, 1875.

'It was resolved that the Road Committee be instructed to provide means for Collecting the Water at the mouth of the Old Mine level into a Tank at such a level as will allow the Water to flow by gravitation into the Water Cart.'

Llandudno Improvement Commissioners, 1875.

'The Inspector reported that Small pox had appeared at Murmawr, Bryncroes, and that he had taken every possible precaution with a view to isolating the disease.'

*Pwllheli Board of Guardians
(Rural Sanitary Authority), 1877.*

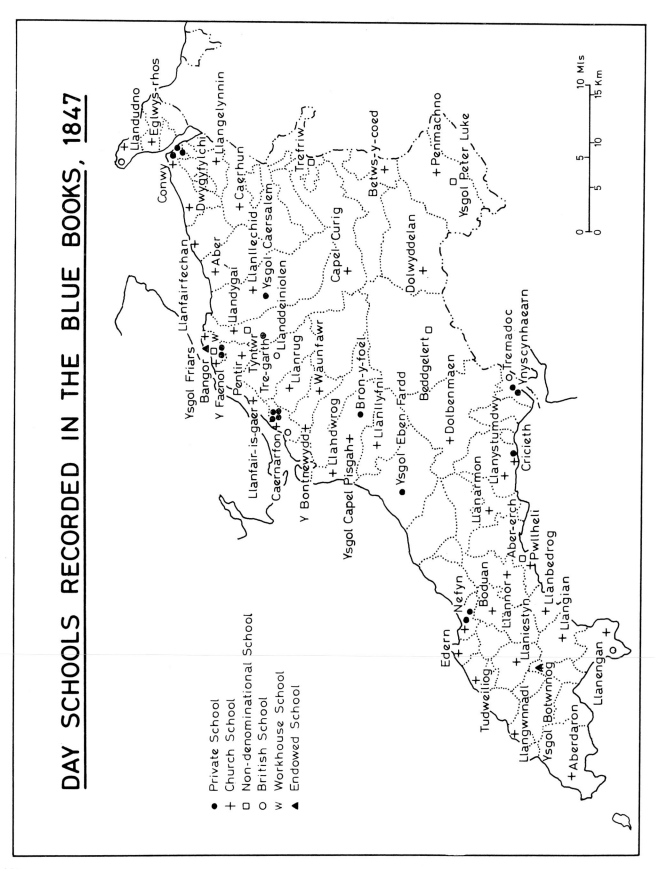

DAY SCHOOLS RECORDED IN THE BLUE BOOKS, 1847

Private School ●
Church School +
Non-denominational School □
British School ○
Workhouse School w
Endowed School ▲

Llandudno
Eglwys-rhos
Llangelynnin
Dwygyfylchi
Conwy
Caerhun
Aber
Llandygai
Llanllechid
Ysgol Caersalem
Trefriw
Betws-y-coed
Penmachno
Ysgol Peter Luke
Llanfairfechan
Bangor
Ysgol Friars
Y Faenol
Pentir
Tyntŵr
Llanddeiniolen
Llanrug
Waunfawr
Capel-Curig
Dolwyddelan
Beddgelert
Llanfair-is-gaer
Tre-garth
Caernarfon
Y Bontnewydd
Llandwrog
Bron-y-foel
Llanllyfni
Ysgol Eben-Fardd
Dolbenmaen
Tremadoc
Ynyscynhaearn
Llanystumdwy
Cricieth
Ysgol Capel Pisgah
Llanarmon
Nefyn
Edern
Boduan
Aber-erch
Pwllheli
Llannor
Llaniestyn
Llanbedrog
Llangian
Tudweiliog
Llangwnnadl
Ysgol Botwnnog
Aberdaron
Llanengan

10 MIs
15 Km
10
5
5

Education 1800-1870

Many of the schools established by eighteenth-century charities continued into the new century, and one new charity school was established, Dr. Hughes's school at Llanystumdwy. In addition to these, there were many private adventure schools kept by old soldiers or sailors who had lost their taste for hard tack, by farmers or craftsmen who had come down in the world, or by a host of unmarried women. These schools had little to recommend them, but the picture would not be complete without naming teachers like Dafydd Ddu Eryri, Ieuan Lleyn, Michael Roberts in Pwllheli, Eben Fardd in Clynnog and David Owen (Brutus) in Aber. Evan Richardson, too, maintained a school of somewhat higher standard in Caernarfon. But the picture seen as a whole is unsatisfactory. A continuation of the eighteenth-century circulating schools would have served the scattered Welsh community much more effectively than these settled schools of unequal standards which followed.

Griffith Jones's ideal of reading the Bible in the vernacular was maintained, however, by the Sunday Schools, and if we accept government statistics, there were 37 of them with 2,651 pupils in 1818. By 1847, the number of schools had risen to 249 with 14,260 pupils under fifteen years of age. Every religious body promoted Sunday Schools, but the Methodists were far ahead with 132 (53%) of the schools and 8,824 (58%) of the pupils. Their work is reflected in the growth of the vernacular press. When *Yr Herald Cymraeg* was first published in 1855, it had a circulation of twelve thousand a week, while the corresponding English newspaper, *The Caernarvon and Denbigh Herald,* sold only twelve hundred. The Welsh newspapers kept the English papers alive!

In 1808, the British Schools Society had been formed, by Nonconformist interests mainly, but progress was slow in Caernarvonshire and it had only two schools by 1840, one in Caernarfon and the other in Tremadog. The National School Society, founded in 1811 in connection with the Anglican Church, had more success through the efforts of Dean Cotton, who did much to establish schools in Bangor, Y Faenol, Llanllechid, Llandygái and Pentir. Other clergymen, such as Edward Hughes, Llanwnda, and Morgan Morgan, Conwy, also strove

diligently, and according to Church statistics, which, unfortunately, are not altogether reliable, there were 41 Church schools with 2,758 pupils by 1839.

Basically, both societies had similar objects, to provide the children of the poor with the elements of learning, with some useful skills, such as plain needlework for the girls, and, above all, to 'civilise' them, that is, to instil in them middle-class moral standards.

The disturbances of the forties, Chartism and Rebecca, frightened and to some extent awakened the consciences of the landowners and other Anglican subscribers, and although Caernarvonshire suffered little directly from the troubles, by 1847 new Church schools had been established in Llanfairfechan, Llanddeiniolen, Betws Garmon, Llaniestyn, Pwllheli, Boduan, Y Bontnewydd, Llanfair-is-gaer, Botwnnog and Llanberis; others were rebuilt in Edern, Llanllechid, Dwygyfylchi and Llanengan, together with three schools in the town of Caernarfon on which a sum of £3,000 was spent within less than three years.

Under the promptings of Hugh Owen, the Non-conformists, too, began to arouse themselves. John Phillips was chosen in 1843 to represent the British Schools Society in North Wales, and schools were founded under local committees, in Llandudno, Clynnog, Y Felinheli, Llanengan, Nant Gwynant, Penygroes, Rhostryfan, Conwy, Edern, Llysfaen and Carneddi. One or two of these, such as Nant Gwynant and Edern, soon failed, but others developed to be among the best schools in the county.

In spite of these efforts, however, the report presented by the Commissioners of 1847 was highly critical. Wide areas were revealed to be without any provision at all; the standard of the teachers was low; buildings were poor and equipment generally non-existent. Apart from men like John Edmunds, who, after some months at Borough Road, became headmaster of Garth, Bangor, before opting for the better prospects of the flour trade, few of the teachers had been to college. In an attempt to improve the situation, the Church established a Training College at Caernarfon (it survives as St. Mary's College, Bangor), and in 1858, through the efforts of Hugh Owen and John Phillips, the Normal College was established at Bangor. Neither had much pretension to culture, but they served a useful purpose at the time by providing sons of the working class with what was in effect a kind of higher elementary education, together with instruction in school management so that they might teach children of the same class.

Side by side with these efforts, 'ragged' schools were founded in some of the towns to provide for less fortunate children, and there were workhouse schools for their pitiful child inmates. There was also a school for army children in Caernarfon. Some schools, founded usually in connection with quarries, are referred to as 'industrial schools', but they differed in name only from the ordinary schools, for there is little evidence that they provided any technical or craft training. William Jones, the Pwllheli shipowner, had indeed called for some kind of technical training in 1846, having navigation more particularly in mind, and suggested the use of the old Pwllheli Grammar School for that purpose, but the school was allowed to die. However, individuals like Eben Fardd in Clynnog and Owen Griffith at Porthmadog did provide a certain amount of instruction in navigation.

One remarkable development in mid-century was the rapid growth of private schools for the children of the middle class, which had grown rapidly in the better economic climate of the fifties. The small manufacturers and shopkeepers who constituted this class had little education themselves, but were determined that their children should acquire some polish — English middle-class polish. To these schools also went the children of the professional middle class, bankers, lawyers, doctors, etc. As many as 200 children out of a total school population of 1,800 in Bangor in 1870 went to these schools. They offered a wide variety of subjects, Music, French, German, Italian, Drawing (pencil and crayon), Water Colour Painting, Plain and Fancy Needlework, Leatherwork and so on. Fees varied from 8-10 guineas a term for boards to 4-5 guineas for day scholars. This did not include payment for special subjects, most of those on the above list, and anyone who visited Professor Hulse in Upper Bangor for instruction in piano playing or singing would have an extra bill for 30s. The motto of one of these schools in Upper Bangor was 'Be not weary in doing good', but all the evidence suggests that the nuances of another theme, 'Bearing towards servants', received more particular attention. As many Nonconformist as Anglican children went to these schools. One or two, like the school known affectionately as 'Ysgol Kirk bach' in Caernarfon, did good work, but by and large they were a debilitating influence on Welsh society.

From the *Reports of the Commissioners of Inquiry into the state of Education in Wales,* London, 1848.

Church School at Llangïan

' The building is in an exposed situation and much out of repair. On the day of my visit there was a great hole in the roof. The floor of the room used for the school is of earth and full of holes. The outbuildings are insufficient, out of repair, full of lumber and inaccessible. There is a separate girls' school-room, but it is used as a receptacle for turf.'

crevices in the door, the place was well ventilated. The floor is of stone, and for furniture and apparatus there are only two rickety desks, barely sufficient for six children to write at, a torn and dirty map of the Holy Land pasted on the wall, and a few ragged books, copies and slates. The room was dirty and I observed a heap of wood for fuel in one corner.'

Church School at Capel Curig

' While some of the scholars were examined, the rest were either playing or staring at me. On my asking the master why he did not teach the scholars in classes, he said he could not for want of proper books. The building is very damp; the earth behind the house resting on the back wall as high as six feet above the level of the floor. Sometimes the place is overflowed with water from the hills. The room is too dark, there being only three small windows, and in these I counted twelve panes of glass broken. Between holes in the windows and

' The " Welsh stick " or " Welsh " as it is sometimes called, is given to any pupil who is overheard speaking Welsh, and may be transferred by him to any schoolfellow whom he hears committing a similar offence. It is thus passed from one to another until the close of the week when the pupil in whose possession the " Welsh " is found is punished by flogging. Among other injurious effects, this custom has been found to lead children to visit stealthily the houses of their schoolfellows for the purpose of detecting those who speak Welsh to their parents, and transferring to them the punishment due to themselves.'

192

BETHEL BRITISH SCHOOL,

AGORWYD EBRILL 11, 1864.

AMCAN y sefydliad yw cyfranu cyfundrefn o addysg Saesoneg fuddiol ac ymarferol, gyda yr hon y cysylltir egwyddorion addysg grefyddol a moesol.

ATHRAW, MR. W. J. WILLIAMS, o'r Normal College, Bangor.

ATHRAWES, MRS. WILLIAMS ei wraig.

RHEOLAU.

I. Ar dderbyniad pob plentyn i mewn, gofynir iddynt dalu y blaen-dal (*entrance money*) o chwecheiniog.

II. Y taliadau—dosparth cyntaf 3*d*.; yr ail 2½*d*.; y trydydd 2*d*.; y pedwerydd 1½*d*.; y pumed 1*d*.

III. Wedi yr ysgrifenir yr enw ar lyfrau yr ysgol, gofynir i bob un dalu, pa un ai presenol ai absenol a fyddo.

IV. Pan y byddo plentyn yn ymadael o'r ysgol, gofynir am rybudd prydlawn, a phe byddai yn ail ymuno â'r sefydliad, gofynir iddo dalu *entrance* fel o'r blaen.

V. Pan y byddo plentyn yn absenol dros dri diwrnod, disgwylir rheswm oddiwrth y rhieni dros yr absenoldeb.

VI. Rhaid i'r plant fod yn drefnus a chyfan eu gwisg, a chadw eu personau yn lan.

VII. O Ebrill y cyntaf, hyd y cyntaf o Hydref, dechreuir an 9 yn y boreu hyd 12eg, ac o 2 yn y prydnawn hyd 4; o'r cyntaf o Hydref, hyd y diweddaf o Fawrth, dechreuir am 9½ hyd 12eg, ac o 1½ hyd 3½ y prydnawn.

VIII. Ni chaniateir i neb ddyfod i mewn i'r ysgol gydag unrhyw gwynion yn ystod yr oriau y bydd y plant yn bresenol.

IX. Bydd gwyliau yr Haf yn parhau am ddwy wythnos, a gwyliau y Nadolig am wythnos.

X. Prydnawniau Mawrth a Gwener dysgir gwniadwaith i'r genethod.

XI. Heblaw y taliadau a nodwyd, disgwylir i'r plant dalu am y llyfrau, yr inc, a cheiniog yn y mis at y tân, cyhyd ag y bydd hyny yn angenrheidiol.

XII. Yr addysg a gyfrenir yn y dosbarthiadau isaf, fydd y Wyddor, Sillebiaeth, Darllen, Ysgrifenu, a Rhifyddiaeth; yn y dosbarth uchaf, Gramadeg, Cyfansoddiant, Cyfieithu, Daeareg, Canu wrth y Nodau, a Hanesiaeth Naturiol (*Natural History.*)

Arwyddwyd dros y Pwyllgor,

Ionawr 11eg, 1865.   ROBERT W. GRIFFITH.

D.S. Gan y bydd Arholydd y llywodraeth yn dyfod heibio yn y mis Mai, erfynir ar i bob plentyn a fyddo wedi rhoddi ei bresenoldeb yn ystod y flwyddyn, i aros heb ymadael hyd nes y byddo yr Arholiad drosodd.

ARGRAFFWYD GAN H. HUMPHREYS, CAERNARFON.

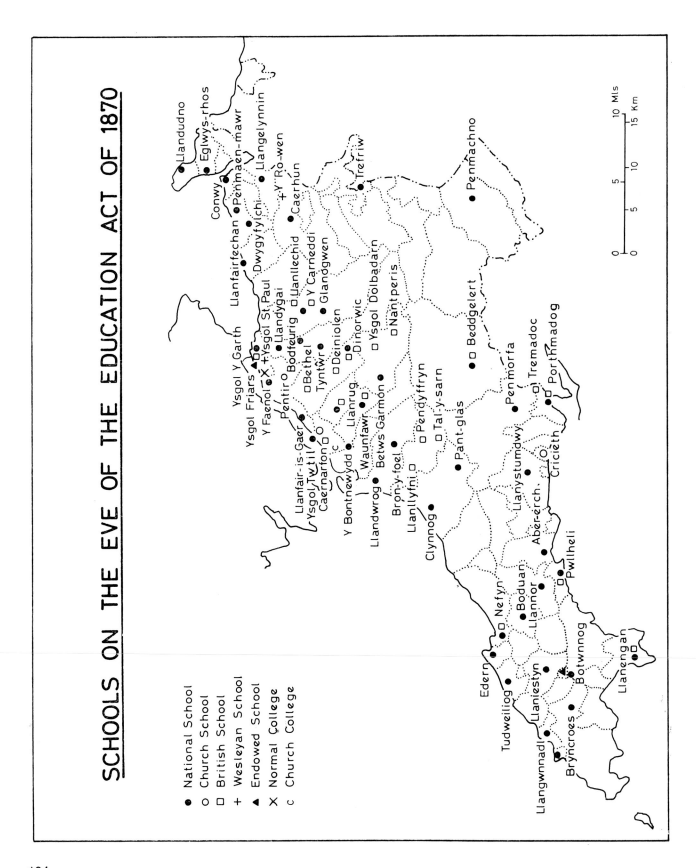

SCHOOLS ON THE EVE OF THE EDUCATION ACT OF 1870

- ● National School
- ○ Church School
- □ British School
- + Wesleyan School
- ▲ Endowed School
- X Normal College
- c Church College

Llandudno
Eglwys-rhos
Conwy
Penmaen-mawr
Llangelynnin
Y Rô-wen
Caerhun
Trefriw
Penmachno

Llanfairfechan
Dwygyfylchi
Llanllechid
Y Carneddi
Glanogwen
Glangwen
Nantperis

Ysgol Y Garth
Ysgol St. Paul
Llandygai
Y Faenol
Bodfeurig
Ysgol Friars
Bethel
Tyntwr
Deiniolen
Dinorwic
Ysgol Dolbadarn
Beddgelert

Pentir
Llanfair-is-Gaer
Ysgol Twtil
Caernarfon
Waunfawr
Llanrug
Betws-Garmon
Pendyffryn
Tal-y-sarn
Penmorfa
Tremadoc
Porthmadog

Bron-y-foel
Llanllyfni
Pant-glas
Llanystumdwy
Criciēth

Clynnog
Aber-erch
Pwllheli

Nefyn
Boduan
Llannor

Ederm
Llangwnnadl
Tudweiliog
Llaniestyn
Bryncroes
Botwnnog
Llanengan

10 Mls
15 Km

Education 1870-1902

The State had interested itself in education for years before 1870, but the Education Act of that year was a bigger step than any taken before. According to its architect, William Edward Forster, its purpose was to close the gap left by the Voluntary Societies. They were given a breathing space of six months in which to act, and if they failed, School Boards were to be established with elected members and powers to raise a rate to support their schools and to enforce attendance.

The Anglican Church saw the boards as a threat to its independence in educating children along traditional lines. On the other hand, Nonconformists were enthusiastic, seeing in the boards an opportunity to break the hold of the National Schools. They intended to transfer their own British Schools to the boards. The Church sought to gain a march during the breathing space, and succeeded in getting grants to build or rebuild schools in many areas, including Llanbedrog, Llangïan, Llanengan, Aber, Clynnog, Penmachno, Llanarmon, Edern, Llangelynnin, Llanfairfechan, Dolwyddelan, Llanfair-is-gaer and Llanllechid. The Nonconformists were equally active in petitioning the government against giving these additional grants to National Schools in a predominantly Nonconformist county.

But the fiercest struggle came over the establishment of the new boards and the election of members. All-important matters such as the quality of the schools, curriculum, training of teachers and even the question of compulsory attendance were lost sight of in the battle between Liberal middle class Nonconformity and the Toryism of Church and landowner. In its essence, the battle was a political struggle for power in the county. The needs and wishes of the unprivileged working classes were lost sight of.

A quick start was made in the towns where middle class Nonconformity was strongest, only to find that 'the principles of freedom' were not always strong enough to overcome the fear of the rate which was essential to support them. As a result, School Boards were turned down completely in Llandudno, Conwy, Nefyn and Porthmadog, while in Bangor, Caernarfon and Pwllheli their hands were tied by a promise given beforehand that they would not raise a rate.

Country districts, too, were resistant. The power of squire and parson still remained strong; farmers objected to the new rate, and to their shame, feared losing the cheap labour of the children. In one country district only was a School Board set up in 1871, in Llangybi, through the influence of the radical clergyman, John Clough Williams-Ellis. The country districts were so slow to act that the authorities in London had to enforce the establishment of boards in Aberdaron, Rhiw, Llanfaelrhys, Bryncroes, Llannor, Penmorfa, Cwm Pennant, Llanbedrycennin and several other country parishes. Even after the establishment of a board there was more concern to keep the rate down than to establish a school.

It was in the industrial areas alone that any genuine enthusiasm was shown for the boards. The new slate-quarrying communities in Llanddeiniolen, Nantlle and Llanberis, together with the granite quarrymen of Trefor, were determined to grasp their new opportunity. School Boards were established enthusiastically in those areas. The only exception was Bethesda, for the good reason that there was sufficient provision there already. A case can be made quite fairly that it was the pressure of social forces rather than Nonconformity alone which was the spur in these areas. Every effort made to improve the standard of the schools in buildings, curriculum, teachers and aids received full support in these areas until the end of the century.

All the towns which had rejected boards at the beginning were forced ultimately to establish them, but as in similar country areas, a tight hand was kept on the purse strings. Not without cause was the Conwy Board nicknamed *Y Bwrdd Sgerbwd* (the skeleton board). One reason for this was, of course, that the middle class in the towns provided for their own children in the private schools which have been noticed already.

The boards did nothing of any significance to establish further education, although an opportunity was provided in the eighties to set up Higher Grade Schools. Not one was opened in Caernarvonshire. They failed also to encourage night-schools

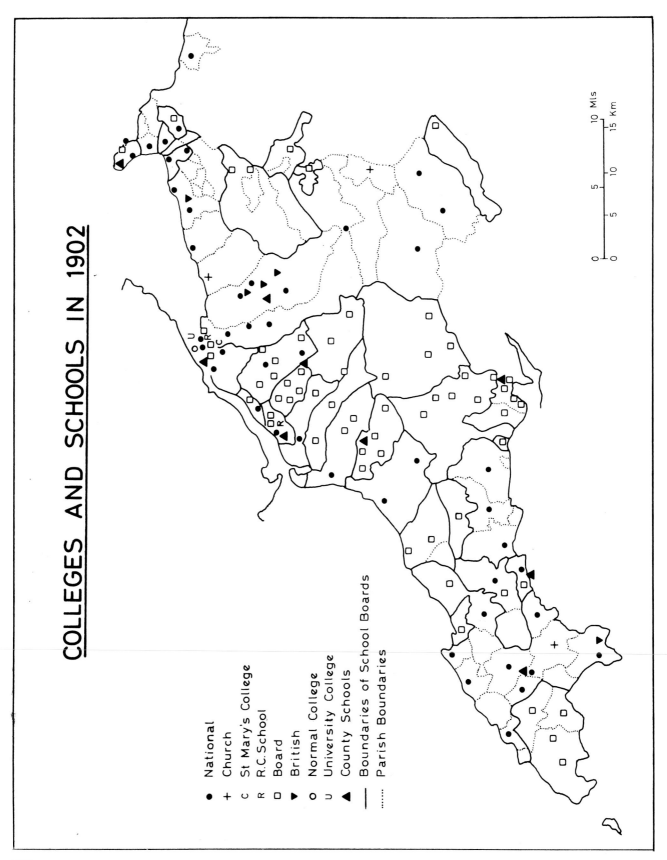

COLLEGES AND SCHOOLS IN 1902

	National
+	Church
C	St Mary's College
R	R.C.School
□	Board
▶	British
O	Normal College
U	University College
◀	County Schools
—	Boundaries of School Boards
⋯	Parish Boundaries

10 Mls
15 Km

until the authorities in London brought pressure to bear. There was a great demand for them. When one was opened at last in Bangor in 1892, 200 young people registered.

The middle class showed more enthusiasm for higher education, realising the opportunities it offered to their own children. The Welsh Intermediate Education Act of 1889 was generally accepted by everyone, both church and chapel, Liberal and Conservative, but the opportunity to establish a broad curriculum linking the schools with the industries and agriculture of the county was lost, and they aped the English Grammar School.

There is no need to emphasise that the 'Welsh Note' was in use in 1870 and for the next twenty years, and that when the Welsh language was finally admitted to the schools it was as a hand-maiden of English. It worried Sir Llywelyn Turner of Parkia that the natives of India were learning English faster than the native of Wales. In Bengal and Trincomalee, the British Schools Society used the native language as a medium for teaching English, and while praising *The Society for the Utilization of the Welsh Language,* it would be naïve to suppose that all its supporters were blind to the lesson of Trincomalee. Dan Isaac Davies, one of the founders of the movement, was not among them. In his evidence to the Cross Commission in 1887, he said, ' If the Welsh are not loyal to their own tongue the new movement will kill it.' It can be argued that permitting the use of Welsh in 1890 was not so much a victory as sowing the seeds of its decline.

It is true that by 1900 some 80% of the children of the county attended school regularly for at least six years, but there was still room to reform the education provided.

In comparison with the rest of Wales, Caernarvon-shire and north-west Wales had been rather well provided with facilities for post-primary education for some considerable time. Within the county, Bangor Friars School had been founded in 1557, Botwnnog in 1616 and Pwllheli *circa* 1736. The last had been discontinued in the eighteen-forties, and by the second half of the nineteenth century this provision was very inadequate and it was not until the passing of the Welsh Intermediate Education Act of 1889 that adequate provision was made in this sector. The Friars School and the Botwnnog School were adopted as County Schools under the new scheme in 1893. New schools followed in quick succession at other centres: Caernarfon, the first in 1894, was followed by Porthmadog, 1894; Bangor Girls' School, 1895; Pwllheli, 1895; Pen-y-groes, 1895; Bethesda, 1895; Llandudno, 1896, and Bryn-'refail, 1900. This basic pattern, with the addition of Aberconwy School, still remains as the main framework for secondary education in the county.

In higher education, the most important event was the founding of the University College of North Wales at Bangor in 1884. Shortly afterwards, in 1886, one of the two Independent Colleges from Bala moved to Bangor, only to be joined in 1890 by the other Independent College from the same town, hence the apellation of Bala-Bangor College ever since. The Baptist College, originally founded at Llangollen, likewise moved to Bangor in 1892. With the Normal College already founded there in 1858, and the coming of St. Mary's Training College to the city from Caernarfon in 1893, Bangor became the hub of a complex of colleges.

BIBLIOGRAPHY

Ellis, T. I., *The Development of Higher Education in Wales,* Wrexham, 1935.

Evans, D., *The Life and Work of William Williams, M.P. for Coventry 1835 - 1847, M.P. for Lambeth 1850 - 1865.* Llandysul, 1940.

H.M.S.O., *Education in Wales, 1847 - 1947,* London, 1947.

Hughes, W. (ed.), *The Life and Speeches of the Very Rev. J. H. Cotton,* Bangor, 1874.

Jones, T. Gwyn, *Cofiant Thomas Gee,* Denbigh, 1913.

Jones, W. R., *Addysg Ddwyieithog yng Nghymru,* Caernarfon, 1963.

Lewis, Henry, *Ysgolion Britanaidd Arfon, Cymru,* 1912.

Morgan, J. V., *Welsh Political and Educational Leaders in the Victorian Era,* London, 1908.

Phillips, T., *Wales: The language, social condition, moral character and religious opinions of the people considered in their relation to Education,* London, 1844.

Thomas, Richard (ed.), *History of the Normal College,* Conway, 1958.

Williams, J. Lloyd, *Atgofion Tri Chwarter Canrif,* London, 1945.

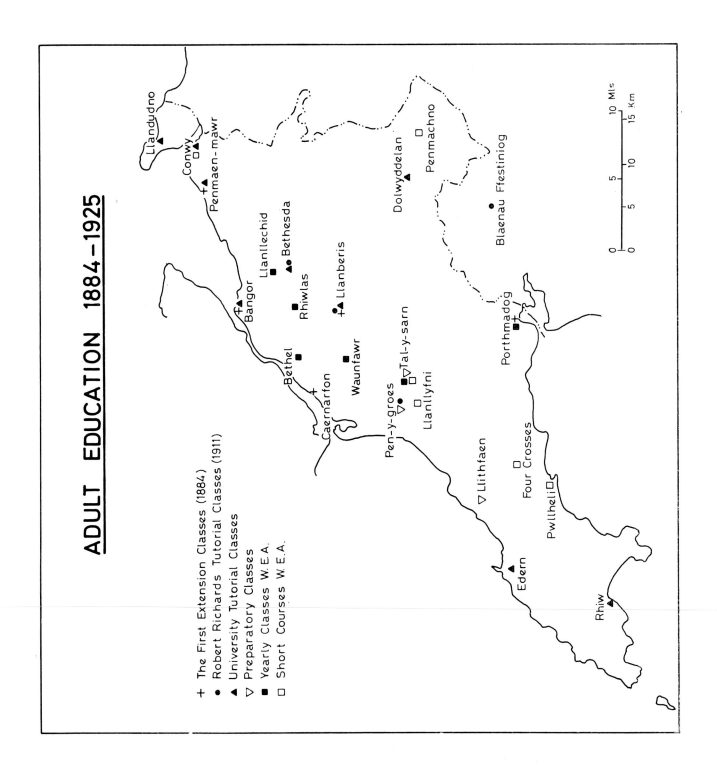

ADULT EDUCATION 1884-1925

+ The First Extension Classes (1884)
• Robert Richards Tutorial Classes (1911)
▲ University Tutorial Classes
▽ Preparatory Classes
■ Yearly Classes W.E.A.
□ Short Courses W.E.A.

Llandudno
Conwy
Penmaen-mawr
Bangor
Llanllechid
Bethesda
Rhiwlas
Llanberis
Bethel
Waunfawr
Caernarfon
Pen-y-groes
Tal-y-sarn
Llanllyfni
Llithfaen
Four Crosses
Pwllheli
Edern
Rhiw
Porthmadog
Dolwyddelan
Penmachno
Blaenau Ffestiniog

10 Mls
15 Km
5
10
5
5
0
0

Adult Education

The university extension movement which began in 1873 at Cambridge was a powerful influence in the establishment of new universities and colleges in England and Wales in the last quarter of the nineteenth century. It was not, therefore, surprising that when the College at Bangor was founded in 1884, it immediately embarked on its own programme of extension courses. Nine courses were organised during the first sessions, and five of these were in Caernarvonshire: at Bangor itself and in Caernarfon, Penmaen-mawr, Porthmadog and Llanberis. This was the start of liberal adult education as we know it today. But the impetus was short-lived. The courses decreased in number from year to year, and by 1892 they had entirely ceased to be provided. Another twenty years passed before the College again began to systematise its extra-mural mission and plan it on a permanent footing.

This time the inspiration came from the Workers' Educational Association, a new movement which began in England in 1903. In 1907, the W.E.A. organised a tutorial class in Wales at Wrexham, with R. H. Tawney as tutor. Three years later, R. Silyn Roberts, then a minister at Tanygrisiau and a member of the College Council, urged the Bangor Senate to establish extra-mural classes ' on the pattern of those promoted by the W.E.A. ', and in the same year, after some negotiations with the Quarrymen's Union, it was arranged for J. F. Rees (afterwards Sir Frederick Rees) to take a preparatory class in Industrial History at Blaenau Ffestiniog. The experiment was a success, and so in the following year the College appointed Robert Richards as a full-time tutor to teach Economics and to develop adult education amongst the quarrymen of Caernarvonshire and Merioneth. He continued with the Ffestiniog class and established new classes at Bethesda, Llanberis and Pen-y-groes.

In 1916, Robert Richards left to take up a post in the War Office, and the classes were discontinued. But the work recommenced at the end of the war on a wider scale than ever. In 1918, Ifor Williams held a class in Welsh Literature at Bethesda. A year later, Robert Richards was back, and the classes at Llanberis and Pen-y-groes had been restored. By 1922, the work had started to spread throughout North Wales. A. H. Dodd and R. Williams Parry were appointed to the College staff as tutors who shared their time between the extra-mural classes and the Departments of History and Welsh respectively. The number of classes increased, and there was a greater variety of subjects studied.

Up to this time, the College alone had been responsible for promoting adult education in North Wales. It functioned in close co-operation with the Trade Unions, especially the Quarrymen's Union. But in 1923 Silyn Roberts was appointed a full-time extra-mural tutor, and he at once saw the need to set up vigorous local organisations to extend the work. He proceeded with great energy to establish branches of the W.E.A., and was so successful that he was able to found, in 1925, a District Council of the Association to direct the movement throughout North Wales. In the new district's first year, the W.E.A. had two branches in Caernarvonshire, at Bangor and Conwy. There were 17 classes organised jointly with the College, and one sessional class and six short courses held by the W.E.A. itself.

When Silyn died suddenly in 1930, he had established seven branches in Caernarvonshire alone, and the Annual Report for that year shows that there were 16 joint classes and 28 independent W.E.A. classes. In the same year the College had one extension course at Bangor. Its tutor was A. H. Dodd, who was by then Professor of History and Chairman of the Joint Tutorial Classes Committee.

Silyn's place as W.E.A. District Secretary was taken by his widow, Mary Silyn Roberts, and under her direction and that of her successor, C. E. Thomas, the work expanded rapidly in Caernarvonshire, particularly in the period immediately after the second world war. It continues to expand under the present secretary, Mr. Raymond Rochell. The College programme has also expanded. Although Bangor was one of the first university colleges to appoint extra-mural staff tutors for adult education, it was not until 1948 that a Department of Extra-mural Studies was established with a full-time Director in charge.

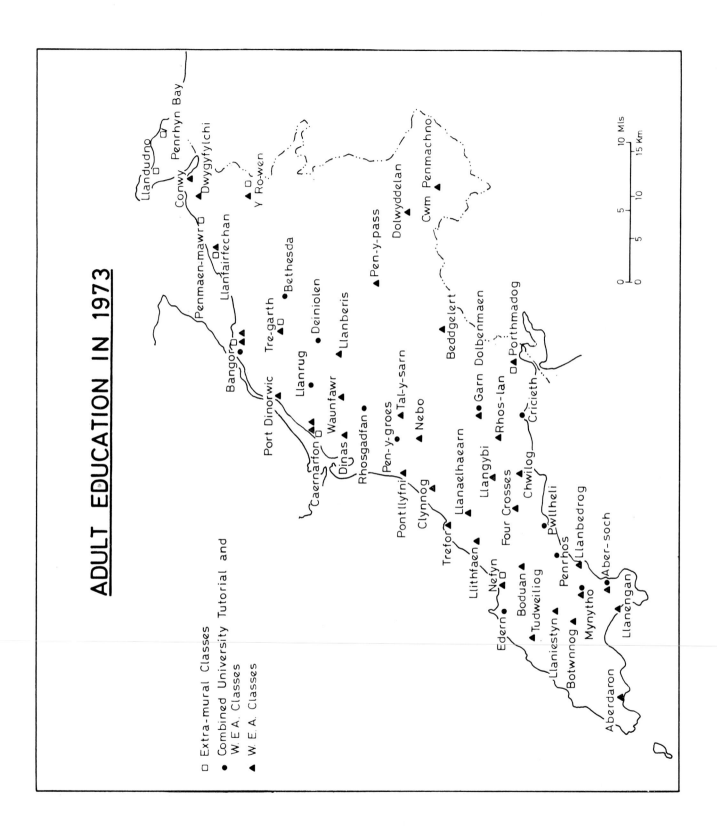

ADULT EDUCATION IN 1973

□ Extra-mural Classes

● Combined University Tutorial and
   W.E.A. Classes

▲ W.E.A. Classes

10 Mls
15 Km

Llandudno
Penrhyn Bay
Conwy
Dwygyfylchi
Y Ro-wen
Penmaen-mawr
Llanfairfechan
Bethesda
Pen-y-pass
Dolwyddelan
Cwm Penmachno
Tre-garth
Deiniolen
Bangor
Llanberis
Beddgelert
Port Dinorwic
Llanrug
Waunfawr
Garn Dolbenmaen
Porthmadog
Caernarfon
Dinas
Rhosgadfan
Pen-y-groes
Tal-y-sarn
Nebo
Rhos-lan
Cricieth
Pontllyfni
Llanaelhaearn
Llangybi
Chwilog
Clynnog
Four Crosses
Pwllheli
Trefor
Llithfaen
Penrhos
Llanbedrog
Nefyn
Boduan
Aber-soch
Edern
Tudweiliog
Mynytho
Llanengan
Llaniestyn
Botwnnog
Aberdaron

200

The following figures show the extent of growth of adult education in Caernarvonshire in the last quarter century:

1948-49

	W.E.A.	Joint	Univ. Coll.	Total
Classes	38	20	1	59
Students	614	317	14	945
Average per class ...	16	18.85	14	

1973-74

	W.E.A.	Joint	Univ. Coll.	Total
Classes	58	14	51	123
Students	780	211	1,071	2,062
Average per class ...	13.5	15	21	

These figures do not, however, show how the pattern of subjects studied has changed to meet new needs in the community nor how varied the demand is today. For instance, the figures under University College for 1973-74 do not include the residential courses held at Bangor during the session.

One other important fact must be mentioned. After the first world war, the Local Education Authorities came to play a more prominent part in adult education, not only by extending financial aid to Universities and to the W.E.A. and other voluntary bodies, but also by making their own provision in evening institutes and by other means. The 1944 Education Act placed the statutory obligation for ensuring adequate provision within their areas for all further education firmly on the shoulders of the Local Authorities. Caernarvonshire took advantage of this to plan as effectively as possible for its citizens. Adult education is now regarded as part of Further Education, and the boundaries between vocational studies or liberal or cultural education are not as closely defined as they were. In many areas, it is the Local Authority which carries today the heaviest burden of work, but in Caernarvonshire the close and happy co-operation between the interested parties ensures that the chief responsibility for organising the liberal education of adults remains with the University College and the W.E.A.

Robert Silyn Roberts

Robert Richards

Photographs by permission of the National Library of Wales and the W.E.A.

Caernarvonshire Newspapers

When one considers the extent and prestige attached to publishing and the adventurous spirit of its publishers, printers and journalists, Caernarvonshire holds a unique place in the history of the periodical press in Wales. Its presses, with their books and pamphlets, their periodicals and, in particular, their newspapers are the most important in the history of the Welsh press. Their essential characteristics are clear from the start for when Thomas Roberts printed *Yr Eurgrawn* in 1807 he included features on religious and moral themes, together with information on market and property prices.

The language of the early Caernarvonshire newspapers was English, *The North Wales Gazette* (Bangor), January 5, 1808; *The Caernarvon Advertiser* (Caernarfon), January 5, 1822; *The North Wales Chronicle* (Bangor), October 4, 1827; and *The Carnarvon Herald* (Caernarfon), January 1, 1831. These were promoted by Englishmen, with an occasional Welshman, like Richard Mathias Preece, with a finger in the pie. The vast majority of the population was Welsh-speaking, but so far the new leaders of Welsh Nonconformity had not acquired sufficient experience or capital to make use of the mass periodical media to lead their people, nor was it possible, before the completion of a railway network, to distribute newspapers in the county, neither had the population become sufficiently centred on the villages and towns to provide the reading public which would make the papers pay. But the greatest fetters on the development of the Welsh press were the three taxes on newspapers which made it difficult to publish any newspaper under fivepence a copy. The tax on newsprint itself was reduced in 1836, and in the autumn of that year *Y Papur Newydd Cymraeg* was launched in Caernarfon — according to its editor, the first Welsh weekly to appear after the reduction of the tax.

It is necessary to wait, however, until the abolition of the tax on advertisements in 1853 and of the stamp tax on newspapers in 1855 before the fetters were finally broken. By mid-century, too, there were a number of well-populated areas in the county and Nonconformity had tightened its hold on the community — a community which had learnt to read Welsh by this time in the Sunday School. Finally, by the seventies a railway network had been completed. It is fair to say that the period 1860 - 1895 was the golden age of newspaper publication in Caernarvonshire.

There were three publishing companies of first significance: *The Chronicle* in Bangor and *Yr Herald* and *Y Genedl* in Caernarfon. The last two companies were exceptionally prolific, publishing a mass of periodical and weekly material of a religious and Liberal colouring for towns as far apart as Barmouth, Holyhead, Rhyl and Llandudno, in addition to papers with a wider circulation, such as *Yr Herald Cymraeg* and *Y Genedl*. The Chronicle Company published newspapers in the Conservative interest, and politics and religion became a bone of contention between the Bangor and Caernarfon papers for most of the century, with no holds barred in the in-fighting between *The North Wales Chronicle* and *The Caernarvon Herald* in the thirties and between *Y Genedl* and *Gwalia* in the eighties. There was much recrimination between papers with more or less the same political approach, too — between *Yr Herald Cymraeg* and *Y Genedl* about the nuances of Nonconformist politics and circulation. Both papers sold around 14,000 copies a week for some years.

The vernacular newspapers were the most important. It is true that much detailed local information was available in the English papers and they published political articles beyond number and some of them were of considerable influence in town politics, but they lacked something. It was probably the zest and exuberance of providing for a whole community together with the consciousness of power and influence within that community which gave to the Welsh newspapers their particular quality.

The material provided by the Welsh newspapers in the second half of the century was wide-ranging. In addition to local news and advertisements, they contained well defined sections for each of the Nonconformist denominations, a column for the poet and musician and pages of national news, together with a mass of political articles. The boundaries between these various interests were well defined and many of the correspondents were little concerned with the material beyond their own immediate interests.

It is unlikely that anyone became rich through publishing and the pay of the journalists themselves was not high, yet there was considerable competition from time to time for some of the posts, especially for the editorship of some of the Welsh newspapers. There was a close connection between the pulpit and the editor's chair, and many men who were prominent in their own denominations were connected with the newspaper offices, among them being such stormy petrels as Herber Evans, Salem, Caernarfon, and Evan Jones, Moriah, of the same town. Literateurs of varying accomplishments like T. Gwynn Jones, Dic Tryfan and Thomas 'Tudno' Jones served on the staffs from time to time; indeed, Tudno had worked for publishers in Caernarfon, Llandudno and Bangor. Professional journalists like James Rees, Daniel Rees and E. Morgan Humphreys were exceptions.

The Welsh newspapers were aimed at a chapel-going, masculine, seriously-minded community for the most part. A weekly like *Briwsion i Bawb*

(Caernarfon), 1885-6, with its jokes and lighter material for every member of the family, was an exception.

Not every part of the county had a tradition of publishing — considering the steady growth of its population, Llandudno was remarkably poor. The truth is that some areas of the county were always outside the influence of these newspapers. By the beginning of the present century one has the impression that many of the old warriors of the vernacular press were still fighting battles which had already been lost or won. World War I was a milestone in the history of both the English and Welsh local press. It is true that they held their ground for some time afterwards, but the education system had ensured that the children of the uneasy post-war years could read the Liverpool and London papers. The railways which had carried *Yr Amseroedd* and *The Observer, Y Werin* and *Papur Pawb* could just as easily carry the *Daily Post* and the pink *Football Echo* to the new bilingual community of the cinema and the radio. It is an aspect of the miracle of survival of the language that part of this tradition of publishing survives — but in a new guise.

LIST OF NEWSPAPERS

Publishing/Printing Centres of weeklies:

1 BANGOR

North Wales Gazette, 1808 (1), 1817 (2)
North Wales Chronicle, 1827 (local editions, 3)
North Wales Gazette, 1850
Original Llandudno Directory and Visitor, 1861
Papur y Cymry, 1863
Cronicl Cymru, 1866 (1)
Llais y Wlad, 1874
Y Celt, 1882 (Bala, 1878)
The Bangor Observer, 1883
Y Clorianydd, 1891 (and Llangefni)
Y Chwarelwr Cymreig, 1893
Cronicl Cymru, 1893 (2)
Holyhead Chronicle, 1905
Bangor Herald, 1907
The Caernarvonshire and Anglesey Advertiser, 1929
Bangor Free Press, 1937
North Wales Motoring Weekly, 1962

2 BETHESDA

Y Wyddfa, 1876

3 CAERNARFON

The Caernarvon Advertiser, 1822
The Carnarvon Herald, 1831

The Carnarvon and Denbigh Herald, 1836 (local editions, 7)
Y Papyr Newydd Cymraeg, 1836
Yr Herald Cymreig, 1855
The Llandudno Register, 1857 (q.v., Llandudno)
Y Goleuad, 1869
North Wales Press, 1871
Y Genedl Gymreig, 1877
North Wales Express, 1877
Y Celt, 1879 (Bala, 1878)
The Holyhead Weekly Mail and Anglesey Herald, 1881
Gwalia, 1881 (Bangor, 1886)
Yr Amseroedd, 1882
North Wales Observer and Express, 1884
Briwsion i Bawb, 1885
Y Werin, 1885
Y Gadlef, 1887
Papur Pawb, 1893 (1)
Yr Eco Cymraeg, 1899
Y Wyntyll, 1903
The Welsh Leader, 1903
Awel Eryri, 1907
Y Gwyliwr, 1907
Y Sylwedydd, 1907
Y Dinesydd Cymreig, 1912
Papur Pawb, 1922 (2)
Yr Herald Cymreig, 1930 (Anglesey edition)

Yr Herald Cymraeg a'r Genedl, 1937
Herald Môn, 1956

4 CONWY

The Weekly News, 1889
The Northern Graphic, 1904
The Deganwy Sentinel/Conway Sentinel, 1915
The North Wales Standard, 1915

5 LLANDUDNO

Llandudno, 1882
Llandudno Advertiser, 1885
The Llandudno Register, 1893 (q.v., Caernarfon)
The Homefinder, 1913

6 PORTHMADOG

The South Caernarvon and Merioneth Leader / Yr Arweinydd 1939 (1), 1946 (2), 1953 (3) — including *Yr Utgorn, q.v. Pwllheli*

7 PWLLHELI

Yr Eifion > Yr Arweinydd, 1856
Udgorn Rhyddid, 1888

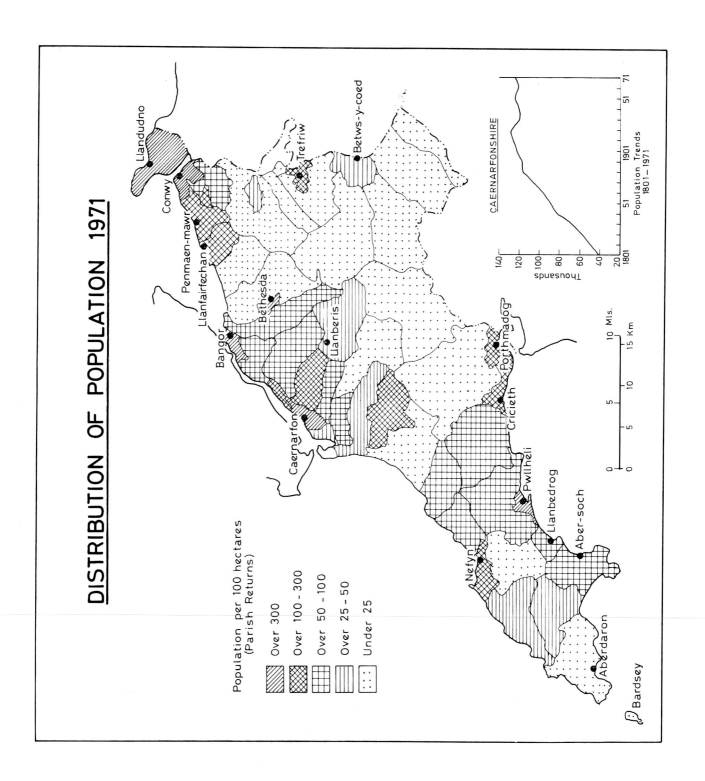

DISTRIBUTION OF POPULATION 1971

Population per 100 hectares
(Parish Returns)

Over 300

Over 100 - 300

Over 50 - 100

Over 25 - 50

Under 25

Llandudno

Conwy

Penmaen-mawr

Llanfairfechan

Bangor

Bethesda

Trefriw

Betws-y-coed

Llanberis

Caernarfon

Porthmadog

Cricieth

Pwllheli

Nefyn

Llanbedrog

Aber-soch

Aberdaron

Bardsey

CAERNARFONSHIRE

Population Trends
1801 - 1971

Thousands

140
120
100
80
60
40
20

1801   1901   71

1801   51   1901   51   71

10 Mls.

15 Km

0   5   5   10   15

Caernarvonshire Population

At the dawn of the nineteenth century, Caernarvonshire was still highly rural in character. Although there were villages or small towns, such as Llandudno, Conwy, Bangor, Caernarfon, Nefyn, Pwllheli and Cricieth along the coast, there were hardly any concentrations of people inland in spite of modest interest in the extraction of lead, copper and slate in certain districts. Conwy, Caernarfon and Cricieth were old castle towns; Bangor was an old ecclesiastical centre, and many of the coastal villages had minor ports and fishing harbours. On the fertile lowlands and sheltered valleys there was a well distributed network of farms and smallholdings, but in the inaccessible highland core with its steep slopes, poor soils and inclement weather, the population was very sparse.

The total population of the county in 1801 was no more than 41,521, but the census returns of the nineteenth century indicated a steady increase to 123,481 by 1901. The population continued to increase in this century to a peak of 128,183 in 1921. Two distinct trends appear in the census returns during the previous century. Up to 1841, the returns showed a significant increase in the total population with intercensal increases of 15% to 21.4%, but thereafter, up to the end of the century, the intercensal increase for the total population was no more than 7% to 12%. The rapid increase during the first forty years of the century can be attributed mainly to the development of the slate quarrying industry. In those inland parishes where quarrying was the principal occupation, the population doubled and trebled, and in the case of Llanllechid it nearly quadrupled itself between 1801 and 1841. The growth of a considerable number of slate-quarrying villages such as Bethesda, Bethel, Llanberis and Nantlle in these parishes was the most important legacy of the Industrial Revolution in Caernarvonshire. Most quarrymen came from the rural parishes of the county, and nearly 90% of the inhabitants in 1841 were Caernarvonshire-born. Nevertheless, up to about 1841, the population returns for most agricultural parishes continued to show a steady increase, but whereas the population of the quarrying districts continued to grow until the end of the century, very many of the agricultural parishes showed a steadily declining population after 1841.

Parallel with this growth of the slate industry and the development of narrow-gauge railways, there was much activity at the little ports of Conwy, Bangor, Port Dinorwic, Caernarfon and Porthmadog. There were active little harbours, too, at Nefyn, Aber-soch and Pwllheli. The population of Bangor, which had been highly static for some four centuries, was only 1,770 in 1801, but with the activities associated with the slate trade in and around Port Penrhyn, it grew to 7,232 by 1841, and similarly Caernarfon, the then most populous town in the county, grew from 3,626 in 1801 to 8,001 in 1841. The coming of the turnpike trusts and better roads did much to open up the county to outside influences at this time, and, in turn, fostered the growth of villages and towns.

From the middle of the century onwards, the construction of main railway lines also furthered the growth of industry and pioneered the development of tourism on a large scale. Of particular interest in this respect was the growth of Llandudno from an insignificant mining village to one of the most popular holiday resorts in the country. In 1851 even, its population was only 1,131, but in half a century it grew up to 9,279 by the 1901 census. Other coastal towns and villages, such as Conwy, Penmaen-mawr, Llanfairfechan, Bangor, Caernarfon, Nefyn, Aber-soch, Pwllheli and Porthmadog experienced further growth for similar reasons. Inland villages at Trefriw, Betws-y-coed, Beddgelert and Llanberis, on account of other attractions, also grew as holiday centres.

The emphasis in the function of the little towns of the county changed with the passage of time, and this in turn influenced the measure of their growth. For instance, Bangor over the ages has functioned as an ecclesiastical centre, a local market town, a little port, a railway centre and an educational centre as well as a catering town. Caernarfon, too, has functioned as a fortress town, an administrative centre, a slate port, a county town, a holiday town and a catering centre. Similar changes have taken place in other towns.

During the present century, the census returns for the county have fluctuated slightly, but the overall trend has been one of a declining population. After reaching a peak figure of 128,183 over half a century ago in 1921, it has not been able to regain that figure, and in the last census (1971) recorded a return of 123,064. [Graph.] Great variations in the returns have occurred within the county. Some of the main towns have continued to grow throughout this period, and Llandudno with a population of 19,077 in the last census takes pride of place. It is followed by Bangor with 14,558, Conwy with 12,206, and Caernarfon, the county town, with 9,260 in the 1971 census. Sadly, however, many other little towns and villages, such as Bethesda, Betws-y-coed, Penmaen-mawr, Cricieth, Porthmadog and Pwllheli, have declined in their population since the Second World War.

Some rural areas show an even more disturbing degree of depopulation, with the Nant Conwy district showing a loss of 15.5% since the Second World War, Llŷn a loss of 14% and Gwyrfai of 11.5% during the same period. Rural depopulation is characteristic in much of Wales, and is usually related to the shortage of suitable job prospects, the fewer amenities, the lack of public transport and the lure of youth to employment in the towns or across the border into England.

Furthermore, the complete collapse of the slate industry since the Second World War has also led to considerable depopulation in the slate-quarrying villages. Families had left for South Wales and parts of England during the years of depression between the wars, and the youth of the county have left in a steady stream to seek employment elsewhere for over half a century. Thanks to the popularity of the motor car and bus transport, the quarrying villages are now dormitory settlements with the majority of the inhabitants in all kinds of employment in towns nearby. Otherwise, the depopulation would have reached much more serious proportions. Of course, the closing of the railways and the curtailment of bus services have in themselves decreased job prospects.

The location of factories at many centres within the county during the last two decades has done much to check the outflow of population, and the steady migration of many retired people into the county helps maintain the levels of the total population. Yet an examination of the population structure reveals many characteristics of an ageing society.

In a county so closely associated with tourism, the seasonal fluctuations in the county's population are very significant. The enormous influx of summer visitors not only to the main resorts but also to the remotest farms and hamlets within the county has been made possible by the coming of the motor car. Every effort is being made to lengthen the holiday season, and this in turn may improve employment prospects. Tourism, however, is too seasonal in character, and many more factories and other sources of employment are urgently required in the county. The construction of better highways, the generation of more power and the direction of industry to the district could help retain the population.

As the map indicates, the present distribution of population continues to be exceptionally sparse in all the mountain areas, in many rural areas such as Llŷn and in the less accessible parts of the county. A moderate distribution prevails along the northern coastal belt and valley lowlands, but the only areas of reasonably dense population are found in pockets along the narrow coastal belt between Llandudno and Bangor, where adequate road and rail services are available.

It is difficult to prognosticate on population trends. Some observers anticipate a growing population, particularly in the Llandudno-Conwy and in the Bangor-Caernarfon areas during the coming decades, but the sudden nationwide fall in the birth-rate, the continual migration of youth to England and the difficulty of attracting industry on a significant scale into North Wales do not make the population or employment prospects for the county as a whole particularly promising during the foreseeable future.

POPULATION STATISTICS (1961 - 1971)

	1961	1971	Intercensal Changes
Caernarvonshire	121,767	123,066	1,297
Bangor	13,993	14,558	565
Bethesda	4,158	4,163	4
Betws-y-coed	788	729	—59
Caernarfon	9,055	9,260	205
Conwy	11,183	12,206	1,023
Cricieth	1,672	1,505	—167
Llandudno	17,904	19,077	1,173
Llanfairfechan	2,869	3,442	573
Penmaen-mawr	3,751	3,991	240
Porthmadog	3,960	3,683	—277
Pwllheli	3,647	3,823	176

Cottage Ruins, Cilgwyn

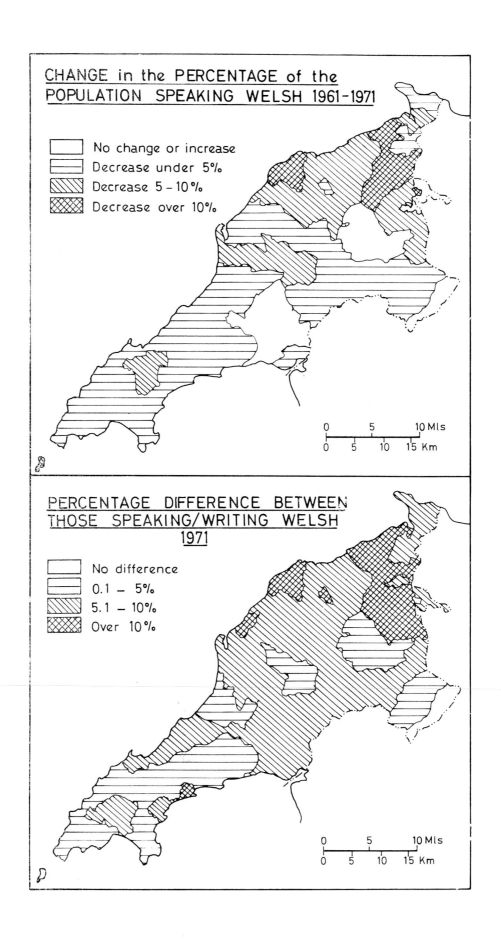

CHANGE in the PERCENTAGE of the
POPULATION SPEAKING WELSH 1961-1971

No change or increase
Decrease under 5%
Decrease 5 – 10%
Decrease over 10%

0   5   10 Mls
0   5   10   15 Km

PERCENTAGE DIFFERENCE BETWEEN
THOSE SPEAKING/WRITING WELSH
1971

No difference
0.1 – 5%
5.1 – 10%
Over 10%

0   5   10 Mls
0   5   10   15 Km

The Position of the Welsh Language

The present position of the Welsh language in Caernarvonshire is represented in four maps. There are two distribution maps, one in which a simple ten per cent interval is used to indicate the proportions able to speak Welsh and a second in which quartiles are used, that is, all the percentages for the parishes are ranged from the highest to lowest and then divided into four groups, each with an equal number of parishes. The third map indicates the change in the proportion able to speak Welsh between 1961 and 1971, and the fourth map depicts the difference between those claiming to be able to speak and those who claim to write Welsh. This last map can be compared with the one indicating change over the last decade since, if a language is in decline, then the ability to write it in a formal fashion will be lost more quickly than the ability to speak it. The maps will not be analysed separately, but the evidence they display will be used to discuss the present patterns of the language.

In 1971, some 62.0 per cent of the population of Caernarvonshire was able to speak Welsh, compared with 68.3 per cent in 1961. This represents a decline of 6.3 per cent, a little more than the decline for the whole of Wales, which was 5.2 per cent. On the other hand, only some 20.84 per cent of the population of Wales was returned as Welsh-speaking, so that the county has one of the highest proportions, but still only taking fifth place of the traditional five core counties of Welsh Wales, largely due to the low Welsh-speaking proportions on the eastern margins. It follows that the dominant general contrast that appears is that between west and east, and this is characteristic of all the criteria, distribution, change and difference. This major contrast is between Llŷn on the one hand and the lower Conwy valley on the other. Between these two there is the more complex area of Snowdonia and Arfon.

The Llŷn peninsula is one of the core areas of Welsh speech, and the proportions remain high, generally over 80 per cent. Most significant is the fact that these high values are maintained along the north coast, and to a lesser degree along the south. Generally in Wales the proportions speaking Welsh are lower on the coasts than in the interior, but in north Llŷn this is not so, and the area demonstrates the only stretch of coastline in Wales with Welsh-speaking percentages generally over 80 and, for much of the length, over 90. There is clearly a reduction along the south coast especially related to the main centres of tourism, areas of second-home ownership, and the towns. This is not reflected in the intercensal change, but does come out in the map of difference between speaking and writing. Generally, however, the maps of change and difference demonstrate how intensely Welsh an area Llŷn remains.

In contrast, the lower Conwy valley and the Creuddyn peninsula show proportions able to speak Welsh only a little over 50 per cent, and this falls to only 19.7 per cent in Llandudno, with 34.7 per cent in Conwy and 46.5 per cent in Penmaen-mawr. This situation is reflected in both change and difference. For example, the proportions speaking Welsh in the parish of Caerhun fell from 73.4 per cent in 1961 to 57.1 per cent in 1971. There are two elements involved in this process of anglicisation. The first is a general one in that influences leading to decline of the language are derived from the border and push westwards, particularly along the coasts and lowlands. Although higher percentages are recorded on the Denbigh moorlands to the east, the tide of anglicisation generally pushes along the coast and up the valleys. More specifically, the development of tourism, as in south Llŷn, explicitly brings anglicisation along with it. The rate of second-home ownership is low in these areas and would not seem to be a significant factor.

The central area is more complex in its condition. There, too, tourism seems to have had an anglicising influence, and an axis of relatively low percentages now extends from Porthmadog through Beddgelert and Capel Curig to link up with the Conwy valley wedge of lower proportions. To some extent, this represents the tourist sphere extending from Betws-y-coed into the upper Conwy drainage and across into the Glaslyn valley and the Vale of Ffestiniog.

The northern part of Snowdonia still retains a high proportion of Welsh speakers, particularly in the

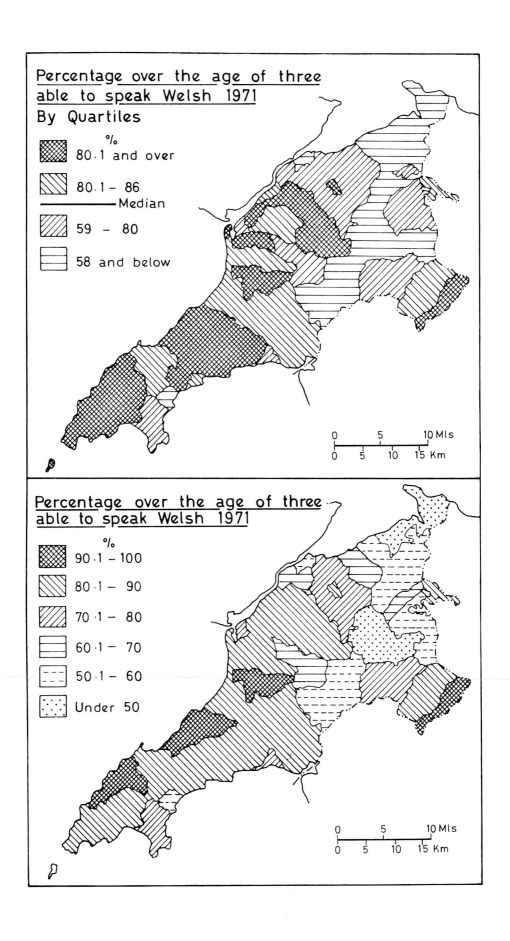

Percentage over the age of three able to speak Welsh 1971
By Quartiles

%
80.1 and over
80.1 – 86
———Median
59 – 80
58 and below

0   5   10 Mls
0 5 10 15 Km

Percentage over the age of three able to speak Welsh 1971

%
90.1 – 100
80.1 – 90
70.1 – 80
60.1 – 70
50.1 – 60
Under 50

0   5   10 Mls
0 5 10 15 Km

former slate-quarrying areas. Llanberis still returns nearly 88 per cent as having the language and has only declined by just under 3 per cent since 1961. The coastal lowland of Arfon, however, displays a greater tendency to decline, particularly about Caernarfon and Bangor, for losses characterise their suburban extensions. This is more apparent in the more easterly town of Bangor, where the percentage at 53.4 has fallen by 12.2 per cent from the 65.6 figure for 1961. Pentir, the parish immediately south-west of Bangor, has also fallen by just over 12 per cent, and both show big differences between speakers and writers.

Finally, the parishes in the extreme south-east, Penmachno and Eidda, in the upper Conwy drain-age, are more remote and provide a link with another core of Welsh speech, Penllyn. Both retain high proportions (84.4 and 96.3 per cent) and show little change (even an increase in the parish of Eidda) and slight differences.

In summary, Caernarvonshire depicts the classic situation of the Welsh language. On the one hand, there is a distinctive and dominant core of Welsh speech, but there is also, on the other hand, evidence of the characteristic forces of diminution, particularly tourism, spreading from the east and particularly along the lowlands and penetrating the valleys. There is a gradual push from the east which is clear on all the four maps presented.

THE LANGUAGE IN NINETEENTH CENTURY SCHOOLS

June 15.

Fine day. One new pupil admitted. A Welsh Card was given out in the I D so as to force the class to talk English. The regulations about it are, that every child who gets 12 marks during the week, is to pay a fine of ½d. and all that will be under, to learn the same number (as they will have marks) of spelling.

At the end of the quarter the mulcts are to be distributed among those that will have had the least number of marks.

From the Log Book of the Llanllyfni British School, 1865.

Sept. 30th.

Could not open school till 9.30 on account of children watching the late master's (Mr. Roberts) marriage. Attendance 40.

Note. I find a great difficulty when giving a lesson to the lower classes, in making them understand my meaning on account of their *very* deficient knowledge of English, and my ignorance of Welsh; in the 1st. classes this difficulty still remains though not to such a degree, one or two boys being able to speak English very fairly, still there are a few from whom it is next to impossible to obtain an answer in English.

From the Log Book of Clynnog National School, 1863.

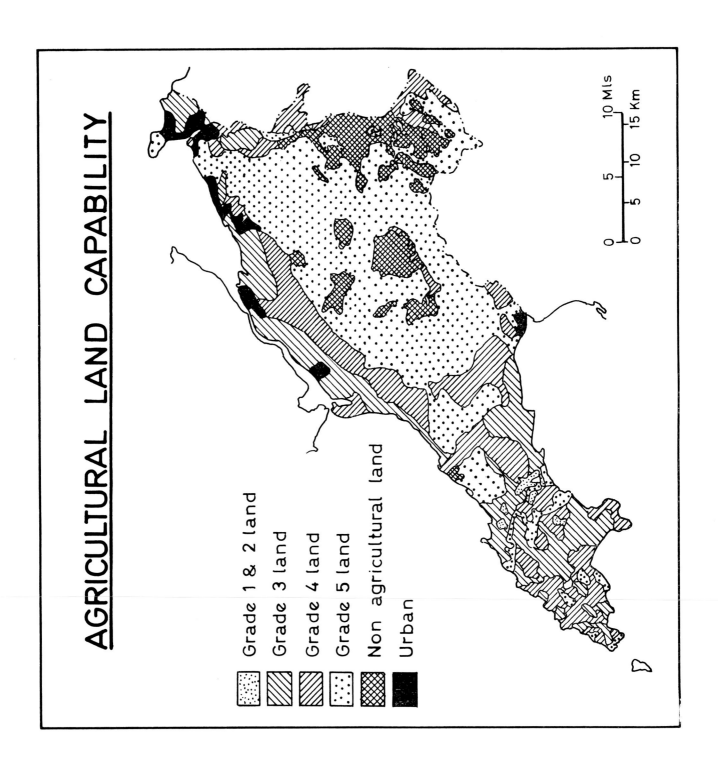

AGRICULTURAL LAND CAPABILITY

Grade 1 & 2 land

Grade 3 land

Grade 4 land

Grade 5 land

Non agricultural land

Urban

10 Mls
15 Km

Agriculture

The agriculture of Caernarvonshire is very clearly livestock based. It was estimated in the early 1970s that about 97% of the gross agricultural output of the county was derived from livestock: beef cattle and stores contributed 43%, dairy cows and milk 23%, sheep 18%, poultry 9% and pigs about 4%. This emphasis certainly reflects the suitability of the local terrain for grassland as against cropping.

Over 60% of the total agricultural area is under rough grazing and this is of very poor quality. The proportion under tillage crops is only 9%. The proportion of land under rough grazing varies considerably, however, from district to district and is a major contributory factor to internal differences within the agricultural economy. In the tract of land enclosed within the National Park in every parish at least 50% of the land is under rough grazing. It also makes up the majority land usage at Dolbenmaen, Porthmadog, Cricieth, Llanaelhaearn and Pistyll. The only areas with less than a quarter of the land under rough grazing are in western Llŷn (excepting Aberdaron), the shores of the Menai from west of Caernarfon to Bangor, the Maenan area of the Vale of Conwy and the Creuddyn peninsula. Tillage crops have a broadly inverse distribution for they are almost entirely absent in Snowdonia and on the tract extending from Cricieth to Dolbenmaen. Only at Llandudno and in six parishes in western Llŷn did they exceed 10% of the total agricultural area.

The fact that these patterns of land-use reflect the inherent physical attributes of the various districts from the point of view of potential for grass and crop production is confirmed when Map (p. 212) is examined. This is a copy of the Agricultural Land Capability map produced by the Ministry of Agriculture. This suggests the potential of various areas where due consideration is given to factors of altitude, aspect, slope, climate and soil. It is included in the atlas along with Map (p. 214) to provide a backcloth to the description of the livestocking pattern.

Indeed, in view of the outstanding importance of livestock farming in the county, it is likely that the more localized characteristics of agriculture can be represented by a map showing the significant livestock enterprises in each parish. Map (p. 216) was produced by applying a standardized system of statistical analyses to the June 1973 Agricultural Census for Caernarvonshire parishes. The dairy cattle, beef cattle, sheep, pigs and poultry have been reduced to a common denominator of livestock units which reflect the amount of fodder consumed by different types of livestock of various ages. The units attributed to the various categories of livestock have then been analysed to identify the characteristic grouping of livestock enterprises in individual parishes.

Accepting the limitations often imposed by significant physical and socio-economic differences which exist within individual parishes, and that individual farm identity is lost, the processed data proves to be interesting.

Centred on Snowdonia is a sheep-rearing territory. It is often associated with very large holdings utilizing largely Grade 5 land. Beef cattle nowhere account for as much as 20% of the livestock units. Dairy cattle are generally even less important — there was not a single dairy cow at Capel Curig. The animals reared generally find their way via local markets to low-lying farms. Many of the young Welsh Mountain ewes are sold in individual farm sales.

The interests of hill sheep farmers are often in conflict with those who require unimpeded access to the mountains for recreational purposes. Extensive tracts of mountain grazing have also been lost to the forester. He also depends heavily on Government subsidies. He is, in fact, very much at the mercy of extraneous forces.

A zone of sheep with beef cattle enterprises virtually encloses this dominantly sheep area. These livestock are dominant in the Snowdonia foothills to the south and west, in the hill country of eastern Llŷn and along the western slopes of the Conwy valley. In these areas altitude is lower, slopes are generally less steep and weather conditions less severe. The agricultural land is a mixture of Grades 4 and 5; the latter predominating near the mountain fringes. Sheep farming is everywhere the leading enterprise, but beef cattle

ROUGH GRAZING

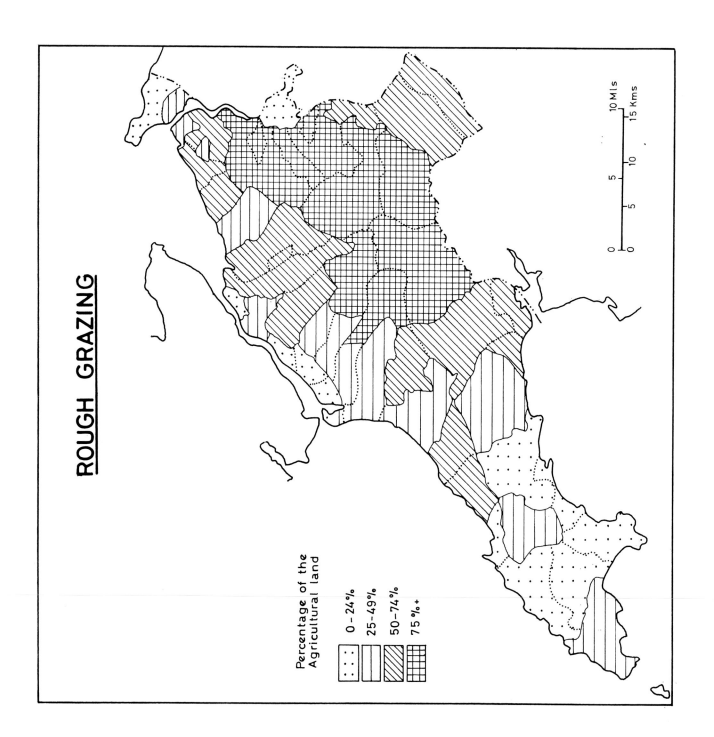

Percentage of the
Agricultural land

0 – 24%
25 – 49%
50 – 74%
75 % +

10 Mls
15 Kms

214

are always significant. In both instances the emphasis is on rearing rather than fattening. At Waunfawr and in many places along the western slopes of the Conwy, however, most of the male cattle exceed a year old and an element of fattening is suggested. These areas have better quality pastures associated with a free draining soil. Elsewhere pastures are poorer and soils heavy and strong.

The marketing pattern is essentially similar to that in the mountains, but without the annual farm sales. The sale of liquid milk is also more significant, but the specialist dairy farmer is very much the exception, reflecting both the poorish quality of pastures and the inducements offered to stock-rearing by the availability of hill farm subsidies.

Much of this sheep and cattle territory contains remnants of former slate quarrymen's holdings. Their abandonment has given the associated stone wall country a distinct derelict appearance.

Sheep, beef cattle and dairy cattle are of comparatively equal importance in an extensive area of the county. (The relative order varies considerably, but the sequences is not particularly important.) This pattern of livestocking characterizes much of western Llŷn, many of the parishes fringing the Menai Strait and Maenan and the Abbey in the Vale of Conwy.

Sheep are virtually ever present on the lowlands (Llanbedrog and Bangor are the only exceptions), but they are usually managed differently to the mountain and hill country flocks. There is a greater emphasis on fattening. Lambs are often produced by crossing Welsh Mountain or half-bred ewes with lowland rams. Beef cattle production contains a store as well as a fatstock element. Cattle fattening tends to dominate in the Creuddyn pensinula, on the shores of the Menai between Llanwnda and Y Felinheli and in an extensive area extending from west of Cricieth to Aberdaron. In these districts Grade 3 and 4 land predominate, but there are pockets of Grade 2 land, and the only Grade 1 land in the county is found at Efailnewydd in Llŷn. Equally, there are patches of very poor land. The generally superior features, however, provide the requisite base for livestock fattening activities. Many farms are also able to produce their own fodder crops. It is interesting that almost two-thirds of what the Ministry regard as 'mixed' viable holdings in the county are to be found west of Clynnog and Dolbenmaen.

At Llanengan and Llanbedrog dairy cattle are comparatively unimportant. This illustrates the fact that cattle fattening and dairying are often mutually exclusive activities on individual farms. The larger farmers concentrate on fattening and larger farms predominate in these two parishes.

Fat stock is sold at local markets, Pwllheli, Bryncir, Menai Bridge, Llangefni and Llanrwst, as well as through buying agencies by national meat companies.

The Llŷn peninsula also stands out as the leading dairying area in the county, for over 60% of the county's specialist dairy farmers, as well as a majority of those regarded as being mainly involved in dairying, are found west of Clynnog and Dolbenmaen. The better quality pastures and fairly long growing season of the peninsula are a definite inducement to the dairymen. These same factors, as well as access to markets, also account for the importance of dairying along the northern coastlands and in the Creuddyn peninsula.

Over nine million gallons of milk was sold off Caernarvonshire farms in 1971 and six million gallons of this was sold through the producer-owned South Caernarvonshire Creamery at Chwilog in Llŷn where nearly two-thirds of the through-put was processed into Cheddar cheese. The remaining output was marketed through the Milk Marketing Board Creamery at Llangefni and the Northern Dairies Creamery at Mochdre. Many of the dairy herd calves are sold to local beef and store cattle producers. A complex interdependence certainly exists in the livestock industry.

The only parishes in the county where poultry are of noteworthy significance are Bangor, Llanwnda, Porthmadog and Llandudno. This is a pattern which suggests an orientation towards a local urban market. The same is suggested by the importance of pig rearing at Bangor.

Within the poultry industry the emphasis is on producing eggs for the local consumer from fairly large production units. The small flock of poultry common to every farm holding is a feature of the past. Apart from the places previously mentioned, those parishes where poultry exceeded 5% of the local livestock units are scattered through the county at Maenan, Henryd, Llanddeiniolen, Llanrug, Llanystumdwy, Nefyn and Llannor.

The effects of a movement towards specialist production units is also apparent when pigs are considered. Between 1961 and 1971 the pig population increased by over a third, and yet only at Bangor, Maenan, Llandudno, Llanbeblig and Llannor do pigs account of 5% or more of the live-

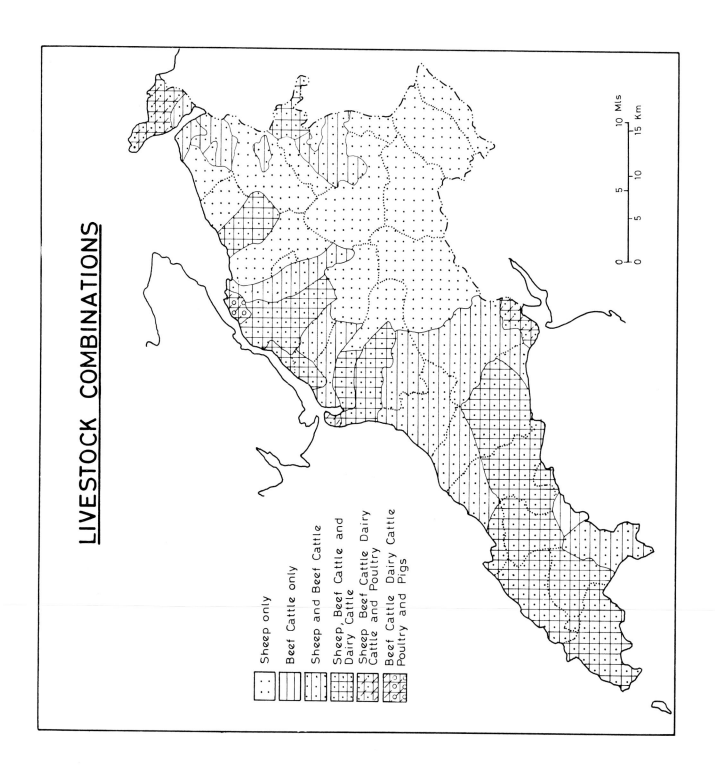

LIVESTOCK COMBINATIONS

Sheep only

Beef Cattle only

Sheep and Beef Cattle

Sheep, Beef Cattle and Dairy Cattle

Sheep Beef Cattle Dairy Cattle and Poultry

Beef Cattle Dairy Cattle Poultry and Pigs

10 Mls

15 Km

216

stock units. In five Snowdonia parishes there were no pigs at all. Well over three-quarters of the pigs produced in the county are sold as weaners through farmer-organized groups at Pwllheli, Tud-weiliog, Llandwrog and Llanrwst.

The sale of cash crops contributes very little to farm income, but the horticultural industry in the Creuddyn peninsula, the early potatoes of Aber-daron and the main crop potatoes of Llanystumdwy and Llannor are worth mentioning.

Livestock farming is not usually labour intensive and this is particularly the case when, as in Caernarvonshire, grass rather than other crops forms the basis of feeding. Small family farms are certainly the lynch-pins of Caernarvonshire farming. Only 140 of the 893 viable holdings exceed 150 acres in size. Indeed, only 35% of the county's 2,553 holdings are deemed capable of offering full-time work for at least one man. The small

holding phenomena is a significant feature of the county's agricultural structure. In the parishes of Trefriw, Dolgarrog, Dwygyfylchi, Betws-y-coed, Llandygái, Bangor, Llanfaglan, Llanwnda, Llan-dwrog, Llanllyfni and Llanbedrog three-quarters or more of the holdings were classified as part-time. These figures do not indicate the proportion of land involved and may also mark the trend towards farm amalgamation. Throughout the county the small farmhouses once occupied by the quarryman-smallholder have a non-agricultural usage in the form of seasonal homes.

The number of people employed in agriculture is declining rapidly. In 1971 the number of farmers was only three-quarters of the 1951 total, and the number of agricultural workers barely more than a third of the 1951 total. It is not without interest that in the early 1970s agriculture accounted for only about 10% of male employment, whilst 86% of the land area of the county was used agriculturally.

Sale of Mountain Rams: Capel Curig

Copyright: Bob Parry & Co. Ltd.

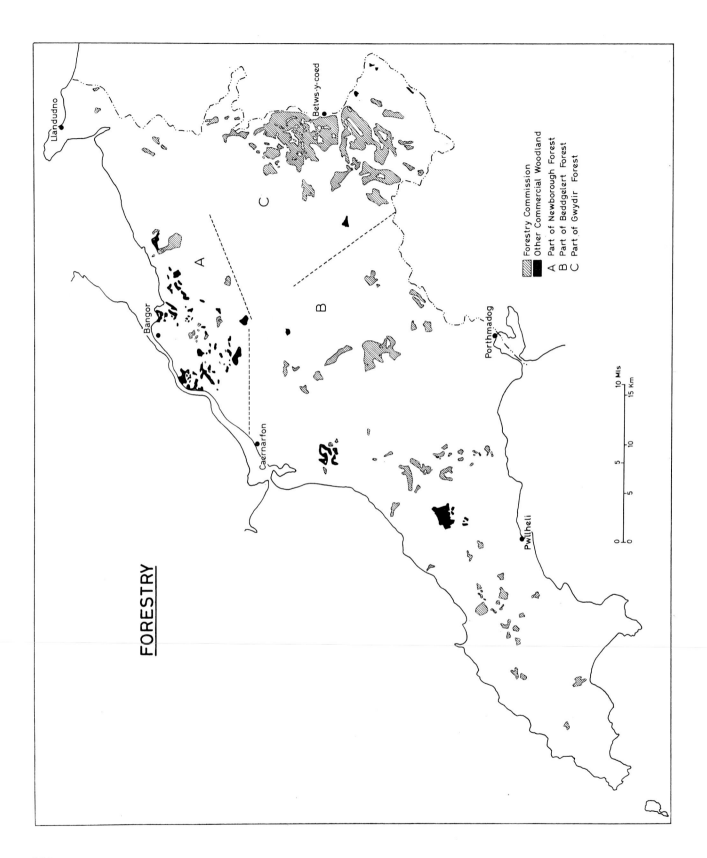

FORESTRY

Forestry Commission
Other Commercial Woodland
A Part of Newborough Forest
B Part of Beddgelert Forest
C Part of Gwydir Forest

Llandudno

Betws-y-coed

C

A

Bangor

B

Caernarfon

Porthmadog

Pwllheli

10 Mls
15 Km

Forestry

As recently as 1895, Caernarvonshire was one of the most poorly wooded counties in Britain. There were only 1,068 acres of plantation covering less than 0.3% of the land area of the county. By 1972 some 23,514 acres or 6.5% of the land area was under some form of managed woodland; comparing with 7.9% of the land surface of the United Kingdom as a whole. The county is, however, one of the most afforested counties in Wales and woodland is a dominant landscape feature in the county's south-eastern extremities.

Significant reafforestation had to await the Forestry Act of 1919 and the establishment of the Forestry Commission. This development was motivated by an awareness of Britain's almost total dependence on imported timber and by a drive to utilize productively the country's extensive areas of waste. The Commission's policy in the inter-war years reflected these factors. Woodland rarely flourishes on land which is totally negative from the agricultural point of view. Particularly attractive to the forester was land classified as Grades 4 and 5 by agricultural scientists. Caernarvonshire has an abundance of this quality land (see section on agriculture) and was thus an attractive domain for the forester.

The Forestry Commission's original acquisition in the county was a lease of 2,400 hectares from the Earl of Ancaster in 1920. Planting in what is now a part of the Gwydir forest commenced in 1921. In 1927 the first planting took place in what is now part of the Beddgelert forest. Extensive tracts of these two forests, together with the Menai beat of the Newborough forest, form the Commission's administrative entities within the county. The main area of the Gwydir forest extends on the west side of Afon Conwy from its Afon Machno tributary to its Afon Cadnant tributary. The main block of the Beddgelert forest lies some three miles south-west of the central Snowdon massif. The plantations of Llŷn are also a part of this forest. The Menai beat of the Newborough forest is located in the area between Aber and Bethesda. Both this beat and the Llŷn plantations are characterized by small and scattered plots which have high management costs. Their acquisition and planting reflected an unfounded optimism concerning potential Forestry Commission activity in these districts.

The Gwydir forest and the bulk of the Beddgelert forest provide an interesting contrast. The former is the best endowed from the sylvi-culturists viewpoint. It is mainly developed on an 800-1,000' plateau and its surrounding steep slopes. The rainfall varies from about 45" per annum on the lower slopes to about 80" on the higher ground. The generally peaty soils support spruces and pines. Douglas Firs dominate on the steeper slopes. Today there are here about 11,700 acres of planted conifers and 2,300 acres of various broadleaved species. The main body of the Beddgelert forest lies on a rocky ridge of varied geology and soils. It is difficult terrain and includes bare rock, irregular steep slopes and thin and deep peat deposits. Rainfall often exceeds 90" a year, but most of the plantations are fairly well sheltered from south-westerly gales. As a result of the generally more difficult conditions, spruce is even more in evidence than at Gwydir.

Gwydir is served by 100 miles of forest roads and 37 miles of shaled tracks as against only 24 miles of roadway in Beddgelert — a reflection in part of the differing dimensions of the forests, but also of contrasting terrain conditions.

An examination of Table 1 shows that the main period of planting in Caernarvonshire was between 1946 and 1970. The planting of new territory is expected to cease before 1981.

AGE CLASS DISTRIBUTION

(Gwydir, Beddgelert and Newborough Forests)

Age Class	Hectares
1971-5	320
1966-70	1,080
1961-65	1,630
1956-60	1,410
1951-55	1,660
1946-50	1,090
1941-45	310
1936-40	650
1931-35	740
1926-30	680
1921-25	140
Pre 1920	70

It generally takes between fifty and seventy years for the Commission's conifers to reach a marketable size, a feature reflected in the fact that felling activity is expected to increase considerably towards the end of the century.

PRODUCTION FORECAST
(GWYDIR, BEDDGELERT AND NEWBOROUGH FORESTS)
— VOLUMES BY SIZE CLASSES

(thousands of cubic metres per year)

	Total	Felling	Thinning
1972	26.7	14.1	12.6
1977	31.5	13.6	17.9
1982	40.6	17.7	22.9
1987	48.5	21.6	26.9
1992	64.9	34.2	30.7

Some of the earlier plantations are currently being harvested and there is a continuous flow of tree thinnings from all areas. The main products are sawlogs and pulpwood. Sawlogs are sent to the sawmills at Conwy, Ellesmere and Wigan. Small roundwood in spruce and pine are received at the integrated ground-wood pulp and paper mill at Ellesmere Port. Roundwood is also marketed as pit props and fencing stakes, whilst some is sent to Chirk for chipboard production.

The activities of the Forestry Commission attracted controversy from the onset. Arguments have raged concerning the comparable profitability of foresting and agriculture, as well as above the aesthetic qualities of coniferous woodlands.

An official report published in 1972 showed conclusively that, in terms of rate of return to investment and on the evaluation of jobs provided per acre in upland areas, forestry is a comparatively poor competitor with hill farming. A comprehensive view of the future of rural areas, however, appreciates the complementary nature of developments in forestry, agriculture, tourism and rural industries.

Much Forestry Commission plantation in Caernarvonshire has been on former agricultural land (Grades 4 and 5) and it is interesting that 5,500 or so acres held by the Commission is being formed at the present time. This feature was encouraged so as to provide smallholding facilities for part-time workers in forestry, to provide fire breaks and, possibly, to placate the agricultural lobby. Over the years, many have failed to attract tenants, and some farm cottages are now let as holiday homes.

The labour demands of forestry are being constantly reduced. In 1971, 146 people worked for the Forestry Commission in the county compared with 265 in 1961. The diminution in planting activity will see a further cut-back in labour requirements. It is likely that the bulk of timber harvesting will be accomplished by using contract labour.

About one in five of the trees in the Commission's plantations are of a broad-leaved variety. This reflects an attempt to break the monotony of extensive coniferous plantation. Yet for years little care was taken over detailed landscaping. Recently considerable efforts have been made to redress this situation. The issue is highlighted locally by virtue of the location of so much of the Commission's plantations within the Snowdonia National Park. The establishment of a Forestry Consultative Panel in 1955 has, however, resulted in widespread co-operation between all parties interested in afforestation within the Park.

Snowdonia lies in fairly close proximity to the populous areas of England and attracts many visitors. In recent decades the Forestry Commission has recognized that the provision of social facilities is one of its main functions. Their woodlands in Caernarvonshire can accommodate 8,000 visitors in one day. Facilities vary from wild-life reserves to picnic places and orienteering courses. It is estimated that in the future 29,000 visitors can be dealt within a day.

Private commercial forestry is comparatively insignificant in the county. Some 3,500 acres are involved under the Dedication and 250 acres under Approved Woodlands schemes. Most plantations are managed directly by their owners, of which the dominant group is Economic Forestry (Wales) Ltd. with nearly 1,200 acres. In general they are more lowlying than Forestry Commission woodlands. The main concentration is in a belt extending from Llanfairfechan to Llanddeiniolen on what is or was the Penrhyn and Faenol estates.

There are quite extensive amenity woodlands in the county and they are usually protected by Tree Preservation Orders. Particularly noteworthy is the Lôn Goed in Eifionydd, immortalized in Williams Parry's poem.

Glasgwm, near Penmachno

221

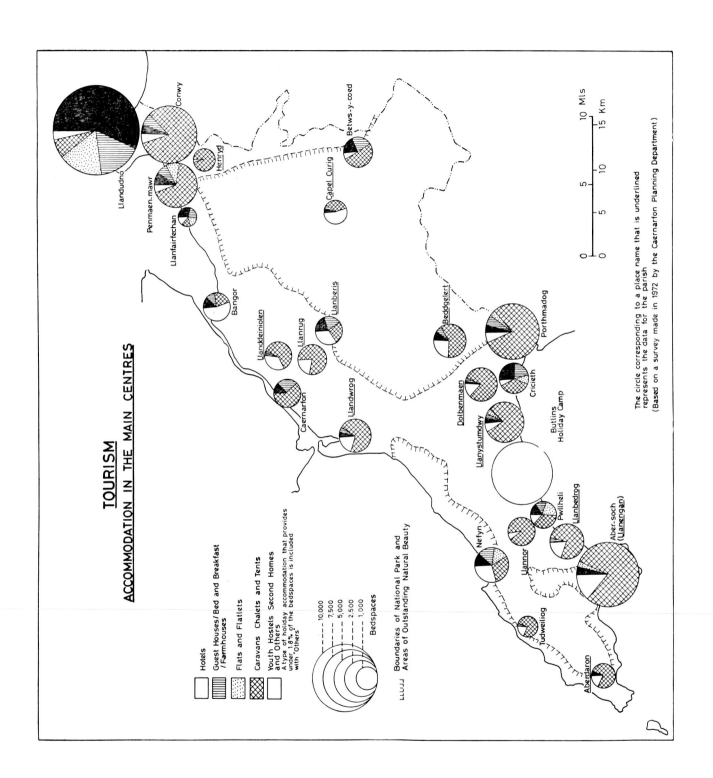

TOURISM
ACCOMMODATION IN THE MAIN CENTRES

Hotels

Guest Houses/ Bed and Breakfast /Farmhouses

Flats and Flatlets

Caravans Chalets and Tents

Youth Hostels Second Homes and Others
A type of holiday accommodation that provides under 1.8% of the bedspaces is included with 'Others'

10,000
7,500
5,000
2,500
1,000

Bedspaces

Boundaries of National Park and Areas of Outstanding Natural Beauty

Conwy
Henryd
Betws-y-coed
Llandudno
Penmaen-mawr
Llanfairfechan
Capel Curig
Bangor
Llanddeiniolen
Llanrug
Llanberis
Beddgelert
Porthmadog
Caernarfon
Llandwrog
Dolbenmaen
Criccieth
Llanystumdwy
Butlins Holiday Camp
Nefyn
Llannor
Pwllheli
Llanbedrog
Aber-soch (Llanengan)
Tudweiliog
Aberdaron

The circle corresponding to a place name that is underlined represents the data for the parish
(Based on a survey made in 1972 by the Caernarfon Planning Department)

10 Mls
15 Km

Tourism

Travellers have been coming to the county ever since the age of the pilgrims. The first to leave behind an account of his journey was Gerald the Welshman. Leland in Tudor times rendered a similar service, whilst early in the eighteenth century we have Dr. Johnson. But he was a townsman with but little feeling for the wild landscape of Snowdonia. It was the Romantic Movement in all its complexity that brought the most interesting travellers. One is aware of the new attitudes in the work of Thomas Love Peacock, ' Headlong Hall '. It was the same change in the intellectual climate that brought Shelley to the county. Yet the most discerning of the travellers of the late eighteenth and early nineteenth centuries are the polymaths of the period, men such as Pennant, Aikin, and Hyde Hall with their interest in botany, geology and history. Their work is a storehouse of knowledge about the county.

But the masses were not attracted, for the roads were too poor. Indeed, the county was barely opened up till the advent of the railway towards the middle of the nineteenth century. Thereafter, activity along the coast increased. Llandudno changed from being a small village dependent on copper mining into a holiday resort. Large boarding-houses and wide promenades appeared along sea-frontages. The visitors in the main were the rich and the well-to-do. They have continued to come, but between the wars, with the new mobility provided by the coach and car after the First World War and holidays with pay more recently, mass recreation has grown to change the pattern.

Tourism now represents one of the largest industries in the county, rivalling agriculture as a source of income. Tourist expenditure within the county in 1972, excluding that by day visitors, is estimated as over £32 million. Much of this money remains in the county and generates additional income reckoned to be from 20p to 70p in the £. About 8,000, including 2,000 self-employed, housewives amongst them, are employed in the industry during most of the summer period, and the total can rise to over 10,000 during the peak visiting months of July and August.

There is a wide variety of types of holiday accommodation. The estimated number of bedspaces in 1972 was 112,435; 50.6% were in caravans, 14.8% in hotels, 8.3% in second homes, 5.8% in flats and flatlets, 5.1% in private houses, 3.1% in guest houses, 2.3% in hostels and 9.6% in other forms, principally in holiday camps. A marina of 400 units has subsequently been developed at Port Dinorwic.

A substantial proportion of the bedspaces is in the Llandudno-Conwy-Penmaen-mawr area. Serviced accommodation dominates in Llandudno, which has two-thirds of all the hotel bedspaces in the county. Conwy and Penmaen-mawr are primarily caravan centres. Caravans predominate also in Llŷn, another area of high concentration of bedspaces. Serviced accommodation in Llŷn is relatively unimportant outside Butlins Holiday Camp. But the camp is a large one, and, together with Llandudno, it accounts for about 90% of the county's bedspaces in serviced accommodation. The caravan sites are more dispersed, and whilst their distribution is changing to include more inland locations, most are still found near the coast with the major concentrations in the three areas of Llandudno-Conwy-Penydyffryn, Llanbedrog-Aber-soch, and Morfa Bychan near Porthmadog.

A caravan holiday, with its comparative cost advantage, has grown enormously in popularity during the past twenty-five years, and since 1960 there has been increasing planning control on the establishment and development of camp sites, particularly within the Snowdonia National Park and the Areas of Outstanding Natural Beauty. Yet the number of touring vans and small sites free from planning control continues to rise.

The coast is the major magnet, and the growing interest in sailing in Conwy, Port Dinorwic, Pwllheli and Aber-soch among other centres is reinforcing its attraction. Mountain-land, however, is nowhere far removed from the sea, and the many visitors to the Snowdonia National Park include hikers and climbers, travellers in coach and car, fishermen, botanists and geologists. Even so, the two most popular special attractions in the county are a legacy of history — Caernarfon castle, with 500,700 visitors in 1973, and Conwy castle, with 278,200. There are, in addition, eight other attractions in the county among the 37 in Wales most frequently visited or used in 1972. They are the Llandudno Bus Tours (243,455); the Regimental Museum, Caernarfon (191,177); the Great Orme Railway, Llandudno (138,230); the Snowdon Mountain Railway (112,200); the Llanberis Lake Railway (91,200); Cricieth Castle (85,500); Penrhyn Castle (71,619), and the North Wales Quarrying Museum, Llanberis (42,200).

The tourist industry brings economic benefit to the county, but it also creates problems. The seasonal influx of visitors can impose excessive demands on public utilities and services, including water supply, and cause acute traffic congestion. It can also endanger the scenic beauty and the local community, and whilst the conservationists tend to place more emphasis on the preservation of the countryside, others deplore the social consequences of the growing number of second homes in localities such as Beddgelert, Betws Garmon, Llanbedrog and Llanengan.

Snowdon and Llyn Padarn   *Copyright: Snowdon National Park Authority*

BIBLIOGRAPHY

Archer, B., Shea, S., de Vere, R., *Tourism in Gwynedd — an economic study* (Welsh Tourist Board, 1974).

Caernarvonshire Planning Authority, *Structure Plan. Subject Report No. 9. Tourism.*

Pryce, W. T. R., ' The location and growth of holiday caravan camps in Wales, 1956 - 1965, *Transactions of the Institute of British Geographers,* 42 (1967).

Welsh Tourist Board, *Tourism in Wales.*

Llandudno

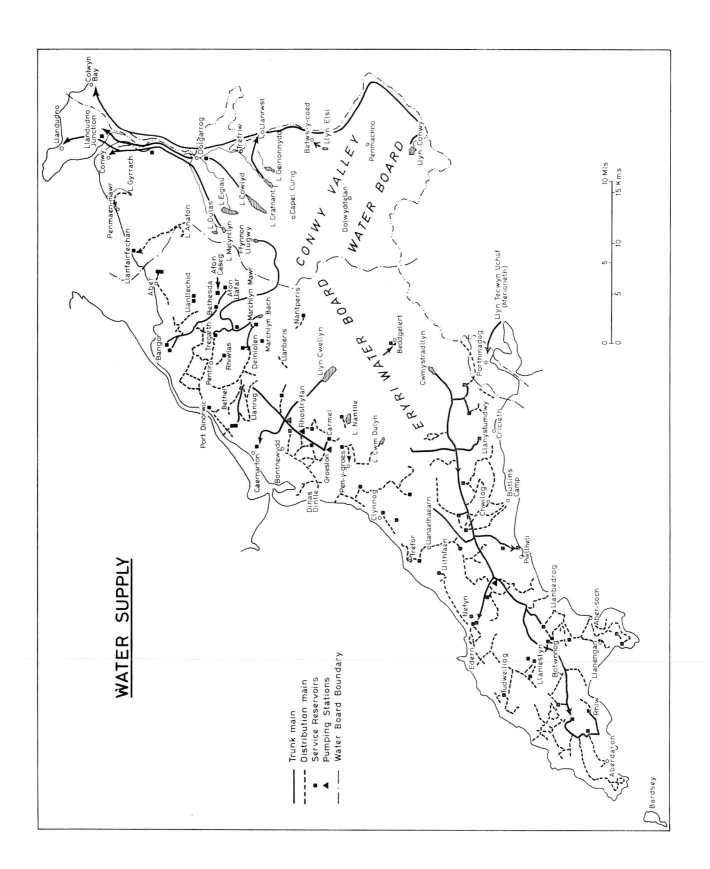

WATER SUPPLY

Trunk main ────
Distribution main - - - -
Service Reservoirs ■
Pumping Stations ▲
Water Board Boundary —··—··—

CONWY VALLEY WATER BOARD

ERYRI WATER BOARD

10 Mls
15 Kms

226

Water Supplies

The average annual rainfall of Caernarvonshire is 1,795 mm. (71.8"), but it ranges from about 750 mm. in the Llandudno area to about 5,080 mm. (200") in Snowdonia. It thus appears that the county has ample water resources, but in practice it is surprisingly difficult to ensure a constant supply to consumers in all areas during a very dry summer. This in part is related to the great loss of water owing to the very rapid run-off on the impermeable surfaces of the county, and in part to the necessity of constructing further reservoirs and pipelines to ensure an adequate regular water supply to all districts. The great influx of visitors to all parts of the county during the summer months is a special characteristic which leads to a very sudden and significant seasonal increase in the water requirements of the area.

Until about a century ago, most of the citizens had to depend on wells and springs fairly close to their homes. Carrying water from the well was a daily chore, and Cynan has immortalised one of the wells of the Pwllheli district:

'Does dim wna f'enaid blin yn iach
Ond dŵr o Ffynnon Felin Bach.

(Nothing can refresh my troubled soul but water from the well at Felin Bach.)

Water was obtained from wells and rivers in towns also in days gone by. The water was often polluted, thus giving rise to epidemics such as typhoid and cholera, which were responsible for hundreds of deaths in the county in the last century.

Gradually people came to appreciate the value of clean water, and the towns constructed their own reservoirs: Bangor in 1854, Caernarfon in 1869, Porthmadog in 1870, Pwllheli in 1879, Llandudno in 1880, Conwy, Llanfairfechan, Bethesda and Cricieth in 1883, and Penmaen-mawr in 1890. Even with the new reservoirs, epidemics still struck some districts, and 42 died of typhoid in Bangor in 1882 because the city's water supply above Gerlan, Bethesda, had been polluted.

Each local authority in the past had been responsible for its own water supply, but in a report to the Caernarvonshire County Council in 1945, the consultant engineer suggested the creation of a comprehensive scheme. Only in Llŷn was the suggestion accepted, and the Cwm Ystradllyn scheme was completed in 1959, though this in turn has become inadequate to meet the increasing demand, especially at the height of the holiday season. Before this, in 1951, the Gwynedd River Board (later the Gwynedd River Authority) had been established to become responsible for the supervision and control of rivers and lakes in the county. As already stated, the county is most fortunate in that the mountains abound in lakes which in very many instances act as natural reservoirs; they are located in unpolluted areas of sparse population, and have a good head-fall which greatly facilitates the flow of water to the network of towns and villages on the surrounding lowlands.

The Conwy Valley Water Board was established in 1965, the Eryri Water Board in 1967, and their first task was to plan more reservoirs and a network of main pipelines. This was essential as the improved standard of living — which meant a demand for more water — and the development of the tourist industry had imposed an enormous strain on the water supply system.

From time to time there was disagreement as the interests of Water Board and River Authority overlapped. This disagreement focussed mainly on the method of supplying water. The Water Boards argued for reservoirs supplying water directly by pipeline, and the River Authority for regulating reservoirs, which meant extracting water lower down the rivers.

In 1974, the two Boards came under the Welsh National Water Development Authority. The Conwy Valley Water Board became the Conwy Valley Water Division with its headquarters at Glan Conwy, and the Eryri Water Board became the Eryri Water Unit (and a part of the West Gwynedd Water Division) with its headquarters at Llanwnda. Further rationalisation is sure to occur in the future.

The new Water Authority's policy is to construct regulating reservoirs to control the flow of water in the various rivers, and though there are about a dozen conventional reservoirs in the county, the Water Authority will be concentrating on three large regulating reservoirs, namely, Cwm Ystradllyn, Cwellyn and Cowlyd. The Cwm Ystradllyn scheme will supply Llŷn and Eifionydd (including Porthmadog, which at the moment receives water from Llyn Tecwyn Uchaf in Meirionnydd), and the Cwellyn scheme will supply the Caernarfon area. Marchlyn Mawr has had to be released because of the Dinorwig hydro-electric scheme, but compensatory water will be piped from Ffynnon Llugwy to new treatment works at Mynydd Llandygái. It is proposed to divert water from Llyn Cowlyd to regulate the flow of the River Ogwen in order to supply the Bangor area — and eventually over into Anglesey.

Here is a list of the county's reservoirs and the areas they supply:

Cwm Ystradllyn	...	Llŷn and Eifionydd
Cwm Dulyn	...	Dyffryn Nantlle
Cwellyn	...	Caernarfon area
Marchlyn Bach	...	Deiniolen area
Ffynnon Llugwy	...	Tre-garth area
Llyn Anafon	...	Llanfairfechan area
Llyn Gyrach	...	Penmaen-mawr area
Dulyn and Melynllyn		Llandudno area
Llyn Cowlyd	...	Dyffryn Conwy, including Llandudno Junction (+ Afon Ogwen)
Llyn Crafnant	...	Llanrwst area
Llyn Elsi	...	Betws-y-coed area
Llyn Conwy	...	Much of southern Colwyn

Melin Nant

Marchlyn

Cwmystradllyn

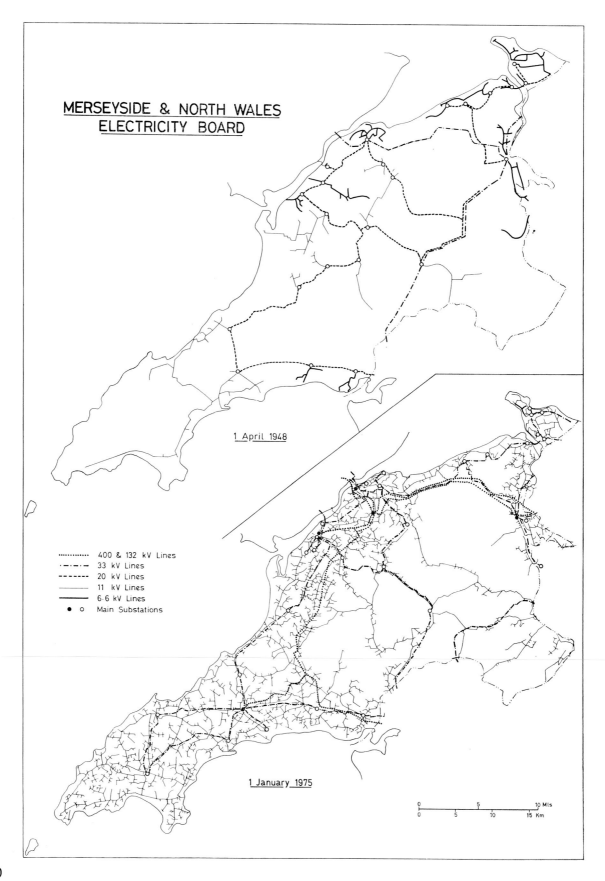

MERSEYSIDE & NORTH WALES
ELECTRICITY BOARD

1 April 1948

400 & 132 kV Lines
.—.—. 33 kV Lines
- - - 20 kV Lines
———— 11 kV Lines
———— 6·6 kV Lines
● ○ Main Substations

1 January 1975

0   5   10 Mls
0   5   10   15 Km

Electricity Supplies

The earliest recorded Authorised Undertaking for domestic electricity supplies in the county was by the Llandudno U.D.C. in 1895. Further Authorised Undertakings commenced, providing electricity supplies as follows: Bangor Corporation (1897), Caernarfon Corporation (1902), Conwy Corporation (1905), Penmaen-mawr U.D.C. (1905), Betws-y-coed U.D.C. (1906), Llanfairfechan U.D.C. (1914) and Bethesda U.D.C. (1925).

In 1904 the North Wales Power Co. was established to provide bulk electricity supplies to the above undertakings and also to provide supplies to the larger industrial enterprises.

In 1906 the first hydro-electric generating station was built at Cwm Dyli by the North Wales Power Co. with a generating capacity of 6.5 MW. The water supply comes from Llyn Llydaw on the slopes of Snowdon, which is approximately 1,150 ft. above the generating station. The water supply to the generating station is carried through two 30" diameter steel pipes.

In 1907 the Aluminium Corporation Ltd., Dolgarrog, constructed a hydro-electric generating station, and it was used exclusively for the production of aluminium, but in 1929 the ownership of the generating station was transferred to the North Wales Power Co. The generating capacity is now 26.5 MW. The water supply to the generating station comes from Llyn Eigiau, Llyn Cowlyd and Llyn Coety, and is carried through two steel pipes.

In 1923 an associated company of the North Wales Power Co., the Electricity Distribution of North Wales and District Ltd., was formed to distribute electricity within the county.

There is no doubt that in the earlier days many small hamlets were provided with electricity for domestic purposes by some of the old quarries generating more than they required, and these supplies continued to be used until they were eventually taken over by the Authorised Undertakings.

The integration of the electricity supply industry in England and Wales was brought about by the Electricity Act of 1947, and on the 1st April 1948 (Vesting Day), MANWEB and 13 other Electricity Boards were created to assume the responsibility of providing and developing supplies of electricity in both urban and rural areas.

The Electricity Act of 1947 requires that 'the Electricity Boards shall secure so far as practicable the extension to rural areas of supplies of the Electricity', and the size of the problem that was facing MANWEB in Caernarvonshire can be seen by reference to Plan No. 1, showing the extent of the distribution networks in Caernarvonshire on 1st April 1948. It will be noticed that apart from the vicinity of the larger towns, there were few distribution lines in the other parts of Caernarvonshire.

During the first five years of nationalisation, electricity development was impeded by a shortage of generating capacity and overloading of the transmission and distribution lines — legacies of war-time restrictions on capital development. Furthermore, most of the distribution networks required reconstruction, and the voltages required to be standardised to enable the network to be interconnected and thus provide improved security.

A further problem facing the Electricity Boards during the first five years after nationalisation was the restriction upon post-war investment which Governments found it necessary to maintain. However, by 1951 permission was obtained to expend additional capital to accelerate progress on rural electrification, and MANWEB undertook to supply 85% of the farms in the rural areas, of which Caernarvonshire is part, by 1968.

This rural electrification programme was completed well ahead of target, and this and subsequent development have enabled 99.8% of farms to be connected to the system.

North Wales, including Caernarvonshire, is now served by a high-voltage distribution network capable of facilitating further economic expansion on all fronts. The Board welcomes all efforts calculated to encourage new development and secure a balanced expansion of the Welsh economy. The extent of the development of

231

electricity supplies in Caernarvonshire between 1948 and 1974 is shown on Plan No. 2.

The picture of electrical progress in the rural areas would be incomplete without mention of the great projects of the Central Electricity Generating Board to harness both water resources and nuclear power in North Wales. In the former neighbouring counties of Anglesey and Merioneth large nuclear generating stations have been built at Wylfa and Trawsfynydd, and a pumped storage generating station has been constructed at Blaenau Ffestiniog. All these advanced generating stations are open to the public and are well worth a visit. These generating stations are also interconnected by the Super Grid Transmission System and there is a major substation in the system at Pentir near Bangor.

In Caernarvonshire a pumped storage generating station is being constructed at Dinorwic near Llanberis, with a generating capacity of 1,650 MW, and this should be completed by 1980.

During recent years there have been official reports emphasising the need to arrest the depopulation of rural areas in Wales by the provision of modern amenities and the absorption of local unemployment by modernising agriculture, expanding existing industries and introducing new ones. The Electricity Supply Industry in North Wales has, without doubt, made a great contribution towards this rehabilitation and development.

(The author gratefully acknowledges that the material contained in this article has been supplied by MANWEB.)

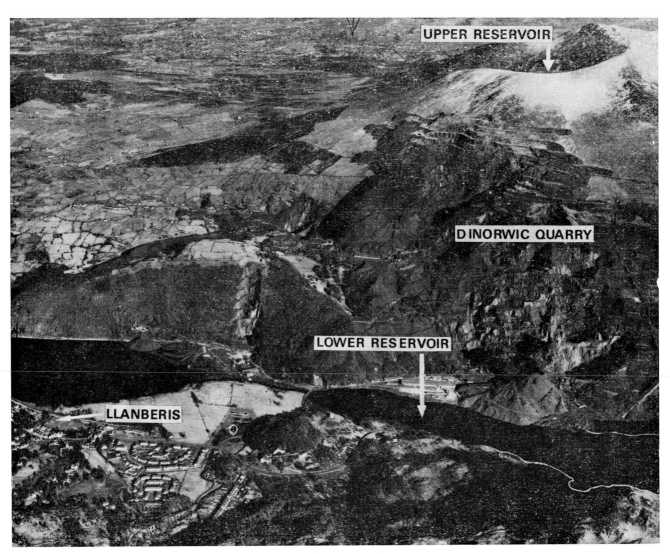

Llanberis Pump Storage Scheme

Copyright: Central Electricity Generating Board